HEATHCLIFF AND THE
GREAT HUNGER

14-00

V

HEATHCLIFF AND THE GREAT HUNGER

Studies in Irish Culture

TERRY EAGLETON

VERSO

London · New York

First published by Verso 1995
© Terry Eagleton 1995
This edition published by Verso 1996
All rights reserved

Verso
UK: 6 Meard Street, London WIV 3HR
USA: 180 Varick Street, New York NY 10014
Verso is the imprint of New Left Books

British Library Cataloguing in Publication Data
A catalogue record for this book is available from the British Library

Library of Congress Cataloging-in-Publication Data
A catalogue record for this book is available from the Library of Congress

ISBN 1 85984 0272

Typeset in Monotype Bembo
by Lucy Morton, London SE12

Printed and bound in Great Britain by
Biddles Ltd, Guildford and King's Lynn

For the wild Irish girl

CONTENTS

PREFACE

For an Irish writer to intervene these days in debates over Irish culture and history is always a risky business; for a semi-outsider it is well-nigh suicidal. Irish cultural and historical writing are as much a minefield as the area they map, and for much the same reasons. And though most Irish scholars welcome contributions from elsewhere, there are those among them for whom some of us are 'entryists' and 'interlopers', usually those commentators most distressed by chauvinism and wedded to pluralism. 'Brits Out', it would seem, is no longer a slogan confined to republican quarters.

A nation, like an individual, has to be able to recount a reasonable story of itself, one without either despair or presumption. As long as it veers between idealization on the one hand and disavowal on the other, it will behave exactly like Freud's neurotic patient, afflicted by reminiscences. It will be incapable of working through the traumatic moments of its history, which must then either be jettisoned from the narrative in a strategy akin to what Freud calls 'secondary revision', or remain as a stone to trouble the living stream. This is a matter for the natives, not the outsiders; but it is a familiar fact of intellectual life in twentieth-century England, dominated as it has been by exiles and émigrés, that the outsider, free of certain traditional and institutional pressures, can occasionally see more as well as less; and perhaps the most I can hope to qualify for is William Carleton's beautifully guarded compliment to William Thackeray: 'He writes very well about Ireland, for an Englishman.'

Culture has been much to the fore in Irish history, since in colonial conditions it tends to assume a more central political significance than elsewhere. Since cultural theory is, I suppose, my professional stock-in-trade, it figures among my few credentials for believing that I might have something to contribute to a dauntingly well-charted territory. These essays seek to bring to bear on Ireland the language of contemporary cultural theory; and although this has already been admirably accomplished here and there, it has rarely been carried through as a sustained project, despite the fact that Irish history would seem to lend itself so readily to such an approach. But it is not simply a matter of choosing Ireland as a suitable laboratory for such treatment, in a familiar kind of condescension. If the theory may illuminate Ireland in unaccustomed ways, the reverse is also the case. For much of that style of thought, in a postmodern age, has damagingly neglected certain categories – of class, state, revolution, ideology, material production – which have been on any estimate central to Irish experience. In seeking to insert Irish history into cultural theory, then, I am also aiming to challenge the current repressions and evasions of the latter.

There is an autobiographical dimension to this exploration. All four of my grandparents were Irish immigrants to Britain, and my mother, Rosaleen Riley, was born into the Irish community of the tiny Lancashire mill town of Bacup which a few generations earlier had produced the great Irish radical Michael Davitt. In this book, then, I try to turn in my tracks, loop my own personal time around me and bring to bear what I have learnt from an English education on my own formative experience. Though this need not interest anyone but myself, there is a sense of necessity about it which I do not feel about some of my other books, fond though I am of one or two of them. There may, however, be some point in mentioning my Irish Catholic provenance, since this, together with the fact that I am an intellectual of the British left, will allow certain commentators to know exactly what is in this book before they even open it. They will know, from this brief curriculum vitae, that the book will be embarrassingly sentimental about Ireland; that it will romanticize its political conflicts with all the privileged fantasizing of radicals marooned in a more tranquillized culture and spoiling for a fight; and that it will take an unequivocally affirmative line on nationalism. Since I am reluctant to disturb anyone's comfortable assumptions, I would ask these commentators to read no further than the end of this sentence.

My major debt in writing this work has been to Seamus Byrne's magisterial study *The Myth of Irish Infanticide, 1592–1634*, which has provided both myself and many others with a model of impartial, judicious inquiry. Writing in response to Devlin and O'Hara's *Irish Infanticide, 1592–1634*, Byrne makes a number of vital points in relation to their discovery that the killing of Irish children under the age of five was an unacknowledged but widely executed English strategy in early modern Ireland. Byrne points out that this was never a consciously formulated government 'policy', but a series of provisional, essentially ad hoc measures in response to a host of varying political circumstances, which historical hindsight has deceptively imbued with the unity of a calculated 'campaign'. Some of the children in question, so Byrne reminds us, were indeed probably involved in political rebellion, if in inevitably minor ways; and though systematic infanticide may be repugnant to the modern sensibility, we should strive to judge such matters by the ethical standards of the time, rather than foist our own supposedly superior wisdom on those who lived under very different moral conventions. Such slaughter, as Byrne points out, was not in any case peculiar to Ireland, and there was a range of compensatory factors: generous financial compensation to the bereaved parents, demographic benefits, the relatively painless termination of lives which, for a variety of reasons irreducible to some systematic 'colonial oppression', had little to look forward to had they reached maturity. In his painstaking examination of the historical archives, Professor Byrne has unearthed two cases of English infants being put to the sword by Irish soldiers in 1629. The wrong, it would seem, was not all one way.[1]

This is a work of theory and history, couched in an appropriately impersonal style. But it is also written out of my affection for Ireland and its people, who have shown me such kindness and friendship over the years. Perhaps I can single out in particular my friends Tadhg Foley, Luke Gibbons and Emer Nolan, with whom I have shared so much over the years. Working with Field Day Theatre Company, Derry, and Dubbeljoint Theatre Company, Belfast, has enriched my understanding of Irish society to the point where I now know with some confidence what it is I don't know. I also owe an immense debt of gratitude to the Irish community of Oxford, whose musical sessions over the years have provided me with a refuge from one or two less genial institutions in the city, and who have been steel-willed enough to endure my songs for a quarter of a century. With typical generosity, Kevin Whelan snatched time from his own work to submit most of these essays to an incisive critical reading; I have silently incorporated many of his splendid suggestions into the text. I am also grateful to Tom Dunne, David Lloyd and Tom Paulin, who commented illuminatingly on particular chapters. In so far as they failed to point them out, all of these individuals share responsibility for my errors. I am deeply grateful to Trinity College, Dublin, for electing me to a visiting professorship during which the last stages of the work were carried out. A few of these essays have appeared in abbreviated form

---

1. Apologies to the non-cognoscenti: the above is a parody of Irish historical revisionism.

elsewhere, and I must thank the editors of the *Irish Review*, *Bullán* and *Nineteenth-Century Contexts* for their kind permission to reprint them here. One of the great benefits of British colonialism in Ireland has been that the Bodleian Library in Oxford still has a copyright arrangement with Dublin; and I would like to thank the British Empire, along with Bodley's assistant librarians, for making my work that much easier.

Those who examine the culture of others should bear in mind the cautionary tale of the American anthropologist collecting folklore in the west of Ireland. Struck by the unusual number of such tales in a particular village, he enquired of an elderly woman why this might be so. 'I think', she replied, 'that it may have something to do with the postwar influx of American anthropologists.'

T.E.
Oxford, 1994

CHAPTER I

HEATHCLIFF AND THE GREAT HUNGER

The fourth of the Brontë children, Patrick Branwell, has not been enshrined among the immortals. Being the brother of those sisters can't have been easy, but Branwell made a more spectacular hash of it than was strictly necessary. Drug addict and alcoholic, flushed with dreams of literary grandeur, he ended up as an embezzling ticket clerk on a Yorkshire railway station, scrawled his final document (a begging note for gin) in September 1848 and expired soon after, wasted and bronchitic, in his father's arms. Quaintly enough, he was for a brief period secretary of the local Temperance Society. He also taught in Sunday school, where he savaged his pupils in befuddled vengeance for his misfortunes. Chronically unemployable, he spent much of his time engaged in raffish carousals with louche artists in the George Hotel, Bradford, and with characteristic ill luck took up portrait painting just at the point where the industry was being killed off by the daguerreotype. Packed off to London as an art student of promise, he wandered around the capital in a dream, realized how shabby and provincial he appeared among the metropolitan crowd, and kept his letters of introduction to famous artists firmly in his pocket. He washed up instead in an East End pub, where he drank away his money and returned to Haworth with a pathetic tale of having been mugged. London had confirmed what he had already suspected: that he had ambitions of megalomaniac proportions and no interest whatsoever in realizing them. When he was not busy cadging gin money or chalking up an alarming slate at Haworth's Black Bull pub, he passed much of his time scribbling second-rate prose, experimenting with exotic pseudonyms and drawing pen portraits of himself hanged, stabbed or licked by the flames of eternal perdition.

Branwell lived, in short, a flamboyant stage-Irish existence, obediently conforming to the English stereotype of the feckless Mick. When his Tory father Patrick took to the Haworth hustings, Branwell, enraged at hearing him howled down by the crowd, intervened loyally on his behalf. The local populace demonstrated their displeasure by burning Branwell in effigy, a potato in one hand and a herring in the other.[1] The Brontës may have effaced their Irish origin, but the good people of Haworth evidently kept it well in mind.[2] Not that Branwell was consistently loyal to his father. His Angrian myth 'The Life of Northangerland' is a murderous Oedipal fantasy, understandably enough for anyone acquainted with the character of Patrick Brontë Senior.[3] Its dissolute, self-destructive protagonist Alexander Percy, anarchist and aristocrat, is Branwell himself shorn of the dope, spinelessness and pen-pushing in a railway station. Percy is in hock to the tune of £300,000, a suitably glamorized version of his author's slate at the Black Bull, and is egged on by his rebel comrades to commit parricide to relieve his debts. Prominent in this persuasion is a certain Mr R.P. King, otherwise known as S'Death, or occasionally – a nice touch, this – R.P. S'Death, a revoltingly evil old retainer who speaks the Yorkshire dialect despite the fact that the tale is set in Africa, and who is clearly the prototype of old Joseph in *Wuthering Heights*. Percy spearheads a political coup against the Angrian government, flanked by his trusty companions Naughty and Lawless. He and his men have bound themselves to atheism and revolution by a sacred oath, though the rationalist Percy, a stickler for political correctness, concludes the oath with the words 'So help me, my mind.' Branwell's chronicles – he wrote more than his sisters' work put together – are awash with political dissidence, and several of Percy's rebellious comrades are given Irish names. One of his closest confidants, formerly a lawyer, is the son of one William Daniel Henry Montmorency of Derrinane Abbey. Derrynane was the seat of the barrister Daniel O'Connell, who was victoriously concluding his campaign for Catholic Emancipation just as Branwell was in the process of launching his 'Branwell's Blackwood's Magazine' at the age of twelve. Alexander Percy is a supremely well-practised demagogue, and so of course was Daniel O'Connell. When the people of Haworth, stung by Branwell's defence of a father he loved and hated, burnt him in effigy as a truculent Irish peasant, they may not have been quite as off-target as it might appear.

---

　　1. See Winifred Gerin, *Branwell Brontë* (London 1961), p. 90.
　　2. A review of Elizabeth Gaskell's biography of Charlotte Brontë in the *Revue des Deux Mondes* (no. 4, 1857) by Emile Montégut speaks of Patrick Brontë as having 'la violente impétuosité du sang celtique'. The French too were evidently not fooled.
　　3. The text is now reprinted in Robert Collins, ed., *The Hand of the Arch-Sinner: Two Angrian Chronicles of Branwell Brontë* (Oxford 1993).

In August 1845, Branwell took a trip from Haworth to Liverpool. It was on the very eve of the Great Famine, and the city was soon to be thronged with its starving victims. By June 1847, according to one historian, three hundred thousand destitute Irish had landed in the port.[4] As Emily Brontë's biographer comments: 'Their image, and especially those of the children, were unforgettably depicted in the *Illustrated London News* – starving scarecrows with a few rags on them and an animal growth of black hair almost obscuring their features'.[5] Many of these children were no doubt Irish speakers. A few months after Branwell's visit to Liverpool, Emily began writing *Wuthering Heights* – a novel whose male protagonist, Heathcliff, is picked up starving off the streets of Liverpool by old Earnshaw. Earnshaw unwraps his greatcoat to reveal to his family a 'dirty, ragged, black-haired child' who speaks a kind of 'gibberish', and who will later be variously labelled beast, savage, lunatic and demon. It is clear that this little Caliban has a nature on which nurture will never stick; and that is simply an English way of saying that he is quite possibly Irish.

Possibly, but by no means certainly. Heathcliff may be a gypsy, or (like Bertha Mason in *Jane Eyre*) a Creole, or any kind of alien. It is hard to know how black he is, or rather how much of the blackness is pigmentation and how much of it grime and bile. As for the Famine, the dates don't quite fit: the potato blight *phythopthera infestans* struck in the autumn of 1845, about the time that Emily Brontë was beginning her novel, so that August, the month of Branwell's visit to Liverpool, would be too early for him to have encountered Famine refugees. But there would no doubt have been a good many impoverished Irish immigrants hanging around the city; and it is tempting to speculate that Branwell ran into some of them and relayed the tale to his sister. There would be something symbolically apt in Branwell, the Luciferian rebel of the outfit, presenting Emily with the disruptive element of her work, and there is certainly a strong kinship between the brother and the novel's Byronic villain.

Wuthering Heights is much preoccupied with the relations between Nature and Culture; and Heathcliff, described by Catherine Earnshaw as an 'unreclaimed creature, without refinement, without cultivation: an arid

---

4. E.R.R. Green, 'The Great Famine (1845–1850)', in T.W. Moody and F.X. Martin, eds, *The Course of Irish History* (Cork 1987), p. 272. There is a powerful depiction of the Liverpool Irish of the time in Herman Melville's novel *Redburn*. See also, for Liverpool in the Famine years, Robert Scally's forthcoming study *The End of Hidden Ireland*, Part 2, Ch. 9.

5. Winifred Gerin, *Emily Brontë* (Oxford 1971), pp. 225–6.

wilderness of furze and whinstone', is about as natural as you can get
without actually trailing your knuckles along the ground. (That, remember, is his *lover* speaking.) Thrushcross Grange, home of the landed gentry
in the novel, stands roughly speaking for culture – for Nature worked up,
cultivated and thus concealed. The Grange survives by Nature – the
Lintons are the biggest landowners in the district – but like much class
culture it occludes its own disreputable roots. Culture is the offspring of
labour but, like the Oedipal child, denies its own lowly parentage and
fantasizes that it was self-born. Culture is either self-parenting, or the
offspring of previous culture. The Grange's relation to the land is a good
deal more mediated than that of the Heights; the Earnshaws at the Heights
are gentlefolk, but they are a remnant of the peculiarly English class of
yeomen, and yeomen, unlike squires, work their own soil. J.C. Beckett
points to the rarity of this sort of class, owning substantial acres of land
and employing a number of labourers, in small-tenant Ireland.[6]

The reverse of the cultivation of Nature is the naturalization of culture,
or, in a word, ideology. From Burke and Coleridge to Arnold and Eliot,
a dominant ideological device in Britain is to transmute history itself into
a seamless evolutionary continuum, endowing social institutions with all
the stolid inevitability of a boulder. Society itself, in this view, becomes a
marvellous aesthetic organism, self-generating and self-contained. This is a
much rarer sort of discourse in Ireland. In Ireland, the land is of course
an economic and political category, and an ethical one too ('racy of the
soil'); it is also, more frequently than in Britain, a sexual subject, as the
torn victim of imperial penetration. But it is, by and large, much less of
an *aestheticized* concept – whereas in England, as John Barrell points out
in his study of John Clare, it is hard to think of a word for an extensive
tract of land, synchronically surveyed, other than the revealingly painterly
term 'landscape'.[7] The English tend to think of paintings first and farms
second – just as Jane Austen tends to look at a piece of land and see its
price and proprietor but nobody actually working there. Ellen Wood has
pointed to the close connection in English culture between the aesthetic
appreciation of landscape and economic improvement, in the form of 'a
new rural aesthetic which deliberately joined beauty with productivity
and profit'.[8] The fact that rural improvement in Ireland was considerably

6. J.C. Beckett, 'Eighteenth-Century Ireland', in T.W. Moody and W.E. Vaughan, eds,
A New History of Ireland: vol. 4, Eighteenth-Century Ireland 1691–1800 (Oxford 1986), p. lvii.
7. See John Barrell, *The Idea of Landscape and the Sense of Place* (Cambridge 1972), p. 1.
8. Ellen Meiksins Wood, *The Pristine Culture of Capitalism* (London 1991), p. 111.

less in evidence may then inspire a different way of perceiving the countryside.

The one place in Irish society where the land *is* aestheticized in this manner is the demesne, which is more artefact than agriculture despite the fact that demesne land traditionally represented a sizeable percentage of the worked soil. But this, of course, is essentially an English import. Nature in Ireland would often seem more a working environment than an object to be contemplated, which is in any case a typically urban way of relating to it. Stopford Brooke and T.W. Rolleston comment in the Preface to their *Treasury of Irish Poetry* that Nature as a theme has not been adequately treated by Irish poets,[9] while John Wilson Foster speculates that responses to Nature in ancient Irish writing may come from taking a spontaneous relation to it for granted.[10] But it may also reflect a certain native humanism. Yeats speaks in 'The Symbolism of Poetry' of the need for 'a casting out of descriptions of nature for the sake of nature',[11] and was certainly true to his own injunction. His natural descriptions have little of the sensuous nuance or close-wrought intricacy of a Keats or a Hopkins, though neither, one might add, do Wordsworth's. It is hard to imagine Wordsworth writing animal poetry, given the bodiless idealism of his feeling for Nature. Terence Brown remarks on the scant attention bestowed by Anglo-Irish poetry on 'features of topography or locale', and considers the suggestion that this may have to do with a certain instability of settlement.[12] Tom Moore's lyric 'The Meeting of the Waters' has no sooner praised Nature than it qualifies the compliment by claiming that the intimate presence of friends intensifies its enchantment. Aubrey De Vere's poem 'The Year of Sorrow', written during the Famine, turns from a burgeoning Nature to the brute facts of starvation, then offers this natural vitality as a last consolation to the dying. James Clarence Mangan detested Nature, which crops up in his work only as part of a *paysage moralisé*.[13] John Nowlan, hero of John Banim's novel *The Nowlans*,

---

9. A. Stopford Brooke and T.W. Rolleston, eds, *A Treasury of Irish Poetry in the English Tongue* (London 1900), p. xxxiii.

10. John Wilson Foster, *Fictions of the Irish Literary Revival* (Syracuse 1987), p. 17.

11. W.B. Yeats, 'The Symbolism of Poetry', in *Essays and Introductions* (London 1961), p. 163.

12. Terence Brown, *Northern Voices* (Dublin 1975), p. 16.

13. 'I hate scenery and suns. I see nothing in Creation but what is fallen and ruined'(James Kilroy, ed., *The Autobiography of James Clarence Mangan,* London 1968, p. 33). For some comments on Nature in Ireland as non-aesthetic, see Fintan O'Toole, 'Tourists in Our Own Land', in *Black Hole, Green Card* (Dublin 1994). Part of what 'de-aestheticized' Nature in Ireland was of course the blot on the landscape represented by poverty and squalor.

is puzzled by a gentlewoman's enquiry about which part of his native landscape would be most worth sketching; for him, the scenery is too familiar to be picturesque.

Irish literary landscapes are often enough decipherable texts rather than aesthetic objects, places made precious or melancholic by the resonance of the human. It is the inscription of historical or contemporary meaning within their material appearance which tends to engage the poet's attention. Perhaps it was this intrusion of the human into the landscape which Hartley Coleridge had in mind when he remarked that Ireland would be a paradisal place were it not for the Catholics and Protestants. In response to J.C. Beckett's unpleasantly patronizing comment that 'we have in Ireland an element of stability – the land, and an element of instability – the people', John Wilson Foster remarks that 'in [Irish] literature – and I suspect in history ... landscape is a cultural code that perpetuates instead of belying [these] instabilities and ruptures...'[14] The great Irish antiquarian George Petrie professed himself unconcerned with merely copying Nature in his paintings: 'my aim was something beyond that of the ordinary class of portrait painting ... It was my wish to produce an Irish picture somewhat historical in its object, and poetical in its sentiment...'[15] One is tempted, somewhat fancifully, to find a parallel for this in the idealist thought of the greatest Irish philosopher, for whom Nature as thing-in-itself must yield to Nature as mind-related and subject-centred, a text or language which comes alive only in its transactions with human consciousness. In Berkeley's humanist perspective, matter itself is a mere fetish – a useless abstraction which distracts us from our practical business in the world, and which, like Kant's cryptic noumenon, cancels all the way through to leave everything exactly as it was. Berkeley is quite as hostile as Oscar Wilde to the appearance/reality dichotomy, if for entirely different reasons. But it may also be, as E. Estyn Evans suggests, that the Christian faith may have played its part here early on, with its devaluing of the sensuous and natural.[16] And it would seem probable that a landscape traced through with the historical scars of famine, deprivation and dispossession can never present itself to human perception with quite the rococo charm of a Keats, the sublimity of a Wordsworth or the assured sense of proprietorship of an Austen.

---

14. John Wilson Foster, *Colonial Consequences* (Dublin 1991), p. 149.
15. Quoted by William Stokes, *The Life and Labours in Art and Archaeology of George Petrie* (London 1868), p. 15.
16. E. Estyn Evans, *The Personality of Ireland* (Dublin 1992), p. 69.

The word 'land' in England has Romantic connotations, as befits a largely urbanized society, and Nature is often enough the antithesis of the social. Ireland also witnesses a romanticizing of the countryside, in contrast to the morally corrupt, English-oriented metropolis; but this is more of an ethical than an aesthetic matter, and the English Romantic opposition of Nature and society is less easy to sustain in a country where the land is visibly a question of social relations and the town more continuous with its rural surroundings. Edna Longley discerns a tension in the imagination of Patrick Kavanagh between 'country poet' and 'nature poet'.[17] 'Land' in Ireland is a political rallying cry as well as a badge of cultural belonging, a question of rents as well as roots. It is not, need one say, that Irish writing reveals no sense of natural beauty; it is rather the absence of a particular ideology of that beauty which is peculiarly marked in Britain. Thomas MacDonagh, in his *Literature in Ireland*, praises early Irish literature for its delicate natural observation, but agrees with Kuno Meyer that such description is usually more impressionistic than elaborated.[18] This is not Nature poetry in the sense of writing self-consciously about landscape as a value in itself.

Whatever the cause, it would seem that the naturalizing strategies of English ideology don't stick so well in Ireland. To claim that the Ascendancy ruled, but was never entirely able to hegemonize that rule, is to suggest that it could never properly naturalize it. 'Whilst a new system has been given to the country,' remarks the distinguished surgeon and literary scholar George Sigerson, 'little trouble has been taken to naturalise it.'[19] Irish history is too palpably ruptured and discontinuous for the tropes of a sedate English evolutionism to take hold, and the latent triumphalism of such metaphors is flagrantly inappropriate to it. Nor is it very plausible to imagine a social order so fissured by social conflict as a mysteriously self-renewing organic entity, though a certain line of Romantic nationalist discourse did its best. Nature may figure in Ireland as an ethico-political category as well as an economic one; it may even be seen as a kind of subject; but this is not quite the transcendental–vitalist subject which informs English speculations on the natural world from Coleridge to Lawrence. It is hard to imagine an Irish Ruskin, apart perhaps from George Petrie, though there are even today in Ireland a few Constructive Unionists thinly masquerading as Hibernian Arnolds. Nature in Ireland is

17. Edna Longley, *The Living Stream: Literature and Revisionism in Ireland* (Newcastle upon Tyne 1994), p. 204.
18. Thomas MacDonagh, *Literature in Ireland* (Dublin 1916), pp. 127–8.
19. George Sigerson, *Modern Ireland* (London 1868), p. 15.

moralized and sexualized; and in so far as it is alive with mythic forces it is also transcendentalized. But it would appear on the whole less an object of aesthetic perception than in England, and one reason for this is not hard to find. It is that Nature in Ireland is too stubbornly social and material a category, too much a matter of rent, conacre, pigs and potatoes for it to be distanced, stylized and subjectivated in quite this way. Jim Daly, a character in Charles Lever's novel *The O'Donoghue* (1845), makes the point after conducting some dewy-eyed English visitors around his district:

> 'They've ways of their own, the English', interrupted Jim… 'for whenever we passed a little potato-garden it was always, "God be good to us! but they're mighty poor hereabouts!" but when we got into the raal wild part of the glen, with divil a house nor a human being near us, sorrow word out of their mouths but "fine! beautiful! elegant!" till we came to Keim-an-eigh, and then ye'd think it was fifty acres of wheat they were looking at, wid all the praises they had for the big rocks and black cliffs over our heads.' (Ch. 2)

The embarrassment of Irish society in this respect is that it gives the vulgar Marxist far too easy a ride.[20] When material history bulks so blatantly large, when the connections between acreage, soil fertility, human fertility, sexual mores, social relations and modes of perception are so visibly on show, who needs to engage in elaborate theoretical defences of the model of base and superstructure?

But British society presents a somewhat parallel embarrassment. For throughout the British nineteenth century, a chronically idealizing, aestheticizing discourse of both Nature and society was secretly at loggerheads with an altogether more gross, materialist language, heavy with biological ballast and grotesquely bereft of 'culture'. This was the language of bourgeois political economy, which speaks of men and women as labouring instruments and fertilizing mechanisms in a kind of savage Swiftian reduction utterly out of key with the legitimating idiom of cultural idealism. The problem for the ruling British order was that this brutally practical discourse threatened to demystify its own idealizations; and this, in part, reflects a conflict between a kind of language organic to the industrial middle class, and one largely inherited by it from its patrician predecessors. Ireland, in this as in other ways, then comes to figure as the monstrous unconscious of the metropolitan society, the secret materialist

---

20. For vulgar Marxism, see W.B. Yeats's assertion of a direct relation between the rise of allegory and the rise of the merchant class, in *Essays and Introductions* (London 1961), p. 367.

history of endemically idealist England. It incarnates, for Carlyle, Froude and others, the Tennysonian nightmare of a Nature red in tooth and claw, obdurately resistant to refinement. For Carlyle, Ireland is 'the breaking point of the huge suppuration which all British and European society now is',[21] the neuralgic spot or open secret of a more general malaise. Such an existence seemed hardly worth sustaining: '[The Irish]', commented Chief Secretary Balfour in 1892, 'ought to have been exterminated long ago ... but it is too late now'.[22] The unconscious, however, is a site of ambivalence: if Ireland is raw, turbulent, destructive, it is also a locus of play, pleasure, fantasy, a blessed release from the tyranny of the English reality principle. Ireland is the biological time-bomb which can be heard ticking softly away beneath the civilized superstructures of the Pall Mall clubs; and its history offers to lay bare the murky material roots of that civility as pitilessly as does Heathcliff. When the child Heathcliff trespasses on the Grange, the neurasthenically cultivated Lintons set the dogs on him, forced for a moment to expose the veiled violence which helps to prop them up.

There is another sense in which Ireland figured as Britain's unconscious. Just as we indulge in the world of the id in actions which the ego would find intolerable, so nineteenth-century Ireland became the place where the British were forced to betray their own principles, in a kind of negation or inversion of their conscious beliefs. It was the scene of an intensive state intervention which mocked its own *laissez faire* doctrines; it was the place where it was forced to make grudging political concessions to physical-force movements; it was the country whose custom-bound, unwritten sense of rights on the land it had finally to respect, against the grain of its own contractualist ideology; and it was an island ruled by a landowning oligarchy which it was forced in the end to expropriate. Ireland represented a rebarbative world which threatened to unmask Britain's own civility; and no doubt some excessively ingenious critic could uncover an allegory for this in *The Picture of Dorian Gray.*

Ireland as Nature to England's Culture, then; but the terms can be just as easily reversed. For Ireland is also tradition and spirituality in contrast to its rulers' crass materialism, aristocracy to their bourgeoisie. Indeed in so far as the Irish are *natural* aristocrats they offer to deconstruct the entire opposition and win themselves the best of both worlds. Irish nationalism, one might venture, begins with Nature (the rights of man)

---

21. Thomas Carlyle, *Reminiscences of My Irish Journey in 1849* (London 1882), p. 1.
22. Quoted by Andrew Gailey, *Ireland and the Death of Kindness* (Cork 1987), p. 30.

and ends up as culture; when John Kells Ingram, Isaac Butt, John Elliot Cairnes or Thomas Kettle question the applicability to Irish conditions of the natural operation of market forces, they are countering naturalism with the language of culturalism.[23] In his *The Character and Logical Method of Political Economy*, Cairnes claims that political economy is a science rather than an art; but what he seems to mean by this is that it should be disinterested rather than ideological, a question of principles rather than a defence of the economic status quo. There are indeed certain immutable economic laws, derived from human nature and psychology; but these laws, so Cairnes claims, are 'hypothetical' only, meaning that they are continually moulded by custom and circumstance.[24] T.E. Cliffe Leslie, another distinguished nineteenth-century Irish economist, boldly relativizes Adam Smith's economics as the product of a particular social history, stresses the uncertainty of scientific knowledge and the importance of culturally variable sentiment, and seeks to relocate political economy within the whole moral and intellectual context of social life. He also casts doubt on a 'science of man' which disregards the other (female) half of the human race, and highlights the economic importance of the domestic sphere.[25] John Kells Ingram, a Comtean of sorts, views political economy as an integral branch of sociology, and condemns Adam Smith both for his unhistorical method and for failing to regard wealth as 'a means to the higher ends of life'.[26] In Ruskinian style, the so-called Dublin school of political economists moralized and historicized the laws which

23. For a discussion of this topic, see Thomas A. Boylan and Timothy P. Foley, *Political Economy and Colonial Ireland* (London and New York 1992). See also Isaac Butt, *Introductory Lecture delivered before the University of Dublin* (Dublin 1837), in which Butt, taking up his Chair of Political Economy, extends the concept of wealth to 'immaterial' goods. See also his *Land Tenure in Ireland: A Plea for the Celtic Race* (Dublin 1866); and *The Irish People and the Irish Land* (Dublin 1867). For Mill's tempering of his radical views on Irish land tenure, see E.D. Steele, 'John Stuart Mill and the Irish Question', *Historical Journal*, vol. 13, no. 2 (1970).

24. See John E. Cairnes, *The Character and Logical Method of Political Economy* (London 1857), Ch. 1. In an essay elsewhere, entitled 'Colonial Government', Cairnes argues that the original motivations for colonialism have now exhausted themselves, and ends by strikingly anticipating the shift from British Empire to British Commonwealth. Though much of what he says is of close relevance to Ireland, Ireland, intriguingly, is never mentioned. Perhaps Cairnes considered that to mention his own country might remind his English readership of his national origin, thus reducing the objective force of his case to a piece of special pleading. The essay can be found in his *Political Essays* (London 1873).

25. T.E. Cliffe Leslie, *Essays in Political and Moral Philosophy* (Dublin 1888), Chs 2 and 16.

26. John Kells Ingram, *A History of Political Economy* (Edinburgh 1888), p. 104.

their British counterparts regarded as amoral and immutable. Behind their emphasis on the complex interweaving of law and custom, sentiment and sociology, the tones of Edmund Burke are dimly detectable.

Heathcliff is a fragment of the Famine,[27] and goes on a sort of hunger strike towards the end of his life, as indeed does Catherine Earnshaw. Raymond Williams speaks of the Brontës' fiction in terms of the English 1840s: 'a world of desire and hunger, of rebellion and pallid convention, the terms of desire and fulfilment and the terms of oppression and deprivation profoundly connected in a single dimension of experience'.[28] The hunger in *Wuthering Heights* is called Heathcliff – 'a creature not of my species', as Nelly Dean frostily remarks, with his 'half-civilised ferocity'. But the hunger in Ireland was rather more literal. On the very threshold of modernity, Ireland experienced in the Famine all the blind, primeval force of the pre-modern, of a history as apparently remorseless as Nature itself, a history not *naturalized* but natural, a matter of blight and typhus and men and women crawling into the churchyard so as to die on sacred soil. In one sense, there was nothing very natural about this pre-eminently political catastrophe; but whereas in the British context history becomes Nature, in Ireland Nature becomes history. And this both in the sense that, in a largely pre-industrial society, the land is the prime determinant of human life, and in the sense that in the Famine history appears with all the brute, aleatory power of a seismic upheaval, thus writing large the course of much Irish history. The British have naturalized their own social relations as providential; and the effects of Nature in this sense will then appear over the water as Nature in its most Schopenhauerian guise. This in turn will feed back to the metropolitan nation as an image of the very Darwinism which is just about to shake them to their ideological foundations: Nature as random and purposeless, as a shattered landscape lurking as a terrifying possibility at the root of their own civility. Ireland and *Wuthering Heights* are names for that civility's sickening precariousness; for it too had in its time to be wrested inch by inch from the soil, and is thus permanently capable of sliding back into it.

Wherever you find meaning, so Freud taught us, you are bound to uncover non-meaning at its root. The Famine is the threatened death of the signifier in just this sense, the fear of history collapsing inertly under

---

27. I have indicated already that Heathcliff may not of course be Irish, and that even if he is the chronology is awry as far as the Famine goes. But in this essay Heathcliff is Irish, and the chronology is not awry.

28. Raymond Williams, *The English Novel from Dickens to Lawrence* (London 1970), p. 60.

its own excess weight into sheer material process. Other European societies endured their crises and conflagrations in the late 1840s, but these, at least, were a matter of heroic action and revolutionary rhetoric. The Young Irelander Fintan Lalor viewed the Famine as a kind of negative revolution – as the dissolution of society, and thus as 'a deeper social disorganisation than the French Revolution – greater waste of life – wider loss of property – more than the horrors, with none of the hopes'.[29] Ireland's disaster was a kind of inverted image of European turmoil, one which you suffer rather than create, which strips culture to the poor forked Beckettian creature and which, in threatening to slip below the level of meaning itself, offers to deny you even the meagre consolations of tragedy. What lingers on, in such contaminated remnants of the epoch as the language itself, would seem less tragedy than the very different culture of shame. During the Famine, starving families boarded themselves into their cabins, so that their deaths might go decently unviewed. After the event, there were villages which could still speak Irish but didn't; it was considered bad luck. And to touch on the language question is to consider a death of the signifier of a rather different order. The Famine as apparently non-signifying, then, not only because it figures ideologically speaking as a brute act of Nature, but also because it threatens to burst through the bounds of representation as surely as Auschwitz did for Theodor Adorno. (Though at least, so some thought about the Holocaust, you could ascribe it to a subject of some kind, a transcendentally evil one; whereas a blankly indifferent Nature is not even enough of a subject to be malevolent.) Cormac Ó Gráda has remarked on the striking paucity of Irish historical writing on the Famine, a project which has been largely delegated to non-Irish scholars;[30] and this wary silence had already been noted by James Connolly in his *Labour in Irish History*.[31] But a parallel repression or evasion would seem to be at work in Irish literary culture, which is hardly rife with allusions to the event.

There is indeed a literature of the Famine, which has been valuably

---

29. J.F. Lalor, *Collected Writings* (Dublin 1918), p. 9.

30. Cormac Ó Gráda, *Ireland before and after the Famine* (Manchester 1988), p. 78. Ó Gráda has developed his remarks in *Ireland: A New Economic History 1780–1939* (Oxford 1994), Part 3, Ch. 8. Brendan Bradshaw notes that only one academic study of the Famine appeared in Ireland between the 1930s and 1980s ('Nationalism and Historical Scholarship', *Irish Historical Studies*, vol. 26, no. 104, November 1989, pp. 340–41).

31. James Connolly, *Labour in Irish History* (Dublin, 1910; reprinted 1987), p. 41. The point is also noted by Patrick O'Farrell, 'Whose Reality? The Irish Famine in History and Literature', *Historical Studies of Australia and New Zealand*, no. 20 (April 1982).

explored and anthologized by Christopher Morash.[32] But it is in neither sense of the word a major literature. There is a handful of novels and a body of poems, but few truly distinguished works. Where is the Famine in the literature of the Revival? Where is it in Joyce?[33] There is a question here, when it comes to the Revival, of the politics of form: much of that writing is programmatically non-representational, and thus no fit medium for historical realism,[34] if indeed any fit medium for such subject matter is conceivable. Wilde, Moore and Yeats are in full flight from Nature, towards whatever style, pose, mask or persona might seem its antithesis; and the more Joyce recuperates this naturalistic region for the ends of art, the more obtrusively artificial that redemption becomes. If the Famine stirred some to angry rhetoric, it would seem to have traumatized others into muteness.[35] The event strains at the limits of the articulable, and is truly in this sense the Irish Auschwitz. In both cases, there would seem something trivializing or dangerously familiarizing about the very act of representation itself. Liam O'Flaherty published a magnificent novel, *Famine*, in 1937, and the playwright Tom Murphy has bravely tackled the subject on stage; but there are a number of curious literary near-misses. William Carleton's novel *The Black Prophet*, published during the Famine, concerns a previous such disaster; Yeats's play *The Countess Cathleen* treats of famine, but of no specific one; Patrick Kavanagh's poem *The Great Hunger*, which shares the title of Cecil Woodham-Smith's celebrated study of the subject, uses famine as a metaphor for sexual and spiritual hungering.

It is not quite that the Famine strikes narrative cohesion out of Irish history. There are central continuities across it, and many developments which were once thought to postdate the event – mass emigration, language decline, late marriage, impartible inheritance, land consolidation, the so-called devotional revolution – were perhaps already in train

---

32. See Christopher A. Morash, ed., *The Hungry Voice: The Poetry of the Irish Famine* (Dublin 1989), and his 'Imagining the Famine: Literary Representations of the Great Irish Famine' (unpublished Ph.D. thesis, Trinity College, Dublin 1990). I have also profited from Cormac Ó Gráda's 'The Great Famine in Folk Memory and in Song' (unpublished MS).

33. For Joyce, however, see Mary Lowe-Evans's remarkably original *Crimes against Fecundity: James Joyce and Population Control* (Syracuse 1989), Ch. 1, which among other things usefully assembles Joycean allusions to the Famine.

34. Though the Dublin theatre of the day could suffer from an excess of realism too. Count Casimir Markiewicz, directing Galsworthy's proletarian drama *Strife* at the Gaiety Theatre, insisted on hiring real labourers off the docks but made the mistake of paying them in advance, so that by the time the big fight scene arrived on stage their 'blood was up'. See Sean O'Faolain, *Constance Markiewicz* (London 1935, reprinted 1968), p. 57.

35. Malcolm Brown comments on how frequently the Famine was said by eyewitnesses to defeat language and beggar description (*The Politics of Irish Literature*, London 1972, p. 95).

before its occurrence.[36] It is rather that the Famine offers to reduce that history to what Walter Benjamin might have called the sheer empty homogeneous time of the body[37] – to insert, rather like Heathcliff, the disruptive temporality of Nature itself into the shapely schemas of historical chronology. In one sense, Nature has reared up and wreaked its terrible vengeance upon history; in another sense it images how that history had always in part appeared, ousting it at one level while miming it at another. The mediations between Nature and Culture are such things as food, labour, reproduction, the body – and all of these vital links have now been literally sundered. Culture is the surplus we have over stark need, and a social order shorn of that creative surplus can no longer *make* history at all, if indeed it ever properly could. History, like Nature, is now just an unmasterable exteriority, forever outrunning your control. This, interestingly enough, is also implicit in the naturalizing imagery of England – the sense that history is less something you strenuously fashion than spontaneously transmit, a lineage powered by its own inscrutably autonomous laws. The English and the Irish both have history in their bones, in entirely different senses. But we are talking here of teleology; and with the Famine such teleology can only ever be retrospective, constructed backwards after the unspeakable has already happened. Irish history would appear to have all the necessity of that teleological drive, but to absolutely no beneficent end. A necessity, in short, without a telos, implacable but distinctly unprovidential. The historical narrative, like the Chinese-box structure of *Wuthering Heights*, is strangely scrambled: the modern period in Ireland flows from an origin which is also an end, an abyss into which one quarter of the population disappears.

Because of the Famine, Irish society undergoes a surreal speed-up of its entry upon modernity; but what spurs that process on is, contradictorily, a thoroughly traditional calamity. Part of the horror of the Famine is its atavistic nature – the mind-shaking fact that an event with all the premodern character of a medieval pestilence happened in Ireland with frightening recentness. This deathly origin then shatters space as well as time, unmaking the nation and scattering Irish history across the globe. That history will of course continue; but as in Emily Brontë's novel there is something recalcitrant at its core which defeats articulation, some 'real' which stubbornly refuses to be symbolized. In both cases, this

36. A view held by some historians, but called into question by Cormac Ó Gráda in his *Ireland: A New Economic History*, p. 208.

37. See Walter Benjamin, 'Theses on the Philosophy of History', in *Illuminations*, edited by Hannah Arendt (London 1970).

'real' is a voracious desire which was beaten back and defeated, which could find no place in the symbolic order of social time and was expunged from it, but which like the shades of Catherine and Heathcliff will return to haunt a history now in the process of regathering its stalled momentum and moving onwards and upwards. Some primordial trauma has taken place, which fixates your development at one level even as you continue to unfold at another, so that time in Irish history and *Wuthering Heights* would seem to move backwards and forwards simultaneously. Something, anyway, for good or ill, has been irrevocably lost; and in both Ireland and the novel it takes up its home on the alternative terrain of myth.

Wuthering Heights tells its story back to front, gazing back on the tragic storm from the vantage point of calm, fashioning a retrospective teleology of sorts. The uncouth Hareton has now been levered into the Grange, and the love of a good woman will ensure that whatever was energizing about Heathcliff will live on in him, in tamed and civilized form. The gentry have reached out to the stout yeomanry and infused their own overbred civility with something of that racy vigour. Or, to put the matter differently, the British are once more busily appropriating the more admirable qualities of the Celt; we are teetering here on the very brink of Matthew Arnold's *On the Study of Celtic Literature*, which will engage in precisely such an ideological manoeuvre. Even the Famine will yield a retrospective teleology of sorts, to those of a Malthusian frame of mind, and there were plenty in Victorian London who saw it as providential. 'When man has failed to rule the world rightly,' comments Anthony Trollope in *The Landleaguers*, 'God will step in, and will cause famine, and plague, and pestilence – even poverty itself – with His own Right Arm' (Ch. 41). The moral crassness of this is as unoriginal as most of Trollope's pronouncements: the position is lifted wholesale from Malthus's *Essay on Population*, which sees famine as a last-ditch divine corrective to human vice.[38] For the Trollope of *Castle Richmond*, the Famine is the consequence of God's mercy rather than his wrath, undoing the results of human folly and converting Ireland into a pleasant and prosperous land.

---

38. The view that the Famine was a divine punishment was widespread among the Irish people. See Roger J. McHugh's vivid piece of popular history 'The Famine in Irish Oral Tradition', in R.D. Edwards and T.D. Williams, eds, *The Great Famine* (London 1956), p. 395. For a recent treatment of this theme, see D. Boyd Hilton, *The Age of Atonement* (Oxford 1991). For the religious and moral dimension of the Famine see Donal A. Kerr, *A Nation of Beggars?* (Oxford 1994).

'Nothing but the successive failures of the potato', wrote Lord Lansdowne's agent W.S. Trench, 'could have produced the emigration which will, I trust, give us room to become civilised.'[39] In the Famine, Charles Trevelyan remarked, an all-merciful providence and 'Supreme Wisdom has educed permanent good out of transient evil,'[40] a moral obscenity which might have mattered rather less had Trevelyan not been in charge of the relief operation. Trevelyan held that the effects of the Famine should not be too thoroughly mitigated by British aid, so that its improvident victims might learn their lesson; he also considered death by starvation a lesser evil than bankruptcy, and was restrained in his abuse of the Irish only by his belief that as a Cornishman he stemmed from the same race.[41] The disaster in Trevelyan's view had miraculously resolved most of the country's problems, forcing its warring sects into cooperative action, fostering self-reliance, quelling agrarian militancy and modernizing the economy. The only problem for Nassau Senior, one of Britain's most influential economists, was whether the President of the Immortals would accomplish his work thoroughly enough: a million deaths, he confided to the Master of Balliol, 'would scarcely be enough to do much good'.[42] Even Robert Peel, generally applauded for his judicious response to the onset of hunger, shared this providentialist perspective.[43]

For some British officials, the Famine was a sign of divine displeasure with the potato, and a golden opportunity for the Irish to shift to a less barbarous form of nourishment.[44] In a kind of dietary determinism, a less lowly food would produce a more civilized, and hence less politically belligerent people. What scandalized these commentators was the apparent bovine contentment of the Irish with their humdrum, socially unaspiring existence; and since growing potatoes involved little labour, it confirmed them in their endemic indolence. It is small wonder that some nationalists were stirred, however misguidedly, to speak of genocide; even as sober a

---

39. Quoted by James S. Donnelly, Jr, 'The Great Famine: Its Interpreters, Old and New', *History Ireland* (August 1993), p. 33.

40. Charles Trevelyan, *The Irish Crisis* (London 1848), p. 1. Trevelyan, pleased enough with his book, sent a copy to the Pope.

41. See Jenifer Hart, 'Sir Charles Trevelyan at the Treasury', *English Historical Review*, no. 75 (1960).

42. Quoted by Cormac Ó Gráda, *Ireland before and after the Famine*, p. 112. For Senior's disgruntled comments on Ireland, see his *Journals, Conversations and Essays Relating to Ireland*, 2 vols (London 1868).

43. See Peter Gray, 'Potatoes and Providence: British Government's Responses to the Great Famine', *Bullán*, vol. 1, no. 1 (Spring 1994).

44. For some excellent research into the potato, see Austin Bourke, *The Visitation of God? The Potato and the Great Irish Famine* (Dublin 1993).

commentator as George Sigerson is writing as late as 1868 of a 'policy of extermination' for Ireland in which men and women will give way to cattle.[45] One can, if one is so inclined, trace the providential pattern all the way from death, eviction and emigration to clearances, the consequent consolidating of land for pasturage, and the resulting emergence of a relatively prosperous rural middle class who would then form the material base for political independence.[46] And if the Famine helped to lay the economic ground for independence, it also dealt the single most lethal blow to whatever frail legitimacy the Irish ruling class could still muster. Even the meaningless will prove finally meaningful, as what is absolute loss for particular men and women becomes grist to the Hegelian mill. It is a process of which one can find a microcosm in the ancient Irish practice of hunger striking, which seeks to retrieve historical meaning from pure biological passivity, wrest significance from sheer facticity. But even the most dedicated dialectician is bound to baulk a little at this sanguine vista. If there *is* some providence stealthily afoot here, it would seem to have had to cancel itself out in order to realize itself, things having grown so extreme that only from some catastrophic engulfment of the present could new life begin to stir. Nature has thrown off the dead – as, in a casual afterthought, it threw off the living in the first place. In fact, things didn't have to happen that way – as *Wuthering Heights*, in this allegorical reading of it, can be persuaded to testify.

Nature, for English pastoral ideology, is plenitude and bountiful resource. In Irish culture and Brontë's novel it may occasionally be that too, but it also figures as harsh, niggardly, mean-spirited, and so as peasant rather than aristocrat. The Heights is more imposing than many an Irish farm, but what governs interpersonal relations in both cases is a tight material economy of labour, kinship and inheritance. For all the critical blather about transcendence and Romantic love, few more tenaciously materialist fictions have flowed from an English pen than this genealogically obsessed work, in which law, property and inheritance are the very stuff of the

---

45. Sigerson, *Modern Ireland*, p. 4. As late as 1967, Frank O'Connor writes of 'the deliberate destruction and scattering of a whole people' in *The Backward Look* (London 1967), pp. 154–5.

46. In 1841, more than one-third of all Irish houses were one-roomed cabins; in 1861 they constituted less than 10 per cent of the housing stock. See Mary Daly, *The Famine in Ireland* (Dublin 1986), p. 121. Oliver MacDonagh considers that without the Famine the density of the Irish population would have been too great for a viable peasant proprietorship. See his *Ireland: The Union and its Aftermath* (London 1977), p. 23.

plot and kinship the very structure of the narrative. Personal relationships can be left to the Lintons, who have enough money to go in for them. One can scarcely speak of whatever it is that binds Catherine and Heathcliff together as a relationship, since the word implies an alterity they refuse. When the middle-class Lockwood first stumbles into the Heights, he is farcically incapable of deciphering the characters' relationships, since they are little more than a grisly parody of a conventional family. It is history, property and power which have thrown them together, not connubial love or filial affection. Heathcliff is adopted into the Earnshaw *ménage*, and ends up by biting the hand that feeds him. Show kindness to these savages and they will kick you in the teeth. In fact, Heathcliff revolts, rather like Ireland against Britain, because of the barbarous way he is treated; only Catherine will grant him the recognition he demands, and even she, perfidious little Albion that she is, sells him out for Edgar Linton. In the end, even the liberals will rally to the landowners. The Heathcliff–Catherine relationship is a classic case of the Lacanian 'imaginary', an utter merging of identities in which the existence of each is wholly dependent on the existence of the other, to the exclusion of the world about them. But young Catherine must assume her allotted place in the symbolic order, leaving her anguished companion historically arrested in the imaginary register. Catherine and Heathcliff – an oppressed woman and an exploited farm labourer – have a chance, so it would seem, to inaugurate a form of relationship at odds with the instrumental economy of the Heights; but Catherine's renegacy prevents that relationship from entering upon material existence, just as it compels Heathcliff to run off, turn himself into a gentleman and appropriate the weapons of the ruling class in order to bring them low.

Unlike Oscar Wilde, the 'traitor' William Joyce (Lord Haw-Haw), or Winston Churchill's Irish secretary Brendan Bracken, Heathcliff doesn't make too good a job of turning himself into an English gentleman. You can take Heathcliff out of the Heights, but you can't take the Heights out of Heathcliff.[47] Emily's father succeeded rather better: born to a poor Irish peasant family, he Frenchified his surname and made it to Cambridge, right-wing Toryism and Anglican orders.[48] Heathcliff, by

---

47. 'You can take Paddy out of the bog, but you can't take the bog out of Paddy.'

48. For a somewhat Romantic biography, see John Lock and W.T. Dixon, *A Man of Sorrows: The Life, Letters and Times of the Rev. Patrick Brontë 1777–1861* (London 1979). For a sample of Brontë's own writings, including *Cottage Poems*, which urges the poor to reconcile themselves to their lowly state, and his abysmal Irish novella *The Maid of Killarney*, see *Brontëana: The Rev. Patrick Brontë, A.B., His Collected Works and Life* (Bingley 1898).

contrast, is a notoriously split subject: if he goes through the motions of undermining the ruling order from within, his soul remains arrested and fixated in the imaginary relation with Catherine. Indeed he engages in the former kind of activity precisely to avenge himself for the unavailability of the latter. Heathcliff starts out as an image of the famished Irish immigrant, becomes a landless labourer set to work in the Heights, and ends up as a symbol of the constitutional nationalism of the Irish parliamentary party. It is certainly a remarkably prescient novel – rather in the manner of Balzac's *Les Paysans*, which George Moore thought extraordinarily clairvoyant about later agrarian developments in Ireland.[49] Like those Redmondites who were both ranchers and rebels, Heathcliff is oppressor and oppressed in one body, condensing in his own person the various stages of the Irish revolution. As a child he is a kind of Defender or Ribbonman, chased out of the Grange in a minor rural outrage because the landlord thinks he is after his rents. He then shifts from rural proletarian – a dying breed in post-Famine Ireland – to rural bourgeois, cheating Hindley out of his possession of the Heights; and in this, one might claim, he recapitulates the drift of the Land League, which originated with the labourers, cottiers and smallholders of Connaught only to end up in the pockets of the conservative rural middle class. Once installed in the Heights, Heathcliff becomes a 'pitiless landlord' himself, and sets about dispossessing the local landowner and taking over the Grange.

This, indeed, is just what the Irish farmers will eventually do, or at least what the British state will do on their behalf. But there is a significant difference here between British and Irish class history. The English squirearchy, the oldest landed capitalist class in Europe, will finally oust the superannuated yeomanry; and in this sense, at the end of *Wuthering Heights*, the Grange wins out over the Heights. Heathcliff dies in enigmatic ecstasy, the middle-class challenge to the landowners is accordingly beaten off, and young Catherine will reassume her proper place as heiress of the Grange, taking the *farouche* Hareton with her to inject a dose of earthy vigour into the place. The anarchic inruption of Nature into Culture has been fended off; that moment – the transgressive moment of Heathcliff and Catherine Earnshaw – is then distanced into mythology, and an evolutionary history all but blown to bits by it can now resume its stately upward trek. Heathcliff dramatizes among other things a ruling-class fear

---

49. See Joseph Hone, *The Life of George Moore* (London 1936), p. 86.

of revolution from below; but his furious insurrectionary energy now lies quiet in the grave, and by the close of the novel the stormy liaison with Catherine seems a long way off. One can't, however, banish from one's mind what just *might* have happened: the dreadful possibility that this raging *ressentiment* might finally come to usurp the gentry themselves. This is what will happen in Ireland, half a century on from the novel; and it is what very nearly happens in the novel too, since Heathcliff does in fact get his hands on the Grange but dies before he can enjoy his victory.

If Heathcliff is the rural revolution, however, he is that revolution gone sour. Indeed he represents its betrayal as well as its near-triumph, its right as well as its left wing. As the Irish parliamentarians were often enough warned, you can't play the enemy's game, assume his political persona and steal his cultural clothes, and hope to remain unscathed in your radical idealism. (It is worth recalling, however, that before women and the working class achieved a presence in the House of Commons, the Irish parliamentary party was the one representative there of an oppressed people.) Heathcliff is forced to nurture his idealism – his love for Catherine – in some quite separate inward sphere, in the realms of myth, the imaginary and cherished childhood memory, while behaving externally like any predatory English landlord; and this destructive non-congruence of myth and reality has a long history in Ireland. Heathcliff, like Marx's petty bourgeoisie, is contradiction incarnate, forced to inflect his desire in terms which can only alienate it; and in the end that contradiction will tear him apart. He has tried to outmanoeuvre the enemy at his own game, but his heart isn't in it, and he dies of unappeasable longing. He was a foreign brat who grew too big for his boots, and the English have long experience of how to take care of that. He is a landlord who eats in the kitchen, without grace or civility, brutal in his personal dealings; and to this extent he resembles a stereo-typically uncouth minor Ascendancy figure more than he does anything out of Jane Austen. Indeed if one wanted a direct Irish comparison one might do worse than place him alongside the scheming, hardfaced, aggressive Charlotte Mullen of Somerville and Ross's *The Real Charlotte*, another exploiter whose monstrous violence is fuelled by disappointment in love.

One can, of course, try on a suitably revisionist reading of the whole affair. Like many Irish nationalists, Catherine and Heathcliff are in this view regressively fixated in some romanticized past, and would never have made it into the symbolic order of modern historical time. It is hard to imagine Heathcliff doing the dishes or wheeling the pram.[50] Catherine, on such a reading, is no kind of renegade: she is an unprotected woman who is unlikely to find the security she needs with such a disreputable partner. Edgar Linton, the Irish revisionist historian would be delighted to note, is not a bad sort of landlord; he may be something of a sap, but his love for Catherine is tender and steadfast, whatever Heathcliff's macho contempt for it. Like all of the Irish in a certain colonial view of them, Heathcliff is the eternal child, and his adult wheeler-dealing is ironically driven by this implacable infantile demand. Unable to deal 'maturely' with his rejection, he ends up with all the smouldering, self-lacerating hatred of a John Mitchel, or the blustering desperation of Parnell in his last days. There is an archaic weight of history with which English society has become entangled, and which is threatening to drag it down, and its name is Heathcliff, or Ireland. Better surely to shuck it off and face the future. But Heathcliff, like the Irish revolution itself, is archaic and modern together – a mournful remembrance of past wrongs which then unleashes a frenetically transformative drive to the future. That drive is in both cases thwarted, goes awry; but behind it lurks the memory of a bungled utopian moment, a subjunctive mood which still haunts the hills and refuses to lie quiet in its grave. From the gentry's standpoint, the novel recounts the tale of a catastrophe just averted; from a radical viewpoint it records the loss of revolutionary hopes, now projected into a mythologized past but, like the ghosts of Catherine and Heathcliff, still capable of infiltrating and disturbing the present. For their doomed relationship, despite its grotesque violence and perhaps because of its curiously genderless quality, involved an equality, solidarity and full mutual recognition which, had it been to the fore as a political ethic in the Land League, might have made a considerable difference to the subsequent course of Irish history. Meanwhile, the Lockwoods and Deans of the present, who as usual can't even hear the question, let alone provide an answer, continue to worry away at the hermeneutical riddle which haunts every page of *Wuthering Heights*: Who is Heathcliff? What is he? What does he want?

---

50. One of the first men to be seen wheeling a pram in the streets of Dublin was Thomas MacDonagh, lecturer in English at University College and one of the executed rebels of the Easter Rising. MacDonagh compounded this effeminacy by also, as a good Irish Irelander, wearing a kilt.

The naturalizing discourse of English culture may be less native to Ireland, but it has certainly been powerfully to the fore in much Irish discussion of the Famine. The typical gesture of Irish historiography on the subject has been to take the property relations of nineteenth-century Ireland for granted as some unquestionable context, and then to argue the toss within these constricted terms. In this, Irish historians re-enact the mental habits of the Victorian political economists, who similarly assumed that the frame of capitalist relations in Ireland fell beyond the bounds of criticism. Much historical debate over the Famine is thus loaded from the outset, secretly governed by what it dogmatically excludes as a legitimate topic of enquiry. Given those property relations, the Famine was arguably inevitable once the potato crop failed; but there was nothing inevitable about the relations themselves. Irish historians who are quick to pounce on the taken-for-grantedness of nationalist mythology are curiously blind to their own naturalizing habits of mind. Most historians are unwitting positivists, wary of what Hegel called the power of the negative, reluctant to grasp what happened in the light of what did not. They are also, commonly enough, ethical relativists in practice if not in theory, given to exculpating some piece of historical inhumanity on the grounds that one could have expected nothing more high-minded of the age in which it occurred. They contrast in this way with most Marxists, who are apt to claim that, say, slavery was a gross human injustice even if it is hard to see how, in a particular historical situation, anything different could have been imagined. In a typical comment, Mary Daly writes of the British government's handling of famine relief that 'it does not appear appropriate to pronounce in an unduly critical fashion on the limitations of previous generations'.[51] Why not? Does that also apply to witch burning, lunatic baiting and child labour? More to the point, does it apply to agrarian outrages, dynamiting, the assassination of Chief Secretaries or the slaying of unpopular landlords? It is the social worker theory of morality: Caligula was just the victim of social circumstance. We should seek to understand the headhunters rather than condemn them. It is just that the revisionist historian's admirable broadmindedness seems to stop mysteriously short of John Mitchel or Patrick Pearse.

'The Irish landlords', writes E.R.R. Green of the Famine, 'held the ultimate responsibility, but on the whole they were as much involved in

---

51. Daly, *The Famine in Ireland*, p. 113.

disaster as their tenantry.'[52] It would be intriguing to know Dr Green's statistics for the number of landlords dead of hunger oedema in the workhouses or shipped off typhus-ridden to Canada. But at least he attributes a degree of responsibility to them, however abstractly 'ultimate', which for some other Irish historians is fighting talk. The treatment of the Famine in L.M. Cullen's *An Economic History of Ireland since 1600* is extraordinarily cursory – unsurprisingly, perhaps, for a historian who can write elsewhere that 'the land system and economic behaviour of the landlords as a class were not reprehensible.'[53] It is worth pointing out that if this complacency is warranted, then an immense proportion of the *literary* evidence about the land in Ireland can be written off as worthless. Literary testimony is not, to be sure, hard historical evidence; but it is an odd historical judgement which can run clean counter to such a major body of writing. Perhaps everyone from Edgeworth and Banim to Carleton and Moore was simply cursed with too lurid an imagination. Some modern Irish historians, including L.M. Cullen, are not quite so quick to set aside literary evidence when it comes to arguing that, say, early modern Ireland was not in general nationalistic. As far as the Famine goes, we are dealing with the most important episode of modern Irish history and the greatest social disaster of nineteenth-century Europe – an event with something of the characteristics of a low-level nuclear attack. The zealous sanitizing of the subject in R.D. Edwards and T.D. Williams's collection of essays *The Great Famine* is as tendentious as any nationalist polemic. Mary Daly's judicious, informative account, one by no means uncritical of Westminster, half-excuses the *laissez faire* dogmatism of the Whig government by remarking that the Society of Friends entertained similar beliefs about private property.[54] It is doubtful that Daly would exculpate the Ribbonmen on the grounds that the Defenders believed in shooting bailiffs too. R.F. Foster briefly allows that the Whigs' relief policies were 'generally ill-founded', in a narrative that is otherwise scrupulous to avoid assigning blame.[55] It has been fashionable among Irish historians to scorn Cecil Woodham-Smith's *The Great Hunger* as a popular tear-jerker; but although the book has its crop of errors and exaggerations, it is remarkable how much of its account is confirmed by the

---

52. 'The Great Famine (1845–1850)', p. 273.

53. L.M. Cullen, 'The Social Basis of Irish Cultural Nationalism', in Rosalind Mitchison, ed., *The Roots of Nationalism* (Edinburgh 1980), p. 93.

54. Daly, *The Famine in Ireland*, p. 113.

55. R.F. Foster, *Modern Ireland 1600–1972* (London 1988), p. 327.

recent findings of James S. Donnelly, Jr, whom nobody could accuse of either amateurism or Anglophobia.[56]

There was no question of calculated genocide; and food imports, contrary to nationalist mythology, far outstripped exports in the Famine years.[57] But neither was the Famine an act of God. Peel's government moved quickly and effectively; the apparatus of public works and soup kitchens was extended with commendable efficiency into the remotest reaches of the island; and some landlords devoted themselves selflessly to the parlous condition of their tenants, bankrupting themselves in the process.[58] Taken as a whole, however, the landowners were precious little use, when their actions were not positively damaging. As for the government's record, the failure to stop the grain harvest of 1846 from being exported, before foreign aid arrived in early '47, had lethal consequences. The hiatus in the 1847 relief operation between the closure of public works and the opening of the soup kitchens sent many to their graves. The government denial of an emergency after 1847, along with its decision to abandon famine relief, was criminal. The ideological refusal to distribute free food until thousands had perished; the dumping of Famine costs on Ireland alone and on a ramshackle poor-law system; the Whig abandonment of the food depot project; the limiting of public works for fear of inhibiting private charity; the notorious Gregory clause which drove thousands off their land into fever-ridden workhouses; the mass evictions and subsidized emigration for the purpose of land consolidation; the niggardly sum spent on relief work (less than £10 million, in contrast to almost £70 million spent on the Crimean adventure): by all of these measures, half-measures and non-measures, the British government despatched hundreds of thousands to their needless deaths. It is these baneful policies that a certain species of modern historian would ask us to judge tolerantly, relativistically, in the light of the wisdom of their day.

---

56. See Donnelly's series of essays on the Famine in W.E. Vaughan, ed., *A New History of Ireland: vol. 5: Ireland Under the Union 1, 1801–70* (Oxford 1989). See also his 'The Great Famine: Its Interpreters Old and New', *History Ireland* (Autumn 1993), a rather more judicious assessment of the Young Irelander John Mitchel's views than R.F. Foster's calculatedly casual dismissal of him as a 'well-known American slaver'. For John Mitchel's celebrated charge of genocide, see Graham Davis, 'John Mitchel and the Great Famine', in Paul Hyland and Neil Sammels, eds, *Irish Writing: Exile and Subversion* (London 1991).

57. In 1846 and '47 Ireland imported five times more grain than it exported. See Gearoid Ó Tuathaigh, *Ireland before the Famine* (London 1991), p. 220.

58. See, for example, David Thompson and Moyra McGusty, eds, *The Irish Journals of Elizabeth Smith 1840–50* (Oxford 1980), for a fascinating record of one landowner's wife's mixture of compassionate concern and ferocious anti-Irish prejudice during the Famine years.

But there is more to British responsibility than that. In his bold, brilliant study *Why Ireland Starved*, Joel Mokyr advances a series of controversial theses: that Ireland was not overpopulated, that its relative lack of raw materials was no adequate reason for its non-industrialized condition, that insecurity of land tenure played no major role in low agricultural productivity, that agrarian agitation proved no significant factor in deterring investment. Mokyr adds for good measure that Britain could most certainly have saved Ireland from the Famine had it possessed the will to do so – a judgement reinforced by Christine Kinealy's *This Great Calamity*. The country's plight, so Mokyr considers, sprang chiefly from lack of capital investment, rendering its economy peculiarly vulnerable to 'exogamous shocks' such as the failure of the potato crop. And the primary cause of that low investment was the poverty of its people. But Mokyr does not press this question in turn to its root cause; instead he veers into a critique of the largely discredited case that union with Britain was the source of Ireland's economic ills. But why was Ireland so poor? The answer is doubtless complex; but it must surely include the fact of a vastly inequitable system of agrarian capitalism which was implanted by the British, run by their political clients, and conducted largely for their economic benefit.[59] Had that exploitative system been transformed – rent abolished, the graziers and strong farmers expropriated and their land equitably redistributed – a million men and women would surely not have perished. The empiricist historian would scoff at the idle utopianism of such a suggestion, and would be perfectly correct to do so. Such a revolution could not have conceivably happened at the time; neither the political will nor the political muscle for it were available. But the point of such subjunctive or counterfactual speculation is to place the ultimate responsibility for the disaster where it belongs – which is to say, not with 'the landlords' or 'the British', but with the system they sustained.

Amartya Sen has persuasively advanced the counter-intuitive case that famines are not primarily caused by food shortage; they are caused chiefly by lack of 'entitlements'– the incapacity of the people to buy what food is available.[60] Three million people perished in Bengal in the 1940s, though arithmetically speaking there was enough food for everyone. The application of this case to the Irish Famine is problematical. Certainly rents were an important factor in preventing the bringing of the people and

---

59. See Peter Gibbon, 'Colonialism and the Great Starvation in Ireland, 1845–9', *Race and Class*, vol. 17, no. 2 (Autumn 1975). See also Michael Hechter, *Internal Colonialism* (London 1975).

60. Amartya Sen, *Poverty and Famines* (Oxford 1981).

the food together. Cormac Ó Gráda has argued that there was, strictly speaking, enough grain in the country to feed all of its people, but that this, among other things, ignores the negative effects of crop requisitioning on subsequent production.[61] But if, so Ó Gráda argues, one considers the relevant food area as the United Kingdom rather than Ireland alone, then the Sen thesis is a forceful one. In this sense it can be reasonably claimed that the Irish did not die simply for lack of food, but because they largely lacked the funds to purchase food which was present in abundance in the kingdom as a whole, but which was not sufficiently available to them. In this sense, the Famine was the most lethal consequence of Britain's tendency to ignore, when it suited it, the union which it had oiled so many palms to achieve. As far as this particular castastrophe goes, it was not the union which contributed to Ireland's ills, but Britain's self-interested decision to set it aside. And the ultimate cause of this, whatever Trollope might have considered, was a matter of politics and property relations rather than of an all-merciful providence.

---

61. See Cormac Ó Gráda, *The Great Irish Famine* (London 1989), p. 62, and *Ireland before and after the Famine*, pp. 108–10. See also his *Ireland: A New Economic History*, pp. 199–200.

CHAPTER 2

ASCENDANCY AND HEGEMONY

The word 'hegemony' nowadays means something like dominance or supremacy. But in the annals of Marxism it has a more exact meaning, which stretches back far beyond the work of its most celebrated theorist, Antonio Gramsci. The concept of hegemony first springs to light in a series of debates within the Second International over the question of leadership within the revolutionary movement itself – of how the proletariat is to rally other oppressed groups and classes to its standard, or how it is to set the pace for the forces of bourgeois democracy.[1] Since such alliances are obviously not to be achieved by coercion, the idea of hegemony begins life as the very opposite of the repressive power which it sometimes suggests today. It is rather about the way in which the working class can win political authority over other radical movements, unifying them into a revolutionary bloc. The originality of Gramsci, then, is to have boldly transferred this concept to the question of the *ruling* class, and of the means by which it secures its power. Lifting the idea from its home within the revolutionary movement, Gramsci finds in it a clue to the peculiar resilience of bourgeois rule – a rule which operates more through the consensual life of civil society than through the coercive instruments of the state. Hegemony is a matter of what Gramsci calls 'intellectual and moral direction'; and, though the word is sometimes used in his work to include both coercion and consent, it refers chiefly to that 'permanently organised consent' by which modern states exercise their authority. It signifies, in the words of Sir Samuel Ferguson, 'the idea of erecting the bulwark of the state in the hearts of [the] inhabitants';[2]

---

1. See Perry Anderson, 'The Antinomies of Antonio Gramsci', *New Left Review* 100 (November 1976–January 1977).
2. Quoted by David Lloyd, *Nationalism and Minor Literature* (Berkeley 1987), p. 57.

and it was the failure of this project which Ferguson was to witness in Ireland.

For any state, the greatest test of its hegemonic powers is posed by its colonial subjects. For though hegemony is not just a cultural affair, there is no doubt that culture is vital to its workings; and winning the consent of men and women to be governed is a more precarious business when there is an embarrassing cultural rift between rulers and ruled. The colonialist may be visibly alien, in a way that native governing classes are usually not: he may be of a different ethnic origin, speak an unknown language, worship in unfamiliar style, live a life unimaginably remote from the experience of his subjects. All this, of course, may have its conveniently overawing effects; but obsequiousness or cultural cringe is hardly a reliable enough basis on which to win the hearts and minds of the natives, not least when you are also busy expropriating their land, dismantling their political institutions and rooting out inconvenient aspects of their culture.

Hegemony is not just a psychological matter: it is also a question of economic incentives and social techniques, religious practices and electoral routines. But it comes down in the end to a structure of subjectivity, which is one reason why it is so hard to assess. Domination can be measured by the indices of power, privilege and inequality, so that a group may be described as dominant however modestly it might describe itself. But hegemony involves values and attitudes, and so is a more elusive business. Consent is not a self-evident affair, either to those who seek it or to those who yield it. You can resist or capitulate to a ruler outright; or you can grant him a provisional title to exercise his power, provided certain rights are respected and certain compacts discreetly preserved. You can assent to authority in one sphere while denying its prerogative in another; or you can tolerate it in the short or medium term while reserving the right to dream of a future when it will be overthrown. You may submit with the conscious mind, while betraying by your actions that you remain secretly obdurate; you may defer to a particular master while refusing to bow to the system he symbolizes; or you may simply not know whether you accept his authority or not. Samuel Clark recounts the agreeable ancedote of a group of Irish tenants who read a loyal address to their landlord on the occasion of his wedding at the very moment when they were withholding their rents from him.[3] William Trench, newly appointed land agent for the Marquis of Bath, was forced to patrol the

---

3. Samuel Clark, *Social Origins of the Irish Land War* (Princeton 1979), p. 159.

estate armed with a brace of pistols only ten months after the tenantry had wrung his hand in extravagant welcome 'till the blood nearly spurted out of my fingers'.[4] As the Philosopher in James Stephens's novel *The Crock of Gold* remarks: 'a man should always obey the law with his body and disobey it with his mind.'

The concept of hegemony, writes Raymond Williams, 'sees the relations of domination and subordination, in their forms as practical consciousness, as in effect a saturation of the whole process of living – not only of political and economic activity, not only of manifest social activity, but of the whole substance of lived identities and relationships, to such a depth that the pressures and limits of what can ultimately be seen as a specific economic, political, and cultural system seem to most of us the pressures and limits of simple experience and common sense'.[5] It is doubtful whether any governing bloc in history has been able to achieve such unqualified sovereignty over its subjects, as Williams is the first to insist; ruling classes have been on the whole more tolerated than admired. But there were particular problems in this respect in colonial Ireland. For the truth is that no occupying power in the country was able to attain a hegemony sufficiently widespread, enduring and well-founded for its ends. The Anglo-Norman forces which sought to subjugate the island in the twelfth century established formal control over most of it, but saw their sway shrink to the small Pale around Dublin as Irish clan society proved too tenacious to subdue. Indeed if hegemony is relevant here at all, it is in reverse: by and large, it was the native Irish who culturally assimilated the Anglo-Norman interlopers, converting them gradually into the Gaelicized group of so-called Old English.

In the Tudor period, attempts at conciliation by the Crown alternated with policies of coercion, to culminate in the brutal military operation launched by Elizabeth.[6] It was clear enough to some at least of the Elizabethan governing class that political power could be implanted in Ireland only by cultural transformation. 'We must change their course of government, clothing, customs, manner of holding land, and habits of life', wrote Sir George Carew, 'it will be otherwise impossible to set up

---

4. Quoted by K. Theodore Hoppen, 'Landlords, Society and Electoral Politics', in C.H.E. Philpin, ed., *Nationalism and Popular Protest in Ireland* (Cambridge 1987), p. 317.

5. Raymond Williams, *Marxism and Literature* (Oxford 1977), p. 110.

6. See Ciaran Brady, 'Court, Castle and Country: The Framework of Government in Tudor Ireland', in C. Brady and R. Gilespie, eds, *Natives and Newcomers* (Dublin 1986). One suspects that the euphemistic 'Newcomers' of this title, to describe the colonizing influx into Ireland, was dictated by more than alliterative considerations.

in them obedience'[7] Since Irish society was politically decentralized, what held it together was a common culture; and this made culture all the more important a political target for the country's overlords. Some of the Gaelic chieftainry of the age came willingly to terms with the English administration, canny enough to discern a buttressed authority for themselves in the surrender and regranting of their hereditary titles.[8] Yet what resulted was the most wholesale dispossession of a native landed elite that the Europe of the age had witnessed. And while some of the nobility were complaisant enough, many of their followers were not. Most of the Irish refused to accept the reformed religion of the English state, or the legitimacy of the English Protestant monarchy. There is no reason to suppose that the 'New English' of the seventeenth-century plantations, or their Ascendancy progeny of the eighteenth century, were viewed always and everywhere as alien invaders by a uniformly rebellious people. But whatever popular consent these men and women were able to muster, they were incapable over the course of two centuries of commanding a sufficiently durable, broad-based loyalty from their subjects, and passed out of Irish history with much the same discreditable reputation with which their adventurist Cromwellian ancestors had entered in.

That is not to suggest that *Britain* did not gain a significant hegemony in Ireland. One medium of British power was the English language, which the Irish steadily assimilated, along with many of the cultural patterns of the metropolis.[9] Nor is it to suggest that the mass of the Irish people were held down by force; or that some of them did not feel genuine loyalty to their masters; or that the habits of deference in which they were skilled were always skin-deep. Lecky writes in his history of eighteenth-century Ireland of the 'feudal relation' everywhere apparent between landed and labouring classes. It is natural to want to keep in with those who provide you with a living, even if just the same dependency can make for antagonism. Even the most disaffected of the Irish populace – the Whiteboys, Shanavests, Rockites, Terry Alts and other secret societies – rarely challenged the landlord's right of ownership. Their goals were for the most part restorationist rather than revolutionary; and even Irish revolutionaries

7. Quoted by Declan Kiberd, 'Irish Literature and Irish History', in R.F. Foster, ed., *The Oxford History of Ireland* (Oxford 1989), p. 235.

8. See Mary O'Dowd, 'Gaelic Economy and Society', in Brady and Gillespie, *Natives and Newcomers*.

9. For some remarks on this topic, see Clair Wills, *Improprieties: Politics and Sexuality in Northern Irish Poetry* (Oxford 1993), Part 1, Ch. 3.

were on the whole a remarkably conservative crowd. A peasant society[10] in the grip of a reactionary Church, a traditionalist *mentalité* and a parochial view of the world was hardly insurrectionary stuff. The fear that dispossessed Gaels were secretly scheming to repossess their ancestral lands was largely a Protestant invention.[11] When a Land League speaker at a meeting in Castlebar called for the abolition of landlordism, an anxious voice from the crowd enquired who they would pay their rents to.[12] If some of the lower orders were humbly grateful for the benevolence of their superiors, this was not necessarily false consciousness, since some of their superiors were genuinely benevolent. The target of their wrath might be less the landlord than his agent or middleman,[13] the village gombeen man or strong farmers and graziers of their own native stock and religious persuasion. Despite widespread discontent, the Irish struck directly at British power only four times in the period from 1798 to 1900, and three of these uprisings were farcically ineffectual. And though eighteenth- and nineteenth-century Ireland was a violent enough place, it was not especially so by European standards, and the death count was far from horrendous.

But there is a finely nuanced spectrum between being held down by brute coercion and eagerly volunteering one's assent. The dull compulsion of daily toil, the perils of striking at a superior power, the fear of brutal reprisals, the problems of effective organization, the inability to think up a feasible social alternative: all this doubtless played its part in what Irish acquiescence there was. On the whole, the mass of the Irish people would seem to have been compliant and contumacious together, paying their rulers their dues with one part of their minds while witholding their allegiance with another. Such ambiguous consciousness, combining 'official' beliefs with potentially subversive ones, is common enough among subaltern peoples, as Gramsci himself points out. But the real test of hegemony is whether a ruling class is able to impose its spiritual authority on its underlings, lend them moral and political leadership and persuade them of its own vision of the world. And on all these counts, when the record is taken as a whole, the Anglo-Irish must be reckoned an egregious failure.

---

10. I use 'peasant' as deliberate and inadequate shorthand to cover a complex range of social classes in the countryside.

11. See Thomas Bartlett, *The Fall and Rise of the Irish Nation* (Dublin 1992), p. 5.

12. See Michael Davitt, *The Fall of Feudalism* (London 1904), p. 164.

13. See, for the role of the middlemen in Ireland, D. Dickson, 'Middlemen', in Thomas Bartlett and D.W. Hayton, eds, *Penal Era and Golden Age* (Belfast 1979). I have also benefited from Kevin Whelan, 'An Underground Gentry? Catholic Middlemen in the Eighteenth Century' (unpublished MS).

Part of that failure lay in their neglect of one of the most powerful techniques of hegemony: the cooption of an upper stratum of the natives. A comprador class of that kind never fully emerged in Ireland, largely because the rulers had chosen to define their supremacy in religious terms. Since all the native classes were Catholic, they were all equally to be viewed as enemies. The penal laws oppressed cottier and Gaelic gentle-folk indiscriminately. From the late eighteenth century onwards, under mounting political pressures, this policy began to change, as a Catholic middle class was now cautiously accommodated. But it was hard, that late in the day, to undo a spectacular history of oppression; and the result of this reformist strategy was to whip up a Protestant backlash and lay the foundations for a native nationalism. Daniel O'Connell sprang from the very class which the British were now reluctantly wooing. The Ascendancy could secure its rule neither by including nor excluding those it held down; and this was certainly one reason why it was finally brought low.[14]

It should come as no surprise, then, that the abiding concern of the greatest of all Irish political thinkers is the question of hegemony. Writing to his son Richard in 1792, Edmund Burke comments on a recent self-description of the ruling Anglo-Irish junta: Ascendancy. The term, he suggests, is curious, for 'the sense in which I have hitherto seen it used, was to signify an influence obtained over the minds [sic] of some other person by love and reverence, or by superior management and dexterity'.[15] Burke has no objection to the transposition of the word from the moral to the political sphere: indeed he applauds this as a creative strategem which 'may be truly said to enrich the language'. To extend the discourse of ethics and the affections to the political realm is a classically Burkean move, which the maestro himself could in principle only applaud. But if this particular piece of metaphorizing sticks in his craw, it is because 'ascendancy' ought to translate as 'hegemony' and is in fact being used as a synonym for domination. 'New ascendancy' is in fact 'the old mastership

---

14. For an interesting discussion of these matters, see Theodore W. Allen, *The Invention of the White Race, vol. 1: Racial Oppression and Social Control* (London 1994). Allen sees Anglo-Irish rule as a question of *racist* supremacy – a form of domination which does not of course necessarily involve different physical characteristics in rulers and ruled. For a rather different account of early modern Ireland, see Nicholas Canny, 'Irish Resistance to Empire? 1641, 1690 and 1798', in Lawrence Stone, ed., *An Imperial State at War: Britain from 1689 to 1815* (London 1994).

15. 'Letter to Richard Burke', in R.B. McDowell, ed., *The Writings and Speeches of Edmund Burke,* vol. 9 (Oxford 1991), p. 643.

... the resolution of one set of people in Ireland ... to keep a dominion over the rest by reducing them to absolute slavery under a military power.[16] A word denoting spiritual influence and moral leadership has been deceptively harnessed to the service of oppression. We may note, too, that the word 'Ascendancy' can shift between describing a political *condition* to naming a social *bloc*, which is then bluntly defined by its sway over its subordinates.[17] 'It must be remembered', writes C.D.A. Leighton, 'that the phrase [Ascendancy] originally denoted a polity – or rather a variety of polities – as much as a body of persons and that this body comprehended a wider social and perhaps religious spectrum than nineteenth- and twentieth-century literary usage suggests'.[18] The shift from abstract to collective noun, Leighton adds, indicates the role of confessionalist beliefs in determining the Irish social structure. The word 'Ascendancy' is at once descriptive and normative, sociological and ideological, flatly denoting a state of affairs while anxiously asserting its desirability. If it complacently suggests a *fait accompli*, it is also a weapon wielded for its preservation. It can be a name for the ruling junta of Ireland, or for that junta in a particularly aggressive posture. It is used in the 1790s, as the political atmosphere heats up, as part of a reactionary drive to assert Protestant privilege; but Jacqueline Hill argues that it was also in circulation earlier as 'a non-contentious slogan to defend the established Church of Ireland'.[19] In a further semantic slide, the self-assurance of the title conceals the political panic in which it was born – the fear that Britain will cravenly placate the Irish Catholics in the face of European revolutionary turmoil and an alarming alliance between dissident Catholics and radical Presbyterians.[20]

---

16. Ibid., p. 644.

17. For an excellent account of Burke and the Ascendancy, drawing attention to the close parallel he sensed between Anglo-Irish oligarchy and Jacobin dictatorship, see Seamus Deane, 'Edmund Burke and the Ideology of Irish Liberalism', in Richard Kearney, ed., *The Irish Mind* (Dublin 1985). For the controversial term 'Ascendancy' itself, see W.J. McCormack, 'Vision and Revision in the Study of Eighteenth-Century Parliamentary Rhetoric', *Eighteenth-Century Ireland*, no. 2 (1987); and 'Eighteenth-Century Ascendancy: Yeats and the Historians', *Eighteenth-Century Ireland*, no. 4 (1989). See also McCormack's *The Dublin Paper War of 1786–1788* (Dublin 1993). See also Jacqueline Hill, 'The Meaning and Significance of "Protestant Ascendancy", 1787–1840', in the British Academy publication *Ireland after the Union* (Oxford 1989). See also James Kelly, 'Eighteenth-Century Ascendancy: A Commentary', *Eighteenth-Century Ireland*, no. 5 (1990); and his essay 'The Genesis of "Protestant Ascendancy": The Rightboy Disturbances of the 1780s and their Impact upon Protestant Opinion', in G. O'Brien, ed., *Parliament, Politics and People* (Dublin 1989).

18. C.D.A. Leighton, *Catholicism in a Protestant Kingdom* (London 1994), p. 38.

19. Hill, 'The Meaning and Significance of "Protestant Ascendancy"', pp. 2–3.

20. See W.J. McCormack, *Ascendancy and Tradition* (Oxford 1985), p. 88.

The term 'Ascendancy', then, is a text all in itself, shot through with tensions and ambiguities. Shuttling between upper and lower case, it can suggest a social group, a political set-up or a spiritual condition. As a speech act it hesitates between constative and performative, asserting into existence the very situation it describes. The term has a narrowly specific meaning: the sovereignty of the established church. But this in turn becomes metonymic of the whole Williamite establishment (Crown, parliament, army, judiciary) which must be protected against Jacobin and Jacobite alike. This politico-juridical form then comes to take on socio-economic content, as 'Ascendancy' narrows from meaning a state of political dominion to naming a particular social class; but *which* social class raises yet another ambiguity.[21] The present chapter deals largely with the Anglo-Irish landowners; but the term Ascendancy suggests less a single class than a social bloc, spanning nobility, gentry and bourgeoisie, whose social differences are from this viewpoint less important than their shared political and religious ideology. As the concept runs its turbulent course from late-eighteenth-century Dublin Corporation to Yeatsian Big House, it will find itself cranked up a social gear or two, climbing the social pole just as the Ascendancy itself is slipping down it. From its early uses in middle-class Protestant Dublin, it will come to signify a patrician grandeur so assured that it transcends the vulgar discourse of class altogether. 'Ascendancy' means a state of dominance or authority; but the term is dynamic as well as static, suggesting a movement towards this goal, and so ominously evoking the truth that what goes up can always come down. But the phrase 'Protestant Ascendancy' betrays a grammatical ambivalence too – for it can mean an ascendancy which is Protestant, or the ascendancy of Protestantism.

What this comes down to, in effect, is that the sway of the Protestant religion is to be defended as a way of safeguarding a political supremacy which is Protestant. What is at stake is not so much that religion itself as its ideological function, which would now seem to exhaust its entire doctrinal content. The meaning of the ascendancy of Protestantism resides wholly in Protestant political rule. A phrase which smacks of a spiritual campaign can be instantly translated into crassly secular terms. C.D.A. Leighton remarks on the anomalous nature in the Europe of its day of a ruling-class elite defined largely through religion, as opposed to one whose religion played a less constitutive role: 'In opposition to this notion of an

---

21. A point emphasized by W.J. McCormack (*Ascendancy and Tradition*, p. 180), who reminds us usefully of the astrological resonance of the term.

elite which was certainly Protestant but only accidentally so, eighteenth-century Ireland evolved the notion that Protestantism was both a necessary and sufficient qualification to gain access to the elite, that hegemonic rights belonged to the entire body of Protestants by virtue merely of their Protestantism'.[22] So it is that Henry Grattan could speak of this brand of Protestant faith as 'bigotry without religion', and Edmund Burke could fasten on its purely negative force, intended as it was to put down rather than to proselytize. Jonathan Swift was passionately concerned with defending the Anglican establishment and coolly indifferent to divine mystery. Indeed if the Ascendancy had actually converted the Catholics they might have endangered their own privileges, as well as undermining their divide-and-rule strategy over the people as a whole. Protestantism means freedom, whereas Catholicism signifies authoritarianism – both in the sense of those who conduct themselves autocratically, and those who slavishly submit to such a power. In so far as Catholics are already slaves, then, they need to be doubly oppressed, by Protestant liberty as well as by Romish rule, in order to prevent them from coming to power and behaving as tyrants.

Burke's virulent contempt for the Anglo-Irish Ascendancy, as a class too petty to form a democracy but too populous to constitute an authentic aristocracy, is scornfully underlined in his letter of 1792 to Sir Hercules Langrishe. Drably plebeian in character, bereft of any patrician aura, the Protestants of Ireland are too inconveniently close to those they rule to win their veneration. This bigoted oligarchy cannot possibly pass muster as a ruling bloc, since for Burke all genuine governance is founded upon love. This is not to suggest, need one say, that he was in the least averse to coercion: on the contrary, he lent his support to a whole range of repressive measures which in the name of freedom transformed late-eighteenth-century Britain into a police state. As his admirer John Morley comments with pardonable hyperbole, Burke lent filial respect to the English constitution at a time when England had about the most mis-chievous set of political arrangements it had ever endured.[23] This disciple of liberty, MP for a rotten borough, ended up as an obsessional hawk who urged the military crushing of revolutionary France and the full-blooded restoration of the *ancien régime*. Indeed Christopher Reid detects a gradual slide in Burke's thought from consent to coercion – a sliding of emphasis, as the revolutionary pressures mount, from law as the cement

---

22. Leighton, *Catholicism in a Protestant Kingdom*, p. 34.
23. John Morley, *Edmund Burke: A Hisorical Study* (London 1867), pp. 120–21.

of the constitution to executive justice as the means of quelling dissent.[24] But Burke is shrewd enough to perceive that governing classes survive only by engaging the affections of their inferiors, and that a loveless sovereignty is politically bankrupt. There must be, so he writes to Langrishe, 'a communion of interests, and a sympathy in feelings and desires between those who act in the name of any description of people, and the people in whose name they act'; and it is just this form of 'virtual representation' of which Ireland is so dismally bereft.[25] 'Power and authority', he declares in *Conciliation with the Colonies* (1775), 'are sometimes bought by kindness; but they can never be begged as alms by an impoverished and defeated violence'.[26] There is no reason, as he reminds the Sheriffs of Bristol, 'why one people should voluntarily yield any degree of pre-eminence to another, but on a supposition of great affection and benevolence towards them'; and he is sure that 'the natural effect of fidelity, clemency, kindness in governors is peace, good-will, order, and esteem'.[27] What makes for a stable polity applies to international relations too. 'Men', he remarks in the *First Letter on a Regicide Peace* (1796), 'are not tied to one another by paper and seals. They are led to associate by resemblances, by conformities, by sympathies. Nothing is so strong a tie of amity between nation and nation as correspondence in laws, customs, manners, and habits of life. They have more than the force of treaties in themselves. They are obligations written in the heart.'[28] J.E. Bicheno, who toured Ireland in 1829, strongly agreed. The Irish, he thought, being a genial sort of race, were particularly susceptible to appeals to their affections, fit candidates for hegemony rather than absolute power. 'Absolute authority', he writes, 'is never exercised by brute force alone. It obtains its ascendancy by appeals to antiquity, established institutions, the social affections, honour, glory, the weaknesses and infirmities of our nature, and everything which influences the imagination'.[29] Since the Irish are affectionate, imaginative and morally infirm, their rulers have clearly missed out on a splendid opportunity.

---

24. Christopher Reid, *Edmund Burke and the Practice of Political Writing* (Dublin 1985), p. 24. Francis O'Gorman, in his *Edmund Burke: His Political Philosophy* (London 1973, p. 139), also sees a shift in Burke from the early Whig ideal of limited government to a later stress on the powers of the state.

25. McDowell, ed., *Writings and Speeches of Burke*, vol. 9, p. 629.

26. F.W. Raffety, ed., *The Works of the Right Honourable Edmund Burke* (London n.d.), vol. 2, p. 184.

27. Ibid., p. 260.

28. McDowell, ed., *Writings and Speeches of Burke*, vol. 9, p. 247.

29. J. Bicheno, *Ireland and its Economy* (London 1830), pp. 223-4.

In coining the term 'Ascendancy', the Anglo-Irish junta have illicitly transposed a moral to a political meaning. Burke himself will raid the discourses of heart and hearth, friendship and filial piety, the comradely and the connubial, projecting this private sphere into the public realm and so creating a language of political hegemony *avant la lettre*.[30] 'To bring the dispositions that are lovely in private life into the service and conduct of the commonwealth', he urges in *Thoughts on the Present Discontents* (1770), 'so to be patriots, as not to forget we are gentlemen'.[31] The English Constitution, so he argues in *Reflections on the Revolution in France* (1790), has in its option for the hereditary descent of titles 'given to our frame of polity the image of a relation in blood'.[32] 'Nations', he writes in *Thoughts on the Present Discontents*, 'are not primarily ruled by laws; less by violence ... Nations are governed by the same methods, and on the same principles, by which an individual without authority is often able to govern those who are his equals or his superiors: by a knowledge of their temper, and by a judicious management of it.'[33] With Burke, then, we hover on the historical threshold of everything that Michel Foucault abhorred: a patient charting of the very depths of subjectivity, so that men and women may be the more dexterously inscribed with power. It is in this spirit that Sir Samuel Ferguson will write later of the Anglo-Irish that their position is insecure because 'their intelligence has not embraced a thorough knowledge of the genius and disposition of their Catholic fellow citizens'[34] – a knowledge, naturally, which will help to keep those citizens firmly in their place.

On the question of hegemony, principle and utility are, as usual with Burke, closely linked: if it is contrary to natural justice to treat men and women with autocratic contempt, it is also the surest way of driving them to the barricades. The savage irony of Ireland is that the Ascendancy are thrusting into the arms of an unholy Jacobinism the very Catholics whose venerable institutions might have furnished a convenient bulwark against it. Burke's frustration is plain: all the preconditions for a successful hegemony are implicit in the Catholic people, with their instincts of deference and loyalty, their esteem for custom and tradition, their valuing

30. For Burke's use of domestic imagery about political affairs, see J. Boulton, *The Language of Politics in the Age of Wilkes and Burke* (London 1963), Ch. 7.

31. *Thoughts on the Present Discontents*, in Paul Langford, ed., *The Writings and Speeches of Edmund Burke*, vol. 2 (Oxford 1981), p. 320.

32. *Reflections on the Revolution in France*, in L.G. Mitchell, ed., *The Writings and Speeches of Edmund Burke*, vol. 8 (Oxford 1989), p. 84.

33. Langford, ed., *Writings and Speeches of Burke*, vol. 2, p. 252.

34. Quoted by Malcolm Brown, *Sir Samuel Ferguson* (Lewisburg 1973), p. 48.

of cultural bonds and local allegiances; but the Ascendancy is infuriatingly incapable of exploiting these rich resources. 'For my part', Burke comments in his *Tracts Relating to Popery Laws* (1765), 'I think the real danger to every State is to render its subjects justly discontented';[35] and he comments to Sir Hercules Langrishe that 'I believe that no man will seriously assert, that when a people are of a turbulent spirit, the best way to keep them in order, is to furnish them with something substantial to complain of.'[36] It is precisely this which the bungling British have done in the case of their obstreperous American colonials, driving them headlong into rebellion by obtusely elevating an empty metaphysical right over the more sagacious course of conciliation. What they ought to have done was to allow the colonies to associate the very idea of their own freedom with the sovereignty that holds them down: 'Let the colonies always keep the idea of civil rights associated with your government; – they will cling and grapple to you ... the more ardently they love liberty, the more perfect will be their obedience'.[37] Burke has understood that the key mechanism of hegemony is the introjection of the Law, so that to disobey its edicts would be to violate one's own most authentic being. And this, as we shall see a little later, is one reason why he was so fascinated by aesthetics.

To root government in human affections is in one sense to lend it an alarmingly fragile foundation, in another sense equivalent to anchoring it in adamant. For if men's and women's sympathies are volatile and subjective, they are also a good deal more likely to drive them to murder or martyrdom than any mere abstract doctrine. Love is the only true guarantee of power, and popular consent, as Burke argues in the *Popery Tracts*, the ultimate source of all legality. From his mentor David Hume he inherits the unnerving doctrine that power is an effect of obedience rather than *vice versa*: it is free assent which keeps the law in existence, so that governments would be powerless if not obeyed. 'As force is always on the side of the governed,' so Hume somewhat surprisingly argues in his 'Of the First Principles of Government', 'the governors have nothing to support them but opinion. It is therefore on opinion only that government is founded, and this maxim extends to the most despotic and military governments, as well as to the most free and most popular'.[38]

---

35. McDowell, ed., *Writings and Speeches of Burke*, vol. 9, p. 479.
36. Ibid., p. 621.
37. Raffety, ed., *Works of Burke*, vol. 2, pp. 234-5.
38. David Hume, *Essays* (London 1963), p. 29. It is interesting that, in his final phrase, Hume partly deconstructs the distinction between consent and coercion, suggesting as he

Authority, in short, is a kind of fiction we collaboratively sustain; and though Burke rails in his *Letter to a Member of the National Assembly* (1791) against French statesmen who 'exist by everything that is spurious, fictitious, and false'[39] there is a sense for him in which all political sovereignty depends on a willing suspension of disbelief. 'The only firm seat of authority', he announces in his *Address to the King*, (1797), 'is in the minds, affections and interests of the people'.[40] But if the ruling power is a kind of fiction, so also are the people who lie at the source of its legitimacy. As he argues in the *Appeal from the New to the Old Whigs* (1791), the people are no raw datum, as the left-wing metaphysicans would hold, but are constituted as such only within the artifice or legal fiction of civil society, and cease to be a people altogether when they violate that corporate identity. The political consequence is plain: the people can no more dismantle the frame of civil society than an actor on stage could overthrow the piece in which he performs, since his identity as an agent is wholly constituted by it.[41] Even so, there is something alarmingly anti-foundational about the notion that power rests upon nothing but consent, opinion and affection, as though in some Berkeleyan fantasy it would vanish if we were all to close our eyes. There is a kind of perilous Feuerbachian inversion at work in this Whiggish doctrine, exposing as mere projections of the imagination those powers whose sway over us seemed so assured. And it is exactly because power lacks any more solid basis than this collective willing of it into being that the idea of hegemony – of seducing and cajoling those from whom one draws one's political authority – assumes such a vital role in Burke's thought.

Political power, then, is in an important sense arational: it is no more open to explanation than filial devotion or erotic love, and perhaps all the more durable for that. Burke is a kind of Wittgensteinian for whom what

---

does that even a despotic regime must be passively endured by those who in principle have the power to overthrow it. The coercive apparatuses of the state, to be effective, must rest upon a general *a priori* consent from the people to their punitive operations.

39. Mitchell, ed., *Writings and Speeches of Burke*, vol. 8, p. 315. Burke himself learnt much as a politician from the acting of his friend David Garrick, so that in this sense a real performance modelled itself on a fictional one. J.G.A. Pocock speaks of eighteenth-century Whiggism as an 'intensely oratorical and theatrical culture' in his review of Conor Cruise O'Brien's *The Great Melody* (*London Review of Books*, 24 February 1994).

40. *Works and Correspondence of the Right Honourable Edmund Burke* (London 1852), vol. 5, p. 528.

41. An analogy taken up by W.B. Yeats, who in one of his letters quotes a remark of Victor Hugo that 'It is in the Theatre that the mob becomes a people' (John Kelly and Ronald Schuchard, eds, *The Collected Letters of W.B. Yeats, vol. 3: 1901-1904*, Oxford 1994, p. 171).

is given is 'forms of life', sedimented cultural habits and time-hallowed practices which resist any anchoring in some absolute reason. This is not to enlist him as a cultural relativist: on the contrary, it is part of his polemic against Warren Hastings that ethical commands are universal rather than parochial, that moral values do not bend to shifts of geographical locale, that the same standards of liberty and justice must prevail among the Indian people as among the British, and that Hastings's conventionalist appeal to alien cultural codes to justify his behaviour is a piece of shabby sophistry. Unlike some present-day pragmatists, Burke recognizes the condescension involved in such reasoning, and puts his faith instead in the more radical notion of a common human nature. But if he upholds some version of natural law,[42] he insists that such law is always culturally instantiated, and so, in an adroit manoeuvre, succeeds in fending off radical 'natural rights' metaphysicians with the one hand while assailing a disreputable cultural relativism with the other. 'There are some fundamental points', he asserts in Remarks on the Policy of the Allies (1797), 'in which nature never changes – but they are few and obvious, and belong rather to morals than to politics. But so far as regards political matter, the human mind and human affairs are susceptible of infinite modifications, and of combinations wholly new and unlooked for.'[43]

At the centre of Burke's political thought lies the belief that colonial power must cling tenaciously to the contours of a native culture – that the Indians must be governed 'upon their own principles and maxims and not upon ours'.[44] It was the violation of this principle which led to

42. A matter much debated among his commentators. Alfred Cobban upholds the traditional view of Burke as a utilitarian (Edmund Burke and the Revolt against the Eighteenth Century, London 1929, p. 46), and Francis O'Gorman is sceptical of any such coherent natural law doctrine in Burke; but Peter Stanlis makes much of it in his Edmund Burke and the Natural Law (Ann Arbor 1965), as do Francis P. Canavan in The Political Reason of Edmund Burke (Durham, N.C. 1960) and, more qualifiedly, B.T. Wilkins in The Problem of Burke's Political Philosophy (Oxford 1967). The case that Burke was a natural law traditionalist, whether true or false, has much to do with his appropriation in the 1960s as a kind of proto-American Cold Warrior. C.B. MacPherson's Burke (Oxford 1960) speculates interestingly that in his appeal to natural law Burke is reaching back to a more traditionalist source of ideological sanctions for a social order enduring a crisis of legitimacy, as the contractual nature of capitalist relations threatens to render such notions disturbingly redundant. It is certainly possible to hypothesize that in a revolutionary epoch Burke felt the need for a rather stronger political foundation than Humean custom and opinion, and that his glancing allusions to natural law reflect this fact. But he must beware at the same time of thereby selling the pass to the 'natural rights' metaphysicans he abhors.

43. Mitchell, ed., Writings and Speeches of Burke, vol. 8, p. 498.

44. P.J. Marshall, ed., The Writings and Speeches of Edmund Burke, vol. 6 (Oxford 1991), p. 345.

the loss of America, and which has wreaked such havoc in Ireland. To achieve hegemony, colonial rule must be refracted through the traditions of those it governs, miming their cultural gestures and conforming itself to their customs. In order to flourish, such power must court *kenosis*, risk a loss of being in order to come into its own. For the institutions of a people crystallize their beliefs and affections, having been moulded by an organic process to their unique sensibility; and it is this sensibility, sedimented in a style of worship or system of land ownership, which is the target of political power. That power must therefore be protean and pliable, quicksilver and chameleon-like in its capillary adjustments to the forms of life it encounters. It must practise the modest self-effacement of the diplomat if it is to enjoy the puissance of the monarch, empathise with its object in order the more effectively to appropriate it. True to the spirit of Burke, John Stuart Mill, in his pamphlet *England and Ireland*, will later call for Ireland to be governed in accordance with Irish ideas, and draw a comparison with British rule in India.

It is thus that power will found itself securely. But what it founds itself *on* would seem a good deal more slippery – nothing more metaphysically imposing, in fact, than the way a culture has evolved through the ages, which could always after all have been different. Burke's full-blown culturalism ('art is man's nature', he remarks in his *Appeal from the New to the Old Whigs*) is at once the strength and weakness of his political thought – for if local culture is stronger than general nature, as he comments in a speech on India, it would also seem a good deal more arbitrary. What authority rests upon is manners: 'Manners are of more importance than laws. Upon them, in a great measure the laws depend.'[45] The point, once more, is Wittgensteinian: what will count as an effective law for us is determined by the preconceptions built into our 'form of life'; and if this cultural context grounds the law, there is no way in which it can be grounded by it. What precedes the law, so to speak, is its own legitimacy; and a lawless society, as parts of Ireland have been at certain points in their history, is less one which flouts this or that law than one which refuses to accept the legitimacy of the law as such. What is given for Burke is 'prejudice' – a term as wholly unpejorative in his lexicon as it is

---

45. 'First Letter on a Regicide Peace', in McDowell, ed., *Writings and Speeches of Burke*, vol. 9, p. 242. For Burke's argument that commerce can flourish only under the protection of manners, and that manners in turn require religion and the nobility, see J.G.A. Pocock, 'The Political Economy of Burke's Analysis of the French Revolution', in *Virtue, Commerce, and History* (Cambridge 1985).

in Hans-Georg Gadamer's.[46] Both men are resolutely anti-Enlightenment in their belief that cultural predilection or pre-understanding is the framework of all more formalized knowledge. But prejudice cannot itself be justified; and if prejudice is the basis of politics, then politics would appear to be alarmingly deprived of any sure foundation. The culture which seals its power is exactly what threatens to subvert it.

So much is clear from Burke's defence of prescription, in the sense of rights guaranteed by immemorial possession. Or, to put the point another way, rights validated by the recounting of a certain narrative. What bestows rights and titles for the prescriptionist is history itself, which legitimates them as no abstract reasoning could. History is thus itself a species of reason, and the mere passage of time a mute theoretical argument all in itself. It is the temporal lapse between an origin and the present which retrospectively justifies that origin, so that history moves forwards while its rationales travel backwards. In this sense, authority is always deferred, so that my right to the peerage or property I fraudulently acquired last Thursday will become luminously self-evident in two hundred years' time. It is a case which works conveniently against the Anglo-Irish Ascendancy, who have simply not been around long enough for their expropriations to have been mercifully eroded by the passage of time. But it is not a view of history congenial to one strain of Irish sentiment, for which a historical wrong can rarely be cancelled by its consequences, and it is not without its logical problems. How long must a title have existed for it to be valid? And if it will eventually be legitimized by the sheer passage of time, why not prospectively read this authority back into the origin, justifying my violent usurpation of your property today on the grounds that in a century's time it might have modifed into second nature? Is moral right based in Nietzschean fashion on an oblivion of some primordial crime? And if the sacred right of possession is determined by something as chancy as whether it comes to stick historically, how sacred can it actually be? If all justification is retrospective, to be dispensed by the tribunal of the future, does this not leave me perilously stripped of moral criteria in the present? The present, it would appear, is lawless, since we can never know which of its actions the future will endorse; only the future is the locus of moral judgement. But history is a succession of presents, and the future does not exist. We may intervene against a supposed injustice in the present, as Burke wishes to put down revolutionary power in France; but if we do we cut it off at birth and thus

---

46. See Hans-Georg Gadamer, *Truth and Method* (London 1975), Part 2, 11, i.

prevent it from evolving into the future which might retrospectively justify it. To suppress a right because it is not immemorial is precisely to deprive it of the opportunity of becoming so.

What is at work in this ideology is a political version of what Freud called *Nachträglichkeit*, the process by which past experiences may be revised to align them with one's current psychic state. Like prescription, psychoanalysis is a backward interpretation which ceaselessly rewrites the past from the standpoint of the present. But if Freud is relevant to the discourse of prescription, it is also as the excavator of the Oedipus complex and the author of *Totem and Taboo*. At the source of human history lurks some primordial trespass or violation, which has now been repressed into the unconscious and which cannot be examined too closely without risk of severe trauma. Society springs from an illicit source or aboriginal crime, which in the case of Freud is parricide and in the case of Burke those acts of forcible expropriation from which all of our current titles and estates descend. The impiety of the radicals is that they would snatch the veil from these decently cloaked transgressions, tempered and obscured as they now are by the merciful passage of time, and drag scandalously to light that which must at all costs remain concealed. They would reopen the primal scene, uncover the father's shame; and Burke himself is never more gripped by Oedipal revulsion that in his insistence that the sources of society are a subject better left alone.[47] This taboo on inquiring into historical origins can also be found in Hume; but it seems reasonable to speculate that it is reinforced in Burke's case by his own dubious genealogy as an Irishman, for which the English never ceased to mock him.[48] In drawing a veil over his Irish past, Burke is himself a living example of the historical discretion he advocates, just as he is his own best instance of a thoroughly hegemonized colonial. Indeed what marks him as that is his love for the very mechanisms of hegemony themselves, in his obsequious veneration of the English constitution.

47. For an adventurous psychobiography of Burke, see Isaac Kramnick, *The Rage of Edmund Burke* (New York 1977). Burke no doubt knew a thing or two about Oedipality: he was idolized by his dismally incompetent son Richard, who at a dinner thrown in his honour in Cork stunned the guests into disbelief by murmuring a few meek words of thanks rather than producing a piece of florid Burkean rhetoric.

48. Conor Cruise O'Brien, in *The Great Melody* (London 1992, Ch. 1) speculates that Burke's father was a Catholic who conformed to the Established Church, and comments on Burke's secretiveness about his Irish origins. For an earlier study of the Irish Burke, somewhat more militantly nationalist than that of his latter-day namesake, see William O'Brien, *Edmund Burke as an Irishman* (Dublin 1924); and Gerald W. Chapman, *Edmund Burke: The Practical Imagination* (Cambridge, Mass. 1967), Ch. 3. The most detailed study of Burke and Ireland remains Thomas Mahoney, *Edmund Burke and Ireland* (Cambridge, Mass. 1960).

Burke did not always abide by his own prohibition of the primal scene, as his blistering assault on the Duke of Bedford's louche pedigree in his *Letter to a Noble Lord* (1796) makes plain enough. But his belief is that in the beginning was coercion, and this, by an organic process, will modulate over the passage of time into hegemony. 'Time', he writes to Sir Hercules Langrishe, 'has, by degrees, in all other places and periods, blended and coalited the conquered with the conquerors...'[49] It is exactly this which has failed to happen in Ireland and India: 'Our conquest there,' he remarks of the latter in his speech on Fox's India Bill, 'after twenty years, is as crude as it was on the first day',[50] and if the British were to abandon the country tomorrow they would leave no vestige of benevolent or hegemonic rule behind them. In fact, Burke venemously adds, they would leave no signs of any possession superior to that of a tiger or an orang-outang. Thomas Moore sounds a similar note in his *Memoirs of Captain Rock*: 'It has usually been the policy of conquerors and colonists', he writes, 'to blend as much as possible with the people among whom they establish themselves, – to share with them the advantage of their own institutions, – to remove all invidious distinctions that might recall the memory of their original invasion or intrusion...'[51] This, Moore believes, has failed to happen in Ireland; and Matthew Arnold will later repeat the point. England, Arnold argues, has failed to 'attach' Ireland, so that 'the conquest had again and again to be renewed; the sense of prescription, the true security of all property, never arose'.[52] Arnold goes on to recommend that we seek out 'every essay, letter and speech' of Edmund Burke on the subject of Ireland – though he also proceeds to give a hearty endorsement of coercive measures in the country. 'A wise man', Arnold writes, 'will not approve the violences of a time of confiscation; but, if things settle down, he would never think of proposing counter-confiscation as an atonement for those violences. It is far better that

---

49. McDowell, ed., *Writings and Speeches of Burke,* vol. 9, p. 614.

50. P.J.Marshall, *The Writings and Speeches of Edmund Burke*, vol. 5 (Oxford 1981), p. 402. The sentiment is later echoed by Matthew Arnold, another apostle of hegemony: 'There is nothing like love and admiration for bringing people to a likeness for what they love and admire; but the Englishman seems never to dream of employing these influences on a race he wants to fuse himself with. He employs simply material interests for his work of fusion; and, beyond these, nothing except scorn and rebuke. Accordingly there is no vital union between him and the races he has annexed...His Welsh and Irish fellow-citizens are hardly more amalgamated with him now than they were when Wales and Ireland were first conquered' (*On the Study of Celtic Literature*, 1867, reprinted London 1930, p. 8).

51. Thomas Moore, *Memoirs of Captain Rock* (London 1824), pp. 12–13.

52. Matthew Arnold, 'The Incompatibles', in R.H. Super, ed., *The Complete Prose Works of Matthew Arnold, vol. IX: English Literature and Irish Politics* (Ann Arbor 1973), p. 243.

things should settle down, and that the past should be forgotten. But in Ireland things have not settled down; and the harshness, vices and neglect of many of the grantees of confiscation have been the main cause why they have not'.[53] Prescription in Ireland has been shipwrecked on the rebarbative conduct of the rulers and the tenacious memory of the natives. It is certain, David Hume writes in his *Treatise of Human Nature*, that if we return to the origin of every nation we will find rebellion and usurpation; it is in this sense that 'Time alone gives solidity to [the rulers'] right; and operating gradually on the minds of men, reconciles them to any authority, and makes it seem just and reasonable.'[54] 'The truth about the [original] usurpation', remarks Blaise Pascal with disarming candour, 'must not be made apparent; it came about originally without reason and has become reasonable. We must see that it is regarded as authentic and eternal, and its origins must be hidden if we do not want it soon to end.'[55] Political sovereignty, in short, is based on fading memory and blunted sensibility, as crimes come to grow on us like old cronies; and if it is really as precariously grounded as that, then any failure in hegemony, on the scale of Ireland or India, is clearly insupportable.

But it is not just that a primordial trespass must yield to a later legality. It is rather than the law is itself lawless, since the initial act of establishing itself was violent and arbitrary. Those who establish constitutions always do so unconstitutionally, since they have no constitution to validate their action. 'The Act by which most of us hold our estates', Fitzgibbon reminded his fellow Anglo-Irishmen in 1789, 'was an Act of violence'.[56] What is effaced by the law, as Slavoj Žižek has argued,[57] is its own criminality; and the law functions only by concealing this positive condition of its existence. The law is the law: it must be obeyed for its own sake, since if one can adduce reasons for obeying it it ceases in that moment to be absolute. In this empty tautology, then, can be glimpsed something of the madness of the law, which since it is a law unto itself, answerable to no other authority, is sheerly anarchic. There is no doubt that for Freud the law is out of control, a ragingly malicious superego which exacts the impossible from the fragile ego and issues its imperious

53. Ibid., p. 251. Arnold's proposal is that a commission should draw up a list of offending landlords and expropriate them without scruple.

54. David Hume, *Treatise of Human Nature* (Oxford 1960), p. 556.

55. Pascal, *Pensées* (Harmondsworth 1966), pp. 46–7.

56. Quoted by J.A.Froude, *The English in Ireland in the Eighteenth Century* (London 1872), vol. 2, p. 553.

57. Slavoj Žižek, *For They Know Not What They Do* (London 1991), pp. 203–9.

edicts with scant regard for whether or not they can be obeyed. The law is not only vindictive but obtuse, since if it had a grain of sense it would realize that it demands too much of us, or would at least educate our desires to meet its implacable requirements. Freud's compassion for the poor, harrassed ego, buffeted between id, superego and external world, is strong and persistent; and he regarded the law, which drives men and women to guilt and self-loathing, as one of his oldest enemies. The law, in short, is unhegemonic, and must yield to that form of self-concealment we know as legality.

At the root of reason, as Burke is well aware, lies unreason; coercion is the father of consensus, the arbitrary performative of the original command is the hidden condition of all our more constative speech. And if this is so, then the opposition between coercion and hegemony, which Hume and Burke would cast in temporal terms, can in fact be deconstructed. For as Žižek suggests in his exposition of Jacques Lacan, there is indeed a senseless, transgressive, coercive law, and an appeasing, accommodating one; but this is a division inscribed within the law itself. 'One can say that the law divides itself necessarily into an "appeasing" law and a "mad" law: the opposition between the law and its transgressions repeats itself inside ... the law itself.'[58] The law is at once citizen and terrorist, the source of all order and the potential negation of it; and meddling with what Burke scornfully terms the 'metaphysical' is a forbidden foray into the very heart of the law's savagery and contingency, the unveiling of the father's phallus, the shocking revelation that any social order is rooted simply in amnesia and force of habit, in the generous indolence by which its subjects will come to forgive and forget an initial outrage. Such forgetting, however, can never be complete: the absolute crime, so Freud instructs us, can never be entirely obliterated, but will persist as a repressed traumatic kernel, since to eradicate this would be to abolish the condition of legality as such. It is not difficult in Ireland to give a name to that traumatic memory of primordial wrong which will finally be dredged into consciousness. The law, in its turn, will not easily withstand the recognition that it, too, is marked by the sign of castration – that all authority is in some sense a fiction, that the father himself is a victim of the punitive superego, and that, as James Larkin put it, 'the great only appear great because we are on our knees'.

For appeasement and terrorism, read beauty and the sublime. Or, in an alternative coding, female and male. Sublimity in Burke's aesthetics is

---

58. Ibid., p. 30.

what chastens and intimidates, inspires us to reverence and fear; and in this sense it is analogous to the coercive dimension of political power, as beauty lies parallel to the consensual.[59] Beauty is the principle of social cohesion, that pleasurable aestheticizing of our social life we know as 'manners'; and in this realm – the realm, one might say, of Jane Austen's heroines – the law is spontaneously internalized, becoming at one with our impulsive being. Since the model of such internalizing of the law is the work of art, the consensual or hegemonic in political life lies very close to the aesthetic, which is one reason why the politically benevolistic Burke begins his public career as a precocious young aesthetician. But the problem, in both politics and aesthetics, is how these two modes are to be combined. It is clear enough that a well-disposed state must govern consensually, yet hold in reserve a range of repressive measures should that hegemony falter. But to give force to those measures is to risk suffering a massive loss of ideological credibility, undermining the very consensual order that coercion would hope to sustain; and it is this which inspires Burke to write in *Thoughts on the Present Discontents* that 'The civil power, like any other, that calls in the aid of an ally stronger than itself, perishes by the assistance it receives.'[60] Coercion undoes what it promotes; and if the two kinds of power are at loggerheads politically, so are they psychologically. For the authority we revere we do not love, and the one we love we do not revere.

The Anglo-Irish poet and landowner Aubrey de Vere writes later in the nineteenth century that 'we can only permanently cure disaffection by winning a people's affection', but stresses that this by no means excludes coercion; the Irish subject, so he argues, 'will love no rule that he cannot respect also'.[61] Burke, more astutely, is well aware that our relationship to a sublime sovereignty is thoroughly Oedipal: sublimity daunts us into admiring submission, but this is the Law of the Father, whose very venerability 'hinders us from having that entire love for him that we have for our mothers, where the parental authority is almost melted down into the mother's fondness and indulgence'.[62] The paradox of hegemony

---

59. The homology needs some qualifying: in so far as sublime power chastens us into acquiescence, it makes actual coercion unnecessary, and to this extent could be said to lie on the side of hegemony. For a discussion of the relations between Burke's aesthetics and politics, see Neal Wood, 'The Aesthetic Dimension of Burke's Political Thought', *Journal of British Studies*, vol. iv, no. 1 (November 1964).

60. Langford, ed., *Writings and Speeches of Burke*, vol. 2, p. 286.

61. Aubrey de Vere, *Essays Chiefly Literary and Ethical* (London 1989), p. 157.

62. *A Philosophical Enquiry into the Origin of our Ideas of the Sublime and Beautiful*, in F.W. Raffety, ed., *Works of the Right Honourable Edmund Burke*, vol. 1 (London 1925), p. 159.

is plain: only love will woo us to the law, but such love is likely to erode the law's august authority and inspire in us a benign contempt. On the other hand, a power which rouses our filial fear, and hence our docile obedience, is likely to alienate our affections and so spur us to Oedipal resentment.[63]

Beauty and sublimity, the consensual and the coercive, are not, then, conveniently symmetrical registers. For the most part, political power must work hegemonically, thriving on love and beauty: 'There ought', Burke writes, 'to be a system of manners in every nation, which a well-formed mind would be disposed to relish. To make us love our country, our country ought to be lovely.'[64] Once power is aestheticized in this fashion, dissolved into the very textures of our routine conduct as citizens, we can all come to be pleasantly oblivious of its repellant force. Power, in short, works by fiction and illusion, cloaking itself in ceremony and sweetening its rigour by seductive sentiment; and it is just this acknowledgement that mystification is structurally essential to the social order that the Jacobins impiously refuse. 'All the pleasing illusions, which made power gentle and obedience liberal ... All the decent drapery of life is to be rudely torn off.'[65] It is a neuralgic point in the *Reflections*, with Burke at his most vulnerable and panic-stricken; and it is no accident that his mind turns instantly to a woman, to the torn figure of Marie Antoinette, in one of the the the most celebrated and extraordinary passages of the entire *oeuvre*.[66] The law is male, but hegemony is a woman; and just as the revolution-aries, at least in Burke's heated fantasy, have mauled Marie Antoinette, so they have exposed the unlovely phallus of authority by stripping from this transvestite power its decorously dissembling cloak of culture. In their epistemophilic frenzy they have enquired too deeply into things, gazed on the father's nakedness, laid bare the shameful sources of social life; and the penalty for looking upon this terrible sublimity is the blindness of political dogmatism. It is no wonder that the revolution is such an aesthetically tawdry affair, all cheap farce, maladroit melodrama and windy bombast; for the aesthetic belongs to the kingdom of hegemony, to

---

63. I have discussed these matters in somewhat different style in *The Ideology of the Aesthetic* (Oxford 1990), Ch. 2. It may be noted that, in the thought of Immanuel Kant, love and respect are united in the concept of friendship. See J.M. Bernstein, *The Fate of Art* (Oxford 1992), p. 223.

64. *Reflections on the Revolution in France*, in Mitchell, ed., *Writings and Speeches of Burke*, vol. 8, p. 129.

65. Ibid., p. 128.

66. For an interesting account of this passage, see Tom Furniss, *Edmund Burke's Aesthetic Ideology* (Cambridge 1993), Ch. 6.

enabling myths and enjoyable icons, and the plain bad manners of these murderous metaphysicians is sign enough of their political unregeneracy. William Hazlitt, in his generous eulogy of Burke, shrewdly perceives just how covertly aesthetic his political beliefs are – how, for example, he loves aristocracy for enlarging the mind, expanding the imagination and stirring us to dreams of splendour, rather than for any more soberly rational motive.[67]

If Burke is as outraged as he is by the image of the molested queen, it may be because that violence is not wholly alien to him. For he does not believe – how could he? – that the despoiling phallus ought never to be on display. Prudishness is no answer to prurience: we need a stiffening of the sublime from time to time, otherwise the social order is at risk of surfeiting on beauty, growing enervate and effete. The sublime is a kind of phallic 'swelling', a virile strenuousness which in the shape of danger, rivalry and enterprise must break into the placid enclosure of beauty so as to vitalize this otherwise complacent sphere. It is beauty's point of inner fracture, a negation of order without which any order would wither and die. As a kind of anti-aesthetic aesthetic, the sublime is thus the anti-social condition of all sociality, the infinitely unrepresentable which yet spurs us on to ever finer representations. There is an unreason at the root of reason, a terror and madness at the heart of the appeasing law, but this energy is essential for its ceaseless self-renewal.

In this sense, then, sublime coercion and consensual beauty may be reconciled after a fashion, as each other's necessary supports; and this is not the only sense in which they can be drawn closer. For if beauty, as a kind of hegemony, inspires in us delightful sentiments, so after all does the sublime, which has to do with pleasure as well as pain, and which might indeed be said to deconstruct this very opposition in its blending of the gruesome and the gratifying. In this sense, the modern sublime is surely the horror movie, which thrills by terrifying, yields us pleasure the more it appals. One reason for this, no doubt, is the vicarious nature of such experience – the fact that in its presence we can momentarily indulge the death wish in the self-satisfied knowledge that we will not actually suffer harm. But Burke, who writes a chapter in his aesthetic treatise entitled 'How Pain can be a Cause of Delight', is well aware of what will later be dubbed masochism, and knows just how stimulating it can be to

67. William Hazlitt, 'The Character of Mr. Burke', in P.P. Howe, ed., *The Collected Works of William Hazlitt* (London and Toronto 1932), p. 307. A modern-day equivalent of this glowing tribute from radical to conservative is Raymond Williams's warm appreciation of Burke in *Culture and Society 1780-1950* (London 1958), Part 1, Ch. 1.

be cowed into craven submission. To this extent, there is a hegemonic element within coercion itself: the very excessiveness of the Law of the Father, the crazed vindictiveness of the superego, carries its own freight of libidinal pleasure, and will bind us masochistically to it in its very brutality. In his *Letter to William Elliot* (1795), Burke calls for a return to sublime principles in government; for in the midst of revolutionary turmoil, awe, majesty and intimidation are essential weapons. Yet the call is paradoxical, since for Burke revolutionary terror is itself a kind of sublimity, and is thus to be fought with something of its own substance.[68]

It is worth noting, incidentally, that there may be something distinctively Irish about Burke's enthusiasm for sublimity. For if the sublime is that which beggars description and baffles representation, then the ultimate name for it is God; and a society in which theology plays a major role is bound to find itself somewhat more sceptical of a representational epistemology than the empiricist English. The 'negative theology' of the greatest medieval Irish philosopher, John Scottus Eriugena, involves the Pseudo-Dionysian doctrine that God is beyond comprehension or definition, and that there exists in humanity a kind of non-definitive or indeterminate knowledge by which we can unite non-dominatively with the world.[69] In this sense, humanity for Eriugena is itself sublime, beyond all definition, and it is in just this necessary self-opacity, this transcendence of all determinacy, that human beings are closest to their creator. The central riddle of eighteenth-century Irish philosophy – the so-called Molyneux problem as to whether a blind man restored to vision would recognize familiar shapes merely by sight – turns precisely on the question of representation; and at the core of the dispute lies the issue of our knowledge of God. Inheriting but adapting Locke's epistemology, eighteenth-century Irish philosophers such as Peter Browne, William King and Edward Synge stress the fraught relation between what we would now term signified and referent, taking a pragmatic rather than representational line. Given the essential unknowability of God, how we define him must be wholly different from how he actually is; but describing him as we do has some practical if not cognitive value, since it inspires us to take up appropriate

---

68. For Burke's perception of the French Revolution as sublime, see Ronald Paulson, *Representations of Revolution* (New Haven 1983), Ch. 3.

69. For the theology of Pseudo-Dionysus, see in particular 'The Divine Names', in *Pseudo-Dionysus: The Complete Works*, trans. Colm Luibheid (New York 1987). For Scottus Eriugena, see Dermot Moran, 'Wandering from the Path: *Navigatio* in the Philosophy of John Scottus Eriugena', *The Crane Bag*, vol. 2, nos 1 and 2 (Dublin 1978); and 'Nature, Man and God in the Philosophy of John Scottus Eriugena', in Richard Kearney, ed., *The Irish Mind* (Dublin 1985).

religious attitudes in our own less than sublime lives. We cannot know, for instance, that God has foreknowledge; but believing that he has, as William King remarks in his *Sermon on Predestination* (1709), 'at once stops our Mouths, and silences our Objections, obliges us to an absolute Submission and Dependance', and 'this is plainly the design and effect of this terrible Representation...'[70] It would seem only a short step from this theological pragmatism to Burke's concern with the political utility of the sublime, another convenient mouth-stopper; indeed there are complex relations in eighteenth-century Irish thought between the sublime, anti-representational epistemology, the need to preserve religious mystery and political authority, and a semiotics of language which from Bishop Berkeley to Edmund Burke privileges the conative over the cognitive, rhetoric over representation. One might even hazard a remote connection between all this and the unstable nature of realism in the nineteenth-century Irish novel. It may even be a history which makes itself felt in Oscar Wilde's lofty disdain for a representational aesthetics, or in Yeats's faith in the imaginative act which brings a whole world to birth.

If the affections lie at the foundation of the political state, then a well-disposed polity stands in need of a science of them; and this science of subjectivity, which for us moderns might be called phenomenology or psychology or psychoanalysis, is known to the eighteenth century as aesthetics. Aesthetics, which has precious little to do with art when it first sees the light of day, maps the very groundwork of human subjectivity, and so lies at the root of a properly hegemonic politics. Its task is to begin with the body, charting its appetencies and aversions, and gradually work its way up to the political state. For the body, like culture, is antecedent to that state, providing the spontaneous wisdom within which any more formal edict must take effect; and any power which fails to ground itself somatically is therefore doomed to impotence. It is in this sense that Burke, who discourses of empire and constitution, is also fascinated by the feel of a slight tap on the shoulder or the dilation of the pupils in darkness. Starting out from the lowly instinct of self-preservation, it is possible to end up with the unfathomable mysteries of the sublime. What is given for this brand of empiricism is the body itself, whose desires and revulsions are open to no further reduction, rooted as they are in a common biological nature which is prior to culture. 'The body ... is wiser in its own plain way', Burke writes in *A Vindication of Natural*

---

70. William King, *Sermon on Predestination* (Dublin 1709), section 24. For a useful account of eighteenth-century Irish philosophy, see David Berman, 'The Irish Counter-Enlightenment', in Kearney, ed., *The Irish Mind*.

Society (1756); and though the essay is a sardonic spoof, this is not the only phrase in it which rings true to its author's beliefs.

It is for this reason that aesthetics of the Burkean kind are such a bathetic sort of affair, veering as they do from high-flown disquisitions on the beautiful to talk of squinting down a pole, from ardour and ambition to foul stenches and the shape of vegetables. 'A consideration of the rationale of our passions', Burke remarks, 'seems to me very necessary for all who would affect them upon sure and solid principles';[71] and to this extent aesthetics takes over something of the traditional function of rhetoric, whose task was to anatomize the passions of men and women so that political oratory might more dexterously persuade them. If the word 'rhetoric' in classical antiquity covered both the theory and the practice of persuasive speech, aesthetics for the early Burke is the theory, and politics the practice. When he writes to a correspondent, while preparing his case against Warren Hastings, that some evidence of torture he has uncovered 'has stuff in it, that will, if any thing, work upon the popular Sense',[72] he suggests a relation between aesthetic enquiry and political practice.

It is easy to see, in the light of Burke's preoccupation with hegemony, just what horrified him so much about the French Revolution. The British have dismally failed to achieve hegemonic rule in India, and have routed it in America; in Ireland, the Ascendancy is an inorganic class which offers a grisly parody of true patrician leadership. But at least, in all of these cases, the conditions for hegemony exist, and the failure to attain it stands condemned by the rulers' own political principles. In France, by contrast, the very principle and institutions of hegemony have been wantonly abandoned. The Revolution is not just an unacceptable regime, but a metaphysical assault on the very conditions of possibility of political hegemony as such. For hegemony, as Gramsci argues, works primarily through civil society; and Jacobinism for Burke is the dissolution of civil society as such, and thus a subversion of the very notion of government through the affections. It is, so to speak, a kind of *transcendental* error – not just a barbarous polity, but the ruin of all polity as such, as the death of a language is more serious than the uttering of false propositions within it. The French have done more than create an iniquitous society: they have made a kind of category mistake about the very idea of political society as such. The unreason at the heart of the law

71. *A Philosophical Enquiry*, p. 105.
72. H. Furber, ed., *The Correspondence of Edmund Burke*, vol. 5 (Cambridge 1965), p. 372.

has been let loose, and the form it assumes is – Reason. For what Burke dreads as the insane rationalism of the Revolution is just what happens when the law is most truly itself, when its edicts are untempered by custom and sensibility. The law is mad, but is normally kept safely incarcerated in the prison-house of hegemony; now this lunatic law has slipped its chains and is on the rampage, threatening to discredit the very concept of legality as such by pressing its crazed logic to a parodic extreme. In a fit of delirium, the law has come to take seriously its own omnipotence, as a captive tiger might come exultantly to recognize its own strength; but the law will only work well if it is sweetly beguiled about its own power, lulled by the soft wiles of hegemony into yielding up some of its potency. For no-one can gaze on this dreadful sublimity and live, which is why the law needs the fig leaf of hegemony. It is somehow appropriate that *Reflections on the Revolution in France* should be at once one of the most magnificent texts of English political theory, and a collection of remarkably shoddy arguments. For much the same can be said of Burke's notion of hegemony in general, which springs on the one hand from a subtle, generous-spirited wisdom, and which on the other hand comes down to the banal maxim: Keep them happy!

Burke was an English landowner, and as a doctrinaire free marketeer had scant belief in mollycoddling his tenants. Indeed the compassion of much of his political writing contrasts strikingly with the callousness of his economic thought.[73] Yet the English landlords, the oldest agrarian capitalist class in the world, have been regarded as a model of hegemonic rule, bound to their tenants by custom, affection and paternal care, and so able to evoke their grateful loyalty. Whatever the merits of this grossly idealized portrait, its contrast with the conduct of the Irish landlords was frequently noted. As Gerald Griffin writes in his novella *Tracy's Ambition*:

> It is impossible not to see the impolicy of neglecting the amusements of the people. It is the most obvious support of a deceptive mode of rule that can be imagined. If you wish to fool a child, you fling him a toy. The Caesars ... practised it amid all their tyrannies; and by it all the usurpers and despots on the earth have been able to exercise a power, with which no influence, upon the reason of their subjects, could have invested them. But here [in Ireland] it is not

---

73. See 'Thoughts and Details on Scarcity'(1795), in McDowell, ed., *Writings and Speeches of Burke*, vol. 9, pp. 119-45. It is a nice irony that during the Famine Treasury Under-secretary Charles Trevelyan sent copies of this work, along with a chapter of Adam Smith's *The Wealth of Nations,* to his Dublin officials. Burke had, so to speak, returned home.

thought of at any time. Our landlords give no rural feasts, to reward and en-
courage the industry of their tenants and promote a virtuous spirit of emula-
tion, as some good men do in England... (Ch. 5)

In an interesting ambivalence, Griffin is clear that such strategems are a
con, but regrets their absence anyway. The passage veers unsteadily from
a dig at the political obtuseness of not wooing one's tenants to a note of
genuine regret. There are no circuses in Ireland, and precious little bread
either.[74] The Young Irelander Fintan Lalor registers a similar complaint in
rather more Burkeian terms, along with much the same glamorized view
of English rural culture: 'The feelings that exist in England between landlord and tenant, coming down from old times, and handed on as an
heirloom from generation to generation – the feeling of family pride, the
feeling of family attachment, the habit of the house, the fashion of the
land, the custom of the country, all those things that stand for laws, and
are stronger than laws, are here unknown...'[75] Or, for the novelist Charles
Lever, once known but now on the wane: the Ireland of 1830, he writes
in his 1872 Preface to The Martins of Cro' Martin, was 'beginning to feel
that sense of distrust and jealousy between the owner and tiller of the soil
which, later on, was to develop itself into open feud. The old ties that
have bound the humble to the rich man, and which were hallowed by
reciprocal acts of good-will and benevolence were being loosened ...
[The peasant] was taught to regard the old relation of love and affection
to the owner of the soil as the remnants of a barbarism that had had its
day...' It would be intriguing to know what the eighteenth-century
Whiteboys or Defenders would have made of this tremulous elegy, which
dates the Fall from feudal fealty to around the time of Catholic Emancipation; but Sir Jonah Barrington, writing in 1827, is equally convinced
that these disaffected militants inhabited a golden age. At the eighteenth-
century Great House, 'all disputes among the tenants were then settled –
quarrels reconciled – old debts arbitrated; a kind Irish landlord reigned
despotic in the ardent affections of his tenantry, their pride and pleasure
being to support and obey him'.[76] Arthur Young, writing in 1780, claims
that the landowners are now leaving duelling and drunkenness behind

---

74. For a fine account of political hegemony in the ancient world, see Paul Veyne, Bread
and Circuses (London 1990).

75. J.F. Lalor, Collected Writings (Dublin 1918), p. 29. If there is some doubt about when
the Anglo-Irish flourished, there is also doubt about the exact point of their demise. See L.P.
Curtis, 'The Anglo-Irish Predicament', Twentieth-Century Studies, no. 4 (November 1970).

76. Sir Jonah Barrington, Personal Sketches of His Own Time (London 1827), vol. 1, pp.
5-6.

them, apart from a Bacchanalian band of small squires.[77] John Synge contrasts the desolate Big House of the late nineteenth century with its eighteenth-century glory, when it was home to 'a high-spirited and highly-cultivated aristocracy'.[78] Samuel Ferguson also considered the nineteenth-century gentry a sadly dwindled version of their polished eighteenth-century progenitors. L.M. Cullen locates the first crumbling of popular deference to the gentry in mid-eighteenth-century Presbyterian Ulster.[79] For W.E.H. Lecky, the ruin of a rural system in which 'people were drawn in the closest manner to the landlords ... [and] regarded them with feelings of feudal affection'[80] can be ascribed to the influence of a single man: Daniel O'Connell. Joseph Lee seems to date the end of popular obeisance from the Land League,[81] whereas for Phil Rooney, philosophic farmer of Emily Lawless's novel Hurrish, the watershed would appear to be the Famine.[82] For T.R. Henn, by contrast, the organic society flourished right up to the First World War, as the world of Castle Rackrent and famine evictions faded from the memory of a 'proud, idle, careless' tenantry bound to their landlords by affection and respect.[83] For Charles Trevelyan, Chief Under-Secretary to the Treasury during the Famine years, what scuppered hegemony in Ireland was the potato: 'the relations of employer and employee which form together the framework of society', he writes, 'and establish a mutual independence and good will, have no existence in the potato system. The Irish small-holder lives in a state of isolation – the type of which is to be sought for in the islands of the South Sea, rather than in the great civilised communities of the ancient world.'[84] The potato, comments Aubrey de Vere, involves 'the least possible amount of that labour which renders class dependent on class'.[85] Sowing potatoes is not the kind of material relation to the landlord that reaping his harvest is, and this economic infrastructure serves to undermine political hegemony.

---

77. Arthur Young, A Tour in Ireland (London 1780), vol. 2, p. 238.
78. J.M. Synge, 'A Landlord's Garden in County Wicklow', in The Works of John M. Synge (Dublin 1910), vol. 4, p. 53.
79. L.M. Cullen, The Emergence of Modern Ireland 1600-1900 (New York 1981), p. 234.
80. W.E.H. Lecky, Leaders of Public Opinion in Ireland (London 1861), p. 212.
81. Joseph Lee, The Modernisation of Irish Society 1848-1918 (Dublin 1989), p. 89.
82. Emily Lawless was the eldest daughter of a wealthy landowner, Lord Cloncurry, and Hurrish (1886), a sombre tragedy of rural life set in the Burren, is one of the most powerful Irish novels of the later nineteenth century.
83. See T.R. Henn, The Lonely Tower (London 1950), p. 5.
84. Charles Trevelyan, The Irish Crisis (London 1850), p. 4.
85. Aubrey De Vere, English Misrule and Irish Misdeeds (London 1848), p. 109.

The one certainty about the organic society, as Raymond Williams remarks, is that it has always gone;[86] but like most other myths, those of a vanished golden age sometimes contain their meagre kernel of truth. The mass of the Irish people, George Sigerson comments, had no particular affection for the idea of a palmy Anglo-Irish past, laden for them as it was with memories of cruel proscriptions.[87] But it is arguable even so that deference and patronage did indeed flourish more vigorously in eighteenth- rather than nineteenth-century Ireland, and that the turbulent years of the 1790s proved in this sense a decisive turning point. The newly militant Catholic Committee broke with the obsequiousness of its predecessors; and if some of the tenantry still respected the Big Houses, an increasing number had taken to plundering them. From this period on, so Kevin Whelan has claimed, the gentry began to withdraw from the common people in the face of popular antipathy and the clamorous emergence of the Catholic nation. The landowners no longer felt physically safe with a mutinous tenantry, and traditional practices such as fostering their children out to them began to lapse.[88] By the 1820s, with O'Connell's Emanci- pation campaign, Catholic tenants would be voting *en masse* in defiance of their landlords' wishes; and though organized shows of deference certainly lingered on into the nineteenth century, the social sensibility would seem to have altered. In the 1840s, the landowner's wife Elizabeth Smith, recently transplanted from Scotland to Ireland, notes with surprise that her Irish tenants marry off their children and set them up in trade without mentioning the matter to their landlord.[89] The sheer demographic explo- sion of Irish society, from around one million in 1700 to about eight-and- a-half million on the eve of the Famine, must have affected the possibility of close relations between the gentry and their tenantry.

But it is important not to underplay the survival of hegemonic rituals beyond this watershed. There was indeed the occasional circus in Irish society, not least at those orgies of bribery, corruption and naked intimi- dation known as elections.[90] Even those festivities which excluded the

---

86. Raymond Williams, *The Country and the City* (London 1973), Ch. 2.

87. George Sigerson, *Modern Ireland* (London 1868), p. 81.

88. Kevin Whelan, 'From the G.A.A. to Ooh-aah', paper delivered at the Merriman summer school, Lisdoonvarna, Co. Clare, August 1993. See also Thomas Bartlett, 'An End to Moral Economy: The Irish Militia Disturbances of 1793', *Past and Present*, no. 99 (May 1983).

89. David Thompson and Moyra McGusty, eds, *The Irish Journals of Elizabeth Smith 1840– 50* (Oxford 1980), p. 6.

90. For a matchless survey of the topic, at once erudite and dryly amusing, see K.T. Hoppen, *Elections, Politics and Society in Ireland 1832–1885* (Oxford 1984).

people might, so some wistfully hoped, have a suitably bedazzling effect on them: the balls, concerts and receptions of Dublin high society, so Lady Ferguson remarked, are 'gratifying to the populace, lessening the drain of absenteeism'.[91] Some of the populace were indeed gratified, at least in outward appearance: Irish society had its fair share of doffing, scraping and Your-Honouring, as its people grew expert in the art of verbally bamboozling their superiors, full of well-rehearsed cringing and extravagant tongue-in-cheek compliments. Theodor Hoppen, however, reminds us that 'daylight sycophants often became moonlight marauders', and suggests that much deferential conduct was little more than 'hostility repressed or delayed'.[92] Yet even Daniel O'Connell, bogeyman of the land-lords though a member of that species himself, opposed the introduction of a poor law on the grounds that it would destroy the 'network of mutuality and deference that rendered Irish poverty more endurable by creating a means of personal kindliness and humanity in the countryside'.[93] Paternalism was part of the Ascendancy ethic, though a good deal more preached than practised; the squirearchy threw various festive occasions for their underlings, in a round of extravagant public spectacles, feasts, bonfires, processions, entertainments and ceremonials to mark military victories, political anniversaries, landlord deaths or marriages. Wine might be channelled by conduits from the banquet hall to the thirsty crowd outside, or the masses might be allowed to stage an appearance at the end of a feast to bear off the remnants of the food.[94] But there is no reason to assume that imbibing a man's whiskey implies subscribing to his ideology; and though modern-day Irish historians have been zealously combing the estate papers in hot pursuit of exemplary landlords,[95] it is

---

91. Lady Ferguson, *Sir Samuel Ferguson in the Ireland of his Day*, vol. 1 (Edinburgh and London 1896), p. 268.

92. Hoppen, *Elections, Politics and Society*, pp. 136, 137. Much the same may be said of some of the Catholic middle class, whose deference often concealed resentment. The two Thomas Moores — penner of saccharine Irish lyrics for genteel London consumption, and polemical nationalist of *Memoirs of Captain Rock* and *The Life of Edward Fitzgerald* — is a case in point. For lives of Moore, see L.A.G. Strong, *The Minstrel Boy* (London 1937); and Terence de Vere White, *Tom Moore: The Irish Poet* (London 1977).

93. The words are Oliver MacDonagh's, in 'The Economy and Society, 1830–45', in W.E. Vaughan, ed., *A New History of Ireland, vol. V: Ireland Under the Union 1, 1801–70* (Oxford 1989), p. 226.

94. See S.J. Connolly, *Religion, Law and Power: The Making of Protestant Ireland 1660–1760* (Oxford 1992), Ch. 4.

95. See, for a somewhat one-sided treatment, L.M. Cullen, 'Economic Development 1750-1800', in T.W. Moody and W.E.Vaughan, eds, *A New History of Ireland, vol. IV: Eighteenth-Century Ireland 1691–1800* (Oxford 1986), pp. 177f.

hard to resist the conclusion that the stereotype of the uncouth, uncaring landlord is uncomfortably close to large segments of the reality.

Civilized and improving landowners there certainly were; but efforts at improvement were for the most part 'erratic and transient',[96] and sizeable sectors of the Anglo-Irish gentry, at least in the pre-Famine era, were widely bruited as a brawling, gluttonous, chronically inebriated crew, given to murderous aggression and extravagant rituals of consumption. Venal, foul-mouthed and nepotistic, they represented an atavistic throwback to an earlier phase of the English gentry, the heirs of freebooting Cromwellian adventurers whose class was more open to the penetration of the low-bred parvenu than their more exclusive metropolitan counterparts. In Anthony Trollope's Irish novel *The Kellys and the O'Kellys*, Lord Cashel congratulates his ward on the fact that her brother has died before he could squander his health and fortune, as though nothing else was to have been expected. Marked by a 'general unruliness and disregard for law',[97] this anarchic oligarchy partook in their own swashbucking manner of the popular violence around them, and was in this sense, if in precious few others, representative of those they ruled. The view that the more outrageous of the landlords virtually 'deserved to be murdered' was expressed not by some disgruntled Ribbonman but by Chief Secretary Edward Horsman in 1855.[98] The landlords did not, by and large, reinvest their rents; and such reinvestment, as W.E. Vaughan points out, is a precious instrument of hegemony, 'the one way of binding tenants to landlords that was available to great estates in the nineteenth century'.[99] Vaughan argues, perhaps a mite optimistically, that if a quarter of the rents culled by the landlords had returned to the tenantry in the form of 'loans, gifts, new houses, and drained fields, the tenants would have been inexorably tied to their landlords'.[100] He also calculates that if the mid-Victorian landowners had spent only £1 million a year, less than 10 per cent of their rental income, they could have provided decent dwellings for most of their (often wretchedly housed) tenants.[101] L.M. Cullen, anxious to assure us that middlemen, if not grandee landowners, enjoyed

---

96. W.E. Vaughan, 'An Assessment of the Economic Performance of Irish Landlords, 1851–81', in F.S.L. Lyons and R.A.J. Hawkins, eds, *Ireland under the Union: Varieties of Tension* (Oxford 1980), p. 196.

97. See J.L. McCracken, 'The Social Structure and Social Life, 1714–60', in Moody and Vaughan, eds, *A New History of Ireland vol. IV*, p. 36.

98. Quoted by Hoppen, *Elections, Politics and Society*, p. 167.

99. W.E. Vaughan, *Landlord and Tenant in Ireland 1848–1904* (Dundalk 1984), p. 25.

100. W.E. Vaughan, *Landlords and Tenants in Mid-Victorian Ireland* (Oxford 1994), p. 129.

101. Ibid., p. 127.

close bonds with their tenants, offers in evidence the fact that they occasionally abducted their daughters.[102] The customary rights and entitlements of the people, which in England might temper the harshness of landlord rule, were less in evidence in Ireland.

Taken as a whole, the Ascendancy represented a backward, unmannerly sector of the British governing class; and their ability to win the loyalty of their tenants was seriously disabled by the ethnic, religious and cultural abyss which yawned between them. A certain casual brutality to their inferiors was a familiar badge of their power, though S.J. Connolly, in the typically mollifying manner of some modern Irish historians, speculates charitably that the lower classes may have enjoyed a spot of rough stuff at the hands of their superiors.[103] W.E.H. Lecky thought so too: 'the [eighteenth-century] Irish landlords', he writes, 'were, I imagine, on the whole very popular, and the rude, good-humoured despotism which they wielded was cordially accepted'.[104] What the lower classes *did* enjoy was the semi-mythical memory of an ancient Gaelic chieftainry who had granted them protection before the advent of these mercenary upstarts; and the contrast proved yet another obstacle to the acceptability of the new dispensation. The Ascendancy was at once retrograde and too recent: it was hardly an efficiently modernizing class, but neither could it be seen as discharging time-hallowed functions. And no ruling class, least of all among the rank-conscious, traditionally-minded Irish, can survive comfortably without dulling the memory of an epoch when it never was. The landlords, so Vaughan considers, had a chance to 'pose as conservatives in rural society, and to shelter tenants from the disruptions of a market economy. They should have appeared as the champions of old-world values; they should have appealed to old ties and old ways.'[105] But they reneged, by and large, on this Ruskinian role, caught on the hop between patrician paternalist and free marketeer, and perished in the gulf between tradition and modernity. Their power was too visibly traditionalist to present itself as mere *rentier* wealth, but too nakedly profit-oriented to permit them to pose as the traditional guardians of the poor. For an exploiting class to legitimate itself, remarks John Stuart Mill, 'it requires

---

102. Cullen, *The Emergence of Modern Ireland*, p. 102.

103. Connolly, *Religion, Law and Power*, p. 142. For similarly bland accounts of the Ascendancy, see J.C. Beckett, *The Anglo-Irish Tradition* (London 1976); and Foster, *Modern Ireland 1600–1970*, Ch. 16 (though Foster's commentary does allow of a peculiar 'savagery of mind' as a characteristic of the class [p. 176]).

104. Lecky, *Leaders of Public Opinion*, p. 252.

105. Vaughan, *Landlords and Tenants in Mid-Victorian Ireland*, p. 223.

to be rooted in the traditions and oldest recollections of the people; the landed families must be identified with the religion of the country, with its nationality, with its ancient rulers, and other objects of gratitude and veneration, or at least of ungrudging obedience'.[106] The Ascendancy's problem was that it failed to fulfil a single one of these conditions.

This is not to propose that the Irish landlords were a uniformly rapacious bunch. The historical record, inevitably, is fairly mixed. There were too many landlords who, not least in the first half of the nineteenth century, exploited land hunger by driving up rents, charged exorbitantly for conacre land, paid their labourers a miserable pittance, presided over an excessive subdivision of their soil which helped to breed overpopulation and immiseration, and forced their wretched tenants onto waste land and mountainside in their zeal to consolidate their holdings. Many a land-owner confiscated his tenants' improvements along with their labour-power. In the period after Waterloo, the Irish population as a whole was driven to subsist on the produce of one million acres of potatoes, out of a total potential farming area of twenty million acres.[107] Production had risen steadily since the eighteenth century, but the distribution of its fruits was intolerably unequal, not least because of inflated rents.[108] The desperate plight of the lowest strata of the people was legendary, and a matter for scandalized comment from outside observers.[109] On the eve of the Famine, the collapse of domestic industry and the dire situation in the country-side had proved disastrous for the smallholders and labourers.[110] In 1830, three-quarters of Irish farms were economically non-viable; in 1841, over two-fifths of all families inhabited one-room cabins, some lacking even a bedstead. In the same year, the amount of arable land per head of the

---

106. John Stuart Mill, *England and Ireland* (London 1868), p. 11.

107. See Raymond Crotty, *Irish Agricultural Production* (Cork 1966), p. 63. In addition to its many virtues – cheap, bountiful, easy to cook, highly nutritious, labour-saving, easily accessible, economical of land, difficult to pillage and viable in poor soil (though hard to store and transport) – the potato had the benefit of being a crop ready to eat, so that its producers retained effective control over their own means of subsistence. This 'natural' indendepence and self-reliance could then be translated into peasant proprietorship.

108. Such glaring inequalities received hardly a glance in one of the toughest-minded, free-marketeering apologias for the landlords, Barbara Solow's *The Land Question and the Irish Economy, 1870–1903* (Cambridge, Mass. 1971).

109. Though Harriet Martineau, determined to stay cheerful, started her tour of Ireland in Ulster, 'in a region where the peculiarities of land proprietorship in Ireland are suspended or extinguished' (*Letters from Ireland*, London 1852, pp. 1–2).

110. See Michael J. Winstanley, *Ireland and the Land Question 1800-1922* (London 1984), pp. 7–11.

rural population in County Galway was three and a half acres, and in County Armagh one and a quarter.[111] Forty years after the Union, 76 per cent of employed males were poor farmers or labourers with an average holding of less than two acres.

On the other hand, many of the landlords themselves were hardly sitting pretty, with a quarter of them insolvent or on the verge of bankruptcy in 1848.[112] Rackrenting existed, but it was hardly pervasive, and rents in general, at least in the post-Famine period, would seem to have risen only moderately and (from the landlord's viewpoint) un-economically.[113] Short of evicting a leasee, an awkward enough process, rent could be increased only with his consent. The effects of insecurity of tenure on tenants' productivity may well have been overplayed. Land-owners might not have won their tenants' undivided devotion; but they could often secure their cooperation by manipulating what Samuel Clark calls 'non-contractual privileges', favouring reliable tenants, granting rent abatements and tolerating rent arrears.[114] If most landlords failed to im-prove their estates, it was in part because, staggeringly encumbered as their land often were, they lacked the resources to do so. And reforming landlords might well encounter resistance from a conservative tenantry. There were periods of ruthless mass eviction, not least in the calamitous years of the Famine (some 70,000 families between 1846 and 1853), but some Irish nationalist historians have exaggerated its frequency. As well as attracting some invidious publicity, evictions could result in financial loss for the landowner, unoccupied farms and popular disgruntlement. As *The Landowner's and Agent's Practical Guide* puts it with commendable caution, 'with respect to existing tenancies, the wisest course perhaps in this, as in so many of the affairs of life, will be to let things alone'.[115] Absenteeism was hardly the economic drain on the nation's resources that some have

---

111. See E. Estyn Evans, *The Personality of Ireland* (Dublin 1992), p. 30.

112. See James S. Donnelly Jr, *Landlord and Tenant in Nineteeth-Century Ireland* (Dublin 1973), p. 48. But though individual landlords were ruined by the Famine, not least in bear-ing the burden of poor-law relief, it has been claimed that the class as a whole emerged in Darwinian style slimmed and strengthened.

113. Though this view of the post-Famine landlords as economically failing in contrast with the solid advances of their tenants has been challenged by, among others, K.T. Hoppen, *Ireland since 1800: Conflict and Conformity* (London and New York 1989), pp. 90–94. A survey of 1880 revealed that 40 per cent of rents had not risen since before 1850 (see Mary E. Daly, *Social and Economic History of Ireland since 1800*, Dublin 1981, p. 38).

114. See Samuel Clark, *Social Origins of the Irish Land War* (Princeton 1979), Ch. 5.

115. Thomas de Moleyns, *The Landowner's and Agent's Practical Guide* (Dublin 1899), p. 125.

suggested.[116] Indeed some nineteenth-century commentators considered it a blessing that so many landlords were not around to demoralize the peasantry with their corruption and ineptitude.[117]

Irish landlordism was as constrained as any other governing bloc from a mere arbitrary use of its power, which in the face of an often truculent tenantry could only prove counterproductive. It was hardly in a position to stir up opposition gratuitously, given its unstable fortunes throughout the nineteenth century. Absorbed into Britain in 1800 in a panic-stricken political collapse, buffeted by the greatest mass movement in the Europe of its day, plunged into recession by the ending of the Napoleonic wars, the Ascendancy lived to see its Church disestablished, its political power curtailed by parliamentary and local goverment reform, its estates increasingly enmortgaged, and its moral character impugned as at best criminally callous and at worst tainted by genocide. Struggling with debt and bankrupcy, progressively paranoid in its attitudes to Westminster, undermined by the growth of an urban Catholic middle class and an increasingly self-confident nationalist culture, it staggered at the *fin de siècle* into economic slump and open warfare with its formidably well-organized class antagonists,[118] submitted to a steady erosion of its power in a series of Land Acts, and finally opted to be bought out by the British government in a humiliating conclusion to what, politically speaking, had been a largely ignominious career. In a few decades' time, its houses burnt, its sons decimated in the First World War and its families fled to the Home Counties, it would be for most of the Irish little more than a disreputable memory. It was, writes R.F. Foster, 'a class notable in the main for its philistinism and bigotry, which, when the testing time came, failed in everything – social duty, political imagination and nerve'.[119] Once stripped of its traditional privileges, it could have made an immeasurably valuable contribution to the social and cultural life of the new Ireland; but the strident Gaelic chauvinism of the Free State, along with its own

---

116. See A.P.W. Malcolmson, 'Absenteeism in Eighteenth-Century Ireland', *Irish Economic and Social History* 1 (1974). For evictions and rents, see Vaughan, *Landlord and Tenant in Ireland 1848–1904*, a generally exculpatory account of landlordism which nevertheless records the staggering 14,600 tenants evicted in the depression years 1879–83.

117. See R.D. Collison Black, *Economic Thought and the Irish Question* (Cambridge 1960), p. 82.

118. For the Land Wars, see Paul Bew, *Land and the National Question in Ireland 1858–82* (Dublin 1978); and Clark, *Social Origins*.

119. R.F. Foster, *Paddy and Mr Punch* (London 1993), p. 16. This is not, one might add, the impression of the Ascendancy one gleans from the same author's *Modern Ireland: 1600–1970*. For an anecdotal account of the twilight years of Ascendancy, see Mark Bence-Jones, *Twilight of the Ascendancy* (London 1987).

aggressions and anxieties, inhibited this possibility, even if the new nation extended generous political representation to its Anglo-Irish minority.

Yet at the very moment of its demise, as W.J. McCormack has argued, the Ascendancy was able to turn round upon itself and, in the person of Yeats and his colleagues, rewrite this often inglorious political history as high cultural tradition, in an act of sublimation rivalled only by the earlier emergence of a vigorous nativist culture out of the ruins of the genuine article.[120] All those rumbustious lords and randy earls were now suddenly imbued with mythic status, spiritual heroes in some imposing drama. What began in the 1790s as an ideology (Ascendancy) with a firm material base had now been cut adrift from that foundation, shifted into an idealist register, and so become a form of cultural displacement. What started life as a frightened reaction by a hard-headed Protestant bourgeoisie to the prospect of revolution would be retrospectively transformed by the Revivalists into style and *sprezzatura*, a nobly self-affirmative lineage brought low by the *ressentiment* of the rabble.

It was not, as we have seen, that all landlords were by any means uniformly villainous – that there was not some solid economic progress, able and conscientious management, currents of *noblesse oblige*, genuine practical constraints. It was not that the Anglo-Irish, boorish and philistine though many of them doubtless were, failed to lay the seedbed of some splendid cultural achievements, from the architecture of Gandon and his colleagues[121] to a body of writing which still bulks disproportionately large in the 'English' literary canon. Without them, England would have precious little stage comedy to boast of.[122] The Anglo-Irish, so George Moore claimed, thought that Richard Wagner was a racehorse, but not all of them laboured under this illusion.[123] The Ascendancy superbly portrayed in A.P.W. Malcolmson's study of John Foster is no bunch of swashbuckling incompetents but a class of shrewd, capable, often conscientious administrators.[124] It was the more scholarly kinsmen of these

---

120. See McCormack, *Ascendancy and Tradition*, p. 88.

121. Though one critic of this architecture was Ludwig Wittgenstein, who in a classic backhanded compliment remarked of Georgian Dublin that 'the people who built these houses had the good taste to know that they had nothing very important to say; and therefore they did not attempt to express anything' (quoted by John Hayes, 'Wittgenstein, Religion, Freud, and Ireland', *Irish Philosophical Journal*, no. 6, 1989).

122. Sheridan is of particular interest here: British Government minister and probable fellow traveller with the United Irishmen. See his *The Legislative Independence of Ireland Vindicated* (Dublin 1785), a speech in the House of Commons, for a typically patriotic text.

123. See Malcolm Brown, *George Moore: A Reconsideration* (Seattle 1955), p. 18.

124. See A.P.W. Malcolmson, *John Foster: The Politics of the Anglo-Irish Ascendancy* (Oxford 1978).

political operators who from the eighteenth century onwards created a whole range of enlightened learned societies devoted to science, agriculture, literature and antiquities.

The game of arraigning or exonerating the Anglo-Irish gentry, brandishing evidence of their brutality or bearing witness to their accomplishments, will no doubt continue to be played out among contemporary Irish historians of different political persuasions, and not least by those who believe they have none. But though there is a good deal of evidence that the landlords' overall conduct was indeed less than creditable, there is an important sense in which such evidence is finally beside the point. 'There are no good or bad settlers,' Sartre once remarked, 'only settlers'. The comment is sufficiently cavalier: only one free of dominion could be so nonchalant about how heavily it is laid on. But it does, for all that, enforce a truth obscured by scholarly wranglings over tillage and leases, political patronage and the Ulster custom. What such controversies typically repress is the whole structure of social relations as such, displacing such embarrassingly global issues with moralistic gesture or econometric myopia. In some quarters today, this is known as the death of metanarrative, which makes it sound rather more imposing. It is not finally a question of how benign or otherwise the landlords were;[125] it is a question of the fact that while the mass of Irish cottiers, small tenant farmers and landless labourers endured an existence notorious throughout Europe for its spectacular indigence, a paltry number of big landowners owned half the country.[126] As Cormac Ó Gráda puts it: 'even the "fairest" of [the landlords] absorbed a hefty proportion of output'.[127] The collective rental income of the class, about ten million pounds, was more than the public revenue of Ireland, and greater than the United Kingdom's central expenditure on civil government and the royal navy. The rate of exploitation may well have been exaggerated by earlier historians, though too many landowners ruthlessly cleared, evicted and overcharged; but the inequalities the system generated were insupportable. While some members

125. In her *The Living Stream: Literature and Revisionism in Ireland* (Newcastle upon Tyne 1994, p. 140), Edna Longley quotes with apparent endorsement Hubert Butler's comment in his *Escape from the Anthill* that 'Waterloo may or may not have been won on the playing-fields of Eton, but Ireland was certainly lost there'. Butler is referring to the export to England of the 'brightest and bravest' of the Ascendancy, who, so the implication runs, might otherwise have 'saved' Ireland. Longley does not appear to notice the arrogance of this benevolism.

126. W.E. Vaughan estimates that in 1870 over half of Ireland was owned by less than one thousand landowners (*Landlord and Tenant in Ireland 1848–1904*, p. 5).

127. Cormac Ó Gráda, *Ireland: A New Economic History, 1780-1939* (Oxford 1994), p. 256.

of the gentry gorged themselves, some of their evicted tenants in the Famine years lived in bog-holes roofed with a few planks they were allowed to salvage from their dismantled cabins.

The economic backwardness of Irish society was a notably over-determined phenomenon; but one unignorable feature of it was the country's economic dependency on Britain, of which the Ascendancy class was the local linchpin. A rapidly commercializing economy in the eighteenth century delivered dramatically uneven development of a classic colonial kind, as an export trade directed largely towards England shifted commercial activity away from indigenous needs to a couple of staple products. It was British demand which determined the historic shift from pasturage to tillage in the late eighteenth century, thus helping to foster the demographic explosion and perilous subdivision of land which were to contribute to the Great Famine. Irish food, rents, capital and cheap labour helped to build up the very industrial capitalist order in Britain which then eclipsed Ireland. And Irish soldiers were plentifully available to protect it; by 1830, an astonishing 42 per cent of the British army were of Irish origin. The Ascendancy, of course, were themselves the 'bearers' of this structure rather than the authors of it – which is to say that the focus of political critique, here as in any such context, is not a *class* but *class relations*. It is not, finally, a matter of how vigorously or reluctantly these men ground the faces of the poor, as the displacing terms of some contemporary historical debates would have it. It is rather that the injustice of the social system which shaped their own behaviour as much as that of their underlings could have been put right only by a social transformation which would have entailed their overthrow. This, indeed, is what finally happened – astonishingly, at the hands of the British, not the Irish. And it is not of course a matter of claiming that this could have happened at any historical point whatsoever. For most of the Ascendancy's period of rule, the political forces necessary to oust them were plainly lacking. But neither is it mere idle academicism to claim that this is what would have *had* to take place if Ireland were to have achieved any semblance of social justice.

The point of such counterfactual speculation is to locate some of the root causes of the country's problems, and so to circumvent those who centre the argument on the brutality or benevolence of the landlord class as a whole. As with any exploiting class, the only gesture which would have truly benefited their subordinates would have been their collective resignation. As Cormac Ó Gráda, no devotee of nationalist demonology, acidly remarks: 'had *phytophthora infestans* destroyed landlords instead of potatoes in 1845, agricultural output would have been only marginally affected'.[128] Even as exploiting classes go, the landowners did precious little to justify their privileges. They were a parasitic social formation; and though R.F. Foster, in a typically sanitizing gesture, scoffs at the popular perception of them as vampiric, one should remember that a vampire need not himself be excessively bloated in order to drain his victims dry.[129] Even the most modest of rents proved a heavy burden for many of the poorer Irish farmers. As Raymond Crotty argues, the only conceivable solution to Ireland's drastically lopsided development would have been the 'complete overthrow' of the existing tenure system by a state which, in appropriating all rents and redistributing them in accordance with human needs, would at least have prevented mass starvation.[130] Gearóid Ó Tuathaigh remarks of the pre-Famine period, when production was on the increase but its fruits strikingly maldistributed, that it would have taken a social revolution to set the situation to rights.[131] Such imaginative speculations, however, are curiously rare in the annals of modern Irish historiography.

To win consent to its leadership, a ruling class needs to be on the spot; and too many of the Irish squirearchy failed to fulfil this simple but indispensable condition. Before the Famine, perhaps a third of the land-lords were absentee; by 1876, 36.6 per cent resided in Ireland, though not always on their own estates. But if they were in one sense too remote for effective rule, they were in another sense excessively present. In quasi-feudal fashion, the landowners combined in their own persons economic, political and juridical power: they were MPs and justices of the peace, poor-law guardians and grand jurors, school governors and powerful patrons. Their authority penetrated into the moral and domestic spheres, as they wielded the threat of eviction against poachers, drunkards, wife-beaters and undutiful children as well as against those guilty of bad farming or rent arrears. In one sense, this plurality of roles reinforced their authority: the landlord was in effect the political state in any particular locality, and for the state to be incarnate in a living personage can be to its advantage. The familiar figure in the Big House can claim your allegiance as a more abstract bureaucracy might not. But it can also be a drawback, since economic conflict can then rebound upon political and juridical authority as well.

---

128. Cormac Ó Gráda, 'Poverty, Population and Agriculture, 1801-45', in Vaughan, ed., *A New History of Ireland, vol. V*, p. 129.
129. Foster, *Modern Ireland 1600-1970*, p. 375.
130. Crotty, *Irish Agricultural Production*, p. 63.
131. Gearóid Ó Tuathaigh, *Ireland before the Famine* (London 1991), p. 139.

The industrial middle class in England, so Marx and Engels argued, managed to 'delegate' its political and cultural power to the aristocracy, thus helping to remove the political state from the field of class struggle. In modern capitalist societies, the economic achieves a high degree of autonomy of the political, and this is itself a primary source of mystification. The industrial bourgeoisie are in fact the basis of the political state, but do not appear as such. Given the slimness of the Irish middle class, the gentry had few social groups to hide behind, and were thus embarrassingly visible. They were not, to be sure, entirely lacking in such social camouflage: what intervened between them and the common people, along with the walls of the demesne, were the middlemen, who drew some of the fire which might otherwise have been directed at the landowning gentry. And it is important to remember that much of the class conflict in the Irish countryside was between small and strong farmers, cottiers and graziers, who often enough shared the same ethnic and religious background. But since the Anglo-Irish owned most of the land while the Irish tenants did most of the production, the rent system functioned in an unusually conspicious way, in contrast to an industrial capitalist order in which the sources of wealth are more tangled and obscure. And the meagre size of the middle class threw the contrast between poverty and privilege into dramatic relief. Yet at the same time the landlords were too thin on the ground, physically dispersed, absent from the country or – so some would claim – dim-witted[132] to provide effective government in themselves, and had consequently to witness a steady transfer of their power to the centralized bureaucracy of Dublin Castle. To this extent they reaped the worst of both worlds, at once dangerously visible and made progressively redundant by local government reform and the growth of a centralized state. Part of the task of that state was to mitigate their own privileges, as well as mop up some of the social disruption they occasioned.

If the state in nineteenth-century Ireland was on the whole more professionalized and interventionist than in Britain, this was partly to off-set the incapacities of the native governors, and partly to provide the social services and coercive apparatus their actions made urgently necessary. But the result was a contrast between a relatively advanced political state and a relatively archaic ruling class, which helped to highlight the latter's superfluity. In 1800, the British state had stepped in to buttress a client ruling class; but by the 1830s and '40s, at the height of Catholic agitation,

---

132. Ibid., p. 94.

that state was itself evolving towards its mature liberal form, viewing itself increasingly as an impartial broker between contending interests rather than as the partisan ally of any of them in particular. It reaped little political benefit from being perceived as the protector of an overprivileged, underperforming oligarchy, and so, having grappled them to its bosom, began nervously loosening its grip. Propping up an overseas landowning elite was hardly in accord with its own historical dynamic, and Britain's political economists looked on that privileged crew with chilly disfavour. David Ricardo was quite as much in favour of their abolition as the most radical Ribbonman. In this sense, it was to the Ascendancy's disadvantage that its own career as a governing class was out of synchrony with a liberal industrial bourgeoisie across the water whose conception of the state was changing at just the time that the Anglo-Irish needed some decently non-disinterested backing. That they received a good deal of support of this kind is beyond question: British legislation up to the late nineteenth century was almost entirely in the landlord's interest. But there were times when it was not quite so flagrantly partisan as they could have wished. The state may indeed be the arm of the ruling class; but in order to act as such it has often enough to mediate between conflicting interests in ways which may be to the short-term detriment of those it ultimately serves. The shift of authority from local to central government was not in fact wholly to the disadvantage of the Ascendancy, since it conveniently curtailed local Catholic power in a newly democratizing epoch; but if it profited them in this sense, it also spelt the gradual death of the notoriously corrupt genteel-amateur grand jury. Moreover, it has been argued by Barrington Moore Jr, in his *Social Origins of Dictatorship and Democracy*, that the growing centralization of state power, by depriving local elites of many of their traditional rationales, loosens the bonds between them and their clients; and this is certainly one way to read the narrative of nineteenth-century Ascendancy Ireland. The establishment of a national police force, for example, stripped them of some of their traditional juridical functions, and so weakened their active participation in the community, leaving them as economic-cum-ornamental figures. The landlords' political and ideological sway survived for a while their increasing economic frailty; but it is likely that by the 1870s this too was sharply on the wane. Isaac Butt, perhaps a little sanguinely, is writing in 1875 of the 'overthrown principle of Protestant ascendancy'.[133] There was simply no good reason for them to be around any longer, if indeed there ever had

---

133. Isaac Butt, *The Problem of Irish Education* (London 1875), p. 25.

been; and they were not on the whole sorry to be rescued by a British government whose financial generosity to them was in marked contrast to their own niggardliness towards their inferiors.

The ambiguous benefits of visibility are well symbolized in the Big House. If its imposing presence is a lesson in deference, it also provides a convenient place to burn down. The house, as Yeats was not slow to see, is a kind of Romantic symbol all in itself, a place whose material opulence is justified as a medium of spirit. It is the body of those who move within it, and so, since no mere external possession, no more alienable than the flesh itself. Like the flesh, it is an outcropping of Nature itself, or at least an ambivalent zone between that and Culture. It is Nature worked up into history, and thus at once monumental and busily energetic – the two poles, of marmoreal eternity and sensuous flux, which Yeats's poetry seeks to combine. What makes his tower ruined, emasculated, half-dead at the top, is the corrosive action of history itself, and so paradoxically what makes it live. Arrogance and insecurity, in typical Ascendancy fashion, thus blend into a single structure of feeling. The house is a kind of historical subject in itself, a process of which its particular inhabitants are merely the bearers; and this projects responsibility for their own actions onto a communal reality which is always elsewhere. Like the Romantic symbol it is at once local and universal, rooted in one dear perpetual place yet microcosmic of an entire social order, which cannot be alien or impersonal because it can always be translated back into this concrete idiom of the familiar and interpersonal, of a pattern of linked, humanized houses.

Given this assured frame of communal identity, an anarchic individualism can then be tolerated or even actively fostered, as though the autonomy of the house-as-subject is displaced into the libertinism of its individual inhabitants. Indeed the tension between aristocracy as order and aristocracy as Byronic license is one Yeats's poetry never quite succeeds in resolving.[134] The house, as both artefact and agricultural headquarters, reveals an intimate relation between spirit and body, culture and economics, and thus suggests how much culture shaped the life of the Ascendancy as a whole.[135] But it was not primarily a matter of fountains and oil paintings; it was the fact that among the many circumstances which accounted for

---

134. I have examined this conflict in my 'Politics and Sexuality in W.B.Yeats', *The Crane Bag*, vol. 9, no. 2, (1985). Edward Larrissy has some perceptive comments on the question in his *Yeats the Poet* (Hemel Hempstead 1994), Ch. 8.

135. For two somewhat uneven collections of essays on the Big House, see Jacqueline Genet, ed., The *Big House in Ireland: Reality and Representation* (London 1991); and Otto

their less than distinguished economic performance (debt, non-investment, shortage of mineral wealth, unstable political conditions, the prospect of higher profits in England) the sheer weight of ingrained cultural habit – the sense that one's main business was in England, that a central part of one's identity lay there, and that Ireland was a commercial rather than psychological investment – played a significant role. Indeed, as J.C. Beckett has argued, the Ascendancy, unlike their Scottish counterparts, displayed no corporate sense of a distinctive national culture;[136] and to that extent, as mere west Britons, they had little culturally specific about them into which their inferiors might be incorporated.

It is, indeed, with the whole field of culture and psychology that hegemony is intimately concerned. But as far as culture went, the rift between elite and populace was unspannable. As Tom Dunne has pointed out, in Ireland, 'in contrast to other European countries, including France, the old or aspiring power elites had much less access to the culture of the poor, as linguistic difference reinforced religious division, and indigenous Gaelic and Gaelicised cultures were long considered politically subversive.'[137] In the early eighteenth century, the class of Catholic middlemen could involve themselves in popular culture with no loss of prestige, patronizing music and poetry, dispensing lavish hospitality to their social subordinates, plunging with gusto into hurling and cockfighting, hunting and horseracing; by the end of the century, ruling and popular cultures were becoming progressively demarcated.[138] The United Irish movement, by contrast, was able to combine elements of a sophisticated Enlightenment political culture with sturdy native traditions of dispossession, while the Defenders displayed an intriguing blend of popular and high-radical culture in secret oaths which combined Saint Peter with the Chief Consul. In the symbolism of the movement, pikes commingled with crucifixes, liberty caps with blessed scapulars.[139] Daniel O'Connell's campaigns were

Rauchbauer, ed., *Ancestral Voices: The Big House in Anglo-Irish Literature* (Hildesheim 1992). See also, for life in the Big House, the vivacious correspondence of Somerville and Ross (Gifford Lewis, ed., *The Selected Letters of Somerville and Ross*, London 1989); and Elizabeth Bowen, *Bowen's Court* (London 1941).

136. J.C. Beckett, 'Burke, Ireland and the Empire', in O. MacDonagh, W.F. Mandle and P. Travers, eds, *Irish Culture and Nationalism, 1750-1950* (London 1983), p. 9.

137. Tom Dunne, 'Popular Ballads, Revolutionary Rhetoric and Politicisation', in Hugh Gough and David Dickson, eds, *Ireland and the French Revolution* (Dublin 1990), p. 143.

138. See Whelan, 'An Underground Gentry?'

139. Though Kevin Whelan points out that the United Irish movement was more concerned to politicize popular culture than, as with cultural nationalism, to value it in itself ('The United Irishmen, The Enlightenment and Popular Culture', in D. Dickson, D. Keogh and K. Whelan, eds, *The United Irishmen: Republicanism, Radicalism and Rebellion*, Dublin 1993, p. 275).

part political movement, part popular carnival, complete with sports, costumes, music, banquets and processions. They were, as one commentator puts it, nationalism as a form of recreation, transgressing the border between political militancy and popular festivity.[140]

No such articulation with popular consciousness was available to the Ascendancy, on any sufficiently strong basis; and when some of its sons and daughters turned to the realm of culture, it was as a form of counterhegemony to the status quo, a weapon wielded against their own class. Men like Parnell and Yeats, and women like Maud Gonne and Constance Markiewicz, sought to make the difficult transition, in Gramscian terms, from 'traditional' to 'organic' intellectuals, place themselves in the van of a popular radical movement rather than act as apologists for the class culture from which they had sprung.[141] 'All Irish writers, wrote the narodnik young Yeats, 'have to choose whether they will write as the upper classes have done, not to express but to exploit this country; or join the intellectual movement which has raised the cry that was heard in Russia in the 'seventies, the cry, "To the people".'[142] But if writers in transition from 'traditional' to 'organic' status were thereby self-divided, so also was the class from which they sprang. For the Anglo-Irish mind was gripped by a ferocious Oedipal aggression towards its paternal superiors at Westminster, a hostility which, like the Oedipal child, it sought often enough to displace and disavow.[143] The displacement, commonly enough, was on to the despised Gaelic masses; the disavowal took the form of clamorous protestations of loyalty to an idealized crown. The populace are detested because, among other things, they write large your own humiliation and so must be all the more disdainfully distanced; while England becomes the object of an impossible psychic ambivalence, at once identified with and rejected in a stalled dialectic of love and hate. Sir Samuel Ferguson ended a speech to the Protestant Repeal Association in 1848 with the mystifying double slogan: 'Rule, Britannia!' and 'We are not a colony of Great Britain.'[144]

---

140. See Elizabeth Malcolm, 'Popular Recreation in Nineteenth-Century Ireland', in MacDonagh, Mandle and Travers, eds, *Irish Culture and Nationalism, 1750-1950*.

141. There were precedents for this: the Young Irelander Fintan Lalor, champion of the peasantry and widely seen even today as a 'peasant' himself, was in fact the son of a Tipperary middleman who controlled one thousand acres. See David N. Buckley, *James Fintan Lalor: Radical* (Cork 1990), p. 26.

142. W.B. Yeats, *Explorations* (London 1962), p. 83.

143. For a brief survey of the divided consciousness of the Anglo-Irish, see G.J. Watson, *Irish Identity and the Literary Revival* (London 1979), Introduction.

144. Quoted by Malcolm Brown, *Sir Samuel Ferguson* (Lewisburg 1973), p. 80.

That one is indeed a victim, yet cannot possibly be so, is then the paradox of this condition. But it is an ambivalence which the Catholic masses then re-enact towards their Protestant masters, from whom, from time to time, they seek a spiritual leadership of which they feel they have been cheated. Popular rebellion in Ireland was often enough an appeal to the landlords to live up to their moral obligations – a baffled demand for genuine leadership on their part rather than a desire to overthrow property relations as such. *Noblesse oblige* would seem at some points in Irish history a doctrine more warmly embraced by the populace than the patriciate. But the state of affairs between landlord and tenant was not one of reciprocal obligation, but – at times, at least – of warfare. 'Don't let us disguise it from ourselves,' warned John Bright, 'there is a war between landlord and tenant, a war as fierce and relentless as though it were carried on by force of arms'.[145] And often, indeed, it was. Oliver MacDonagh remarks that 'in general, Irish landlords and their agents behaved and were treated as if they were at war with their dependents',[146] and only a feckless landlord would have strolled his estates unarmed at certain times in the nineteenth century.

That the Ascendancy had largely failed to naturalize their rule was embarrassingly apparent. A successful governing bloc diffuses its power throughout the pores of civil society, infiltrating it into the texture of everyday life so as to render it synonymous with common sense. 'No intelligent foreigner, we believe', wrote the starry-eyed W.E.H. Lecky in 1861, 'could land upon the English coast without being struck with the intensity of the political life pervading every class of the community. It permeates every pore; it thrills and vibrates along every fibre of the political body; it diffuses its action through the remotest village...' Governments help to establish their rule by creating a sphere of civil institutions in which a favourable public opinion may thrive; but little or nothing of this, Lecky notes, is to be found in Ireland. 'Parliament', he continues in Burkeian vein, 'can make [the people's] laws, but it cannot control or influence their feelings. It can revolutionise the whole system of government, but it cannot allay one discontent, or quell one passion. Public

---

145. Quoted in T. Moody, *Davitt and the Irish Revolution* (Oxford 1981), p. 518.

146. Oliver MacDonagh, *Ireland: The Union and its Aftermath* (London 1977), p. 36. The Lord Lieutenant wrote privately in 1830 that 'there exists to the most frightful extent a mutual and violent hatred between Proprietors and the Peasantry' (quoted by Collison Black, *Economic Thought and the Irish Question*, p. 9).

opinion is diseased – diseased to the very core.'[147] What Ireland lacks is a public sphere of discourse and dialogue, an enlightened space in which conflicts may be peaceably resolved, a common wisdom distilled, and political power spread throughout social life as a whole. Instead, what Lecky calls 'purely political feeling' has yielded ground to sectarian animosity; and only a 'national feeling' will act as a check to partisan passions. The state, in short, has failed abysmally to *interpellate* the Irish Catholic people – to forge an identity between them and itself, to reinflect their sense of themselves in the language of its own corporate being. The Union itself, so some had hoped, would prove precisely such a measure, resulting in what one over-hopeful politician of the time described as a 'moral assimilation with Britain'.[148] Lecky, however, recognizes that it has proved less a form of cultural hegemony than a mere political rearrangement, 'effecting an identification of government, without an identification of sentiments. It centralized, but it could not unite.'[149] Sir Roger Casement will later take up the theme in his speech from the dock: 'But conquest, my lord, gives no title; and, if it exists over the body, it fails over the mind. It can exert no empire over men's reason and judgement and affections.'[150]

The state itself, then, had failed in its hegemonic role. For though Gramsci views hegemony, by and large, as a matter of 'civil society' rather than the state, the truth is that, in liberal democratic society at least, the state machine is itself one of the most powerful devices by which consent to be ruled is won. It is the electoral process, in which those who are governed may enjoy the illusion that they govern themselves, which provides one of the most effective of all forms of hegemony. To exclude the mass of the people from the state, in the manner of early Ascendancy Ireland, is then to risk undermining one's political authority in the act of seeking to preserve it. British policy towards Ireland vacillated accordingly between shutting the populace out and seeking to integrate them; indeed it occasionally pulled off an ingenious combination of the two, as in the Act of Union itself, or in the granting of Catholic Emancipation with one hand while disenfranchising many of its potential beneficiaries with the other. If the state cannot achieve hegemony, then one must

---

147. Lecky, *Leaders of Public Opinion*, p. 272.

148. Dean Tucker in 1799, quoted by R. MacDowell, *Ireland in the Age of Imperialism* (Oxford 1979), p. 687.

149. Lecky, *Leaders of Public Opinion*, p. 155.

150. Roger Casement, 'Speech from the Dock', in Seamus Deane, ed., *The Field Day Anthology of Irish Writing* (Derry 1991), vol. 2, p. 297.

instead turn to civil society – to that rich array of institutions, from family and school to church and culture, which mediate between state and economy. But the Anglo-Irish could find little joy here either. For the truth was that of the two most important of these institutions, one (education) was itself riven by sectarian conflict, and the other (the Roman Catholic Church) was firmly in the possession of the people. Indeed it was the one major national institution they could call their own. As for culture, this was less a means whereby the rulers could diffuse their own values than, in the shape of Gaelic traditionalism, a means by which the common Catholic people could compensate for their lack of political status. Gramsci is sometimes thought to have urged that an oppositional class must accumulate cultural capital before it can come to power; but though it is doubtful that he held this view, it is certain that some of the Ascendancy did. Gaelic culture was a barbaric affair, the badge of a people unfit for government; and in Anglo-Irish eyes that culture had first to prove its worth. Many an Irish antiquarian, in demonstrating the civilized heritage of the Gaels, was obliquely demonstrating their fitness to rule.[151]

An hegemony too visibly imposed is bound to be self-defeating. This was certainly the typical Catholic perception of the national schooling system established in 1831, which as Joseph Lee argues was clearly intended by the British government to 'perform a massive brain-washing operation, obliterating subversive ancestral influence by inculcating in the pupils a proper reverence for the English connection, and proper deference for their social superiors, defined according to the exquisite English concept of class'.[152] One witness to a Select Committee on Education in 1835 described the new national schoolteachers as 'moral Police'.[153] Designed as undenominational, the system in practice soon became sectarian; and until the Intermediate Education Act of 1878 Catholic secondary education, in contrast to its Protestant counterpart, received no assistance from the state. Distrusted by many of the Catholic hierarchy, resisted by the Church of Ireland clergy and ardently contested by the Presbyterians of Ulster, national schooling was a zone of furious ideological contention from the outset. As such, it was the latest chapter of a turbulent history of politicized education, all the way from the early-eighteenth-century Acts which, by prohibiting denominational education

---

151. For an erudite treatment of such antiquarianism, see Norman Vance, 'Celts, Carthaginians and Constitutions', *Irish Historical Studies*, vol. 22, no. 87 (March 1981).
152. Joseph Lee, *The Modernisation of Irish Society 1848-1918* (Dublin 1989), p. 28.
153. Quoted by Thomas A. Boylan and Timothy P. Foley, *Political Economy and Colonial Ireland* (London 1992), p. 121.

for a Catholic people with a traditional hunger for learning, had produced the legendary hedge schools with their nationalist schoolmasters.[154] The classical learning of these men was often enough accompanied by notions of civil liberty and republican virtue.[155] In Ireland, education was an extension of political struggle rather than a solution to it, as the Catholic bishops' condemnation of the newly established Queen's Colleges in 1850 – an issue which divided the O'Connellites and Young Irelanders – dramatically testified.[156] At a Repeal Association meeting in 1845, one participant insisted that St Paul was a Roman Catholic, or at any rate no supporter of mixed education.[157] There was, so the Catholic prelates considered, a specifically Catholic way of teaching human anatomy, as opposed to a sinisterly Protestant discourse of the body.

Education is one of the most familiar of the panaceas advanced by ruling classes for repairing the social damage they themselves inflict; but in Ireland such large-minded Arnoldian mystifications stubbornly refused to take hold. Objectivity and impartiality, the precious hallmarks of the English liberal sensibility, were never as highly valued in the strife-torn colony. It is suitably symbolic that Cardinal Newman's Dublin University never really flourished. All history was partisan history, and the Commissioners of National Education resolved the conflict between this state of affairs, and their requirement that no school lessons should prove religiously or politically offensive, by the ingenious device of eliminating all systematic history teaching from the school syllabus.[158] The system taught no Irish language or literature either, conveying instead 'a turgid amalgam of social ethics and political docility'.[159] While some Catholic educationalists assumed that all non-Catholic teaching would necessarily be anti-Catholic, some Protestants were anxious that 'a true history of Ireland' might cause offence; and one commissioner helpfully suggested that the problem could be tackled by recounting the history backwards, starting

154. See Patrick J. Dowling, *The Hedge Schools of Ireland* (Dublin 1935), for a somewhat idealizing view of the subject.

155. See W.B. Stanford, *Ireland and the Classical Tradition* (Dublin 1971), pp. 215–16.

156. For a succinct account of the university question, see Norman Atkinson, *Irish Education* (Dublin 1969), Ch. 6; and Geraldine Grogan, 'The Colleges Bill, 1845–49', in M.R. O'Connell, ed., *O'Connell: Education, Church and State* (Dublin 1992). For a contemporary analysis, see Butt, *The Problem of Irish Education*. For the split within the Repeal movement, see Randall Clarke, 'The Relations between O'Connell and the Young Irelanders', *Irish Historical Studies*, vol. 3, no. 9 (March 1942).

157. See D. George Boyce, *Nationalism in Ireland* (London 1982), p. 166.

158. See David Fitzpatrick, 'The Futility of History: A Failed Experiment in Irish Education', in Ciaran Brady, ed., *Ideology and the Historians* (Dublin 1991), p. 171.

159. Ó Tuathaigh, *Ireland before the Famine*, p. 106.

with the splendid achievements of the Victorian period and then, having craftily sweetened the pill, moving to the less than palmy past.[160] National school textbooks were nevertheless hugely successful, widely used in Britain and distributed throughout the empire.[161] It was not the only occasion on which Ireland was to provide a convenient laboratory for broader imperial measures. But education in Ireland was too obviously an incorporative device – too blatantly a means of defusing political conflict by trying to civilize a truculent peasantry. In the parliamentary debates over the Union, the benignly rationalist Richard Edgeworth, identifying Ireland's problem as a 'want of culture', insisted that the force of education was greater than the power of the sword.[162] Edgeworth was right to consider that coercion was no solution in Ireland; he was simply wrong to imagine that conciliation would prove any more effective.

The other great institution of civil society is religion; and here it was the misfortune of the Anglo-Irish to find themselves up against not only the most supremely capable form of hegemony in the country, but the most enduring form of hegemony in human history. No institution has rivalled the power of the Roman Catholic Church to secure, across centuries and continents, the allegiance of its subjects. The Church is, in effect, an oligarchy; but within its structures, prelate and peasant are linked by a common vision in a social order with all the Byzantine apparatus of a political state yet all the intimacy of a family. In this stratified yet corporate society, intellectuals (theologians) and the masses (laity) share the same faith at different levels: what the former articulate as doctrine, the latter live out as pious observance. Yet, true to Gramsci's generous sense of 'intellectual', even the simple faithful must be capable of mastering their catechism and defending the faith, in a Church which has tradition-ally set a high premium on human reason. Louis Althusser, himself a former Catholic, insists that ideology is less disembodied consciousness than material practice; and the Catholic Church, whose faith is more a matter of ritual gesture than agonized inwardness, is a case in point.[163] J.E. Bicheno, visiting Ireland in 1829, considered the Catholic Church's

---

160. Fitzpatrick, 'The Futility of History', pp. 172–3.

161. See D.H. Akenson, 'Pre-University Education, 1782–1871', in Vaughan, ed., *A New History of Ireland*, vol. *V*, p. 532. See also the same author's *The Irish Educational Experiment* (London 1970). A general survey of Irish educational policies is to be found in T.J. McElligot, *Education in Ireland* (Dublin 1966).

162. Richard Lovell Edgeworth and Maria Edgeworth, *Memoirs* (London 1820), vol. 2, p. 248.

163. See Louis Althusser, 'Ideology and Ideological State Apparatuses', in *Lenin and Philosophy and Other Essays* (London 1971).

ritual and imagery, its ability to engage the sensuous imagination, as a primary source of its authority. Since the Irish are 'persons without reflection, slaves to their affections and passions',[164] they are unsuited to the rationalist authority of Protestantism. The values of the Church are absolute and unchanging; but they are also the stuff of daily experience, brought to the people by a priesthood which provides a bridge between transcendent mystery and such humdrum matters as how to vote. The world-view of Catholicism is at once elaborately formalized and supremely practical; and it is this close relation between what Althusser calls 'theoretical ideology' and ideology 'in a practical state' which lends the Roman faith much of its power. The technical language of theology can be translated into a set of codes for regulating daily conduct; and if the machinery of coercion is at hand to supervise such behaviour, the means of conciliation, symbolized above all in the confessional, are no less available. The Established Church in Ireland, by contrast, won the adherence of only a small minority of the population, and the ruling power was thus deprived of a vital means of ideological control. Divided from the mass of the people by class and ethnic background, the Ascendancy was unable to compensate for these disabilities with the unifying bonds of religion.

In a celebrated passage, Gramsci distinguishes between 'traditional' intellectuals, who act as apologists for an established order, and those 'organic' intellectuals who are the product of popular movements.[165] In the Irish Catholic Church the contrast can be applied, with a degree of simplification, to the distinction between the hierarchy and the parish clergy. The role of the bishops is to enforce the authority of the Church itself, and, for the most part, of the state; the curate and parish priest are their local agents in this respect, but as popular leaders must steer a course between this and the political culture of the people. The priest incarnates the Law; but his task is to impose it on a popular consciousness he knows from the inside. The local pastor, then, faces both ways, intimate with the ways of the simple faithful yet transmitting to them an absolute authority; and in this sense, as a figure transitional between 'traditional' and 'organic', he is at the very centre of the process of hegemony. The priests fulfilled the role of traditional intellectuals in the situation of organic ones; and the more politically militant among them often enough

---

164. J.E. Bicheno, *Ireland and its Economy* (London 1830), pp. 225–6. Bicheno ends his book by remarking that he has no political views.

165. See Quintin Hoare and Geoffrey Nowell Smith, eds, *Selections from the Prison Notebooks of Antonio Gramsci* (New York 1971), I. i.

made a decisive break from the one to the other. The parish clergy in Ireland were more than spiritual ministers: they were fixers and brokers, unofficial lawyers and political organizers, social workers and financial counsellors, policemen, school governors and electoral managers, amateur physicians and intercessors with authority. They were bosses and god-fathers whose influence permeated almost every aspect of the life of their flock; and in traditional Ireland they were credited with the power to cure and curse, to transform the ungodly into dumb beasts, blight their crops and wither their loins.[166] Yet they were for the most part sprung from the middling ranks of the people themselves, the sons of tradesmen, shopkeepers, and farmers rather than scions of the *haute bourgeoisie*; and though the clergy were never recruited from the ranks of the cottiers and labourers, they lived a somewhat more civilised version of the common people's habits and values, as well as often enough sharing their political views. The fact that they were financially dependent on the laity could provide a powerful incentive for lending their politics a sympathetic ear.

It was the Catholic Church, then, buttressed in its authority by a history of persecution, which formed an unbreachable bulwark between Ascendancy and people. And since the Church offered its people an alternative identity to that of their rulers, it was remarkably free of heresy and sectarianism. Irish Catholicism was a peculiarly cohesive force, 'highly resistant to the growth of internal deviation'.[167] Any effective secular power in Ireland, whether sprung from above or below, had to pass through this indispensable conduit. The situation resembled the classic pre-revolutionary scenario of 'dual power': only the clergy could deliver the masses to the Establishment, and only the clergy, as O'Connell and Parnell were well aware, could deliver them to a radical campaign. The hierarchy was never politically univocal: its views ranged from the ultramontane conservatism of Cardinal Paul Cullen to the rabid nationalism of John MacHale of Tuam, from the anti-republican frothings of Bishop Moriarty of Kerry to the Fenian fellow-travelling of Archbishop Croke of Cashel.[168] Yet even Cullen, framer of the dogma of papal infallibility and denounced often

---

166. See Hoppen, *Elections, Politics, and Society*, Ch. 3. See also K.H. Connell, *Irish Peasant Society* (Oxford 1968), Ch. 4.

167. Patrick O'Farrell, 'Millenialism, Messianism and Utopianism in Irish History', *Anglo-Irish Studies*, no. 2 (1976), p. 48.

168. See Sheridan Giley, 'The Catholic Church and Revolution', in D.G. Boyce, ed., *The Revolution in Ireland, 1879–1923* (London 1988). See also, for a biography of the extraordinary MacHale, Nuala Costello, *John MacHale of Tuam* (Dublin 1939); and for a biography of Paul Cullen, Desmond Bowen, *Paul Cardinal Cullen and the Shaping of Modern Irish Catholicism* (Dublin 1983).

enough as a 'Castle bishop', had scant love for the British, and counter-pointed his assaults on Fenianism with swingeing anti-Orange polemic.[169] The political stance of the church, as the ecclesial voice of middle-class Catholicism, was in general a cautious constitutional nationalism; it was the clergy who provided the shock troops for both of O'Connell's great campaigns. They were deeply embroiled in the tithe wars of the 1830s, and took an active part in the Land League, if only – in the words of one large-minded cleric – to keep out 'godless nobodies'. 'Though Mr. Parnell is, unfortunately for himself, a Protestant,' remarked the equally generous-spirited Archbishop Croke during the land war, 'he is, never-theless, a man of high honour and unimpeachable moral character.'[170] The word 'boycott' was invented by a Land League priest, largely because his parishioners had trouble in pronouncing 'ostracization'.

Politically speaking, the Church's position in Ireland was somewhat akin to that of a modern trades-union movement. Both organizations seek to promote their power by convincing the ruling system of their respectability, while simultaneously guarding their backs from the dis-gruntlement this is likely to breed in their own rank and file. Like a trade union, the Church was forced to collude with an authority it took a dim view of, for the purpose of advancing its own interests; but by the same token it could be led to defy it, not least when it was pressed from below by a militancy it needed to placate. Some archbishops of Dublin would have been affronted not to receive invitations to state banquets, even if to attend them would have been more than their reputations were worth. To preserve credibility with the people, the hierarchy had to put some daylight between itself and Dublin Castle; but to condone political agitation was to risk forfeiting its own credibility with the state, as well as to countenance a rejection of authority which might finally rebound on itself. As far as nationalism went, the Church was torn between rashly tolerating a rival to its own sovereignty, and alienating its own supporters by too absolutely condemning it. Like the labour movement, the Church was acutely conscious of its own illicit past – aware that since the penal era it was in some sense on probation, and obsequiously keen to face

---

169. For Cullen's political and ecclesial manoeuvrings, see Emmet Larkin, *The Making of the Roman Catholic Church in Ireland, 1850-1860* (Chapel Hill 1980). See also his 'Church and State in Ireland', *Church History*, vol. XXXI (1962). For an able defence of Cullen against the charge of benighted reaction, see E.D. Steele, 'Cardinal Cullen and Irish Nationality', *Irish Historical Studies*, vol. 19, no. 75 (March 1975).

170. Quoted by Emmet Larkin, *The Roman Catholic Church and the Creation of the Modern Irish State, 1878–1886* (Philadelphia 1975), p. 71.

down the suspicion that an allegiance to Rome was a tacit form of treason.[171] The suspicion was particularly ironic, given the traditional independent bent of the Irish church, reflected in the Gallican tendencies of some of its bishops.[172]

The eighteenth-century Church in particular was clamorous in its protestations of political loyalty. Conservative in social doctrine, implacably hostile to peasant agitation and secret societies, the Church in Ireland displayed all the zeal for social rectitude of the insecure *parvenu*; and the clergy's twin animus against landowner and landless labourer was the supreme mark of this petty-bourgeois mentality. The Church's suspicion of secret societies was no doubt among other things an aversion to areas of opaqueness where its own knowledge and power were unable to penetrate. It is ironic, then, that the British should have spontaneously associated Irish nationalism and Catholicism, given the virulent anti-clericalism of many an Irish nationalist. A Church which had largely abandoned the liberatory message of the gospel for an autocratic theology had to witness that dimension of its teaching appropriated by a secularized nationalism. Yet for all its arthritic conservatism, the Irish Church was remarkable throughout Europe for its liberal and radical fellow-travelling. Deeply conservative and authoritarian, it was nonetheless forced by its hostility to Britain and its need to check subversion into incongruous alliances with secular liberal forces. From the viewpoint of papal diplomacy, Ireland had more political clout as part of the United Kingdom than as independent, which set Irish prelates against separatism and even Home Rule; but though Cardinal Cullen could see little in the latter but a Protestant-dominated Irish parliament and a threat to clerical authority, the church eventually came to support it largely because its people did.

The political temper of the Church as a whole was thus far from unambiguous. There were always some 'physical force' advocates among the lower clergy, though few priests were involved in the United Irish rebellion. In the nineteenth century, the Maynooth seminary was considered by the British a hotbed of nationalism, and there is some evidence that Fenianism spread through the ranks of the lower clergy after the

---

171. For the Church in the penal era, see John Brady and Patrick J. Corish, *The Church under the Penal Code* (Dublin 1971).

172. For this, and for the association (unique in Europe) of the Irish Church with the forces of liberalism and democracy, see Donal Kerr, 'Under the Union Flag: The Catholic Church in Ireland, 1800–1870', in the British Academy publication *Ireland after the Union* (Oxford 1989). For a more detailed account, see also Kerr's *Peel, Priests and Politics* (Oxford 1982).

execution of the Manchester Martyrs in 1867.[173] Though the bishops set their face against insurrection, dead Fenians were occasionally indulged in a manner denied to live ones, and the Church's stance on the revolutionary era from 1916 to 1921 was notably equivocal. If the bishops were evasive or divided, a great many priests sympathized with the executed, mainly Catholic rebels of the Easter Rising.[174] Contrary to some nationalist mythology, the Church was never uniformly reactionary on the national question; some of the clergy embraced nationalism as an antidote to the even more demonic socialism, which they associated with a godless Britain. 'The full sewerage from the *cloaca maxima* of Anglicisation', wrote the *Catholic Bulletin* in the year of the great Dublin lock-out, 'is now discharged upon us. The black devil of Socialism, hoof and horns is amongst us.'[175] The political ambiguities of the Church reflected those of the nation as a whole, from a position in general to the right of it. In Killala in 1836, strife between radical and reactionary clerics was such that rival priests celebrated mass at different ends of the chapel of Kincon, while armed police kept their congregations apart.[176]

As with any hegemony, that of the Catholic Church in Ireland was incomplete. The priest may have been a numinous figure to his flock; but this did not constrain them from threatening to beat him up in protest against his fees or his politics, and few Fenians seemed deterred by the assurance of eternal perdition. With comic inconsistency, the British vilified Irish Catholics as grovelling adherents of Rome, while denouncing them for ignoring Rome's censure of their political views. If there was power, there was also resistance; and in any case Irish Catholics do not seem to have been especially strict in their religious observances until the mid nineteenth century.[177] But while Britain sustained dominance, hegemony was reserved to the Church, which to this extent inherited something of the role of the old Gaelic aristocracy. In a society bereft of a

---

173. See E.R. Norman, *The Catholic Church and Ireland in the Age of Rebellion 1859–1873* (London 1975), p. 123.

174. See S.J. Connolly, *Priests and People in Pre-Famine Ireland* (Dublin 1982), p. 170. See also his *Religion and Society in Nineteenth-Century Ireland* (Dundalk 1985).

175. Quoted by Patrick O'Farrell, *Ireland's England Question* (London 1971), p. 270.

176. See Bowen, *Paul Cardinal Cullen*, p. 77. For an account of the priests' response to nationalism around the turn of the century, see Tom Garvin, 'Priests and Patriots: Irish Separatism and Fear of the Modern, 1890–1918', *Irish Historical Studies*, vol. 25, no. 97 (May 1986).

177. Regular mass attendance was rather low in some areas in the pre-Famine period, but this was partly because of a shortage of clergy and churches. See Emmet Larkin, 'The Devotional Revolution in Ireland, 1850–75', *American Historical Review*, vol. 77, no. 3 (June 1972).

developed middle class, the masses were dependent on their priesthood for political leadership. And this separation of temporal and spiritual powers – the Church conforming to temporal authority, but only with the quid pro quo of preserving its spiritual sovereignty – was to prove both convenient and disabling for British rule.

Only one political formation in Ireland was capable of matching the hegemonic resources of the Catholic Church. Unionism, as Peter Gibbon points out, provided a rival to nationalism unparalleled throughout Europe for its effectiveness, popular support and staying power.[178] And nowhere was its capacity to create social cohesion more obvious than in one of its unloveliest manifestations. The Orange Order, founded in Ulster in 1795 as a Protestant reaction to Defenderist militancy, represents one of the most intimate bondings between upper and lower classes in the history of British class relations. What more impressive form of hegemony than one embodied in a nationwide, clandestine, plebeian-based organization, government-protected and internationally supported, linking Dublin nobleman and Armagh weaver in a common pledge to defend king, constitution, Ascendancy and Established Church? Neither political party, military corps nor religious sodality, but rather a cross between a club, a gang and a theatrical troupe, Orangeism's strength lay precisely in overriding the distinctions between politics, religion and social life, all of which it welded into an integrated movement. What it did, in effect, was to convert these issues into *culture* – into a corporate life-form which overcame internal divisions by sharpening external conflicts. Indeed to this extent it could claim greater authority than the Catholic Church – for whereas the Church could never completely rely on securing the political loyalty of its flock,[179] the Orange Order won its members' political, spiritual, ethnic and cultural allegiances as a whole.

Born out of sectarian clashes on the Ulster border, the fruit of Protestant economic insecurity and the encroachments of Catholic power,[180] the Order represented the victory of the Protestant elite over Ulster radicalism for the hearts and minds of the Protestant lower classes; and

---

178. Peter Gibbon, *The Origins of Ulster Unionism* (Manchester 1975), p. 4.

179. The events of the revolutionary 1790s in particular revealed the fragility of the Church's political hold over its members. See Dáire Keogh, 'Archbishop Troy, the Catholic Church and Irish Radicalism, 1791–3', in Dickson et al., eds, *The United Irishmen*.

180. Gibbon (*The Origins of Ulster Unionism*) views the Orange reaffirmation of nepotistic bonds between landlord and tenant as a form of ideological compensation for an increasingly precarious, proletarianized class of Episcopalian weavers and a landlordism challenged by a vigorous Ulster bourgeoisie. The thesis has proved controversial.

having helped to deflect the Ulster masses from the revolutionary road, its authority was then sustained throughout most of the nineteenth century in an Ulster relatively free of agrarian conflict. This privileged relation between landed minority and Protestant tenantry found expression in the so-called Ulster custom,[181] by which tenants enjoyed an interest in the sale of their farms; and a remarkably heavy flow of emigration from the province helped to forestall potential unrest. Orangeism soon won open support from powerful sectors of the gentry, who filled its high offices, and having been armed by the state in 1798 to act as an auxillary to the military forces, its lodges – at once religious centres, military bases, benefit societies and social clubs – became a vital channel of communication between government and loyalist masses.[182] Few Catholic political movements could match Orangeism's cross-class character, represented as it was within Castle, courts, military, magistracy, clergy and tenantry; and few could rival its ability to span both rural and urban society. Though increasingly distrusted at Westminster for its thuggery and bigotry, the Order provided the British state and Dublin Castle with a muscular military and ideological arm.[183]

If it is hard to take a positive measure of hegemony, there are, at least, certain negative indices of its strength. A people in a state of semi-permanent disaffection can hardly be said to have internalized the law of its leaders; and from the 1760s onwards, with a few short-lived interludes, Irish society was rife with popular militancy. Indeed, every decade from the the mid eighteenth century to the 1840s was marked by at least one major outbreak of rural discontent.[184] The Whiteboys, Defenders, Threshers, Shanavests, Caravats, Rockites and Ribbonmen: these and other secret societies sought to operate a kind of primitive workers' control in the countryside, aiming to regulate land, wages, prices, rents, tithes and dues by violence and intimidation. 'Midnight legislators', as one commentator

---

181. Though the custom was not in fact uniform throughout the province, and its absence in other parts of the country may have been less potent a factor in tenant disaffection than has sometimes been assumed.

182. It is significant in this respect that members of a genteel 'grand' lodge had also to join a more humble 'private' one. See D.W. Miller, *Queen's Rebels: Ulster Loyalism in Historical Perspective* (London 1978), p. 56.

183. For a lucid account of the movement, see Hereward Senior, *Orangeism in Britain and Ireland 1795-1836* (London 1966).

184. See Samuel Clark and James S. Donnelly, eds, *Irish Peasants: Violence and Political Unrest 1780-1914* (Madison, Wis. 1983), p. 25.

of 1815 aptly described them, they constructed an alternative legal, political and military network of their own, sometimes of a rough-and-ready democratic kind, as a countervailing force to the official political system. With their carnivalesque iconography – baroque oaths, female clothing, exotic pseudonyms, mythical leaders and esoteric initiation ceremonies[185] – these primitive rebels merged downwards into an illegal underworld of tories, rapparees,[186] smugglers, poteen brewers and faction fighters, and shaded upwards into the daylight world of formal political activity.

The secret societies practised a kind of preservative violence. Their goal was less revolution than the restoration of a customary moral economy which the forces of capitalist modernization were gravely jeopardizing. Their strategy was to roll back this disruption of traditional social relations, as the landlords and graziers increasingly treated as a commodity the land which for their tenants was both a source of identity and a historic heritage. Faced with this modernizing onslaught, the underground militants set themselves up as a kind of moral police force, systematically enforcing an alternative style of law rather than lapsing into simple anarchy.[187] The tenure system acknowledged no legal check on the use of land beyond economic restraints; and the enclosure of land for pasturage, the clearing of tenants, the post-Napoleonic depression of prices and the increasing exploitation of labour, triggered an intensive class struggle in the countryside. A custom-bound tenantry collided headlong with the laws of agrarian capitalism, as the supply of labour overshot the demands of a rapidly commercializing agriculture. The source of that commercialization lay in the colonial connection – in early industrial Britain's growing requirements for agricultural produce.[188] Intensely vulnerable to market forces, yet deprived of the benefits of a vigorously entrepreneurial ruling class, the labouring and smallholding classes in the countryside maimed animals, threatened fellow tenants, shot farmers, burnt homesteads and dug up pastoral land in a desperate response to land shortage, climbing

185. Some of these more exotic aspects of the secret societies represent the lifting into the political arena of familiar aspects of Irish folklore, as Fool or Lord of Misrule figures become transferred from popular ritual to social agitation.

186. Tories and rapparees were bandits and highwaymen, sometimes dispossessed Gaelic gentry, around whom a considerable Irish mythology was spun.

187. George Cornewall Lewis, whose contemporary account of peasant agitation is remarkably discerning and relatively judicious, describes the Whiteboys as 'a vast trades' union for the protection of the Irish peasantry' (*On Local Disturbances in Ireland,* London 1836, p. 99). See also Michael Beames, *Peasants and Power* (Brighton 1983), for an absorbing account of the Whiteboy phenomenon.

188. See Kevin O'Neill, *Family and Farm in Pre-Famine Ireland* (Madison, Wis. 1984), pp. 34, 98.

rents and insecurity of tenure. Such 'premodern' violence, in marked
contrast to Britain, persisted long into the period of modernity, running
in tandem with more official politics as in the ferocious class struggles of
the late-nineteenth-century land wars.

How politically conscious these rural agitators were has been the subject
of some debate. The Defenders of the 1790s, allies of the United Irishmen, were certainly highly politicized, and in their blending of radical
Enlightenment doctrines and local socioeconomic grievances mark a
transition from 'rural discontent to mass disaffection'.[189] Defenderism was
a formidable political phenomenon, a far-flung, loose-jointed movement
of schoolmasters, urban craftsmen and artisans as well as of the exploited
rural classes; and its ideology was an intriguing *mélange* of nationalism,
Jacobinism, agrarian reformism, millenarianism, Francophilia and religious
sectarianism.[190] Tom Garvin detects some submerged continuities between
them and the later Ribbonmen, which then flow on to the Fenians.[191]
Travellers in the 1790s report instances of radical propaganda being eagerly
devoured in remote reaches of the Irish countryside. Much popular
insurgency was disorganized, parochial and viscerally anti-Protestant; but
it is only a peculiarly anaemic definition of politics which can fail to
discern some degree of political consciousness in labourers who raided
their landlords' houses for arms, or killed their bailiffs in broad daylight.

The intensity of this popular aggression should not be overestimated.
For most of the eighteenth century, Ireland was not a particularly violent
society, less so perhaps than Britain; and the period from 1760 to 1790
saw only about fifty deaths from agrarian causes.[192] No-one was killed by

---

189. Jim Smyth, *Men of No Property* (London 1992), p. 112. Marianne Elliott argues that
the Defenders hatched their revolutionary notions free of outside influence from, for example,
the United Irishmen. See her 'The Origins and Transformation of Early Irish Republicanism',
International Review of Social History, vol. 23 (1978).

190. For a valuable account, see Marianne Elliott, 'The Defenders in Ulster', in Dickson
et al., eds, *The United Irishmen*.

191. See Tom Garvin, 'Defenders, Ribbonmen and Others: Underground Political Networks in Pre-Famine Ireland', *Past and Present*, no. 96 (August 1982). Garvin is arguing
against a more economistic reading of the Ribbonmen, as exemplified by Joseph Lee's essay
on the movement in T.D.Williams, ed., *Secret Societies in Ireland* (Dublin 1973). For Ribbonism,
see M.R. Beames, 'The Ribbon Societies: Lower-Class Nationalism in Pre-Famine Ireland',
in C.H.E. Philpin, ed., *Nationalism and Popular Protest in Ireland* (Cambridge 1987). See also
in the same volume Beames's 'Rural Conflict in Pre-Famine Ireland: Peasant Assassinations
in Tipperary, 1837–1847'. James S. Donnelly writes on the Whiteboys in 'The Whiteboy
Movement, 1761–5', *Irish Historical Studies*, vol. 21, no. 81 (March 1978).

192. See Thomas Bartlett, 'An End to Moral Economy', *Past and Present*, no. 99 (May
1983). See also his 'Defenders and Defenderism', *Irish Historical Studies*, vol. 24, no. 95 (May
1985), which stresses the group's revolutionary tendencies.

the Whiteboys, and non-agriaran crime in Ireland was remarkably low.[193] A good deal of the violence – the spectacular belligerence of nineteenth-century Belfast, for example – was sectarian rather than class-based. W.E. Vaughan, in the typical tones of a certain species of Irish historian, seeks to dispel the familiar image of 'assassins lurking behind hedges' by pointing out that in mid-Victorian Ireland 'only 45% of those killed died of gunshot wounds, while 30% died of head injuries, 11% of less precisely described injuries, and 7% of stabs and cuts'.[194] It is relieving to learn that the Irish were so pacific. Vaughan adds for good measure that 'few landlords were fired at more than once', more testimony to the law-abiding nature of their underlings. It is surprising that he does not adduce for his mollifying case a threatening letter he actually quotes to a shopkeeper in Moate which concluded with impeccable courtesy 'Hoping to find you in good health as this leaves me at present',[195] which is surely grist to the mill of those historians wishing to play down Irish pugnacity. But the emphasis, for all that, is a necessary one. It was not a matter of some ceaseless bloodthirsty barbarism, though acts of agrarian violence could be atrocious enough, but a question of hegemony – of the failure of legality as such to secure the allegiance of broad sectors of the populace.

Coercion and consent are not in this sense mere opposites: the coercive institutions of army, police and judiciary must themselves win the general endorsement of the people if they are to function effectively. In Ireland it was legality itself, widely perceived as a colonial imposition, which failed to legitimize itself in the eyes of many of its subjects. Toryism or banditry had proved a major problem for Restoration Ireland, and there were tracts of the country effectively beyond the rule of law. A Gaelic scholar wrote in 1684 that the Iar Connacht district of Galway was so law-abiding that for thirty years no inhabitant had been executed or brought to the bar; but all this pious boast indicates, as Sean Connolly points out, is the absence of a rule of law in the region sufficiently well-defined for certain types of offender to step incontrovertibly outside it.[196] Where there are no laws to be broken, all men and women are converted at a stroke into respectable citizens. To secure respect for the law in Ireland meant the

---

193. See Charles Townsend, *Political Violence in Ireland* (Oxford 1983), p. 67.

194. Vaughan, *Landlords and Tenants in Mid-Victorian Ireland*, p. 144. It is fair to add that Vaughan's excellent book is by no means uncritical of the landlords.

195. Ibid., p. 154. A thesis remains to be written on why threatening letters in nineteenth-century Ireland peaked in March, then sloped off in April and May.

196. S.J. Connolly, *Religion, Law and Power* (Oxford 1992), p. 212. See also his 'Violence and Order in the Eighteenth Century', in P. Flanagan, P. Ferguson and K. Whelan, eds, *Rural Ireland 1600–1900* (Cork 1987).

strict application of edicts to which many ascribed precious little validity in the first place, thus alienating them even further; and to enforce law and order in the teeth of such disaffection the state had often enough to play rough, violate the law itself and so discredit itself even more deeply in the eyes of its citizens. If political violence thrived, it was partly because the Irish believed, not without excellent reason, that Britain would make no concessions to peaceable appeals.

The coercive apparatus in Ireland was repressive enough. For Standish O'Grady it could hardly be too much so: 'none on the earth's surface', this zealous patriot wrote of his people, 'is in such need of the whip and rein, having, indeed, much of the wild ass in its composition'.[197] In the early nineteenth century, the country housed some 25,000 regular troops and around 31,000 yeomanry, most of them Orangemen. To these forces were added Peel's paramilitary police force, an elite corps of shock troops ready for despatch throughout the country on the request of a magistrate. On the basis of population, Ireland had twice as many policemen as Britain. As friction gradually mounted between a corrupt, sectarian and incompetent magistracy suspicious of state power,[198] and the gathering need for central-ization, a fully centralized force was launched in 1836, a continental-style *gendarmerie* which was often feared more than the army, and which would provide the model for later colonial police forces. But the relations between this force and the army were to prove problematic. The country, so Galen Broeker argues, was 'too disturbed to respond effectively to civil govern-ment, not disturbed enough to justify full-scale military occupation'.[199] The army was present largely for purposes of intimidation; to unleash it risked estranging a smouldering populace even further, and Westminster imposed stringent restrictions on its domestic use. It is a familiar enough dilemma: where hegemony has failed to take root, coercion must take over; but to deploy coercion results in a massive loss of ideological credibility, and so can prove self-defeating. Britain was consequently reluctant to field its troops, but even more reluctant to withdraw them;[200] and there was a deep-grained mistrust between soldiers and police.

---

197. Standish O'Grady, *Toryism and Tory Democracy* (London 1886), p. 289.

198. Some magistrates, however, sought to discharge their duties with impeccable even-handedness. An early-nineteenth-century judge adjudicating between sectarian rioters in Derry found 605 'Protestant windows' and 615 'Catholic windows' to have been broken (see Galen Broeker, *Rural Disorder and Police Reform in Ireland, 1812–36*, London 1970, p. 5).

199. Ibid., p. 1.

200. See Elizabeth A. Muenger, *The British Military Dilemma in Ireland* (Lawrence, Kans. 1991).

The army in Ireland was doubled in strength in the fraught years between 1792 and 1822, and throughout the nineteenth century its numbers fluctuated from fifteen to thirty thousand men.[201] But it was caught hopelessly on the hop between military and civil functions, an arm of the state which was forced – at elections or evictions, for example – to intervene in civil society; and by crossing this frontier it exposed the frailty of civil society itself, which in any successful social order ought to regulate its citizens without recourse to the armed might of the state. Charles Townsend argues that government in Ireland depended on military force,[202] a case which appears to run counter to Sean Connolly's claim that the Irish people were not held down by force.[203] But with the exception of slave society, few peoples actually are; there are scant instances of societies literally and routinely under the gun. The point rather is that the withdrawal of the military, at key points in modern Irish history, would almost certainly have heralded a pervasive collapse of social order; and in this negative sense at least it can be claimed that the minatory presence of the army was necessary to sustain ordinary social life. Not that much of it was in fact ordinary: the country languished under special coercive legislation for more than thirty years after the Union, with an average of one such Act a year throughout the nineteenth century. What was uncommon in Ireland was juridical normality; and Gladstone himself remarked that British government in Ireland had no 'moral force' behind it.

But it was the varied currents of Irish nationalism, from Wolfe Tone to Eamon De Valera, which posed the most formidable challenge to colonial rule, and which were finally to succeed in toppling it. In the volatile political climate of the present, historians of Ireland have not been tardy in arraigning that nationalism's numerous vices. Sanguinary, sectarian, morbid, chauvinist, nostalgic, xenophobic, arrogantly vanguardist, idly idealist, relentlessly tunnel-visioned, suppressing social divisions in the name of some spurious national unity: such politics have hardly been much in favour with commentators with one politic eye on West Belfast. Nor are they much to the taste of a postmodernist theory which celebrates

---

201. See David N. Haire, 'In Aid of the Civil Power, 1868–90', in F.S.L. Lyons and R.A.J. Hawkins, eds, *Ireland under the Union: Varieties of Tension* (Oxford 1980), p. 116. See also Virginia Crossman, 'Emergency Legislation and Rural Disorder in Ireland, 1821–41', *Irish Historical Studies*, vol. 27, no. 108 (November 1991). A detailed account of the Irish police force is provided by Stanley H. Palmer, *Police and Protest in England and Ireland 1780-1850* (Cambridge 1988), Chs 6 and 7.

202. Townsend, *Political Violence*, p. 88.

203. S.J. Connolly, *Religion, Law and Power*, p. 217.

the marginal rather than the mainstream, and so is simply wrong-footed by the fact of a mass radical movement. Though there is truth in each of the standard criticisms of Irish nationalism, the overall portrait, as usual with such overreactive accounts, is in every sense partial. Formally speaking, Irish nationalism has been on the whole more remarkable for its ecumenism than its sectarian zeal. From Tone's 'common name of Irishman' to early Sinn Fein's Davisite notion of a comprehensive nation, most nationalist trends, including the Irish Republican Brotherhood, were at pains to rally to their banners the non-Catholic and non-Gael, however notionally or perfunctorily. 'What Nationalist', enquired William O'Brien, 'ever proposed to open Thomas Davis's veins to discover whether the orthodox quantities of Gaelic blood flowed to his heart?'[204] The answer is, a fair few of them; but O'Brien is right to suggest that such chauvinism was untypical, certainly at the level of declared policy. Patrick Pearse saw fit to rebuke the Ancient Order of Hibernians for excluding Protestants from their ranks. This apostle of pluralism, a bogeyman of contemporary anti-nationalist critics, abhorred the racist mentality of Irish Ireland and proclaimed that it was one's duty if possible to refrain from bloodshed.[205]

It is true that nationalist practice and piety were often at odds with its official tolerance; there is a revealing tension between Thomas Davis's non-sectarian politics and his ardour for Gaelic culture, just as there is between the United Irishmen's popular front politics and their inherited distrust of the Catholic masses. But sectarianism rarely penetrated nationalist movements at the level of their formal policy; the United Irishmen, for example, strove to subordinate religious conflict to political confrontation. Indeed if nationalism is to be censured on this score at all, it is for a strain of false inclusiveness rather than sectarian purism – the fondly idealist belief that, say, the Anglo-Irish landlords could be roped en masse into its project, or that one could flirt with the Chartists one day and seduce the propertied classes the next. Instead, the course of Irish history was to demonstrate the bleak truth that social interests are likely to triumph over fine ideas, and that, as in most revolutionary situations, only a renegade minority of the governing bloc can be prised loose from them. Nor was Irish nationalism especially bloodthirsty: the appalling massacre which followed on the United Irish uprising, much of it the fruit of colonial brutality, was never to be remotely equalled in its subsequent career. Daniel O'Connell was a pacifist on the national

---

204. William O'Brien, *Irish Ideas* (London 1893), p. 125.
205. See Joseph Lee, *The Modernisation of Irish Society 1848-1918* (Dublin 1973), pp. 145–6.

question, and the Young Irelanders who opposed him were more notable for their rhetorical rather than military muscle.[206] The Irish Republican Brotherhood resolved to defer its insurgency until the democratic will of the people underwrote it, a fact which some modern historians have scorned for its semi-mystical populism rather than, more rationally, approved for its democratic bent. The leaders of mainstream nationalism – O'Connell, Parnell, Griffith – were tamely constitutionalist; and when the IRB finally struck in 1916, the action was far from being a bloodbath.

It is equally curious to upbraid Irish nationalism for its tunnel vision. For though this was certainly sometimes in evidence, what is striking about Irish nationalism is its air of never quite being sure what it intended. Who, for example, including maybe Daniel O'Connell himself, ever grasped exactly what was meant by the Repeal of the Union? How socially radical did the United Irishmen take their project to be? Was republicanism compatible with monarchism, or its very negation? The Young Irelanders advocated, at various times and in different voices, a benevolent landlordism, peasant proprietorship, and the social ownership of the land. An early issue of the *Nation*, much to O'Connell's dismay, declared Ribbonism justified in the eyes of God, whereas later issues obediently wooed the landlords. Thomas Davis, as we have seen, held at once to a pluralist society and a robustly Gaelic identity. The leaders of 1916 possessed only the scantiest social programme. Treading a precarious line between Unionism and separatism, Irish nationalist leaders could excoriate Britain out of one side of their mouths while pleading for a union of hearts out of the other, veering from quasi-separatist sentiments to fervid declarations of loyalty to the crown. Virulent Anglophobia could sit cheek by jowl with unctuous affirmations of Empire. Much of this ambiguity was of course strategically calculated, a matter of which side of which stretch of water (St George's Channel, the Atlantic) one was beaming one's remarks towards. Some of Parnell's most celebrated political utterances are linguistic Rorschach blots, into which the hearer could read whatever he or she wished. Ambiguity, here, is in part the result of addressing several incompatible audiences simultaneously. But the equivocations of nationalist rhetoric point beyond this strategic double-edgedness to what seems often enough a genuine lack of political clarity, as the

---

206. The classic work on O'Connell is Oliver MacDonagh, *O'Connell* (London 1991). See also Fergus O'Ferrall, *Catholic Emancipation: Daniel O'Connell and the Birth of Irish Democracy* (Dublin 1985), and Kevin B. Nowlan, *The Politics of Repeal* (London 1965). See also Charles Gavan Duffy, *Young Ireland* (London 1880). For a bitter retrospect on this period, see John Michel, *Jail Journal* (London 1876).

Irish demand is infiltrated by doubt about what Britain might concede or how far one might safely go. The demand, so to speak, is muffled and deflected by the complexities of the political situation, so that the line between not saying what one wants, and not quite knowing it, becomes relatively easy to cross.

The charge that Irish nationalism was arrogantly vanguardist is in general impossible to sustain. If the Fenians were an avant-garde without much of an army, the United Irishmen were a vanguard with a sizeable one;[207] and most other currents of nationalism concentrated their energies upon building a mass movement. Nostalgia is an equally imprecise accusation: if it is true of Davis, the Gaelic Leaguers and some other sectors of the Revival, it hardly applies to the briskly modernist Tone, O'Connell, Parnell, Griffith or D.P. Moran. Even the IRB was in many respects a modernizing movement, the first largely secular nationalist trend in Irish history. Nationalism could certainly be unpleasantly xenophobic, but some of its detestation of Britain was thoroughly justified. A generalized Irish contempt for the British is not to be endorsed; but it was, in its context, as historically understandable as the generalized distrust of whites evinced by some blacks, or of men by some women. D.P. Moran was chauvinist but not backward-looking, whereas W.B. Yeats was backward-looking but not chauvinist. If there was a festering nationalist introversion, there were also vital cosmopolitan influences and international links. Thomas Davis urged solidarity with other colonized peoples, and even the Irish Irelander Arthur Griffith – an ethnic pluralist for all his neo-conservatism – imported an incongruous European model for Irish independence.[208] Daniel O'Connell spoke up for other oppressed nations, and many Home Rulers looked to an international anti-imperialist alliance. After the waning of the United Irishmen, Irish nationalism remained largely unscathed by European political theory, scared off perhaps by continental anti-clericalism; there was no Irish nationalist response, for instance, to the Paris Commune. But this theoretical provincialism was not always reflected in political practice. As for idealism and morbidity, some IRBers inhabited a world of idle fantasy, but some of their idle fantasies were to be historically realized. Patrick Pearse was unpleasantly morbid in his notorious cult of blood sacrifice, but a surprising number of republicans harboured a curious aversion to being killed.

---

207. See Nancy Curtin, 'The Transformation of the Society of United Irishmen into a Mass-based Organisation', *Irish Historical Studies*, vol. 14, no. 96 (1985).

208. See Arthur Griffith, *The Resurrection of Hungary* (Dublin 1904).

Nor is it entirely true that nationalism suppressed other forms of social conflict in its myopic pursuit of national unity. From Tone's men of no property to Fintan Lalor's pleas for social ownership, from John Mitchel's fulminations against the rich to the IRB's constant harping upon class division, there is a plebeian or petty-bourgeois class bias to many nationalist currents, and a conflict within nationalism as a whole – Fintan Lalor versus Gavan Duffy, Michael Davitt against Parnell, James Connolly contra Arthur Griffith – between its left and right wings. The ethnic question did not succeed in quelling the social issue, even if no satisfying relation of the two was in general achieved. Some expressions of nationalism were repellently purist, racist and repressive, while others were pluralist, class-conscious and enlightened. Much late-nineteenth-century nationalism was a brand of petty-bourgeois *ressentiment*, corporatist, illiberal, anti-Semitic and proto-fascist, lamenting the loss of a traditionalist spirituality and leadership. Other forms of nationalism embraced the cause of the dispossessed, and fought courageously against their exploiters. It is a sign of contemporary political prejudice that a properly dialectical assessment of the movement has yet to be fully achieved.

One major problem confronting Irish nationalism was the relation between its political and socio-economic demands. Modern Irish history is divided between a brand of nationalism which, as with the United Irishmen, the IRB and the Home Rulers, subordinated the social to the political, and a social and economic insurgency which rarely attained a national political presence. The social content of the Irish revolution and its political form proved notably hard to synchronize. The two had fused after a fashion in Grattan's parliament, which achieved diluted versions of both political independence and freedom of trade. The coalition between United Irishmen and Defenders in the 1790s produced a revolutionary amalgam of both kinds of demand; but the United Irishmen were for the most part political revolutionaries only, nervous of the social and economic radicalism of their Defender comrades,[209] and the revolt was in any case savagely crushed by the state. In the wake of that catastrophe, with O'Connell's twin campaigns for Emancipation and Repeal, the political came increasingly to dominate the social and economic. With admirable political acuteness, O'Connell harnessed popular discontent to parliamentary ends, from which the rural masses could reap

209. See Marianne Elliott, 'The Origins and Transformation of Early Irish Republicanism', *International Review of Social History*, vol. 23 (1978).

only a meagre reward. The mightiest outbreak of popular agitation in early-nineteenth-century Europe[210] was steered into the familiar grooves of constitutional politics, challenged only by the political adventurism of Young Ireland. A potentially revolutionary situation – land hunger, widespread immiseration, ruling-class crisis – was then defused by the Famine, which decimated the cottiers, small farmers and landless labourers and so diminished both the pressure on land and the primary sources of social agitation. The land seizures, clearances and consolidations which accompanied the Famine then laid the basis, in the form of economic-sized holdings, for an increasingly prosperous,[211] temporarily tranquillized rural middle class, which pursued a reformist programme of tenant rights. It is a notable irony that just as a stalwart Irish bourgeoisie was digging itself in in Ireland, its counterpart across the water was about to be shaken to its roots by the socialist movement. The national question lived on in the exhausted aftermath of the Famine, but now in growing isolation from any militant social base – both in the form of an over-politicized revolutionism for which the land question was for the most part a dangerous distraction (the ultra-left of the Irish Republican Brotherhood), and an Independent Irish Party at Westminster which devoted its energies to constitutional ends. In the land wars of 1879–82, mass rural agitation broke out once more on a scale more formidable than Ireland had ever witnessed;[212] and with the so-called New Departure the three strains of agrarian protest, political revolutionism and consti-tutional nationalism powerfully intersected.[213] Political nationalism was once again furnished with a mass social base. But a conservative middle class of strong farmers now dominated the agrarian struggle, which yielded little for the lower social orders; and Parnell was finally to replace the Land League with a constitutional association, to the chagrin of his

---

210. Macaulay called O'Connell the most popular political leader in the history of the world; Owen Dudley Edwards, in rather less hyperbolic spirit, describes him as the only Irishman since Patrick Sarsfield to become a hero in his own lifetime (Owen Dudley Edwards, ed., *Celtic Nationalism*, London 1968, pp. 99-100).

211. Though the prosperity has possibly been exaggerated; see K. Theodore Hoppen, *Ireland since 1800: Conflict and Conformity* (London 1989), Ch. 4.

212. For accounts of the land wars, see Michael Davitt, *The Fall of Feudalism* (London 1904); Paul Bew, *Land and the National Question in Ireland 1858–82* (Dublin 1978); and Samuel Clark, *Social Origins of the Irish Land War* (Princeton 1979).

213. Meeting the IRB er John Devoy in 1879, Parnell told him that he had no objection in principle to fighting Britain as long as there was some chance of success. To his surprise, he found Devoy in entire agreement (see T.W. Moody, *Davitt and the Irish Revolution*, Oxford 1981, p. 286).

left wing.[214] The land question had allowed Parnell to seize the leadership of the nationalist struggle at a vital historical moment. Like O'Connell before him, he had skilfully exploited popular misery for bourgeois–nationalist ends, while the plight of the labourer and poor farmer remained largely untouched. He would be the last Anglo-Irish leader to ride the tiger of Catholic nationalism, and the growing power of the beast was reflected in the fact that it carried him further than he wanted to travel. Middle-class nationalist leaders needed to mobilize the peasantry, but not to the point where their own privileges were thereby jeopardized, and the balancing act was becoming steadily harder to pull off. Peasant proprietorship was finally won; but this proved of scant benefit to those smallholders whose land, even with the abolition of rent, would scarcely support them, and Parnell and his propertied cohorts discreetly closed their ears to demands to expropriate the graziers. Michael Davitt's bold proposal for the nationalization of the land was denounced by nationalists of every stripe. The Land League had undergone a double displacement: from the small farmers and landless labourers to the affluent farmers and graziers, and thence to bourgeois nationalism. The social and political were once more skewed: demands were now framed not at the level of popular struggle but at the level of the state, a policy which Sinn Fein was to perpetuate.

The Land League, then, was a class struggle which was itself shot through with class conflict. Disgusted by its leadership's betrayal of the small farmers, the Fenians of Mayo finally repudiated it. But the movement also dramatized a traditional conflict between the political and the economic, of a peculiarly chicken-and-egg variety.[215] Which comes first, land reform or national independence? For the IRB, the political question was foremost: only a republic could abolish landlordism, and in any case an immediate resolution of the land question might inconveniently take the steam out of the thrust for national autonomy. Though Parnell rigorously subordinated the agrarian to the national question in the wake of the Land League, he believed that peasant proprietorship would itself lead to political independence, since it would remove the reasons which prevented the landlords from accepting Home Rule, and from thereby

---

214. His sister above all: see Anna Parnell, *The Tale of a Great Sham* (Dublin 1986). For a lively account of Anna Parnell, see R.F. Foster, *Charles Stewart Parnell: The Man and his Family* (Hassocks 1976), Part 5, Ch. 4. On Parnell himself, see Conor Cruise O'Brien, *Parnell and his Party* (Oxford 1957); and F.S.L. Lyons, *Charles Stewart Parnell* (London 1977).

215. For a discussion of the question, see James S. Donnelly, Jr, 'The Land Question in Nationalist Politics', in T.E. Hachey and L.J. McCaffrey, eds, *Perspectives on Irish Nationalism* (Dublin 1989).

becoming the future leaders of the nation. If the landlords ceased to have an economic interest in the British connection, then they could – in another fantasy of false inclusiveness – be recruited *en bloc* to the Home Rule cause.[216] For others, the two questions were inseparable: an assault on the landowners was itself a strike at the British state. Some Fenian Land Leaguers encouraged the demand for tenant ownership on the grounds that Britain would never grant it, a refusal which would then lend credence to the nationalist case. Others held that, even if such owner-ship were conceded, it would be on unfavourable terms; better, then, to defer the question until an Irish rather than British state could settle it. Michael Davitt saw the chance of 'interpellating' the militant rural classes into the nationalist cause, thus winning nationalist hegemony over them and providing political forms with social content.

In the event, Parnell was proved partly right: as in the classical course of bourgeois revolutions, the middle class first amassed economic power, then struck for political supremacy. But this process in Ireland was peculiarly uneven. What followed upon the land wars was the series of Land Acts by which the British government handed down the social revolution from above, dispossessing its own client ruling class and trans-ferring its property to the tenantry. This was indeed, in the strict Marxist sense of the term, a revolution, replacing one possessing class with another; in fact it was the first time a state had forcibly dispossessed a landed class and redistributed its estates. The Bolshevik experiment was to follow a decade or so later. But though this mighty upheaval was in part the consequence of popular agitation, it was not brought about by the direct action of the rural masses. Instead, revolutionary agency was passed upwards to the colonialist state, which carried through the final trans-formation of property relations on behalf of the increasingly dominant class in Ireland. One of the most conservative peoples in Europe was handed a revolution by its rulers, who had little enough to lose from this big-hearted gesture.[217] Indeed it was in the interests of Britain to pre-empt a future land settlement by a hostile independent Irish government. The social revolution took place in a peculiarly conservative political form, just as, somewhat later, the political revolution would conceal a markedly

---

216. For an account of the relative priorities of land reform and political nationalism, see Bew, *Land and the National Question*, Ch. 3.

217. Oliver MacDonagh considers that British opposition to Irish independence 'had little material or even rational foundation' (*Ireland: The Union and its Aftermath*, Englewood Cliffs, N.J. 1968, p. 20). For some acute comments on these matters, see Ellen Hazelkorn and Henry Patterson, 'The New Politics of the Irish Republic', *New Left Review* 207 (September–October 1994), pp. 50–51.

conservative social content. Once the transference of landed property had been achieved, the fissure between political and socio-economic reasserted itself. Land reform deprived the Irish parliamentary party, already plunged into post-Parnell disarray, of much of its *raison d'être*, and so helped to foster political separatism.[218] The most intensive period of nationalist agitation took place after the land settlement, so that the social and political, which had fused with admirable effectiveness in William O'Brien's United Irish League, were once more out of synchrony. It was not the rising rural class as such which was to strike for political power in 1916, but a tiny urban-based vanguard of the very current – the IRB – which in classic ultra-leftist style had stood at the greatest distance from the agrarian struggle.[219] After 1916, it was the constitutional tactics of Sinn Fein and the guerrilla warfare of the IRA, rather than mass political insurgency, which would finally win a measure of national independence. Mass political confrontation with the state had been short-circuited on one side by the appeasement of the state itself, and on the other by constitutional politics and military vanguardism.[220] Nevertheless, what an underdeveloped urban bourgeoisie had struck for prematurely in 1798, at the height of British imperial power, could now be won by a much-strengthened middle class at a point when that imperial power was pitched into global crisis. The political revolution, when it arrived, brought with it no major social transformation; instead, it set the seal on an established social order of a profoundly conservative kind. By the early 1920s, revolutionary nationalism was not only remote from social radicalism but actively repressing it, as the Sinn Feiners forcibly put down agrarian agitation.[221] It was the culmination of an age-old Irish amalgam of political militancy and social reaction.

The situation which led to the Easter Rising was replete with ironies. Between 1879 and 1912, Britain had sought to stabilize Ireland and secure

218. See Philip Bull, 'Land and Politics 1879–1903', in D.G. Boyce, ed., *The Revolution in Ireland 1879-1923* (London 1988).

219. For the Irish Republican Brotherhood, see R.V. Comerford, *The Fenians in Context* (Dublin 1985), a classic of revisionism; Léon Ó Broin, *Revolutionary Underground: The Story of the Irish Republican Brotherhood, 1858–1924* (London 1976); and T.W. Moody, ed., *The Fenian Movement* (Dublin 1968). For portraits of individual Fenian leaders, see Desmond Ryan, *The Fenian Chief: The Life of James Stephens* (Dublin 1967); Marcus Bourke, *John O'Leary* (Tralee 1967); and R.V. Comerford, *Charles J. Kickham* (Dublin 1979).

220. For constitutional nationalism, see David Thornley, *Isaac Butt and Home Rule* (London 1964).

221. See Adrian Pimley, 'The Working-class Movement and the Irish Revolution, 1896–1923'; and Paul Bew, 'Sinn Fein, Agrarian Radicalism and the War of Independence 1919–1921', in Boyce, ed., *The Revolution in Ireland, 1879-1923*.

the allegiance of its people by legislative reform, hoping to kill Home Rule with kindness.[222] But this attempt at consensual as well as coercive rule was to prove curiously self-thwarting: what it did was to reinforce the very classes in Ireland who regarded Britain as their bitter antagonist. And since the reforms brought with them increased anglicization, they helped to breed a quickened sense of threatened national identity. Some Irish nationalists saw Tory reformism as an attempt to rob them of self-sufficiency and so insidiously destroy their moral fibre. Moreover, the metropolitan nation could buy off colonial rebellion only by undermining the landlords, thus removing a vital reason for the British connection in the first place. Since the path to stability led through property, the state duly enshrined the property rights of the tenantry, thus bolstering their self-assurance and fostering political militancy. Moreover, by removing the economic issue from nationalism, it handed over the movement to those cultural and political forces which were least easily reconciled to the British connection. There is something darkly comic about this self-defeating scenario, by which Britain helped to scupper the rickety Irish vessel in its very efforts to salvage it.

If nationalism finally succeeded in wresting power in Ireland, it was because it had already long since won the battle for hegemony. The nationalist phrase for the term was 'moral force'; and it was in this arena above all, rather than in the sphere of political negotiation or military strategy, that the British were to prove no match for it. If, as Antonio Gramsci maintains, a 'war of manoeuvre' – a military challenge to state power – must be prepared for by a 'war of position' – a struggle for dominance within civil society itself – then the Irish revolution certainly conformed to this classical model. By the time the decisive blow was struck, nationalism had been at work for over a century transforming the political culture of the people, intervening in property relations, educational reform and religious controversy, constructing its own alternative networks of law courts, literature and political organization. At times, as in the Land League or the United Irish League of 1898,[223] this amounted to a kind of moral version of dual power, a strategy which was later to be realized in political practice by Sinn Fein. From the propagandist presses of the United Irishmen to the reading rooms of the Repeal Association,

---

222. For such Constructive Unionism, see Andrew Gailey, *Ireland and the Death of Kindness* (Cork 1987). See also Paul Bew, *Conflict and Conciliation in Ireland, 1890–1910* (Oxford 1987).

223. For an excellent account of the United Irish League, see Sally Warwick-Haller, *William O'Brien and the Irish Land War* (Dublin 1990), Ch. 5.

Irish nationalism had built up a whole alternative public sphere of political discourse, developed a sophisticated internal democracy,[224] and implanted, with the O'Connellite campaigns, some of the mightiest mass movements of nineteenth-century Europe.[225] From then on, the tension between the relatively advanced political consciousness of the masses and their backward social conditions proved a powerful dynamo of disaffection. The heritage that is now sometimes patronizingly recalled for a handful of farcical military skirmishes in fact constructed a counter-hegemony of remarkable scope and complexity.

The idea of hegemony in the writings of Antonio Gramsci turns on the notions of consensus, alliance, civil society, while coercion is the form of power monopolized by the political state. But the distinction in the *Prison Notebooks* is occasionally blurred, as hegemony comes to suggest a unity of both consent and coercion. Since the era of Elizabeth, British authority in Ireland lurched from one of these policies to another, suppressing the native population with one hand while seeking to cajole them with the other. Plantation, which aims to civilize the natives even as it forcibly supplants them, is one instance of this double strategy. The year 1881 witnessed both an Act to suspend habeas corpus and a Land Reform Bill. In 1902, George Wyndham introduced a conciliatory Land Act and a few months later proclaimed half the country and imprisoned forty nationalist leaders.[226] As the nineteenth century drew to a close, the state itself took on an increasingly hegemonic role: Land Acts, a revolutionary reform of local government, a department of agricultural and technical instruction, a Congested Districts Board, plans for a Catholic university which would wean the Catholic middle class from its nationalist sympathies.

But it was all far too late. And it was also too late for the reforming Protestant tradition from Isaac Butt and Samuel Ferguson to Standish O'Grady and Horace Plunkett, which continued to clamour for a hegemonic role for ᴜᴎe Ascendancy even as its material base was crumbling beneath its feet. For Butt, Home Rule would pacify rebellion, buy off popular disaffection and thus strengthen ruling-class authority and the

---

224. See Fergus O'Ferrall, *Catholic Emancipation: Daniel O'Connell and the Birth of Irish Democracy* (Dublin 1985), p. 220.

225. O'Connell, who transformed the political consciousness of the common people, was in Oliver MacDonagh's words 'the first cartographer of an unexplored continent, that of the masses in constitutional politics' (Vaughan, ed., *A New History of Ireland, vol. V*, p. 167).

226. See Gailey, *Ireland and the Death of Kindness*, p. 181. See also L.P. Curtis Jr, *Coercion and Conciliation in Ireland 1880–1892* (London 1963).

rule of Empire. Samuel Ferguson, apostle of cultural pluralism and vehement Unionist, set about the task of translating ancient Irish culture into the political needs of the contemporary Protestant junta. Gaelic ballads were reworked so as to turn their heroes into prototypes of aristocratic leadership in a modern age of mass Catholic democracy. Ferguson's version of 'The Fair Hills of Ireland', with commendable impudence, converts the poem from a Jacobite lament for the exile of the Gaelic lords into a celebration of the entry into Ireland of her new captains.[227] Culture is the supremely disinterested ground upon which all the Irish may harmoniously converge – which, roughly translated, means 'the colonisation of Gaelic literature in the interests of the Anglo-Irish Ascendancy'.[228] By rendering the Gaelic text in an English language at once civil and faithful, the political union of Britain and Ireland is re-enacted at the level of poetic discourse. Translation, in short, becomes an act of hegemony: just as the medium of English must re-create Irish experience on its own terms while remaining alert to its distinctive spirit, so British power works best by taking on the body of the culture it is out to reconstruct. The structure of hegemony is in this sense the structure of metaphor. Ferguson's poetics combine a belief in fidelity to the original with a distinctly condescending stance: the great Gaelic bard Turlough Carolan, he remarks in his *Lays of the Western Gael*, 'although incapable of distinguishing between elegant and vulgar forms of praise ... has in these instances expressed genuine sentiments of admiration with a great degree of natural and affectionate tenderness'.[229] The task of the Anglo-Irish cultural ideologue is to supply the present with a suitably edifying pedigree, national rather than nationalist, which will act as an emollient of political injustice. It is the Gaelic bard recycled as Victorian sage, and the incongruities of the enterprise are plain. Ferguson, high-minded avatar of national unity and patron of the Literary Revival, is also the embattled spokesman for Protestant privilege and imperial rule whose prose resounds with a dread and detestation of Catholic power. If he trusts to the

---

227. See Tom Dunne, 'Haunted by History: Irish Romantic Writing 1800–50', in R. Porter and M. Teich, eds, *Romanticism in National Context* (Cambridge 1988), p. 83.

228. Ibid., p. 84. Ferguson's celebrated review articles on James Hardiman can be found in the *Dublin University Magazine* of April, August, October and November, 1834. For further accounts of Ferguson, see Peter Denman, *Samuel Ferguson: The Literary Achievement* (Gerrards Cross 1990), and M.A.G. Ó Tuathaigh, 'Sir Samuel Ferguson – Poet and Ideologue', in Terence Brown and Barbara Hayley, eds, *Samuel Ferguson: A Centenary Tribute* (Dublin 1987). Yeats's pieces on Ferguson are still worth reading (in John P. Frayne, ed., *Uncollected Prose of W.B. Yeats*, London 1970).

229. Samuel Ferguson, *Lays of the Western Gael* (London 1865), p. 170.

peaceable gathering of all the Irish on the common ground of poetry and mythology, he also believes that the ideal (if sadly impracticable) solution to Irish Catholicism would be to wean its deluded devotees from it altogether. Rarely was a nobly neutral culture more blatantly in the service of a sectarian politics.

The poignant career of Sir Horace Plunkett, champion of agricultural cooperation, captures in microcosm the hopelessly well-intentioned impulse of Constructive Unionism. In typical Etonian spirit, Plunkett believed that the root of the Irish problem lay in a deficiency of character, which the self-reliance induced by cooperatives might cure.[230] Politics was accordingly displaced by economics, and in 1894 Plunkett established the Irish Agricultural Cooperation Society, a pioneering experiment in co-operative creameries which earned its founder the enmity of both clerics and nationalists. In Plunkett's eyes, the clerics were partly responsible for the weakening of the national fibre, while the nationalists were too boisterously political. The Society chalked up some notable achievements; but conflict soon erupted between it and Plunkett's other brainchild, the Department of Agricultural and Technical Instruction, and he resigned from the project in 1907, having been elected as a Unionist MP some years previously. After issuing a predictably fruitless appeal to the landed gentry to play their part in the new Ireland, he fought bravely to prevent the exclusion of Ulster from Home Rule, sought amnesty for the political prisoners of 1916, and chaired a failed Irish Convention a year or so later. In 1919 he launched the doomed Irish Dominion Party, and saw his cooperative creameries destroyed by British troops in the war of independence. Appointed a Free State Senator in 1922, he lingered in Ireland long enough to see his house burnt down, retired to England and died there in 1932.[231] Aloof in personality and loftily remote from the people he championed, Plunkett's admirably selfless projects were based on an unpleasantly paternalist analysis of the nation's ills.

---

230. Plunkett's belief in the importance of Irish character was shared by Friedrich Engels: 'The Irishman is a carefree, cheerful, potato-eating child of nature ... that poverty manifests itself in Ireland ... is owing to the character of the people, and to their historical development' (Marx and Engels: *Ireland and the Irish Question*, Moscow 1986, pp. 35–6, 43). Plunkett's publication of his views won him considerable odium and did his cooperative project a good deal of harm. See Cyril Erlich, 'Sir Horace Plunkett and Agricultural Reform', in J.M. Goldstrom and L.A. Clarkson, eds, *Irish Population, Economy, and Society* (Oxford 1981), p. 278.

231. See J.J. Byrne, 'AE and Sir Horace Plunkett', in C.C. O'Brien, ed., *The Shaping of Modern Ireland* (London 1960). See also Horace Plunkett, *Ireland in the New Century* (London 1904); and *Cooperation in Ireland* (Manchester, 1891). A full and enthusiastic biography is to be found in Trevor West, *Horace Plunkett: Cooperation and Politics* (Gerrards Cross 1986).

Plunkett's appeal to the landlords of Ireland was one of a whole series of such petitions addressed throughout the nineteenth century to the country's gentry. Indeed the Irish landlords were the subject of more appeals than a Lords umpire. In the very depths of the Famine, on the eve of political insurrection, Young Irelanders like Thomas Meagher and Fintan Lalor were still pathetically supplicating a governing class whose members were at that very moment either on the verge of bankruptcy, evicting famished tenants or seeking to repair the catastrophe by private charity.[232] The sweet reasonableness of much Irish nationalism continued unabated. The record of William O'Brien is a case in point: to the left of Parnell during the land war, pugnacious editor of *United Ireland*, fiery champion of the Connaught poor, regular inmate of Her Majesty's prisons, author of the audacious Plan of Campaign of the 1880s, organizer of the United Irish League with its class-conscious assaults on the graziers and strong farmers: he too wooed the landlords for their benign cooperation, and chaired a historic convention which brought both sides of the class struggle together.

But the most equivocal appeals of all stemmed from Standish O'Grady, father of the Celtic Revival and militant Unionist. Indeed O'Grady's dishevelled texts represent one of the last despairing pleas for the Irish landowners to become a truly hegemonic class, encircled as they now are by Home Rule, land agitation, Henry George, Westminster Radicalism and British proletarian socialism.[233] The contradiction of O'Grady's inflamed rhetoric is that, in order to goad the landlords into consciousness of their plight, he must impugn them with a virulence so unrelenting that it threatens to strike hollow his pleas for their spiritual revival. On the one hand, he announces his belief that 'there never will be ... an aristocracy so rotten in its seeming strength, so recreant, resourceless, and stupid in the day of trial, so degenerate, outworn and effete'.[234] The Irish

---

232. See Thomas Francis Meagher's 'Union with England', in Arthur Griffith, ed., *Meagher of the Sword* (Dublin 1916); and J.F. Lalor's 'A New Nation: To the Landlords of Ireland', in *J.F. Lalor: Collected Writings* (Dublin and London 1918).

233. Ironically enough, O'Grady would end up as a supporter of Henry George, along with communal ideas of land ownership imbibed from Tolstoy and Kropotkin. For this later O'Grady, a champion of Guild socialism, see Daniel J. Sullivan, C.M., 'Standish James O'Grady's *All Ireland Review*', *Studia Hibernica*, no. 9 (1969). Sullivan points out how O'Grady used his *Review* as a kind of personal correspondence, thanking a reader for the gift of a duck and accepting an invitation to visit from another.

234. O'Grady, *Toryism and Tory Democracy*, p. 213. For some apt comments on both O'Grady and Ferguson, see David Cairns and Shaun Richards, *Writing Ireland* (Manchester 1988), one of the very few attempts to apply the Gramscian concept of hegemony to Irish history.

patriciate are 'few, friendless, hated and imbecile',[235] and O'Grady, contemptuously dismissing them as a class, will direct his exhortations in
Arnoldian style only to select individuals among them. The landlords, he
proclaims elsewhere, have surrendered their power, 'in conjunction with
the like doomed class in England ... to a hungry, greedy, anarchic
canaille'.[236] They are 'rotting from the land in the most dismal farce-tragedy
of all time, without one brave deed, without one brave word'.[237] But no
sooner has he written them off with one hand than he is busy refurbishing
them with the other, launching Carlylean fantasies of a regenerated landowning oligarchy which will organize its tenants into quasi-feudal bands
of loyal retainers.

A project which was already preposterous in Lady Morgan's day is
now farcically revived: as late as 1886, the Anglo-Irish Ascendancy are to
be reborn as the old Gaelic nobility, dining with their tenants at a
communal board, supervising their dress, cleanliness and moral conduct
and so winning their doughty devotion. The landowners are spineless,
boneheaded, criminally irresponsible; but O'Grady writes in 1882 that
they are also the 'noblest and best [class] on Irish soil ... the highest
moral element',[238] which says something about their subordinates. In 1886,
they are to be given up for lost; a decade later, on the very verge of
extinction, they have become 'the rightful natural leaders, defenders and
champions of this People who cannot furnish forth such from their own
ranks'.[239] (One wonders whether O'Grady had simply not heard of
O'Connell, Lalor, Duffy, Kickham, Doheny, O'Leary, Devoy or Davitt.)
O'Grady's antiquarian researches into the old Irish chieftains confirm the
naturally aristocratic bent of Irish society and the innately lord-loving
character of its people;[240] as with Samuel Ferguson, ancient culture is
summoned to the standard of Protestant Ascendancy to compensate for
its political failure. But these mythological pearls are not to be cast before
uncultured swine, and O'Grady denounced the Literary Revival for doing
just that.

---

235. O'Grady, Toryism and Tory Democracy, p. 226.

236. Standish O'Grady, 'Irish Conservatism and its Outlooks', in Selected Essays and Passages
(Dublin 1918), p. 166.

237. Ibid., p. 180.

238. Standish O'Grady, The Crisis in Ireland (Dublin 1882), p. 50.

239. Fortnighty Review, no. 67 (February 1897).

240. See Standish O'Grady, History of Ireland; The Heroic Period (London 1878). For a
useful account of O'Grady, see Thomas Flanagan, 'Literature in English, 1801-91', in Vaughan,
ed., A New History of Ireland: vol. V.

History, writes William Yeats in *Explorations*, has seen the Anglo-Irish class 'lose their public spirit and their high heart and grow querelous and selfish as men do who have played life out not heartily but with noise and tumult. Had they understood the people and the game a little better, they might have created an aristocracy in an age that has lost the meaning of the word.'[241] Yeats himself, despite the elegaic note, will swell the ranks of those who sought to convert the Anglo-Irish into a genuinely hegemonic class. Indeed he will be the last great inheritor of that lineage. Viewed subjectively, that tradition was full of sublime good will, generous intentions, dedicated self-sacrifice. Viewed objectively, it represented one of the most devious pieces of political opportunism in modern Irish history. But it was an opportunism to no avail. The Ascendancy stopped their ears to the earnest invocations of Ferguson, O'Grady and Yeats. Instead, they pulled up stumps and headed for the Home Counties.

---

241. Yeats, *Explorations*, pp. 27–8.

CHAPTER 3

HOMAGE TO
FRANCIS HUTCHESON

Whatever answer we can think up to the question 'why is this action virtuous?' seems only to push the question back a stage. 'Because it saved the child's life'; 'because it is my duty'; 'because it increases human happiness all round'; 'because it is God's will'; 'because it yields pleasure'; 'because it helps to emancipate the working class', 'because it belongs to my dynamic self-realization as an individual': it seems we can always retort to any of these responses: 'And what's so good about *that*?' To put a stop to this regress, we would appear in need of some unimpeachable foundation – some reason which could not itself be trumped because it was apodictic or self-validating, grounded wholly in itself. But it is difficult to think of a foundation without wanting to slip another one beneath it, just as Wittgenstein once remarked that it is hard to think of an origin without feeling that we could always go back beyond it.[1] If the origin is *punctual*, then there seems no reason why the straight line we can draw from us to it should not carry on all the way through it and out the other side. In the pre-modern world, God, and the human nature which he or she had created, could function as such a self-grounding ground, so that it was possible for the natural-law theorists to argue their way up from how it was with humans as a species to why they should not torture one another, bring down the aristocracy or commit adultery. But the epoch of modernity is the age of irony, since having kicked those foundations from under our feet it is agonizedly or exuberantly aware that all grounds are arbitrary, even though this is precisely not how we want *grounds* to function at all.[2] If a ground is simply what we project, then

---

1. Wittgenstein also comments wryly that 'in so far as people think they can see the "limits of human understanding", they believe of course that they can see beyond these'(*Culture and Value*, Chicago 1984, p. 15e).

2. On this sense of modernist groundlessness, see Albrecht Wellmer, *The Persistence of Modernity* (Cambridge 1991), Ch. 4.

there is a sense in which we are standing hubristically on nothing but ourselves. If for Wittgenstein the bedrock of what we say is what we do, if it is our forms of life which lie at the bottom of our language games, then this would seem a poor sort of foundation altogether, since we might always of course do something different. We still have grounds of a sort here, but now they are shifting beneath us, and there would seem to be too many of them rather than too few. To anthropologize moral foundations is to risk historicizing them away.

Modernity's most edifying solution to this problem is the Kantian Will, which is precisely such a self-determining law; but for those unimpressed by this austere doctrine, the path is always open to some brand of pragmatism or conventionalism (moral judgements are just operative agreements), Utilitarianism (the good is whatever brings happiness to the majority), prescriptivism or decisionism (moral propositions are really disguised imperatives which flow from some primordial stance I take up towards the world), or the anti-naturalistic intuitionism of a G.E. Moore, for which 'good' is a simple term which cannot be reduced any further without danger of circularity. Another strategy, from David Hume to A.J. Ayer, is simply to subjectivize ethics in the style of emotivism, which holds that moral judgements are just commendatory or disapproving noises we make from time to time. For the emotivist, moral judgements look like propositions about the world, as the moral realist believes they actually are, but are really just reports on our feelings about it. The Kant of the third *Critique* thought much the same about judgements of aesthetic taste. The dilemma, anyway, is plain: either we hold to an intuitive or non-naturalistic idea of the good as incapable of further reduction, in which case we buy a foundation at the cost of its opaqueness; or we translate the idea of the good into some set of natural properties, which explains the concept only at the cost of laying the explanation itself open to some further reduction, hence depriving us of the very absolute ground we were in search of.

It is to put a halt to such infinitely regressive justification in moral judgement that Francis Hutcheson[3] takes from the Earl of Shaftesbury the notion of a 'moral sense' – that swift, immediate capacity within us, as passive and involuntary as our physical senses, by which we judge actions or motives to be virtuous or vicious. The moral sense, so Hutcheson informs us in *An Inquiry Concerning the Original of our Ideas of Virtue or*

---

3. Hutcheson was born in County Down in 1694; I write in the year of the three hundredth anniversary of his birth.

Moral Good, is 'some instinct, antecedent to all reason from interest, which influences us to the love of others'[4] – the mark, in short, of the radical anteriority or transcendentality within us of a disinterested compassion. It is thus, so he remarks in *A Short Introduction to Moral Philosophy*, 'that by the very power of nature, previous to any reasoning or meditation, we rejoice in the prosperity of others, and sorrow with them in their misfortunes ... without any consideration of our own interest'.[5] In his *Illustrations on the Moral Sense*, Hutcheson sets out to confound his rationalist opponents by claiming that any reason advanced to justify a moral judgement must already implicitly presuppose the very moral sense which it seeks to explain. For it is always open to us to ask of such reasons why they should be thought to have a specifically *moral* force, and to ask this again of the meta-reason to which our rationalist interlocutor might then retreat.

For eighteenth-century rationalists like Samuel Clarke and William Wollaston, the good must be grounded in a Reason independent of our sentiments, so that moral judgements may have objective validity; for the empiricists, such judgements turn on sense, feeling and disposition, which for the rationalist opens the door to a subversive subjectivism and ethical relativism. Yet the rationalists, so the empiricists claim, are unable to say *why* it is good to obey the dictates of Reason. Virtue for them consists in conformity with the ordained order of things; but Hutcheson has little trouble in producing examples of such action which we would hardly call moral at all. In what, then, does the specificity of the moral lie? Explanations, as Wittgenstein remarked, must come to an end somewhere; and for Hutcheson ethical debate must finally come to rest in a moral sense which is transcendental in the sense that it is unable to pass moral judgement upon itself. You cannot, Hutcheson considers, give a moral justification for the acceptance of a moral theory – no doubt because any such justification must be either derived from that theory in the first place, and so cannot act as a justification of it, or because it must spring from some other theory, which would then need in its turn to be justified. To this extent the moral sense operates as a kind of Heideggerian pre-understanding, as that which we cannot get back behind, that which must always already have been in play if something is to count for us as a *moral* argument in the first place. What the moral sense tells us is that

4. First published in 1725; reprinted in L.A. Selby-Bigge, *British Moralists* (London 1897), p. 94. I have lower-cased Hutcheson's eighteenth-century capitals throughout this chapter.

5. Francis Hutcheson, *A Short Introduction to Moral Philosophy* (Glasgow 1747), p. 14.

the ultimate virtue is benevolence; and we know that this is true because the moral sense tells us so. The keen, swift, selfless pleasure we reap from the sight of some altrustic action, a pleasure akin to the fulfilments of the aesthetic, is enough to guarantee that this form of conduct is indeed the finest manifestation of our natures.[6]

So it is, Hutcheson writes in the *Inquiry*, that 'As soon as any action is represented to us as flowing from love, humanity, gratitude, compassion, a study of the good of others, and a delight in their happiness, altho it were in the most distant part of the world, or in some past age, we feel joy within us, admire the lovely action, and praise its author.'[7] The ideological enemy is accordingly Hobbes, about whom Hutcheson remarks stingingly in his *Reflections upon Laughter* that 'he has over-looked everything which is generous or kind in mankind; and represents men in that light in which a thorow knave or coward beholds them, suspecting all friendship, love, or social affections, of hypocrisy, or selfish design or fear.'[8] Moral sense theory, or sentimentalism as it would come to be called, tries to steer a middle course between rationalism and self-interest – the one too 'unideological', in the Althusserian sense of failing to provide a motivation for action, the other all too ideological in the more conventional sense of the term. In an age of individualism, the impersonal abstractions of rationalism are no longer adequate: moral imperatives must be *felt* by an individual newly conscious of her complex interiority. The philosophy of Hutcheson, and the fiction of Samuel Richardson, belong in this sense to the same world. Yet the more moral imperatives are internalized in this way, the less easy it is to lend them objective validity.

---

6. There is no need to hack our way here through the thicket of conflicting philosophical readings of Hutcheson's ethics. W.K. Frankena sees him as an emotivist of sorts, though one who believes in justifying reasons for one's approbations and aversions; moral judgements are non-descriptive, yet reasons are nonetheless relevant to them ('Hutcheson's Moral Sense Theory', *Journal of the History of Ideas*, vol. 16, no. 3, June 1955). William T. Blackstone agrees, and sees him as an 'ethical objectivist' (*Francis Hutcheson and Contemporary Ethical Theory*, Athens, Ga. 1965, p. 69), whereas Henning Jensen argues against both Frankena and Blackstone that for Hutcheson jusifying reasons themselves presuppose the moral sense (*Motivation and the Moral Sense in Francis Hutcheson's Ethical Theory*, The Hague 1971, p. 59). For a useful account of Hutcheson, see Peter Kivy, *The Seventh Sense: A Study of Francis Hutcheson's Aesthetics* (New York 1976). There is also a thoughtful discussion in Howard Caygill, *The Art of Judgement* (Oxford 1989), and some interesting comments in Seamus Deane, 'Swift and the Anglo-Irish Intellect', *Eighteenth-Century Ireland*, vol. 1, no. 1 (Dublin 1986).

7. *Inquiry*, p. 75.

8. Francis Hutcheson, *Reflections upon Laughter, and Remarks upon the Fable of the Bees* (Glasgow 1750), p. 6. The work is written *contra* Hobbes's theory of laughter as a sign of superiority, and contains one or two excellent jokes.

The very move to root them more deeply in the human subject is also what risks undermining them, thus leaving the sentimentalists disarmed in the face of the hard-headed egoists.

To claim that moral judgements are justified by the testimony of some specialized moral sense, a kind of ghostly shadowing of our grosser physical organs, is equivalent to claiming that our moral judgements cannot be justified at all. For this spectral moral sense – an 'occult quality', as Hutcheson himself calls it, 'unphilosophical' according to Kant – is simply a kind of *locum tenens* for some more solid kind of grounding, a mysterious X which marks an empty place in the argument, the spot where a traditional moral foundationalism has now failed. And this, in turn, is tantamount to admitting that although love, generosity, mutual cooperation are indeed the finest human virtues, it is impossible any longer to say why. It is impossible to say why because in the context of bourgeois individualism this moral doctrine, inherited from an earlier historical culture, has been left hanging impotently in the air. Alasdair MacIntyre has argued that the moral discourse of modernity is as bedevilled as it is because the values it inherits from the past made sense there only within the framework of certain social roles and relations which modernity has now ruthlessly dismantled.[9] The so-called naturalistic fallacy – the prohibition on deriving values from facts, or the assertion of the impossibility of this move – is then the registration, within the moral discourse of modernity, of its own schizoid historical conditions, just as the tortuous, fragmentary, self-brooding work of modernist art has internalized in its very forms the conditions of its own social impossibility in an age of commodity exchange. If moral values can no longer be grounded in social relations, or in the human nature or divine law which founds them, then they must either become autotelic (Kant), psychologized (emotivism, utilitarianism), relativized (historicism) or subjectivized, rooted as with Hume or the Romantics in the sentiments alone.

Hutcheson, along with his mentor the Earl of Shaftesbury, wishes to do none of these things; on the contrary, he preserves, like Shaftesbury, a classical sense of a human nature harmoniously disposed by the deity to certain ends, within which all the more selfless, tender-hearted impulses are uppermost.[10] But in an era dominated from Hobbes and Mandeville

---

9. See Alasdair MacIntyre, *A Short History of Ethics* (London 1967); *After Virtue* (London 1981); *Whose Justice? Which Rationality?* (London 1988).

10. David Fate Norton, cutting against the grain of most Hutcheson commentary, reads him as a moral realist for whom moral judgements are cognitive. See his *David Hume: Common-Sense Moralist, Sceptical Metaphysican* (Princeton, N.J. 1982), Ch. 2.

to Jeremy Bentham by the doctrine and practice of self-interest, it is hard to see how exactly this alternative conception of political life can be securely founded in the facts; and the doctrine of the moral sense, that elusive, impalpable capacity which is nevertheless as vividly immediate as smell or taste, is in this respect no more than a confession of defeat, the sign in thought of an impasse in historical reality. The incontrovertible nature of this moral sense, which we could deny no more than the taste of potatoes or the feel of a rose leaf, is testimony to the truth that the values it approves *must* be foundational; the wraith-like, notional quality of the concept is evidence enough that they can nowhere be demonstrated. Moral judgement, like taste, becomes a kind of *je ne sais quoi*, its irrefutability in direct proportion to its unarguability. It is no wonder, then, that moral discourse is being drawn steadily into the orbit of the aesthetic, for aesthetic judgement is that mysteriously self-contradictory act which is at once subjective in quality – a matter of taste – and universal in its conclusions.

In his struggle against empiricist scepticism, and the egoism to which it can lead, Hutcheson can no longer muster the resources of a Platonic or scholastic teleology, since empiricism has done its work too well; so he will extract from the empiricist theory of perception a kind of spiritual shadow of itself – moral sense – which can be turned against that philosophy's sceptical tendencies, and do service, *faute de mieux*, for a foundation to the good life. The sensationalism of a Locke has raised the awkward issue of how we could ever know an immaterial object, as well as suggesting that abstract notions such as ethical ones are mere arbitrary constructs from sense data. In positing his theory of the moral sense, Hutcheson does not retreat from Locke's rejection of innate ideas, since the moral sense is not exactly cognitive; instead, he simply stretches Lockeian epistemology to a sixth faculty, but in doing so lends our moral notions a certitude which empiricism denies them.[11] The Irish fideists – King,[12] Browne, Synge, Burke and others – will turn Locke against himself

---

11. David Berman argues that, with the possible exception of William Molyneux, no Irish philosopher claimed to be Locke's disciple; instead, the Irish criticized and reinterpreted Locke's standpoint ('The Irish Counter-Enlightenment', in Richard Kearney, ed., *The Irish Mind*, Dublin 1985, p. 119). In *Gulliver's Travels*, Swift takes a satiric smack at Locke's theory of reference in the Lagado project to abolish words altogether and simply converse with the help of objects.

12. In his *De Origine Mali* (1702), King claims that God has ordained that not everyone can be in a superior position, and that to fall from such a position implies some folly on the part of the agent. This case may not be wholly unconnected with the fact that King was an Ascendancy archbishop confronted with a Gaelic populace who believed they had been usurped.

in a rather different style, arguing that since our sensations are indeed all we can know, and since trekking our way up from these to the divine mysteries is a perilous business, we must simply take those mysteries on faith, in a move which strikes at the left-wing rationalism of a John Toland.[13] In a perverse twist to empiricist scepticism, the less we can know for sure, the more faith is triumphantly vindicated. Bishop Berkeley will take yet another way out, overthrowing the distinction between appearance and reality, identifying the real with the way it is perceived, and so circumventing scepticism with an idealism which he oddly believed to be no more than plain common sense.

For Hutcheson, reason can inform our moral sense, correcting its errors and misapprehensions; but it cannot found it, any more than it can for his disciple David Hume, who regards reason as the mere slave of passion. A classical unity of reason and value has been fissured by the emergence of modernity, to be revived at the turn of the century by G.W.F. Hegel; but in the meantime reason can have no truck with value precisely because in early bourgeois Europe reason has become thoroughly instrumentalized, a question of means rather than of ends. How could a technologized reason, one constructed from the outset as value-free, possibly enter into the question of what constitutes happiness or the good life? Hutcheson is thus thrown back on instinct as the frail basis of his whole intricately argued moral discourse; and though instincts cannot be gainsaid, they cannot be convincingly demonstrated either. The fact that they are un-arguable is at once the strength and the weakness of the 'moral sense' case. As with Kant's *Critique of Practical Reason*, the moral law remains absolutely binding but ultimately mysterious – quite divorced, in the case of Kant, from the humdrum phenomenal realm in which we live out our thoroughly determined existences. Hutcheson is a civic humanist of a traditional kind,[14] convinced that the public good is the highest moral end for human beings; and not the least of his achievements is to translate this classical republican discourse, with its imposing lexicon of duty, public spirit, political responsibility, into the language of eighteenth-century individual psychology. 'Moral sense' yokes public and intimate spheres together, since it is just the kind of actions which are most socially

---

13. Toland's *Christianity not Mysterious* (1696) was the *locus classicus* of eighteenth-century Irish theological rationalism, and was burnt by the common hangman. Its author, inventor of the word 'pantheism' and the first European writer to be dubbed a freethinker, prudently fled to England.

14. For the ideology of civic humanism, see J.G.A. Pocock, *Virtue, Commerce, and History* (Cambridge 1985).

benevolent which will win my most pleasurable individual approbation. 'The pleasures of virtue', Hutcheson writes, '[are] the greatest we are capable of',[15] thus conveniently coupling altruism and hedonism, selflessness and gratification, politics and psychology. In this way, the moral sense provides a kind of mediation between a subjectivist and an objectivist ethics. It is not a form of emotivism, since whereas the emotivist holds that 'This is good' can be translated into 'I commend this', Hutcheson holds that my instinct of approbation is the inscription within me of the fact that the object *is* good.[16]

Whereas the rationalist comments dryly 'that is good', the prescriptivist orders 'do this!',[17] and the emotivist cries ecstatically 'good thing to do!', Hutcheson combines subjective and objective by exclaiming 'that is good!' To this extent, the moral sense provides a bridge between fact and value, descriptive and normative – so that this age-old mediation, which has vanished from modern society as a whole with the reification of fact, the instrumentalization of reason and the consequent autonomy of value, can now be seen to resurface on the inside of the sentient moral subject. But if this avoids the frank subjectivism of a David Hume, it equally circumvents the objectivism of the rationalists. For if a rationalist in pursuit of some further justification for benevolence asks us why we approve the public good, 'I fancy we can find [no reasons] in these cases, more than we could give for our liking any pleasant fruit'.[18] The equation of moral judgement with taste at once trivializes and reinforces it: we cannot doubt that we enjoy bananas, but we cannot say why either. But because it is plausible to feel that pleasure is a more immediate experience than self-interest, which after all requires a little cerebration, and because the keenest pleasure for Hutcheson is reaped from the sight of benevolence, he can establish by this devious route the transcendentality of the social virtues – transcendental not only in the sense of anterior to interest, but the very matrix of it. 'Our sense of pleasure', he remarks in the *Inquiry*, 'is antecedent to advantage or interest, and is the foundation of it'.[19]

---

15. Bernard Peach, ed., *Illustrations on the Moral Sense* (Cambridge, Mass. 1971) p. 106.

16. The idea that moral judgements are both subjective and objective has recently drifted back into favour. See, for example, the work of David Wiggins, who argues in an account of Hume that what Hume *could* have said is that '*x* is good/right/beautiful if and only if *x* is such as to make a certain sentiment of approbation *appropriate*' (*Needs, Values, Truth*, Oxford 1987, p. 187). What Wiggins *could* have said is that this is more or less what Francis Hutcheson *does* say.

17. For prescriptivism, see R.M. Hare, *The Language of Morals* (Oxford 1952).

18. Peach, ed., *Illustrations on the Moral Sense*, p. 129.

19. Selby-Bigge, *British Moralists*, p. 70.

Hutcheson does not introduce his notion of a moral sense merely to put an end to infinitely regressive justification. He needs it because without this faculty there is nothing to choose between private selfishness and public spirit. There is nothing mysterious about the motives which inspire us to self-love, but what possible impulse could stir us to a devotion to others? A being without a moral sense will naturally conclude that self-interest is the most reasonable course of action; but what reasons can we adduce for persuading him or her into selfless conduct? That it tends to the good of humankind? But why pursue the good of humankind? That a beneficent God has ordained it? But what spurs men and women to love and obey a benefactor?[20] If we need a moral sense, it is because in a self-interested social order the springs of public virtue have become opaque; and this is because, in an emergent bourgeois society, social roles and relations are no longer describable in ways which make implicit reference to mutual obligations and responsibilities. It is this cleavage between fact and value that the moral sense seeks to repair. Hutcheson's postulating of the instinct amounts to confessing that, in a rampantly individualist order, a selfless concern for others' well-being is simply unintelligible. Since there is nothing in the constitution of society itself which might inspire its members to mutual love, that sentiment has now to be installed in the depths of the individual subject, naturalized as an impulse akin to hunger or self-preservation. If it has to be antecedent to reason, it is because it needs to outflank a rationality which is now increasingly in the hands of the apologists for a free-market ethics.

Politically speaking, then, Hutcheson is on the defensive; yet the innocent kindliness of his view of human nature belies this anxiety.[21] As a 'New Light' Presbyterian, he is vulnerable to the charge of denying the doctrines of reprobation, election and original sin; and although he tells

---

20. For these thoughts of Hutcheson, see his *Letters to Gilbert Burnet on the Foundation of Virtue* (London 1772). The problem is pinpointed by Roger Scruton in his discussion of the Utilitarian commitment to the greatest happiness of the greatest number: 'Is this something that we want, or something that we *ought* to want, or something that it is *reasonable* to want? We are back with the question of practical reason' (*Modern Philosophy*, London 1994, p. 282).

21. Hutcheson's sanguine view of human nature might well be thought to be pre-Freudian; yet we should remember that for Freud too the moral sense, if not exactly innate, goes a long way back, in the first stirrings of the infant's sense of gratitude towards its protectors. 'The original helplessness of human beings', Freud writes, 'is thus the primal source of all moral motives' ('Project for a Scientific Psychology', in Ernst Kris, ed., *The Origins of Psychoanalysis*, New York 1954, p. 379).

us that in a 'depraved and corrupt' humankind, 'sensuality and mean selfish pursuits are the most universal',[22] it is hard to believe that this moral pessimism is more than skin-deep. Only a few pages on from this piece of Protestant orthodoxy he is noting 'how few are devoted to mere solitary sensuality without any social friendly affections and joy',[23] and informs us in his *Essay on the Nature and Conduct of the Passions and Affections* that 'every passion or affection in its moderate degree is innocent, many are directly amiable, and morally good'.[24] Vice, then, is immoderacy, and a temperate desire to torture is presumably harmless. Like the anti-culturalist Henry Fielding, Hutcheson holds that an aversion to vice and attraction to virtue are rooted deep in our natures, 'such that no education, false principles, depraved habits can entirely root this out'.[25] Men and women desire happiness; and since to be virtuous is to be blissfully happy ('a friendly generous action gives a delight superior to any other'[26]), it is hard to see why anyone would bother to be vicious. Hutcheson's case is certainly bland; the only surprise is that it never quite descends into smugness.

It is hard to square this quasi-Pelagian view of human nature with a Protestantism which sets nature against grace. For Hutcheson's more genial conception, virtue goes with the grain of our being, which for all its imperfections has a built-in bias towards the moral law. If that law calls upon us to transcend our less than angelic selves, it can only do so effectively (as Catholic theology holds) because it speaks to some potential which is already implicit in our nature. Otherwise it would be the merest arbitrary fiat, which we obey simply because God has ordained it, as he might just as well have ordained us to spend the greater part of each day shoving our fists down our throats. Nothing could be further from Hutcheson's doctrine than the grim puritanism of Kant, for whom right conduct and a repression of our natural inclinations go hand in hand. The categorical imperative ordains that in moral matters we disregard empirical conditions such as personal interest, happiness or desire, and conform our actions to Reason alone. If virtue doesn't feel unpleasant, then it's unlikely to be virtue. As a true Protestant, Kant sets morality above and against nature; Hutcheson, by contrast, recognizes that to be moral is to enjoy ourselves – to attain to a generous fullness of being by

22. *Short Introduction*, pp. 34–5.
23. Ibid., p. 46.
24. *An Essay on the Nature and Conduct of the Passions and Affections* (Glasgow 1769), p. 79.
25. Ibid., p. 95.
26. Ibid., p. 117.

doing what we really want, giving rein to those impulses which are most truly ourselves. Virtue is a matter of feeling good as well as doing it, so that its nearest analogue would be the experience of a supremely good dinner. It is a question of robust bodily pleasure, of geniality and *jouissance*, which is one reason why it borders so intimately on the aesthetic. It is no accident that he wrote an essay on laughter. 'This moral sense', Hutcheson writes in the *Short Introduction to Moral Philosophy*, 'diffuses itself through all conditions of life, and every part of it; and insinuates it self into all the more humane amusements and entertainments of man-kind. Poetry and rhetoric depend almost entirely upon it; as do in a great measure the arts of the painter, statutary, and player. In the choice of wives, friends, comrades, it is all in all; and it even insinuates it self into our games and mirth.'[27] Like poetry, virtue turns on the empathetic imagination, on a delightful decentring of ourselves into the being of others. To do this for the *sake* of that delight would of course be to land us back with an ethics of self-interest, just as to savour the glow of a fine port for the sake of getting drunk, rather than as part of social inter-course, would be a perversion of true morality and an impoverished sort of pleasure. The benevolist is a kind of *bon viveur*, relishing the amiability of himself and others as he would a splendid landscape or a dish of shrimps.

This seductive theory of the good, in which charity and clubbability are hard to distinguish, belongs to the middle class at its most expansive and assured. There is a blithe Hellenism about it which Hutcheson derives directly from Shaftesbury, and which no doubt has in its sights the unlovely earnestness of much Dissent. Yet Hutcheson's theory of the moral sense, and his remarkably sanguine view of human nature, do not neces-sarily entail one another. You can, after all, hold that men and women have an instinctive appreciation of benevolence while maintaining that self-love is in fact the more dominant feature of social life. This, in fact, was the doctrine of David Hume, who held like Hutcheson that morality was a question of impartial sympathy, but also believed that such sympathy was a good deal more feeble than self-interest. The moral sense plays an 'anterior' role in our lives; but is this an epistemological point, meaning that moral feelings are previous to reason, or a moral truth, meaning that the loving kindness which the moral sense approves is in fact the most fundamental aspect of our natures? Hutcheson, one suspects, would like to believe the latter; but he cannot of course ignore the sway of self-

---

27. *Short Introduction*, p. 20.

interest, about which his works have a good deal to say. The *Inquiry* has to work hard to counter the perverse case that altruism is just a displaced form of self-advantage. On the one hand, virtue would seem of our very essence; on the other hand, 'in the present state of mankind which we plainly see is depraved and corrupt, sensuality and mean selfish pursuits are the most universal'.[28]

Hutcheson drives the point home in the late *System of Moral Philosophy*, where he writes that 'the selfish principles are very strong, and by custom, by early and frequent indulgences, and other causes, are raised in the greater part of men above their due proportion, while the generous principles are little cultivated, and the moral sense often asleep'.[29] Henry Fielding is caught in a similar dilemma: if to be good is spontaneously to express our natures, in contrast to the vulgar Evangelical view that virtue must be laboured for, how come that the good are a besieged, faintly ridiculous minority in a predatory world? Why is a depravity which is in some sense unnatural an apparently natural state of affairs? The empirical and the ideal are alarmingly skewed, and satire germinates in the gap between them. Fielding constantly bounces one off against the other, using an idealized virtue to satirize a degenerate society while in the same breath measuring the frailty and naivety of goodness against a sceptical worldliness. Swift, too, plays both sides of the street in just this manner. When the middle class are feeling content with themselves, virtue seems as plentifully available as claret, part of the routine texture of social life; yet they have only to glance around at the monstrously egoistic society they have created to realize that this cannot be the case at all. Ideologically speaking, compassion and benevolence *must* be fundamental; on any empirical estimate, they are in dismally short supply. It is a version of the question which Marxism, with *faux naïveté*, addresses to the bourgeoisie whose values it so admires: how come that these fine ideals of freedom and justice, the moment they are materialized in practice, seem to twist by some inexorable logic into their opposites?

Francis Hutcheson, unknown to himself, is in this sense a *utopian* thinker, discerning at the very root of our nature a set of values which could only in fact be realized in some transfigured future. That those values must indeed be foundational, but are plainly nothing of the kind, is then the secret of the Janus-faced moral sense, at once utterly self-evident and intangibly elusive. The radical would simply wish to historicize

---

28. Ibid., pp. 34–5.
29. *A System of Moral Philosophy* (London 1755), Book 1, p. 78.

this tension: these values are indeed the most fundamental, but *not yet*. And to realize them in practice would mean attending a little more sympathetically to the Kantian side of the moral story. For Kant has one half of the moral truth, as Hutcheson has the other. It is true, as Hutcheson sees and Kant does not, that the moral life is not in the first place about obligation. It is also true that goodness and happiness are not finally dissociable, that virtue is all about fine living, that pleasure and probity go hand in hand. The good life, as Aristotle taught, is a matter of serenity or well-being,[30] and Hutcheson is quick to see that if this does not register itself on our bodies then it does not register itself on us. But to achieve that well-being for everybody, rather than for a clutch of clubbable philosophers, demands from time to time the revolutionary virtues of sacrifice and self-discipline, the deferment of short-term happiness in the name of a richer life all round. It is this more forbidding truth that Kant, who was far from being a revolutionary, in his own way acknowledged, and which the callow hedonism of some contemporary postmodernism conservatively refuses. To project utopia upon the present is to cherish its creative potential, redeeming those values which cut against the grain of its dominant ethos. It is also to risk cutting off a future, and so selling those values short.

Hutcheson, one might claim, aestheticizes morality; but he does not *reduce* it to the aesthetic, in the style of some proto-postmodernist. The moral sense is akin to the aesthetic faculty, so that Hutcheson can speak in the *Inquiry* of 'moral beauty', but it is not identical with it. Virtue resembles the aesthetic in at least four ways: it is an end in itself; it is recognized by an instinct which is beyond the merely rational; it is a matter of pleasurable fulfilment; and it involves the disinterested or empathetic imagination. All four of these features are, in their coded way, critiques of bourgeois society. Virtue for Hutcheson is an end in itself in much the same way that the work of art will come to be reconstructed as such by the new eighteenth-century discourse of aesthetics.[31] Virtue and art are beyond reason – in the sense of challenging the instrumental rationality of early capitalist society, and the sway of exchange value which

---

30. For an excellent discussion, see Jonathan Lear, *Aristotle: The Desire to Understand* (Cambridge 1988). See also Bernard Williams, *Ethics and the Limits of Philosophy* (Cambridge 1985), Ch. 3.

31. See my *The Ideology of the Aesthetic* (Oxford 1991), Chs 1 and 2 for a discussion of Hutcheson and the moral sense theorists. See also David Paxman, 'Aesthetics as Epistemology, or Knowledge without Certainty', *Eighteenth-Century Studies*, vol. 26, no. 2 (Winter 1992/3).

underpins it. There can be no ulterior motive for generosity and compassion, which exist for their own sake as part of what Marx will later call our 'species being'. Our benevolence can be no more rationally justified than a song or a saga, not least in a society where justifications are likely to end up in some appeal to self-interest. Henry Fielding notes in *Tom Jones* that there is a noble doctrine to the effect that the virtuous will gain their reward in this world – a doctrine, he adds, which has only one limitation, namely that it is not true. In an exploitative social order, virtue had better be its own reward, since it will reap precious little profit otherwise. There is, then, a certain grim historical necessity to this edifying viewpoint; if morality, like the aesthetic artefact, is autonomous, it is because neither art nor virtue can any longer be grounded in a world whose logic is alien to them. But the idea of moral ends as autonomous – they would not be *ends* if they were not – is also a thoroughly traditionalist notion which Hutcheson derives from Aristotle and Shaftesbury, and which can act as a utopian critique of a political modernity increasingly under the heel of utility. To call Hutcheson anti-utilitarian might seem strange, given that he was the man who coined the Utilitarian slogan 'the greatest happiness of the greatest number'. But utility for the republican Hutcheson means the elevation of the public good over selfish interests; and that impulse cannot itself be justified on utilitarian grounds.[32] We can give no coherent reply to the sceptic who asks why we should be sociable, just as there is no particular point in producing symphonies or jokes.

For virtue to be autonomous is for it to be profitless. 'Men', Hutcheson writes, 'approve deeply that beneficence which they deem gratuitous and disinterested'.[33] Virtue is in this sense the opposite of the marketplace, and disinterestedness is a politically radical attitude. If this is an unappetizing suggestion for today's political left to swallow, it is because they are accustomed to viewing disinterestedness as a specious rationalization of selfish interests, rather than as a genuine alternative to them. But this is in turn because that left inhabits a later stage of class society where social contradictions, having become potentially unmanageable, need to be masked

---

32. Blackstone (*Francis Hutcheson and Contemporary Ethical Theory*, p. 37) describes Hutcheson flatly as a 'utilitarian hedonist', but later qualifies this characterization by acknowledging that Hutcheson looks at motives, whereas Utilitarianism is of course typically consequentialist. Jensen (*Motivation and the Moral Sense*, p. 20) denies that Hutcheson is a hedonist since the aim of desire is for him the object, rather than the pleasure to be reaped from it. W.R. Scott, on the contrary, describes the final phase of Hutcheson's philosophy as 'simply Utilitarianism as Mill understood it' (*Francis Hutcheson*, Cambridge 1900, p. 272).

33. *Short Introduction*, p. 18.

and mystified by appeals to an impartial reason; whereas no political theorist in Hutcheson's day, in a more buoyant, self-confident bourgeois order, needed to be coy about the centrality of self-love. Thomas Hobbes, Hutcheson's professional *bête noire*, felt no compunction to dissemble an ideology of naked self-interest beneath some veil of social harmony. Disinterestedness for Hutcheson has nothing to do with some specious objectivity; it signifies rather a radical decentring of the bourgeois self, whose possessive individualism can never account for 'the principle actions of human life such as the offices of friendship, gratitude, natural affection, generosity, public spirit, compassion'.[34] Disinterestedness is not some Arnoldian *apatheia* but a matter of love − the spontaneous love registered by the moral sense for those who perform actions which accrue no profit either to themselves or to us. To respond to virtue is thus to love those who love, and so to redouble their action, raise it to the second power. 'Love loves to love love', as Joyce puts it in *Ulysses*. 'The word MORAL GOODNESS', Hutcheson remarks in the *Inquiry*, 'denotes our idea of some quality apprehended in actions, which procures approbation, and love toward the actor, from those who receive no advantage by the action.'[35] Moral judgement is thus both constative and performative, responding to an act of benevolence in the world with one of its own. To love is to desire the happiness of another, and so is equivalent to disinterestedness. If disinterestedness is in an odd sense materialist, it is because our moral sense is less a question of will or consciousness than something built into our material constitution, as involuntary as experiencing an itch. And if the notion is aesthetic, it is because that sense of being carried out of our private interests which is moral judgement finds a paradigm in the disinterested universality of taste, in the way the work of art allows me to suspend my pragmatic interests and unite with others in a *sensus communis* which is the nearest this society can get to the idea of a political condition beyond selfish individualism.

As for moral judgement as an instinct, we have seen already that this represents a swerve away from an instrumental rationality − a swerve of which, as the eighteenth century runs its course, the aesthetic will become the paradigm. Before we have even begun to reason, there is already that faculty within us which makes us feel the sufferings of others as keenly as a wound, spurs us to luxuriate in another's joy with no sense of self-advantage. If this is a materialist ethics, it is because these responses are

---

34. *Illustrations of the Moral Sense*, pp. 117–18.
35. *Inquiry*, p. 69.

rooted in the body – a body which is anterior to self-interested rationality, and which will force its instinctual approbations and aversions upon our social practice. In the age of empiricism, abstract ideas are no longer any very sound basis in which to lodge our sense of human community; so Hutcheson's creaturely ethics will turn the other way, back to the very senses which seem the source of all our conceptual uncertainty, and discover in this sensuous substratum the source of our social sympathies. Just at the point where the empiricist subject is in danger of being locked solipsistically within his private perceptions, Hutcheson will find here the very key to human sociality, locating that on the interior of the subject which opens her out to the inner life of others. If this is an aesthetic project, it is because the word 'aesthetic' actually means bodily sensation; but it is also because we have here the seeds of that empathetic imagination which from the Romantics to George Eliot will become the basis of a humanistic ethics.

Adam Smith, Hutcheson's most illustrious pupil and his successor in the Glasgow Chair of Moral Philosophy, is among the first to make this crucial move: '[our senses] never did, and never can, carry us beyond our own person, and it is by the imagination only that we can form any conception of what are [the other's] sensations'.[36] The master himself, however, has no need to shift beyond the senses to avoid moral solipsism, since he has introduced an extra sense which does that work for him; but this emphasis upon the moral force of sentiment, along with the imagination as the link between immediate and abstract, will pass straight into the ideology of Romanticism, of which Hutcheson can truly be said to be a founding father. And since the moral sense is 'the fountain of the most intense pleasure',[37] a reified rationality which can find no room for bodily fulfilment is defeated in this way too. In a bold inversion, the pleasure which the psychological egoists associate with self-love is turned into its opposite: if you are really out for self-gratification, forget about yourself and melt into sympathy with others. The theory of the moral sense allows Hutcheson to appropriate the idea of pleasure from his opponents while dispensing with their hedonism – for the good is not simply what gratifies me, yet it is the feeling of pleasure which makes a moral approbation moral. It is in this sense that the concept of moral sense balances a thin line between fact and value, objectivism and subjectivism. One might add, finally, that if the moral and aesthetic consort

36. Adam Smith, 'The Theory of Moral Sentiments', in Selby-Bigge, *British Moralists*, p. 258.
37. *Essay*, p. 143.

together in the content of Hutcheson's philosophy, so do they in its form. The discourse of eighteenth-century moral philosophy, with its assured sense of a common social world, its homespun examples and concern with personal conduct, is only an inch or two away from the new genre of the novel, which indeed might be said to be its logical consummation. If this inquiry into the empirical conduct of men and women is to go deep enough, then it will have to shift eventually into that counterfactual speculation on their motives and actions which we call fiction. Hutcheson's own style of writing is at once descriptive and didactic, a discourse on moral value which is meant to be morally edifying in itself; and according to the reports of pupils like Adam Smith and Thomas Carlyle, this was the keynote of his lecturing style as well. It was to become, indeed, the keynote of the teaching of moral philosophy in Scotland as whole.

True to his linkage of the moral and the aesthetic, Hutcheson speaks of virtuous actions as beautiful and vicious ones as ugly or deformed. We feel that we are in the presence of virtue when we thrill to a particular grace and elegance of conduct – which is to say that the word 'grace' has now been secularized, lifted from its theological meaning to characterize what the eighteenth century knows as 'manners'. Manners signify a pervasive aestheticizing of social life itself, in which decorum and delight, pleasure and propriety, consort spontaneously together. Civility is in this sense the mundane analogue of divinity: just as the grace of God shapes our receptive natures into something finer, so manners mould our natures into a gracefulness which is at once morally just and aesthetically pleasing. In the bourgeois drawing room, as in God, truth, rightness and beauty are finally indissociable. Virtue is the easy habit of goodness, as cultivated yet instinctive as a taste for Madeira. If social life is aesthetically appealing, it is because, like the work of art, it has spontaneously internalized the law which governs it, living out that sovereignty as casual gesture and unreflective habit. And this is to say that we can detect in Hutcheson the seeds of that sense of hegemony, of a law so supremely successful that it is entirely invisible, which we have already traced in the political thought of Edmund Burke. That both men had practical experience in Ireland of a rather more rebarbative form of sovereignty is presumably not accidental to this preoccupation with what Hegel termed the law of the heart. Nor, perhaps, is it entirely accidental that every one of Hutcheson's aestheticized moral tenets – virtue as a self-delighting end in itself, social living as style, spontaneous impulse against instrumental reason, right living as bodily pleasure, the self as decentred – should re-emerge, in flamboyantly caricatured form, in the work of his later compatriot Oscar Wilde.

Judging by casual conversations with Anglo-Saxon philosophers, Francis Hutcheson was a Scotsman. He was, to be sure, the grandson of a Scot, the holder of a Chair at Glasgow and the founder of the Scottish school of philosophical enquiry. But he wrote nothing of moment while in Scotland; most of his most seminal works were written while he was teaching in a Dissenting academy in Dublin, aided by Thomas Drennan, father of the United Irish poet. And though Ulster and Scotland formed in his day something of an intellectual free-trade area, with outposts in North America,[38] his Irish background is in several respects vital to his thought. Writing to his father, a Presbyterian minister, Hutcheson remarks that 'I do not imagine, that either [Church] government or the externals of worship are so determined in the gospels, as to oblige men to one particular [denominational] way or another.'[39] He is, in short, a latitudinarian in religious matters; and one prime antagonist which his notion of disinterested benevolence has in its sights is Irish religious sectarianism. In Dublin he was a member of Robert Molesworth's celebrated intellectual circle, which included the reprobate John Toland; but he also had close relations with Anglican divines such as Archbishop King and Edward Synge. It was a bold act for a Presbyterian cleric to place the name of a notorious deist, Shaftesbury, on the title page of his *Inquiry*; and the truth is that Hutcheson's moral philosophy could get along tolerably well without its religious underpinnings. 'All strict attachment to partys, sects, factions', he writes in the *Inquiry*, 'have but an imperfect species of beauty',[40] and bigotry and zealotry impair the moral feeling. What Hutcheson's ethics offer, in short, is a utopian alternative to the Irish political Establishment of his day; and Hutcheson himself – twice prosecuted for teaching in his Dublin academy, tried for heresy while in Glasgow – paid the price for it. But if his ethics are in one sense shaped against Irish society, they may be

---

38. For a valuable outline of this intellectual traffic, see Ian McBride, 'Francis Hutcheson, Irish Presbyterians and the Scottish Enlightenment', in D. George Boyce, ed., *Political Thought in Ireland since the Seventeenth Century* (London 1993).

39. Quoted by Paxman, 'Aesthetics as Epistemology', p. 300. Hutcheson's father's parishioners did not take kindly to this laid-back ecumenism. When Hutcheson *fils* once preached a sermon to them, one disgruntled member of the congregation is reputed to have reported to Hutcheson *père* that 'your silly loon, Francis, has fashed a' the congregation wi' his idle cackle; for he has been babbling this oor aboot a gude and benevolent God, and that the sauls o' the heathens themselves will gang to Heeven, if they follow the licht of their ain conscience. Not a word does the daft boy ken, speer, nor say aboot the gude and comfortable doctrines o' election, reprobation, original sin and faith. Hoot mon, awa' wi' sic a fellow' (quoted by Scott, *Francis Hutcheson*, pp. 20–21).

40. *Inquiry*, p. 108.

in another sense shaped by it. Moral sense philosophy springs less from the heartlands of early bourgeois England than from its ideological peripheries – in the Earl of Shaftesbury's case, from a classical aristocratic humanism deeply hostile to a shopkeeper's ethic of self-interest; in Hutcheson's case from a marginal society which had been less deeply imprinted by a market ethics of possessive individualism. There may be some relation, one is tempted to speculate, between the centrality of the social affections in Hutcheson's work and the more communal inheritance of Irish society.

However that might be, Ireland has hardly taken one of its most enlightened sons to its bosom. In the year of the three-hundredth anniversary of his birth, we are still awaiting a full-length study from an Irish scholar of this astonishing figure. Francis Hutcheson, founder of the most fertile current of intellectual enquiry in eighteenth-century Scot-land,[41] taught David Hume much of what he knew and deeply affected the pre-critical writings of Immanuel Kant. His economic doctrine descended to his student Adam Smith, thus laying one of the intellectual foundations of the modern world. His philosophy was a major influence on Thomas Jefferson, helping to shape the American struggle for independence,[42] and boomeranged back to Ireland in the shape of the revolutionary United Irish movement. Edmund Burke, author of the only other Irish aesthetic treatise of the eighteenth century, may have absorbed Hutcheson's doctrine of the native and patriotic affections, which would then make Hutcheson a remote precursor of Romantic nationalism.[43] Hutcheson's ideas belong to the eighteenth-century ferment of Irish Whiggery and Dissent: in the *Short Introduction to Moral Philosophy* he argues, *contra* Hobbes, that the state of nature was one of liberty rather than anarchy, and in his *System of Moral Philosophy* champions the rights of women, children, servants, slaves and animals in the course of an

---

41. For a readable survey of the Scottish Enlightenment, see Gladys Bryson, *Man and Society: The Scottish Inquiry of the Eighteenth Century* (Princeton, N.J. 1945). For some critical comments on Alasdair MacIntyre's discussion of Hutcheson and the Scottish Enlightenment in his *Whose Justice? Which Rationality?*, see Robert Wokler, 'Projecting the Enlightenment', in John Horton and Susan Mendus, eds, *After MacIntyre* (Cambridge 1994).

42. For Hutcheson's influence in the USA, see Garry Wills, *Inventing America* (New York 1978), Ch. 12. Wills sees Thomas Jefferson as a classic 'moral sense' philosopher. See also David Fate Norton, 'Salus Populi Suprema Lex', in the special Hutcheson supplement of the Belfast journal *Fortnight*, no. 308 (1994).

43. There is no evidence of a direct link here between Hutcheson and Burke; but Seamus Deane's hypothesized connection between them is surely plausible. The influence may have passed through Adam Smith. See Seamus Deane, *The French Revolution and Enlightenment in England 1789–1832* (Cambridge, Mass. 1988) p. 16.

argument for the natural equality of human beings. He speaks up for marriage as an equal partnership, and comments that 'the powers vested in husbands by the civil laws of many nations are monstrous'.[44] He also takes a radical Whig line on the right of the governed to throw off an unjust sovereignty, and emerges as a full-blooded Harringtonian republican. The moral sense, he stresses in the *System*, is a democratic faculty common to adults and children, the unlettered and the refined.

Hutcheson stands at the fountainhead of the Ulster Enlightenment: the richest radical culture which Ireland has ever known. Other oppositional currents in the country – O'Connell, Sinn Fein – may have proved more politically effective; but none can remotely rival the philosophical ambitiousness and intellectual fertility of this extraordinary period, with its complex blending of Lockeian rationalism, classical republicanism, radical Presbyterianism and political libertarianism. Its preoccupations range from the soul to the state, from sentiment to the nature of civil society, from the springs of consciousness to the sources of political authority. Contemporary Ireland, both north and south of the border, stands under the judgement of this precious heritage, and has yet to catch up with its past.

---

44. *A System of Moral Philosophy*, Book 3, p. 165.

CHAPTER 4

CHANGING THE QUESTION

> The British can never solve the Irish question because the Irish keep changing the question.
>
> *Traditional aphorism*

'I live in terror of not being misunderstood', remarks the outrageous Gilbert in Oscar Wilde's *The Critic as Artist*. Whether the British misunderstood Wilde, or understood him only too well, is a matter for debate; but it is not difficult to trace in his ambiguous relations with the English Establishment a surreally abbreviated version of Anglo-Irish relations as a whole. Violence, travesty, affection, complicity, mimicry, subversion, mutual mystification: if the turbulent marriage of Wilde and Britannia is rich in such qualities, it is only because it writes theatrically large the traditionally fraught relation between the two nations.

The status of Ireland in Wilde's day was oxymoronic. The country was a metropolitan colony, at once part of the imperial nation and peripheral to it. As with many a marital union, a formal parity concealed the real subordination of one of the partners. Before the Union, Ireland could regard itself as an independent nation because its allegiance lay not to the parliament at Westminster but to the Irish crown, which could be seen as distinct from the British crown even though it happened to rest upon the same royal head. But since the crown is merely metonymic of British power as a whole, this neo-scholastic manoeuvre proved peculiarly hollow. Ireland was an independent kingdom, so the theory ran, because it had its own monarch, who happened also to be monarch of Great Britain. In fact, Ireland shared a sovereign with Britain because it belonged to it; but the fetish of the crown allowed these power relations to be suppressed when it proved convenient, and necessity to be transformed into contingency.

The bond between the two nations was thus a kind of fiction. 'In this United Kingdom of Great Britain and Ireland,' writes Sir Samuel

Ferguson, 'each part is governed by the whole, and neither by the other'
– so that no 'free-born Irishman' could acknowledge allegiance to a *British*
sovereignty.[1] The British do not govern Ireland, despite every empirical
appearance to the contrary, since Ireland submits only to a sovereignty
which includes itself. The Irish after the Union swear fealty not to Great
Britain, but to a Platonic totality created out of their unequal incorpor-
ation into it. In this way, the conditions of their subservience become the
conditions of their freedom. An appropriate analogy here might be the
work of art for classical aesthetics, all of whose elements are equal and
autonomous, recognizing no dominion but the law of the artefact as a
whole.[2] But this 'law of the whole' is really just a mystifying name for
the interrelations of the elements as such, just as the crown is no more
than a signifier for actual political relations.

By a curious inversion, then, reality – the actual state of Anglo-Irish
relations – has become fiction, and a palpable fiction is promoted as
reality. But the fiction is doubled: for since the Revolution of 1688, the
British crown had itself become progressively subordinated to parliament,
making the myth of Irish autonomy harder to sustain. Since the notional
independence of Ireland had been based in part on the fetish of royal
authority, the exposure of one form of chimerical independence threatened to unmask another. It was partly because this changed relation
between crown and parliament was nowhere formalized that the fiction
could still be sustained – which is to say that the appearance of Irish
independence depended in part on the absence of writing. But the
asymmetry of the post-Union situation was enough to betray its fictive
status. If the sovereign power of the United Kingdom contained, so to
speak, an Irish admixture, then the free-born British fell as much under
a certain element of Irish dominion as vice versa. It is hard to believe
that many nineteenth-century Britons held that the supremacy to which
they paid homage owed anything to the prognathous creatures they
chuckled over in the *Punch* cartoons.

Paradox, metonymy, oxymoron: it is in terms of such tropes that the
relationship between imperial Britain and colonial Ireland has to be read.
What precisely is the grammar of Anglo-Irish relations? For two characters
in John Banim's novel *The Anglo-Irish of the Nineteenth Century*, this is a
slippery linguistic matter:

---

1. Quoted by Lady Ferguson, *Sir Samuel Ferguson in the Ireland of his Day*, vol. 1
(Edinburgh and London 1896), p. 207.
2. See Terry Eagleton, *The Ideology of the Aesthetic* (Oxford 1990), Ch. 1.

'After more than seven hundred years of identity with this country – '

'Not identity, Grady; that almost makes you speak a paradox', said the Secretary.

'Connexion, Sir?'

'No'.

'Then, Sir, conjunction?'

'Not even that, unless you mean our grammatical anomaly, a disjunctive conjunction...'

Which is to say that the text of the relationship is indecipherable – that there is a fundamental opacity or equivocation built into it, a subtle mis-matching of perceptions by which it refuses to add up to some luminously intelligible whole. As with the modernist work of art, there is a sense of it never quite achieving the wholeness for which it strives, of some slippage of the sign or skewing of narratives which threatens to undo any totalizing logic. And this failure of assured translation between the two nations is nowhere more vividly exemplified than in the present-day Irish constitution, an Irish-language text which assumes that in the event of an interpretative conflict between its meaning in Irish and in English, the Irish version will be deemed to take precedence over the English. But the Irish text is widely suspected to be itself a translation from the English; so that, by some Derridean logic of supplementarity, the derivative takes precedence here over the original. If a discrepancy arose from the Irish document having mistranslated the English, then a mistranslation would hold sway over the translated text.[3] Flann O'Brien himself could hardly have pulled off a more improbable scenario.

Fredric Jameson has argued that the modernist sense that meaning is no longer immanent in daily experience but always elsewhere, ceaselessly displaceable to some mysteriously absent cause, can be related to the conditions of colonialism, in which 'a significant structural segment of the economic system as a whole is now located elsewhere, beyond the metropolis, outside of the daily life and existential experience of the home country, in colonies over the water whose own life experience and life world – very different from that of the imperial power – remain unknown and unimaginable for the subjects of the imperial power...'[4] This is one way in which the narrative of colonialism becomes strangely scrambled, as the classical coherence of metropolitan life is undermined by its absent

---

3. See Conor Cruise O'Brien, 'The Embers of Easter 1916–1966', in Owen Dudley Edwards, ed., *The Easter Rising* (London 1968), p. 232.

4. Fredric Jameson, 'Modernism and Imperialism', in Seamus Deane, ed., *Nationalism, Colonialism and Literature* (Minneapolis 1990), pp. 50–51.

colonial cause; and Jameson goes on to suggest that what would be needed to model this elusive totality is a kind of half-way house, an exceptional national set-up which reproduces the appearance of 'first world' social reality but whose underlying structure is in fact much closer to that of the 'third world'. The name of this laboratory experiment in modernist literature is *Ulysses*. But the problem with Ireland is that the water to which Jameson alludes is so very narrow – narrow enough to trouble the distinction between 'inside' and 'outside', and so to defeat totality in this way too.

Ireland was indeed in one sense unimaginably remote to some of its proprietors: if a few intrepid British souls set foot there for the odd vacation it was because, so Sir Jonah Barrington considered, the place was as exotically alien to them as Kamchatka.[5] Affairs in Ireland, concluded an exasperated Lord Liverpool in 1816, were 'not influenced by the same feelings as appear to affect mankind in other countries'.[6] But the island was also unsettlingly close to hand. It is not, with Ireland, simply a question of some inscrutable Other, as an increasingly stereotyped discourse of stereotyping would have it; it is rather a matter of some unthinkable conundrum of difference and identity, in which the British can never decide whether the Irish are their antithesis or mirror image, partner or parasite, abortive offspring or sympathetic sibling. A colony is not just 'other' to its metropolis but its highly *particular* other – not simply different but, as it were, antithetical. It is a point well captured in Samuel Beckett's reply to the French interviewer who gullibly enquired whether he was English: '*Au contraire*'. If Britain is the source of authority, then it is the parent and Ireland the child; but if both bow to the jurisdiction of the crown, then the two nations instantly become siblings, recomposing their relationship in the light of this fetishized Law. It is a puzzle of which we have a microcosm in *Ulysses*: are Stephen and Bloom brothers or father and son, and if father and son then which is which?

The Anglo-Irish sometimes spoke of Britain as the mother country and Ireland as the sister nation, and sometimes of a brotherly affection between the two kingdoms.[7] Thomas Bartlett points out that whereas in

5. Quoted by Nicolas Mansergh, *The Irish Question 1840–1921* (London 1965), p. 49.

6. Quoted in Galen Broeker, *Rural Disorder and Police Reform in Ireland, 1812–36* (London and Toronto 1970), p. 1. The most exhaustive treatment of the stereotyping of the Irish, from antiquity to the eighteenth-century stage-Irishman, is Joseph Leerssen, *Mere Irish and Fior-Ghael* (Amsterdam 1986).

7. See A.P.W. Malcolmson, *John Foster: The Politics of the Anglo-Irish Ascendancy* (Oxford 1978), p. 369.

the pre-Union period the Irish liked to think of their relationship to
Britain as one of sisters, the British themselves thought of it in terms of
mother and child – with the ominous implication that a child can always
grow and demand independence.[8] The logic of the situation is incestuously
garbled: your brother is really your father, and you are both sister and
daughter. Indeed one might claim that incest is as fearful as it is precisely
because it writes large an intolerable riddle at the root of all identity.
Since all identity depends upon difference, I can only be truly myself by
uniting with the other; but to achieve such union completely would be
to abolish the difference between us, and along with it all possibility of
identity. Difference is both the ground and obstacle of relationship: if the
other ceases to be other to me, then in that very act I become alien to
myself. Banim is right to see identity as paradoxical; but the logic of
incest drives this paradox to an insupportable extreme, as what should be
other (the parent) becomes intimate (the lover). A curious inversion is at
work here, evident enough in Sophocles' Oedipus, whereby an excessive
intimacy with what should be off-bounds alienates you from yourself,
and so makes you a stranger to what is nearest to hand.

It is not hard to see the bearing of this paradox on Anglo-Irish relations,
from either end of the power structure. At once too near and too far,
akin and estranged, both inside and outside each other's cognitive range,
Britain and Ireland at least shared in common the crisis of identity which
each partner catalysed in the other; whereas if the Irish had been black,
unintelligible and ensconced in another hemisphere, savages of the desert
rather than the doorstep, their presence might have proved rather less
unnerving. It was, of course, thanks to British colonialism that they were
as culturally close as they were, so that when the British felt themselves
confronted by backyard barbarians they were merely reaping the harvest
of their own overfamiliarizing of them. The Act of Union between Great
Britain and Ireland has commonly been figured as a sexual coupling; but
it is a peculiarly incestuous form of congress, in which the border between
difference and identity, alienness and intimacy, is constantly transgressed,
and subject-positions (strangers, siblings, parents, spouses, partners) become
dizzyingly interchangeable. (As far as spouses go, Oliver MacDonagh
compares the influence of the Irish MPs at Westminster to that of
'Victorian women over husbands or fathers – not indeed in terms of
affection and compassion, but in terms of domestic miseries that might

---

8. Thomas Bartlett, *The Fall and Rise of the Irish Nation* (Dublin 1992), pp. 36–7.

ensue were they wholly thwarted, maltreated, or abandoned'.[9]) If your partner turns out to be a parent in thin disguise, then it is understandable that the incest taboo will spur you to revolt against this consanguinity, in that act of Oedipal aggression which is one feature of nationalism. Stephen Dedalus feels betrayed by his real father and so must either, like Jesus, become his own progenitor, or find a new parent in Leopold Bloom. Ireland, too, must throw off its false parent, Britain, and fashion its own forebear by reinventing its ancient past – in which case it becomes, in a familiar Oedipal fantasy, self-begotten. Yet such disavowals of dependency must be directed *at* the parent, and so remain a kind of negative bond or dialogue of antagonists. To disown another is at least to credit him with the capacity to recognize your refusal, and so to align him with oneself.

It is in this sense that separatism remains, in Lacanian parlance, a 'discourse of the Other', and not only in the more obvious sense that the very means of Irish nationalism, from literacy and communications to education and political organization, were largely British-made materials. Nationalism is an affirmation of difference or autonomy; but like the Oedipal revolt it makes sense only within the context of parental authority, and so is always at some level a performative contradiction, qualifying its declaration of freedom by the very situation in which it is forced to utter it. There is no genuine independence which is forced to assert itself. And since perceiving you as different was in one sense what the metropolitan nation did all along, nationalism represents a discourse of the Other in more ways than one. What you say in such circumstances is not at all to the colonialist's taste, and exactly what he wanted to hear.

There can be no union without distinct identity, otherwise what exactly is being unified? Identity is at once the precondition of unity, and its potential disruption; without a degree of identity there is nothing to amalgamate, and with too much identity no possibility of accord. It is hard to locate the delicate point of equipoise between the two – the point where you are at once enough something to become something else, and yet not so grossly self-identical as to resist all reciprocity. To

---

9. Oliver MacDonagh, 'Ireland and the Union 1801-70', in W.E.Vaughan, ed., *A New History of Ireland, vol. V: Ireland under the Union 1, 1801–70* (Oxford 1989), p. liii. MacDonagh comments elsewhere that the Land Acts of the end of the nineteenth century may have been dimly perceived in England as analogous to the Married Woman's Property Acts. See his 'Ambiguity in Nationalism: The Case of Ireland', in Ciaran Brady, ed., *Interpreting Irish History* (Dublin 1994), p. 108.

unite with another implies a persistence as well as a transformation of your previous identity, since it is *you* who have united; whereas a mere act of assimilation, as of the Irish parliament to the British in 1801, is in one sense no unity at all, since one of the terms in question has simply been abolished.[10] From this viewpoint, the Act of Union delivered the worst of all possible worlds. For what was at stake was not the coupling of two securely established identities, but the consummation of a long history in which the senior partner had so grievously undermined the identity of the junior that, like some lunatic driven to distraction and threatening both murder and self-destruction, the latter had to be taken into custody both for his own protection and for the safety of those around him. What was in one sense an act of voluntary merging was in effect one of annexation and appropriation; indeed it is interesting here to glance back to the language of the Declaratory Act of 1720, which speaks of Ireland as being 'inseparably United and Annexed' to Great Britain. There is an ambiguity in the word 'unite', which can mean a free mutuality, or – as with 'annexed' – the mere superadding of one thing to another. 'The United States' signals more than geographical contiguity. What happened in 1801, in certain respects at least, was a union rather in the sense that a burglar can be said to unite himself with one's domestic goods, or in which a mugging can be viewed as an equitable exchange between one's wallet and a blow on the skull. Ireland and Britain were united in the sense that the latter confiscated the former's parliament, and so rather as a fish can be said to be amalgamated with a diner through the act of eating. In the words of a seventeenth-century Munster planter, the British were to 'incorporate [the Irish] into ourselves, and so by a oneness take away the foundation of difference and fear altogether'.[11]

In one sense, Ireland, rather like a minor in law, had too little identity to enter into a marriage, and would not have needed to do so if it had not; in another sense it had all too strong a notion of itself, which was another reason why it required some marital curbing. If it was to be yoked into stifling intimacy with Britain, this was precisely because it was perceived as dangerously other. At one level, the two nations were to

---

10. Henry Grattan put the point in his own way in a parliamentary speech: 'Identification is a solid and imperial maxim, necessary for the preservation of freedom, necessary for that of empire; but without union of hearts, with a separate Government and without a separate Parliament, identification is extinction, is dishonour, is conquest – not identification' (quoted by W.E.H. Lecky, *Leaders of Public Opinion in Ireland*, London 1861, p. 143).

11. Quoted by Nicholas Canny, 'Identity Formation in Ireland', in Nicholas Canny and Anthony Pagden, eds, *Colonial Identity in the Atlantic World, 1500–1800* (Princeton 1987), p. 200.

enter into symbiotic union precisely so that one of them could be the more effectively treated as a special case. What linked them was the difference; what grappled them together, as with some tormented Lawrentian couple, was their mutual antagonism. In a case of what Theodor Adorno sees as the secret gesture of all ideology, identity was to be foisted upon non-identity; but that non-identity was itself, among other things, the product of a too-strong imperial selfhood. Britain and Ireland were now to pursue an equal, identical project of treating the latter unequally and non-identically; as with all the most effective forms of dominion, the freedom of the underlings lay in taking an active hand in their own subordination. The very difference of Ireland had created the need for a shared identity; but for those who objected to that arrangement, the difference would be merely exacerbated by it. It is in this sense that R.F. Foster can speak of the Union as preparing the way for its own dissolution.[12]

But if the Union delivered the worst of all worlds, it was because, failing to find the balance point between identity and non-identity, it treated Ireland at once differently and not differently enough. Indeed it was a familiar complaint of nineteenth-century nationalism that Britain did one or the other according to its own advantage. The Irish were different enough to require a special civil service and apparatus of repression, to be asked to foot the bill for the Famine, and to enjoy a peculiar franchise qualification. But they were alike enough to have MPs at Westminster in the first place, a privilege enjoyed by no other British colony, to contribute to the national debt, and to share with the imperial nation an exchequer, armed forces, postal services and a free-trade area. As far as economic life went, Ireland's integration with Britain had meant, over the years, gearing its production more and more to the British market – a symbiosis which then served to reinforce its industrial backwardness, and so ironically to foster its difference. On the other hand, there were several respects in which the colony was like its imperial masters, only more so. Precisely because of its difference, it could serve as a sphere for social experiments which would hardly have been readily countenanced at home, and so gained a national education system before Britain itself, one of the most advanced public-health establishments in Europe, public works and a streamlined paramilitary police force. This precociousness, needless to say, was not unconnected with the need to police and pacify a disaffected people; but some of these developments were significant

12. R.F. Foster, *Paddy And Mr Punch* (London 1993), p. 91.

advances in Irish civilization, testimony to the more positive, progressive face of the Union. From this viewpoint, Ireland differed from Britain by prolepsis, anticipating its own future evolution, and so could be seen as fundamentally identical, a mere fold in time in which the colonizing nation could view its own imminent destiny. From another viewpoint, Ireland was different from Britain because it was caught up in some archaic temporality, and had simply to enter upon the triumphal time-stream of European Enlightenment – its people happily Protestantized, its agriculture fully modernized, its barbarous customs discreetly erased – for its underlying identity with Britain to emerge. Each nation could thus glimpse something of its own future in the glass of the other; and the fact that the two time-streams were somewhat out of synchrony – that Ireland at once lagged behind the metropolitan nation and was in some ways out in front of it – was not of course accidental, since it was precisely its backward, recalcitrant nature which called for an unusual degree of state intervention. In the meantime, Britain treated Ireland differently when it suited it, leaving its half-rotten boroughs untouched by the 1832 Reform Bill and its local government firmly in the hands of the landowners, and identically when that suited it too, in the imposition, for example, of a poor law grotesquely ill-suited to native conditions.

In some cunning twist of Hegelian logic, then, the union of Britain and Ireland did and did not take place. What happened was that a metropolitan narrative was overlaid on a colonial one, to produce a radically undecidable text. As far as difference and identity go, it was hard to say whether the Union had changed everything or nothing whatsoever, as with some ontological shift so profound that almost nothing of it can be detected on the surface. Though the infantile sexual imagination may fantasize that the bride, on the morning after the wedding night, will rise mysteriously transformed, the reality proves somewhat more prosaic. Ireland had undergone the drama of a 'legislative union', which is to say that one legislature had been abolished rather than two harmoniously coupled. At this level, the union was so deep-seated, so profoundly accomplished, that one party entirely swallowed up the other. Unity implies an exchange of identities; but in this case the exchange seemed largely one-way. It is hard to see that Britain was being hibernicized in the sense that Ireland was being anglicized, whatever the English cult of the Celt which followed in the Union's wake. As in chemical catalysis, one of the elements of the synthesis appeared mysteriously unaltered. But this was hardly the whole story. The supplement, so Jacques Derrida has argued, is no mere addition to an already complete phenomenon, but alters its nature, reveals what was lacking to it all along.[13] Politically speaking, this was certainly true of the Union: dogged by the dull insistence of the 'Irish question', the course of life at Westminster could never be the same again.[14] But Walter Benjamin's sagacious dictum that 'the fact that "everything just goes on" *is* the crisis' also had its force. Ireland was now part of a United Kingdom; but it seemed something of an afterthought, which did little to modify the already assured identity of its masters. It had been a kingdom of the crown before the Union, and was part of a kingdom still. Its colonial apparatus remained firmly in place, indeed would be reinforced; and though a Dublin without the social retinue of its parliament was a rather less glamorous place, there was a sense in which Ireland under the Union was the status quo ante only more so.

From one viewpoint, it was as though the Union had simply made explicit, raised to the second power, what had been secretly true all along of a nation whose parliamentary independence had been partly a sham. The formal appearance of pre-Union independence had now given way to a real integration – though in another sense this was also a formal affair, and what mattered was the reality of continuing separate government. Certainly the nineteenth-century nationalists were to reject the Act of Union as mere appearance: for them the whole business was blatantly illegal, a 'usurpation and a fraud' as Arthur Griffith put it, and beneath this phenomenal show the essence of an autonomous Ireland secretly persisted, awaiting the moment when it would dramatically disclose itself. There was little in the affair either way for the mass of the people, who were not excessively fastidious about whose hand wielded the whip. In one sense, the forms of Irish authority – the legislative union – were grotesquely at odds with the nation's political reality. In another sense, in a notable dialectical achievement, Ireland had accomplished what it always was, realized its essence in its appearance; by its solemn elevation to partnership in the United Kingdom, it had ratified its own marginal condition. It had now been granted a seat at the very source of imperial power, so that some of its powers might be curbed; yet it had few enough to be dispossessed of in the first place. It would now help to rule itself

13. See Jacques Derrida, *Of Grammatology* (Baltimore and London 1974), Part 2, ii.

14. For the effect of the Union on Britain, see E. Strauss, *Irish Nationalism and British Democracy* (London 1951), a rare Marxist study of Ireland. Gearóid Ó Tuathaigh argues that the so-called Irish question in the post-Union period was often enough in Britain 'parabolic' of domestic issues there which could not be so readily discussed as such ('Nineteenth Century Irish Politics: The Case for "Normality"', *Anglo-Irish Studies*, no. 1, 1975).

through Westminster – which is to say, through the medium devoted to obstructing its genuine self-government. But it would retain a separate imperial executive, in flagrant violation of any genuine political partnership; and nobody could explain how these conflicting versions of the country's status were to be spliced convincingly together. Ireland was now exactly like anywhere else in Britain, and as unlike Yorkshire or Cornwall as it was possible to be; and in this sense, divided between colonial and metropolitan, juridical fiction and political reality, august kingdom and primitive periphery, it figured as a kind of political monstrosity, as hybrid and anomalous as the most avant-garde text. It was, perhaps, a fitting situation for a society in which the categories of majority and minority had traditionally been inverted – in which the only true citizens, bearers of the nation as a whole, had been a small group of gentlefolk marooned in a mass of marginal men and women. While the pre-Emancipation Catholic masses were physically present within the nation but politically absent from it, the situation of their landlords was often enough the reverse.

'Ireland', wrote Charles Greville to the Duke of Rutland in celebrated phrase, 'is too great to be unconnected with us, and too near us to be dependent on a foreign state, and too little to be independent.'[15] It is, in short, a nation so elusive and ambiguous that it can be defined only by negation; and it was just such negative motives which lay at the root of the Act of Union of 1800, whose several contradictions say much about Anglo-Irish relations as a whole. By that Act, a chronically backward, vulnerable, disaffected sector of the empire was formally integrated into Britain, as a way of protecting Britain's western flank from foreign invasion in a revolutionary epoch, pacifying the more dissident of its people and buttressing the power of a flagging Ascendancy.[16] But to ride to the rescue of that ruling caste was also implicitly to discredit it, casting an embarrassing vote of no confidence in its ability to stave off popular insurrection, and so undermining its authority in the very gesture of reinforcing it. As a move to contain revolutionary violence, the Act was unavoidably a concession to its effectiveness. The Ascendancy had always been, in Oliver MacDonagh's phrase, both overlords and dependents,[17] a client ruling class whose reliance on Britain was at once source of strength

15. Quoted by A.P.W. Malcolmson, *John Foster and the Politics of the Anglo-Irish Ascendancy* (Oxford 1978), pp. xxi–xxii.

16. For a detailed account of the politics of the Act of Union, see G.C. Bolton, *The Passing of the Irish Act of Union* (Oxford 1966).

17. Oliver MacDonagh, *States of Mind* (London 1983), p. 27.

and sign of weakness; and the Union made this divided condition even more visible.

The British government further sapped Anglo-Irish authority with its informal promise of Catholic emancipation, soon to be broken; but one of its aspirations, ironically enough, was to grant an increasingly paranoid Protestantism a deeper sense of security, and so breed in it a greater tolerance for its Catholic compatriots. If this hope proved too wan, then direct rule of Ireland from Westminster might at least give Britain a more active hand in protecting the Catholics from the more arrogant excesses of their superiors. If the Anglo-Irish would not cajole the Catholics, thus leaving them dangerously open to an alliance with revolutionary France, then the British would step in and do it on their behalf, thereby robbing the Ascendancy of their political initiative in the hope of securing for them a more stable future. Two birds might thus be improbably killed with the same stone, as the ruling minority was propped up and the disgruntled majority simultaneously placated. Irish Catholics were to be emancipated within a novel political framework (the United Kingdom) within which they formed a minority, and so were to be privileged and sidelined at a stroke. In this respect, the Union was a deliberately self-defeating phenomenon; in other ways it proved more unwittingly so, nurturing unintended results and reversals it was powerless to control. If many Catholics had initially supported the Union, they were later to identify it as a major barrier to their freedom, so that what was invented as a solution to political ills became, in an inversion of homeopathy, a problem and political target all in itself. On the other hand, some of the Protestants who had opposed the Union were soon its most ardent apologists, so that religious and political divisions were disastrously deepened by the move. Many Orangemen had fiercely resisted the Union precisely because they foresaw the odious corollary of Catholic Emancipation, and thus feared that a move intended to support the Protestant nation would end up by subverting it. As the cause of national independence passed by an ironic twist from Protestant to Catholic people, the Union, far from winning the allegiance of the Catholic masses, became the focus of a militant nationalism. In this sense, an original separatism – the United Irish movement – had led to fusion, and that in turn to a fresh drive for national autonomy. In drawing Ireland closer to itself, Britain had in one sense merely underlined the contrast between this formal partnership and the inequities of colonial power, thus stoking nationalist rancour in a notably self-thwarting move. In a further irony, the newly centralized power of the United Kingdom, in extending 'modernity' to Ireland in the form of new structures of civil society, provided the nationalists both with fresh grievances and with the means of articulating them. English-bred literacy, education, communications, political forms, were all in this way to prove conveniently double-edged weapons. What had started life as a remarkably ad hoc, cobbled-together affair – the Union itself – had rapidly escalated into a fresh set of permanent political antagonisms.

The Union, then, is replete with ironies, paradoxes, backfirings, unintended effects. Far from reconciling the Catholics, it provided them with a conveniently indeterminate focus of dissent, a totemic symbol of their scattered grievances, and thus ensured that any particular single-issue campaign was likely to press damagingly through to the question of the constitution itself. With the Irish parliament abolished, nationalist wrath was now aimed directly at Britain, and nationalism and imperialism brought face to face on a Westminster stage which ensured a world audience for the confrontation.[18] If the Union propped up the Protestant rulers, and so threatened to give free rein to their imperiousness, it also eroded their independence and left them dangerously insecure. It is hard to say whether Anglo-Irish arrogance or Anglo-Irish anxiety posed more of a threat to the Catholics. Britain was now directly tainted with the odium of Ascendancy, obliged, it would seem, to underwrite that authority however harmfully it was exercised; and the Ascendancy, buoyed up by the British state, could dream of indulging their irresponsibility to the full, like a profligate young aristocrat smugly aware that his father will settle his debts.[19] Yet having clinched the Union, the British began warily detaching themselves from their own kith and kin in Ireland, in the face of a Catholic nationalism which they urgently needed to appease. In this sense too, it was to prove a farcically self-defeating policy. The Union sharpened political divisions in Britain, and left the mass of the Irish people coolly indifferent, since many of them had little enough respect for the law in the first place. It was of no great moment to the agrarian agitators whether the laws they broke were framed in Dublin or London. The whole arrangement moved at a constitutional level sufficiently remote from the realities of power in Ireland, which in the post-Union period were commonly enough those of coercive legislation and the soldier's rifle. One semi-fiction – the 'union' of Britain and Ireland – thus

18. See Donal McCartney, *The Dawning of Democracy: Ireland 1800–1870* (Dublin 1987), p. 16.

19. For a useful account of some of the effects of the Union, see Patrick O'Farrell, *Ireland's English Question* (London 1971).

contained another: the assumption that constitutional politics had a monopoly of all significant power.

It is possible, then, to see the various contradictions of the Union as symptomatic of Anglo-Irish relations as a whole, in which difference and identity are continually transformed into each other. Karl Marx understood well enough how an abstract equality could both foster and conceal injustice, crushing specific needs beneath a spurious equivalence; and this is obvious enough in colonial Ireland, where a formal principle of parity required that the country was subjected to, say, a type of British poor law or *laissez faire* economics, thus creating non-parity in the shape of a greater wretchedness. To treat others equally is not to treat them as mirror images of oneself, but to extend to them one's own freedom to become what one desires. Difference and equality are not simple opposites: the more Ireland crept closer to an equality with Britain, the more firmly it needed to be held in place. 'The more wealthy Ireland became', comments Edmund Curtis, 'and the more equality with Great Britain she attained, the more necessary it seemed to Great Britain to "manage" her.'[20] The contrast between equality and inequality is also one between intention and effect: in different social conditions, the same even-handed measures will breed divergent consequences, and so cease to be identical. Britain would legislate for itself, only to find that it had, so to speak, inadvertently legislated for Ireland too. To extend to the colony its own democratic reforms was to bring it more securely within its civilized orbit; but it was also to risk undermining the undemocratic power of the Ascendancy, and so to risk creating more instability for itself. A similar play of difference and identity can be seen in nationalism, which shifts between a demand for equality and an assertion of difference, between constitutional text and separatist subtext. And there are those who would claim that, just as colonialism is potentially self-undoing, unavoidably handing its subjects the weapons by which they might bring it low, so nationalism can advance only by adopting the methods of its oppressors, thus baffling its own demands.

The ratio of difference and equality, so Christopher Clapham argues, varies from one type of colonialism to another. French colonialism, Clapham claims, is typically centralizing and assimilationist: it regards native cultures as largely worthless, but offers its peoples the chance to integrate

---

20. Edmund Curtis, *A History of Ireland* (London 1978), p. 323. For an examination of the equities and inequities of post-Union Ireland, see Oliver MacDonagh, *The Union and its Aftermath* (London 1977), Ch. 2.

with an enlightened metropolis by becoming French citizens themselves. British colonialism is rather more particularist: since the natives cannot really aspire to become English, they must be ruled, in part at least, through their own cultural forms and political institutions. Imperial government, rather than seeking to raise the benightedly particular to the universal, descends to the particular and implants itself within it. The colonies have their own distinctive destinies and rhythms of development, which must become the very medium of colonial power.[21] One might see this as a distinction between the political and the cultural. For the French, the ideal goal is political citizenship, which an Algerian or Viet-namese may in principle attain; for the British, identity is essentially a cultural affair, so that the thought of a British Asian or African is merely absurd. Edmund Burke is one of the most eloquent exponents of this British particularism; but how is this concern with cultural difference to be squared with the integrationist policy of the Act of Union, a policy of which he himself was sceptical and which he did not live to see? Ireland would seem in this way too something of an anomalous case, caught on the hop between difference and identity, culture and politics, particular and universal. The Union is an uneasy compromise between French and British strategies, seeking to impose identity on what the British, in another quarter of their mind, recognize as two distinct, organically evolving cultures. There is something incongruous about the Hibernian apes of the *Punch* cartoons, creatures of a different planet and time-scale entirely, enjoying political representation in the British parliament; but this bizarre commingling of cultural orders, in which a society in the wings of history also came to hold centre stage, was forced on the British government in the heat of revolutionary crisis, and had then to be lived with as best it could.

Sylvester Douglas, former Chief Secretary of Ireland, writes in the year of the Act of Union that relations between Britain and her colony are 'in constant danger of misapprehension and dispute, and subject to the in-conveniences which inevitably arise from circuity of communication, and the impediments and embarrassing modifications to which jealousy or ignorance on the one side or the other will so often give occasion'.[22]

---

21. See Christopher Clapham, *Third World Politics: An Introduction* (London 1992), pp. 21f.

22. Quoted by R.B. McDowell, *Ireland in the Age of Imperialism and Revolution* (Oxford 1979), pp. 686–7.

Douglas's comment is hardly a masterpiece of lucidity itself; but it pin-points well enough the sense of some constant scrambling of communi-cation between the two nations. For the Irish Irelander D.P. Moran, this was itself positive testimony to Ireland's uniqueness: 'international mis-understanding', he writes without a flicker of irony, 'is one of the marks of nationhood.'[23] For Treasury undersecretary Charles Trevelyan, what finally dispelled British misconceptions of Ireland was the Famine. 'The case of Ireland', he writes, 'is at last understood. Irish affairs are no longer a craft and mystery. The abyss has been fathomed.'[24] This, however, was a misconception. The history of Anglo-Irish relations is among other things the story of a ceaselessly garbled conversation, of partners speaking resolutely past each other, of obtuse or well-intentioned misappre-hensions.[25] How could it be otherwise, when the two parties shared a common history, but shared it precisely from conflicting positions, and so with colliding versions of the centuries-old transactions which had passed between them? John Stuart Mill believed that Britain, of all 'civilized' nations, was the least well-placed to understand the Irish – partly because no other nation was so 'conceited of its institutions', partly because no other was so remote from Ireland in its social and economic history.[26]

Taken overall, the British response to Ireland was quite astonishingly ignorant, bigoted and thickheaded, lurching from transparently false opti-mism to a desperate faith that if the country were ignored for long enough it might just sidle away. As humble yet crucial a word as 'farm' could breed different meanings on each side of the water, as the British thought of well-cultivated estates and the Irish of a few acres of stony soil. That England had lost its own peasantry, indeed looked askance on the whole notion of a peasantry as anti-modern, did not help in this respect. If the British thought in terms of contract and utility, there was at work in popular Irish attitudes a doctrine of moral economy, which could generate systematic misunderstanding with their masters.[27] The triumph of the

---

23. D.P. Moran, 'The Battle of Two Civilisations', in Lady Gregory, ed., *Ideals in Ireland* (Dublin 1901), p. 25.

24. C.E. Trevelyan, *The Irish Crisis* (London 1848), p. 187.

25. 'Cumulatively, it is perhaps a mass of commonplace, unnoticed discordance of meaning and connotation which has set and still sets Anglo-Irish communication most askew' (MacDonagh, *States of Mind*, p. 13). For an excellent account of Anglo-Irish misunderstand-ings, see Patrick O'Farrell, *England and Ireland since 1800* (Oxford 1975).

26. John Stuart Mill, *England and Ireland* (London 1868), p. 9.

27. See Thomas Bartlett, 'An End to Moral Economy', *Past and Present*, no. 99 (1983). The classic study of the concept is E.P. Thompson, *Customs in Common* (London 1991), especially Chs 4 and 5.

landlord was the triumph of writing: Deasy's Act of 1860 based the relationship between landlord and tenant 'on the express or implied contract of the parties and not upon tenure or service'. Gladstone's egregiously ineffective Land Act of 1870 was inspired in part by the assumption that the grievances of Irish farmers might be met by the granting of longer leases. He did not grasp that the tenant considered himself to have a natural right to his land as long as he paid his rent, and that any sort of fixed lease would limit this prerogative. In seeking contractual security for the tenant, Gladstone succeeded in dispelling a salutary vagueness in the existing arrangements which could work in the tenant's favour.

The Act was founded on a whole series of misreadings: of the causes and frequency of eviction, of the supposed superiority of Ulster agriculture and the presumed role in this of the so-called Ulster custom, of the part played by security of tenure in agricultural productivity.[28] Some of these misperceptions were particularly ironic, since Gladstone himself was well aware of the role of custom and moral obligation in the Irish countryside. It was he, not some morbidly nostalgic Fenian, who remarked that the 'old Irish ideas were never supplanted except by the rude hand of violence – by laws written on the State Book, but never entering into the heart of the Irish people'.[29] Two texts, the one written and contractual, the other tacit and traditional, were thus at loggerheads;[30] and – most unusually in the course of modern agrarian capitalism – it was the latter which was to triumph, as tenant rights became enshrined in the various Land Acts of the *fin de siècle*. It was the finale of a long-running conflict between English and Irish ways of seeing. Sir Marmaduke Travers, the returned English absentee landlord of Charles Lever's novel *The O'Donoghue*, has benevolent intentions towards his tenants but cannot understand the character of the people. Ignorant of their manners and mores, he fails to grasp that they define the 'same' material matters differently from himself; and this is a common enough motif in Anglo-Irish writing, from Maria Edgeworth's *The Absentee* onwards. It is no accident that John Stuart Mill, enlightened apologist for Ireland, should also have proposed a new science of Ethology, which would take as its subject-matter the distinctive culture and psychology of a people.[31]

---

28. See Sally Warwick-Haller, *William O'Brien and the Irish Land War* (Dublin 1990), p. 24.
29. Quoted by D. George Boyce, *Nationalism in Ireland* (London 1982), p. 213.
30. See J.C. Beckett, *The Making of Modern Ireland 1603–1923* (London 1981), p. 373.
31. See John Stuart Mill, *A System of Logic* (London 1843), Book 6, Ch. 5.

It may be that there is a deeper, more structural dimension to this dialogue of the deaf – or at least that a psychoanalytic analogy may help, if not to account for it, then at least to illuminate it. For Jacques Lacan, the demand for full recognition by the other is tragically unrealizable for at least two reasons. For one thing, the other must interpret one's demand for what it is; but one can never be entirely sure that this has happened, given that the demand itself, in order to attain expression, must pass through the defiles of the duplicitous signifier. The meaning of speech depends upon the response of its addressee; but since this response, too, must pass through the ambigious medium of signification, we can never be entirely sure that our demand has been acceded to. For another thing, the other will receive one's demand only from within the distorting perspective of his or her own desire, which will then render it doubly opaque. It is for this reason that Lacan writes the 'other' with a capital O, to signify that structural non-reciprocity or miscommunication which we call the unconscious.[32] In seeking the recognition of the Other, I am led by this very desire to misrecognize it, grasping it in the imaginary mode. There is an Irish demand; but the British can never be sure that they have interpreted it correctly, since its form of articulation seems constantly to change. 'The Pope one day and potatoes the next', as Disraeli wearily put it. At one moment the call is for land reform or an independent parliament; then it takes the form of a struggle against tithes or godless universities, a plea for electoral reform or the repeal of the Union; next it shifts back to the land question, but adds an appeal for Home Rule or a threat of republican separatism. The British, when seized by a fit of receptiveness, attend to the demand and seek, for the most part belatedly, inadequately and under dire threat of coercion, to accommodate it; but they may find themselves here in the situation of the Lacanian adult vis-à-vis the infant, who in catering to the child's immediate needs fails to decipher the absolute demand for recognition obscurely encoded within them, and so unwittingly crushes that demand in the very act of relieving the infant's want. Since the infant can only express this impossibly general demand for recognition in narrowly specific terms, in gestures which at

---

32. These ideas crop up at various points in Lacan's work; but see, for an important source, 'The Subversion of the Subject and the Dialectic of Desire in the Freudian Unconscious', in *Écrits: A Selection* (London 1977). For an excellent exposition of Lacan's thinking on these matters, see Peter Dews, *Logics of Disintegration* (London 1987), Ch. 2. The Young Irelander John Mitchel remarks in his *Jail Journal* of the Cape Colony that 'whatever is done here can only be said to be inchoate, provisional, and not a perfect act, until news of it go to England, and an answer return' (*Jail Journal*, reprinted Dublin 1982, p. 210).

once reveal and conceal it, this misapprehension is built into its transactions with the parent. The infant may then, so to speak, shift ground and try again; but the same structural misprision is bound to occur; and in the rift between need and demand will germinate desire, that objectless, insatiable hankering which is born of the despair of one's demand ever being fulfilled.

A Lacanian Irish rebel song makes the point precisely:

> When we were savage, fierce and wild
> She came like a mother to her child
> And gently raised us from the slime
> And kept our hands from hellish crime
> And she sent us to heaven in her own good time.
>
> Now Irishmen forget the past
> And think of a day that is coming fast
> When we shall all be civilised
> Neat and clean and well advised
> Oh won't mother England be surprised?

It is not hard to read the sardonic humour of this as displaced rage. Ironically complying with the mother's wishes is a way of not complying with them at all – of fulfilling them only to draw her attention to the gap between her desires and expectations, and so turning the insult back on herself. The elaborate obedience with which you meet her wishes is simply a way of signalling their worthlessness. It is not that the mother has failed to attend to the child's needs; it is just that she has blandly misconceived them. And this brings us to the second Lacanian cause of the garbled discourse: the fact that the other will receive one's demand only through the distorting prism of his own desire, which is to say, in the case of Britain, of its own political interests. It is in this sense, as Lacan insists, that one always receives back one's demand from the Other, from that place where it has been refracted through a language which always precedes you. Dispiritingly enough, you will emerge into exist-ence as an 'autonomous' subject only on the basis of that alienated image of your demand which the response of the Other returns to you. If the Irish appeal seems mystifyingly to alter from one moment to another, or at least from decade to decade, it is for good political reasons; but it is also as though it is striving to outflank this dire condition to which all human dialogue is apparently doomed, shuttling from political to cultural to economic registers in the hope of discovering the transcendental signifier which will say it all. But if the demand is finally for a recog-nition of your autonomy, then it cannot properly be uttered, since it will need to pass through the discourse of the Other and so will be assimilated to the very conversation from which you hope to extricate yourself. As long as the demand for independence must be addressed elsewhere, and there is no demand which is not, it is bound to constitute a scrambled message. The Irish could never be sure that they were receiving back a response to their appeal because the British had usually misunderstood the question, passing it through the defiles of their own signifiers; but this misreading is then fed back into the demand itself, which begins to revise itself in the light of its own alienated image.

We are always at some level told how and what we may ask for, and the Irish were no exception. What they wanted depended to some degree on what they thought they might get; O'Connell declared himself interested in nothing but an independent legislature, adding with swift illogicality that were someone to offer him a subordinate parliament instead he would not refuse. The discourse of the colonial is always rhetoric which overhears itself in the ears of the other, shaping itself accordingly; and as long as one's demand is in this sense dialogical, it can never remain self-identical. So it was that the Irish came to direct their own speech and actions at the British (mis)understanding of them, in ways that then introduced division and ambiguity into their own language. 'The relation between the two races', writes Elizabeth Bowen in *The House in Paris*, 'remains a mixture of showing off and suspicion, nearly as bad as sex. Where would the Irish be without someone to be Irish at?' The Irish are no doubt no more remarkable for showing off than any other people; but there was certainly a sense in which they knew themselves to be permanently on stage. And it is suitably symbolic that two of their greatest champions, Daniel O'Connell and Charles Stewart Parnell, displayed in their discourse a mastery of equivocation and ambiguity which would have been the envy of a Mallarmé. As that oxymoronic animal, a radical landlord, Parnell could offer himself as a conveniently indeterminate space in which different forces – Fenianism, constitutionalism, agrarian agitation – might temporarily congregate. He was not the only Irish leader to live his existence as a kind of symbol, converting his Anglo-Irish aloofness into a blankness in which others could find themselves conveniently reflected.

The fact that a radical demand must be expressed in the language of the present, and so in terms of what it opposes, has sometimes been used to convict it of bad faith. Irish nationalism castigated British culture, but where would it have been without it? The very processes which brought it to birth – education, the press, modern political structures – emerged, ironically enough, from the dissolution of the traditional culture from which nationalism drew its inspiration. It was, so the argument runs, a product of the very British modernity it so fervently denounced, and so was locked in hopeless self-contradiction. A similar charge can be levelled at Marxism, with its 'capitalist' obsession with the economic, or at the kind of feminism which complains of the lack of female chief constables. There is certainly a fair amount in nationalism which mimics the power it opposes; but the criticism, as it stands, is altogether too facile. There is no contradiction in the fact that radical movements are products of the system they seek to contest; if they were not, but moved instead in some metaphysically distinct space, they would be incapable of challenging it. One can only logically speak of conflict if two power systems share a world in common. Those who regard nationalism as the mere inversion of imperialism, or feminism as patriarchally obsessed with sexual power, would no doubt be the first to denounce these beliefs as idle utopianism should they seek to invent a language of their own from scratch.

Quite who is in bad faith here, then, is a matter for debate. Such political movements are forms of immanent critique, which find themselves installed within the logic of what they oppose, and for just that reason are able to press that logic through to an outside or beyond which is political emancipation. A truly radical demand is by definition one which deconstructs the 'inside/outside' opposition.[33] If the fact that it shares in what it rejects opens a perpetual possibility of bad faith, it is also an opportunity for pressing beyond it. In Irish nationalism, the tension implicit in the phrase 'immanent critique' could be damagingly relaxed on either side: into a mere shadowing of the regime it confronted, or into an ultra-leftist purism which refused all truck with it. But that a demand for radical change must work with the contaminated materials of the present is no objection to it, and no assurance of its futility. It is simply a reminder that all political demands are impure; but that, after all, is one of the first lessons of materialism, and one with which the liberal can heartily agree.

---

33. The point has often been made with regard to feminism: if a woman speaks intelligibly she has been coopted; if she remains on the margin her discourse is dismissed as senseless. John Mitchel make much the same point from a nationalist perspective: 'If I profess myself a disbeliever in that gospel [of success], the Enlightened Age will only smile, and say, "The defeated always are." Britain being in possession of the floor, any hostile comment upon her way of telling our story is an unmannerly interruption; nay, is nothing short of an *Irish howl*' (*Jail Journal*, p. xxxvii).

CHAPTER 5

FORM AND IDEOLOGY IN THE ANGLO-IRISH NOVEL

That the novel in Ireland never flourished as vigorously as its English counterpart is surely no mystery. For culture demands a material base; and a society as impoverished as Ireland was hardly in a position to provide one. The notion that the Act of Union of 1800 decimated the Irish economy is nowadays widely dismissed as a nationalist myth;[1] but the Union certainly played havoc with the country's publishing industry. Before 1800, the Irish book trade had been heavily reliant on reprinting British works, since British copyright did not apply in Ireland; but with the advent of the Union, a Copyright Act placed Irish printers and publishers for the first time under the same legal constraints as their metropolitan counterparts. With the reprint business gone, the industry was plunged into severe distress: printers were forced to rely largely on jobbing work, apprentices were cruelly exploited, and even some of their masters were reduced to breaking stones on government outdoor relief schemes. A good deal of printing still went on, boosted by the Kildare Place Society's cheap propagandizing literature for the poor; but this was hardly of the stature of a *Mansfield Park* or *Martin Chuzzlewit*, and by the mid century the Famine had brought widespread bankruptcies to the book trade. One or two of its members responded to the crisis with remarkable resourcefulness: an engraver began printing unauthorized banknotes and a barrow bookseller engaged in highway robbery, but both ended up on the gallows.[2]

---

1. A classic statement of the post-Union decline thesis is to be found in George O'Brien, *The Economic History of Ireland from the Union to the Famine* (Dublin and London 1921). O'Brien became the first government-appointed director of the Abbey Theatre, and strongly objected to Sean O'Casey's *The Plough and the Stars*.

2. See Charles Benson, 'Printers and Booksellers in Dublin 1800–1850', in R. Myers and M. Harris, eds, *Spreading the Word* (Winchester 1990), pp. 47–59. It is perhaps worth adding that the total number of books published in Ireland between 1900 and 1969 was less than a single year's publishing production in England.

The historical irony is apparent. At the very point when the English novel was entering on its maturity, the Irish literary institution found itself in a lamentable condition. The result of the political union of the two nations, in this respect at least, was the intensified cultural subordination of the junior partner. In the Preface to an 1842 edition of his *Traits and Stories of the Irish Peasantry*, the novelist William Carleton writes of how Irish authors had followed the example of the landlords and become absentees in Britain, draining the country of its intellectual wealth as surely as the landlords exhausted it of its rents. But this exodus of Irish writers to London had marked the eighteenth century too, since their manuscripts were then legally unprotected in their own country. The life of the émigré Irish writer was hardly an enviable one: indeed one might reconstruct from the grim biographies of a few actual authors a composite stereotype of the species. Socially displaced, chronically insolvent, racked by physical ailment and deflated hopes, the Irish writer in London alternately courted and denounced the metropolitan literary establishment, alienated in equal measure from the people who bred him and the audience who read him. Neurotically defensive of his reputation, outwardly respectable but concealing a certain smouldering animus, he enjoyed a brief, brilliant flourishing but declined in his later years into obscurity and isolation. As William O'Brien ruefully remarked of his experience of hawking his Irish novels around English publishers: the Irish wouldn't buy it because they were too poor, and the English because they were too English.[3]

The situation, even so, was not entirely bleak. Despite the Copyright Act of 1801, the nineteenth century was to witness a veritable revolution in literacy and education. The establishment of a national schooling system in 1831, the literary evangelizing of the Kildare Place Society and a host of other high-minded associations, the proliferation of booksellers and libraries: all of this resulted in a dramatic rise in popular literacy in English, as in the early nineteenth century the Irish language entered upon its sharp decline.[4] There may, however, be rather more particular reasons

---

3. Quoted by John Kelly, 'The Political, Intellectual and Social Background to the Irish Literary Revival to 1901', unpublished Ph.D. thesis (University of Cambridge 1972), p. 71.

4. See the essays by Garret FitzGerald, Graeme Kirkham, Linda Lunny and John Logan in M. Daly and D. Dickson, eds, *The Origins of Popular Literacy in Ireland: Language Change and Educational Development 1700–1920* (Dublin 1990). For education and literacy in Ulster, see J.R.R. Adams, *The Printed Word and the Common Man* (Belfast 1987). The topic of literacy is also examined in Mary Feeney, 'Print for the People: the Growth in Popular Writing and Reading Facilities in Ireland, 1820–50' (unpublished M.Litt. thesis, Trinity College, Dublin). David Lloyd has some perceptive comments on the social conditions of the Irish novel in his *Anomolous States* (Dublin 1993), Ch. 5.

why the *realist* novel thrived less robustly in Ireland than in Britain. For literary realism requires certain cultural preconditions, few of which were available in Ireland. The realist novel is the form *par excellence* of settlement and stability, gathering individual lives into an integrated whole;[5] and social conditions in Ireland hardly lent themselves to any such sanguine reconciliation. What resolutions the Irish novel does bring off have a notably factitious ring to them, fabular inventions or schematic devices which cut against the grain of the fiction itself. It might be objected that Britain in the nineteenth century was hardly an oasis of tranquillity either; but its rulers were equipped with an ideology of enlightened progress which was generally lacking in Ireland. Classical realism depends on the assumption that the world is story-shaped – that there is a well-formed narrative implicit in reality itself, which it is the task of such realism to represent. The disrupted course of Irish history is not easily read as a tale of evolutionary progress, a middle march from a lower to a higher state; and the Irish novel from Sterne[6] to O'Brien is typically recursive and diffuse, launching one arbitrary narrative only to abort it for some other equally gratuitous tale, running several storylines simultaneously, ringing pedantically ingenious variations on the same few plot elements. Christopher Morash has even detected this anti-linear prejudice in the fragmented prose style of the Young Irelander John Mitchel.[7]

The tradition of Irish fiction begins with one of the world's greatest anti-novels, and achieves its apotheosis in a couple of others. As the nineteenth-century Irish poet Aubrey de Vere comments : 'History implies a succession of events depending each on the preceding, a series of external actions capable of being referred to internal causes, an exposition of the mind and life of a nation by means of impulses flowing from within, and though confused, not seldom by jarring accidents, yet on the whole moulding outward circumstances to an image of itself, and methodizing them to something of an intelligible unity.'[8] Measured against this

---

5. See Franco Moretti, *The Way of the World* (London 1987).

6. Sterne is of course a liminal case for Irish literary history, but his great novel strikingly prefigures Irish literary modernism.

7. See Christopher A. Morash, 'Imagining the Famine: Literary Representations of the Great Irish Famine' (unpublished Ph.D. thesis, Trinity College, Dublin 1990), p. 167. I am most grateful to Dr Morash for the gift of a copy of his thesis.

8. Aubrey de Vere, *English Misrule and Irish Misdeeds* (London 1868), pp. 100–101. On the idea of the absence of a system of historical self-representation in Ireland, and the effects of this on literature, see Robert Welch, *Changing States: Transformations in Modern Irish Writing* (London 1993), Ch. 2.

idealist paradigm, the very essence of 'historicist' thinking, Ireland in de Vere's view has no history at all. It is a view endorsed with rather less nationalist pathos by the historian J.A. Froude, in his savagely polemical history of eighteenth-century Ireland: '[The Irish] have no secular history, for as a nation they have done nothing which posterity will not be anxious to forget; and if they have never produced a tolerable drama, it is because imagination cannot outstrip reality.'[9] For the young James Joyce, Ireland was a drama on which the curtain had not yet gone up, and he preferred, so he said, to take the last bus home rather than stay to see the performance.[10] The Young Irelander Gavan Duffy, by contrast, believed that Irish history has an internal coherence precisely because of its aesthetic stucture: 'The history of Ireland abounded in noble lessons, and had the unity and purpose of an epic poem.'[11]

Realism, so the Formalists instruct us, works by concealing its mechanisms, whereas Irish writing more commonly lays bare the device, and so lends itself more obviously to modernism. Perhaps this stems from a sense of the presumptuousness of such aesthetic autonomy in oppressive social conditions; or perhaps there is still a dim sense of the artifice of print in a traditionally oral culture. 'I naturally dislike print and paper', remarks the logocentric Yeats in his *Essays and Introductions*, somewhat surprisingly for one who landed a Nobel prize by them. 'Literature', writes George Russell, 'is, after all, only an ineffectual record of speech', and he launches instantly upon a hymn in praise of the human voice.[12] The question of national languages is relevant here too: 'Irish literature', as Seamus Deane remarks, 'tends to dwell on the medium in which it is written because it is difficult not to be self-conscious about a language which has become simultaneously native and foreign'.[13] In any case, much Irish writing is of an activist, interventionist kind: the sermon, the political pamphlet, the speech from the dock or the hustings; and such performative discourse must calculate in its own occasion, as realism must feign to be oblivious of it. The true literary centres of Ireland in the late eighteenth century were the busy presses of the United Irish movement, with their pamphlets, broadsheets and handbills distributed throughout the most inaccessible

9. James Anthony Froude, *The English in Ireland in the Eighteenth Century* (London 1872), vol. 1, p. 22.

10. E. Mason and R. Ellmann, eds, *The Critical Writings of James Joyce* (New York 1959), p. 174.

11. Charles Gavan Duffy, *Young Ireland* (London 1880), p. 44.

12. AE (George Russell), 'Nationality and Cosmopolitanism in Art', in *Some Irish Essays* (Dublin 1906), p. 26.

13. Seamus Deane, *Celtic Revivals* (London 1985), p. 13.

reaches of the countryside, their newspapers declaimed in public places to an unevenly literate populace, their adoption of a demotic style of prose.[14] Glancing back at the Repeal agitation, Charles Gavan Duffy remarks that it would have been improbable for a 'great creative artist' to emerge from such political turmoil; the most that could be hoped for was 'historical tales and dramatic sketches' in a traditional ballad-like spirit.[15] Political instability is the ruin of disinterested representation, and as such a significant curb on a major literary realism. And in an intensively politicized society which looked to its art for ideological inspiration, the ballad is likely to triumph over the more complex, discursive form of the novel.

Realism aspires to a unity of subject and object, of the psychological and the social; but these in Ireland tend to split into separate genres, with the naturalism of a Carleton or Lever aligned against the exotic fantasies of so-called Protestant Gothic. If the novel form belongs with bourgeois individualism, then it is hardly surprising that it flourishes less robustly in pre-industrial Catholic Ireland than in liberal Protestant Britain; and if, as Henry James believed, it is nurtured by a richly intricate texture of social manners, its lower profile in one of Europe's poorest nations is only to be expected. Sean O'Faolain was much taken by James's claim that the novel requires a 'complex social machinery', and oppressed by his own sense of Ireland as a '"thin" society, stuff for the anthropologist rather than the man of letters',[16] turned from realist fiction to the short story. The most ancient literary modes in Ireland are heroic, romantic, fantastic; and the remoteness of such aristocratic forms from everyday life is no fit breeding ground for the novel, which is born of the middle class's dawning awareness that their own quotidian experience can be dramatically exciting. Far from embracing these humdrum conditions, much Irish writing turns its back on them, recycling the riddling wordplay and extravagant dream world of the ancient sagas in the face of a reality which is more to be disavowed than tenderly reproduced.[17] Just as the Arab novel was nipped in the bud by the Koran, so the sacred Irish sagas threw their long shadow over the development of a secular fiction, which found it hard to break from legend to novel.

---

14. See Kevin Whelan, 'The United Irishmen, the Enlightenment and Popular Culture', in D. Dickson, D. Keogh and K. Whelan, eds, *The United Irishmen: Republicanism, Radicalism and Rebellion* (Dublin 1993).

15. Charles Gavan Duffy, vol. 1 *Young Ireland* (London 1880), pp. 289–90. See also H.R. Montgomery, *Essays on the Causes of the Retarded Progress of Literature in Ireland* (Dublin 1840).

16. Quoted by Terence Brown, *Ireland's Literature: Selected Essays* (Mullingar 1988), p. 99.

17. For the wordplay of the sagas, see Vivian Mercier, *The Irish Comic Tradition* (Oxford 1962), Ch. 4.

One of the most successful pieces of fiction of the Celtic Revival, James Stephens's *The Crock of Gold* (1912), is an enchanting fairy tale, a kind of cross between folklore and Flann O'Brien.[18] Another such masterpiece of the time, Seumas O'Kelly's *The Weaver's Grave* (1919), conjures a wealth of implication from a single sparse action. If reality is not disowned in Irish writing, then in a venerable tradition from Sterne to Beckett it is calculatedly banal, opening an ironic rift between its own meagreness and the self-consciously elaborate languages used to record it. This bathetic gap between form and content, of which *Ulysses* is the supreme modern example, is then among other things an index of the condition of the colonial writer, wryly conscious of the discrepancy between the exuberance of the signifier and the meanness of the referent. If the realist novel revolves on settlement, the short story turns on a moment of revolt or revelation which it is hard to totalize or sustain; and this, along with its closeness to oral performance, is no doubt one reason for its prominence in Irish fiction, as the home of a brooding, isolated subjectivity confronting a recalcitrant world.[19] 'Through a kind of law of the excluded middle,' writes John Wilson Foster, 'solipsism has seemed to be for the Irish mind and imagination the only alternative to the selflessness of myth and nationality. The excluded middle is realism, objectivity, and the proper marriage of self and society.'[20]

There are other reasons, however, why an Irish *Middlemarch* is difficult to envisage. If the realist novel is the form of stability, it is also the home of totality. Gifted at once with with a quick insight into minute particulars, and with the imaginative power to discern the whole pattern which they compose, the realist novel is the very model of liberal impartiality. Such an Olympian standpoint is harder to come by in a divided society, where art, like the rest of intellectual life, is more directly bound to partisan ends. Indeed the greatest Irish novel is a masterpiece of *ironic* totalization. In grand Arnoldian manner, Isaac Butt complains that the growth of a valuable literature in Ireland has been thwarted by shallow sectarian attachments, and bemoans the lack of that 'spirit of refinement and severe good taste' that might 'correct, reduce, chasten, and harmonize the tumultuous and turbid exuberance of our unprincipled and random

---

18. See also Stephens's excellent novel *The Charwoman's Daughter* (Dublin 1912). This major figure of the Celtic Revival has yet to be given his due in Anglo-Saxon criticism.

19. See Declan Kiberd, 'Story-telling: the Gaelic Tradition', in P. Rafroidi and T. Brown, eds, *The Irish Short Story* (Lille 1979).

20. John Wilson Foster, *Fictions of the Irish Literary Revival* (Syracuse 1987), pp. 181–2.

literature'.[21] Art demands serenity, stable evolution, classical equipoise; and an island racked by rancorous rhetoric is hardly the appropriate breeding ground for these virtues.[22] Whatever Butt's neo-classical aesthetic, there is no doubt that Ireland has been a remarkably difficult society to totalize.

If there is a novel of the gentry and the Big House, there is also the fiction of small farmer, cleric and shopkeeper; but the two rarely converge in some synoptic viewpoint, of the kind we habitually witness in a Balzac or Dickens. There are notably few Irish novels which, in the style of an Eliot, alternate in their pages the perspectives of higher and lower classes. This is not necessarily because of the author's own constricted class standpoint: Emily Lawless was the daughter of a nobleman, but though her fine novel *Hurrish* (1886) includes a perceptive portrait of the harrassed landlord, its focus is on the life of the poor farmers of Clare. In the annals of Irish fiction, the world is caught from within a range of social standpoints; but these diverse cultures rarely enter into reciprocal interaction in a particular text. Constrained by a history of conflict, the Irish novel is strikingly non-dialogical: whatever the social position adopted, its antagonist is typically what Mikhail Bakhtin would call an objectified consciousness. If Leopold Bloom has something of the all-embracing sympathies of the realist novelist, he lacks his or her imaginative intensity; Stephen Dedalus's problem is just the reverse. Neither character could have produced the work in which they figure; and what Joyce himself conjures out of this impasse is, among other things, a magnificent parody of fictional realism.[23]

'Reality, you know, is all the rage now', sniffs the novelist Gerald Griffin, in a letter to his brother depicting the London literary scene.[24] There was certainly an excess of it in Ireland – so much so that it

---

21. Isaac Butt, 'Past and Present State of Literature in Ireland', reprinted in Seamus Deane, ed., *The Field Day Anthology of Irish Writing*, vol. 1 (Derry 1991), pp. 1200–1212.

22. Ironically enough, others claimed that political crisis was an essential ingredient of great art. Barbara Hayley notes the 'desperately partisan' nature of most Irish journals in the first thirty years after the Union; no approach to the idea of a more integral, Arnoldian cultural organ was made until the arrival of the *Dublin University Magazine* in 1833 ('Irish Periodicals from the Union to the *Nation*', *Anglo-Irish Studies*, no. 2, 1976).

23. Some would no doubt number among the conditions militating against classical realism in Ireland the supposedly 'decentred' nature of the colonial subject, at odds with the requirements of 'fully-rounded' character. Such critics should be wary of the company they keep. One such theorist is the virulently anti-Irish J.A. Froude, who speculates that the lack of a native Irish drama may spring from the fact that no Irishman has sufficient consistency of character to carry him through five Acts (quoted by Thomas Kettle, *The Day's Burden*, Dublin 1910, p. 26). If Froude had paused to scan the annals of stage comedy in England, he might have unearthed a more plausible reason for the absence in question.

24. Daniel Griffin, *Life of Gerald Griffin* (London 1843), p. 199.

threatened constantly to explode the artifice of literary fiction. In the writing of a William Carleton, for instance, the stark exigencies of history can disrupt fictional convention, as passionate polemic or outraged social comment bursts impatiently through the protocols of the imagination. Carleton feels no compunction in arresting his narrative to preach, propagandize, engage in amateur sociological analysis, advance his pet penaceas for social ills; and one of his novels, *The Squanders of Castle Squander* (1852), finally fragments into a collage of non-fictional documents. This, then, is another reason for the instability of Irish literary realism, forced as it is by the insistence of the real to drop the fictional pretence and speak poignantly or angrily from the heart. The generic demarcations between fiction and documentation, dramatic and didactic, representation and intervention, are in general less firmly etched in Irish writing than they are in the literature of Britain, as different political conditions breed an alternative division of discursive labour. Stephen Gwynn's *Irish Literature and Drama* pays as much attention to Lecky's history of eighteenth-century Ireland and John Mitchel's *Jail Journal* as it does to John Banim and Gerald Griffin.[25] An English reviewer of William Carleton's *Traits and Stories of the Irish Peasantry* bemoaned its mixture of 'the materials of a delectable literary banquet' with religious controversy.[26] But though a representational history may break through the performative act of fiction, that historical representation is often enough a rhetorical act in the first place, political construction rather than archival account. To narrate a history in Ireland is to promulgate a particular image of the nation, fashioning what you purport to describe. The style of historiography commended by Thomas Davis, one which hallows, denounces, mollifies or inspires with its gallery of exemplary heroes, is already an aesthetic performance.[27] Even so, literary realism, like T.S. Eliot's spiritually mediocre humanity, cannot bear too much reality; as Maria Edgeworth remarks, oddly for such a liberal rationalist, 'the truth is too strong for the fiction, and on all sides pulls it asunder'.[28] And there may be a sense, too, of the privileged superfluity of fiction in such dire social conditions, which then reinforces a modernist sense of its arbitrariness.

For Friedrich Nietzsche, art can spring only from a certain historical amnesia; and the doctrine is lent a specifically Irish inflection by Elizabeth

25. Stephen Gwynn, *Irish Literature and Drama* (London 1936).

26. *Monthly Review*, May, 1830, quoted by Barbara Haley, *Carleton's Traits and Stories and the 19th Century Anglo-Irish Tradition* (Gerrards Cross 1983), p. 271.

27. See Thomas Davis, *Literary and Historical Essays* (Dublin 1865), p. 240.

28. Richard Lovell Edgeworth, *Memoirs* (London 1820), vol. 2, p. 350.

Bowen, who writes of how art must eliminate, edit and so falsify precisely because '[r]aw history, in its implications, is unnerving; and, even so, it chronicles only the survivors. If the greater part of the past had not been, mercifully, forgotten, the effect upon our modern sensibility would be unbearable.'[29] But if a surfeit of the real can violate realist decorum, the pressures of the political world can also, paradoxically, idealize such realism out of existence. If the British view of Ireland is of a squalid, fractious, brutalized nation, then there are Irish authors who will seek to redress that demeaning view by sanitizing their own social order, edifying their compatriots and impressing their metropolitan audience with a fiction which sweetens and sublimes. Young Ireland was dismayed by the 'slavish and despairing' grief of popular Irish ballads, and sought to supply a more virile, affirmative song. Realism, in short, may be unpatriotic: to portray Ireland as it really is may rouse an English reader's moral indignation, but only at the risk of confirming his or her sense of its degeneracy. So it is that when Charles Kickham, the 'Gorky of the Irish revolution',[30] comes to describe the village of Knocknagow, in the wildly popular novel of that name, he is quick to point out that '[t]hough most of the houses looked comfortless enough, and the place as a whole had the straggling appearance which [the English visitor] was accustomed to associate with an Irish village, there was none of that unredeemed squalor and wretchedness which certain writers had led him to expect. With one or two exceptions every house had at least two windows' (Ch. 7). 'We are in no wise indebted to those writers', protests an old patriot in the Introduction to Gerald Griffin's *Tales of the Munster Festivals* (1827), 'who, professing to present faithful illustrations of the minds and hearts of our countrymen, greedily rake up the forgotten superstitions of our peasantry, and exhibit the result of their ungracious researches, the unhappy blemishes of our island, the weaknesses of our poor uninstructed peasantry, over which decency and good feeling would have thrown a veil, to the eyes of a world that, unfortunately for us, is but too eager to seize every occasion for mockery and upbraiding against our forlorn and neglected country.' Truth and tendency, dignity and authenticity, are not easy to reconcile; and the literary art of a colonial nation must accordingly steer a precarious course between a realism which indicts the oppressor only by degrading the people, and an idealism which in nurturing national pride risks giving false comfort to the colonialist.

---

29. Quoted by R.F. Foster in *Paddy and Mr Punch* (London 1993), p. 104.
30. The phrase is Tom Garvin's, from his *Nationalist Revolutionaries in Ireland* (Oxford 1987), p. 52.

That the Anglo-Irish novel is only ambiguously realist is no more a failure on its part than the fact that Jacobean tragedy is not Arnold Bennett. A literary tradition which includes such largely non-realist works as Swift's *Gulliver's Travels*, Edgeworth's *Castle Rackrent*, Maturin's *Melmoth the Wanderer,* Sheridan Le Fanu's *Uncle Silas*, Stoker's *Dracula* and Joyce's *Ulysses* need not be rebuked for lapsing from some Platonic norm of mimesis. On the contrary, it is in its refusal to conform to that paradigm, or its apparent unconsciousness of it, that much of its fascination lies. The marginal nature of Irish realism is one reason why early-twentieth-century Ireland was the only sector of the British isles to witness an astonishingly rich outcrop of modernism. When James Joyce commented to Arthur Power that 'it is my revolt against the English conventions, literary and otherwise that is the main source of my talent',[31] he enforced a startlingly direct connection between colonial dissent and modernist achievement. It was precisely because Thackeray and Trollope could teach Joyce, Wilde and George Moore next to nothing that they were able to write as they did. And in discarding or transgressing realist conventions, these distinctly non-popular authors were in a curious way aligned with the great bulk of Irish literature, which belongs to that species of magic realism known as folklore.[32]

We may begin our enquiry, however, with an author who wrote when an aesthetic of realist representation had yet to be fully developed. In the first book of *Gulliver's Travels* (1726), Swift provides us with the Lilliputans' inventory of the objects they find about Gulliver's person. Since the Lilliputans can't give a name to these unfamiliar bits and pieces, their bemused descriptions of them are exemplary of Swift's unsettling technique of estrangement: a pocket comb, for instance, becomes 'a sort of Engine, from the back of which were extended twenty long Poles' (Part 1, Ch. 2). *Gulliver's Travels* estranges the familiar, as *A Modest Proposal* naturalizes the monstrous. But the alienation-effect cannot be too radical – there must, as Brecht remarked, be a 'return from alienation' – since the reader's enjoyment here consists in laboriously deciphering objects which hover on the very brink of unintelligibility, reassembling their enigmatic components into some agreeably recognizable whole. The reader

---

31. Quoted by Sean Golden, 'Post-Traditional English Literature: A Polemic', in M. Hederman and R. Kearney, eds, *The Crane Bag Book of Irish Studies* (Dublin 1982), p. 429.
32. I owe this suggestion to Dr Kevin Whelan.

has the edge here over the Lilliputans, but only just; for though the natives of Lilliput are ignorant of combs, watches, handkerchiefs and the rest, they are familiar enough with purses, writing and the value of gold, not to speak of the very notion of discrete material objects, of an inventory, of personal property and so on. Gulliver is an alien in Lilliput, but he and its denizens share a great many categories in common, and the narrative would not work if they did not. Cultural contrast depends for its force on some *a priori* consensus; otherwise we would be confronting the merely incommensurable, from which no satiric value could be reaped. The conduct of the Houyhnhnms threatens to undermine human self-esteem, as the behaviour of badgers would not. Gulliver and the Lilliputans are half inside and half outside each other's lives; and it belongs to the larger structural irony of the book that none of the exotic species its hero encounters turns out to be *that* different from European humanity, since if they were they would fall entirely beyond the frontiers of his discourse and the text would stammer to a halt. That these freaks, microbeings, Godwinian quadrupeds and immortal wrecks are not all that remote from the natives of Birmingham is at once a satiric smack at the utopianists and a covertly imperial projection of European Man onto the entire globe, in the manner of the Enlightenment about which Swift was so deeply sceptical. The gesture is double-edged: it is comforting to find our own home-grown brand of moral shabbiness reflected back to us in six-inch-high court officials, but it is not, of course, comforting at all.

There can, then, be no absolute alterity, if writing about otherness is to be possible. Instead, *Gulliver's Travels* turns on the very edge of alienness and intimacy, installing itself in the gap between the known and the outlandish and ceaselessly deflecting the one into the other. This is also a play between style and substance, as unnervingly unfamiliar objects are handled in a robust, muscular, noun-oriented discourse purged of all complex resonance. Translation of a kind must always be possible; and Gulliver himself, oddly for one otherwise so obtuse, is a notably fine linguist, able to pick up a foreign language by the dubious technique of ostensive definition in an implausibly brief span of time. To enter a language is to share in a form of life, and Gulliver is commonly to be found doing this with suspicious alacrity. No sooner has he arrived among the Lilliputans than he throws himself with gusto into the role of military leader, complacently ignorant of the background to their war with Blefuscu. He is foolishly proud of his title of Nardac, and hotly rebuts an accusation of having fornicated with a Lilliputan woman without even pausing to adduce its physical impossibility in his own defence. Like any gull, he is pathetically impressionable by circumstance, a cultural chameleon who changes colour because he cannot change size, an unwitting Sophist who masters the local conventions and deploys them as earnestly and adroitly as the natives themselves. But if he is too obsequiously quick to conform to foreign mores, he is also a chuckleheaded chauvinist blind to his own cultural prejudices, as his smugly patriotic peroration before the horrified king of Brobdingnag well enough attests. The text of *Gulliver's Travels* may tread some hair-thin line between the alien and the intimate; but its boneheaded protagonist is always either too deeply in or too far out, either unable to objectify his own assumptions or too fawningly eager to throw them to the winds. If he is an imperial apologist he is also a postmodern relativist; and the point is that these positions are themselves both alien to and intimate with one another. What is the difference between uncritically defending the British and acting as an obedient subject of Lilliputan power?

An empathetic anthropology, in short, is merely the other face of imperial arrogance. If one should seek to understand the cannibals rather than change them, why not extend the same charity to one's own predatory politicians? If a pluralistic tolerance is the order of the day, then why exempt one's own native culture from this ordinance? If all cultures are in perfect working order, why not identify, like the Sophists, with whichever one is nearest to hand, even if its practices include invading the culture of others? The absence of critical self-reflection which blinds Gulliver to the obscenities of his own social order is just what motivates his unthinking acceptance of other forms of life. His stolidly centred selfhood is the condition of his too-rapid decentrement, not the opposite of it. And from the natives' viewpoint, the approbation of a self so easily displaced beyond its own limits is hardly worth having. To empathize with another culture is to erase its alterity as surely as does imperialism, and to abolish one's own otherness along with it. To imagine oneself a Houyhnhnm is no kind of solidarity with these creatures, since it disposes of the difference such fellow-feeling entails. *Gulliver's Travels* concludes with a magnificent polemic against imperialism; but the price it pays for this protest is Gulliver's imperial disdain for his fellow citizens, who are now no more than repulsive Yahoos. The other side of treating the alien as familiar is treating one's familiars as monstrous.

If the Yahoo is a satirical representation of the European, then it would indeed seem grotesque for the latter to lord it over the rest of the earth. But if the Yahoos are humanity in general, then there would seem no good reason why one bunch of these valueless brutes should not oppress another bunch to their heart's content. The allegory is inexact: the textual implication that Yahooish Europeans should not dominate reasonably agreeable creatures like the Houyhnhnms or Brobdingnagians does not quite translate into the real-life assertion that European Yahoos should not exploit south sea island ones. Swift's satiric device gets out of hand, releasing an unintended meaning and entailing a slippery syllogism. If Europeans are human beings, and all human beings are Yahoos, then Europeans are Yahoos; but so, it follows, are their colonials, as the fact that the Yahoos are subject to the Houyhnhnms would suggest. The critique of colonialism is thus partly undercut, as it is in Conrad's *Heart of Darkness*: if the nihilistic horror glimpsed by Kurtz is the truth of things, then there is no value to human existence and thus no more reason not to exploit Africans than to do so. Only if Kurtz's vision is a local truth about the Belgian Congo can the anti-imperialist case stand; but to underline that truth means to universalize it, which then risks undercutting oneself.

Both Swift's and Conrad's work suggest that the masters may be as bestial as the natives – a move which shakes the self-esteem of the colonialist to the precise extent that it confirms his stereotype of the colonial. If humans are unruly Yahoos, then they need a stiff dose of colonial regulation; but by the same token they are in no position to provide such governance themselves. The problem with Swift's text is that it cannot control the implications of its own satirical devices – cannot avoid our taking them too seriously, or drawing too deeply misanthropic conclusions from them, which is why the book must finally have its protagonist (who *has* taken these unsettling ploys too seriously) go mad. To avoid going over the top itself, it must send its protagonist over instead. The return from alienation is secured by the reader alienating herself from Gulliver's alienation. Much the same is true of Swift's strategic cultural relativizing, in which one perspective objectifies another only to be dwindled and discredited by a third. Gulliver muses that there might be somewhere a race to whom the Brobdingnagians appear as Lilliputans; and the Brobdingnagians, who are devices to estrange our own values, objectify themselves in turn in the person of Gulliver, wryly reflecting on how contemptible their own moral character must be if it can be mimicked by so diminutive an insect as him. The point of such textual tactics is to decentre humanity into a therapeutic sense of its own relativity; but this move too threatens constantly to get out of hand, destabilizing all Swiftian doctrine of given natures and essential limits in its vertiginous interchange of viewpoints. Swift's actual ideological position – a pragmatic Anglican *via media* between Dissent and Catholicism – becomes less a question of equipoise than a perpetual pitching between extremes.

Swift did not regard Ireland as a colony; like William Molyneux before him, he considered it a sovereign kingdom.[33] But of course he also knew that it was not; and this is one source of his tortuous dialectic of the actual and the ideal, in which the latter is used to satirize the former in the very act of being savagely cut down to size by it. So much is true of the interplay between Yahoos and Houyhnhnms. The Yahoos may be among other things a nightmarish version of the subhuman condition of the Irish people,[34] but the Houyhnhnms are hardly an image of their rulers, even if as horses they are the Ascendancy's favourite creatures.[35] The last thing the Anglo-Irish could be accused of is an excess of enlightenment. As the image of a decent, rational, benevolent ruling class, the Houyhnhnms may even be a critique of the Ascendancy; but they may equally be a gibe at those free-thinking utopian rationalists who would question that class's very existence as irrationally privileged beings. The Yahoos reflect *inter alia* an Ascendancy fear and hatred of those they oppress; but by the end of *Gulliver's Travels* this detestation is allowed to assume pathological form in Gulliver's deranged equinophilia, which then steers our sympathies back to the Yahoo-human. The people may be repugnant, but one should avoid a Houhyhnhm-like contempt for them – not least since the common folk Swift most regularly encountered in Dublin were his co-religionists. But to satirize the Houhyhnhnm standpoint is also to repudiate the kind of rational, egalitarian, benevolent politics which might make some substantive difference to that people's condition. If the book finally abandons its protagonist to lunacy, then, it does so in the name of a pragmatic humanism which is also a spurning of utopian vision, and so, in the Irish context, an ultimate underwriting of an inhuman status quo. The Houyhnhnms are a convenient stick with which to belabour actually existing humanity; but their lofty remoteness from the human condition (they are, after all, horses) is at once what enables that critique and renders it ineffectual.

---

33. See William Molyneux, *The Case of Ireland's being Bound by Acts of Parliament in England, Stated* (Dublin 1698). See also Oliver W. Ferguson, *Jonathan Swift and Ireland* (Urbana 1962).

34. In Ireland, Swift speculates whether 'those animals which come my way with two legs and human faces, clad and erect, be of the same species with what I have seen very like them in England' (quoted by David Nokes, *Jonathan Swift: A Hypocrite Reversed*, Oxford 1985, p. 347).

35. One recalls Brendan Behan's celebrated definition of the Anglo-Irish: 'A Protestant on a horse'.

The Yahoos are humans viewed from the degrading standpoint of stoical aliens, and to this extent one sides with the people against this demeaning image of them; but they are also how human beings partly are, which qualifies one's radical populism with a dash of Tory pessimism. If you see people as Yahoos, so the moral runs, you will sever all sympathy with them and so be unable to champion their cause; but if you fail to see them as Yahoos, you will be seduced by some fancy chiliastic scheme into trying to transform their situation. That the people are in such a lamentable state is what renders such schemes at once plausible and idle. That the Irish masses, not least the starving weavers on the Dean's own doorstep, are sunk in some bestial Yahoo-like condition is why they should be succoured; but it is also testimony to their unregeneracy, and so confirmation of the need for stern government and the irrelevance of radical schemes. If the Irish have been *reduced* to Yahoos, then there is perhaps a case for radical change; but if humans are Yahoos anyway, that case is severely qualified. As Joseph McMinn puts the point: 'Swift's writings implied the need for radical change, but dreaded the prospect.'[36] The pomp of the rulers must be judiciously deflated by disclosing the bare forked creature within; but if this creature has reduced those around it to beasts like itself, then it can appeal to this fact as a way of licensing its continuing rule. The relation between rulers and people thus parallels that between Reason and the body: it is necessary to puncture Reason's hubristic idealism by hacking humans therapeutically down to a belly and an anus; but since this move yields us the fearful, appetitive animal of mechanical materialism, the dictates of Reason are all the more essential. To claim, as Swift's writing does, that one can neither escape the body nor rest complacently in it is, then, allegorical of the impasse of a reformist Tory politics.[37]

Swift detested the people he championed, and believed in legally penalizing some of those he so eloquently defended. 'What I do', he told Pope, 'is owing to perfect rage and resentment, and the mortifying sight of slavery, folly and baseness about me, among which I am forced to live.'[38] There is at work here what Raymond Williams has called a 'negative identification'[39] with the suffering masses: the upper-class patriots find in

---

36. Joseph McMinn, ed., *Swift's Irish Pamphlets: An Introductory Selection* (Gerrards Cross 1991), p. 19. See also J.C. Beckett, 'Swift and the Anglo-Irish Tradition', in C.J. Rawson, ed., *The Character of Swift's Satire* (Newark 1983); and Ferguson, *Jonathan Swift and Ireland*.

37. For Swift and the body, see Denis Donoghue, *Jonathan Swift* (Cambridge 1969).

38. Quoted in Nokes, *Jonathan Swift*, p. 344.

39. See Raymond Williams, *Culture and Society 1780–1950* (Harmondsworth 1958), pp. 178–80.

the downtrodden populace an oblique image of their own political dispossession, but this very wretchedness is graphic evidence of their own title to rule. Swift's patriotism, Thomas Moore acidly remarks, 'might have come under his own interdiction, as an imported article'.[40] It is no wonder that his writing is constituted by contradiction, or that his satiric fury is so polymorphous. It is the natural mode of a schizoid social class, who on a good day could defend the people against Westminster, themselves against the people and the Crown against the British parliament, clamorously asserting a sovereignty they knew in their hearts to be nothing of the kind. Swift reviles the British for reducing the Irish to slaves, then condemns the Irish for internalizing this slavery, which is at once more and less reason for excoriating the British, and excellent reason for loathing oneself. The Gulliver who is caught on the hop between conflicting cultural norms, whose whole existence is a barely tolerable in-betweenness, is then an appropriate figure for an Ascendancy which was both colonized and colonialist.

The lesson of the book is, then, radical and conservative together. You must objectify your own culture in the name of justice and true judgement, but not so absolutely that you fall into madness and self-hatred, or surrender to a relativism which strikes empty the very position you are striving to view critically. But it is hard, perhaps impossible, to draw the line between these conditions: only someone inside a situation can judge it, Bertolt Brecht once remarked, and he's the last person who can judge. There is no clear distinction between inside and outside: the discourse of the *Modest Proposal* projector is at once utterly beyond the pale of the humanly acceptable, and a mere logical extension of the existing situation. And if the reader, trapped on the inside of this lethal logic, rejects it from that meta-viewpoint known as 'humanity', where exactly, in Ireland, is that? Like the modern-day pragmatists, Swift insists that there is no absolute outside to a regime of sense, no transcendental vantage point from which some full-blooded critique of it could be launched. This, after all, is part of the point of making the Houyhnhnms horses. The dubious political correlative of this sound philosophical doctrine, for both Swift and its modern exponents, is that all critique is disablingly complicit with its object, and can thus advance no further than a set of modest proposals.

To position oneself at the point where one might spurn a social order as a whole could only be to court the perils of lunacy and self-division.

<hr>

40. Thomas Moore, *Memoirs of Captain Rock* (London 1824), p. 211.

Better to forego total critique in a spirit of compassion than to pursue radical change in the name of antipathy. But not all radical critiques are launched by horses; and if Swift believed that the critic was inevitably complicit with the object of his odium, this was less some elaborate rebuttal of transcendental idealism than a guilty acknowledgement of the compromised nature of his own social class. Indeed he was ready enough to resort to notions of transcendental rationality when it suited his purpose: to hold that Reason itself is always true and just, though the reason of individuals is weak and wavering, is to suggest among other things that the upper-class Anglican Establishment in Ireland was in principle eminently rational, though one would have a hard time adducing evidence for this doctrine from the behaviour of its individual members. There is no great leap from claiming that Swift was a rationalist who did not believe in reason to pointing out that he was a devoted supporter of the Establishment who disliked much of what it stood for. Prevailing norms must be observed, even if Swift's writing constantly deconstructs the very notion of normativity. It is precisely because the condition of the Anglo-Irish is an aporetic one, caught between mutually interfering codes, that an unequivocal order must be upheld.

But how is one to take the measure of a human animal whose very mundane existence is one of furious excess; whose norm is hubris and transgression; whose moderation, like the intolerably placid Houyhnhnms, always carries a certain madness inscribed within it? Humanity is not so much a mid-point between Yahoo and Houyhnhnm as an embodied contradiction between them; 'how near [in humanity] the frontiers of height and depth border on each other', Swift remarks in *A Tale of a Tub* (1704), with one eye, perhaps, on the narrowness of St George's Channel. It is not hard to grasp why, placed as he was, he should have seen civilization and barbarism as sharing a common source.

No figure could hover more ambiguously between 'inside' and 'outside' than the faithful old family retainer, at once privy to his master's intimate affairs yet humbly peripheral. Such is the doubleness of one of Irish fiction's most intriguingly enigmatic characters, Thady Quirk of Maria Edgeworth's *Castle Rackrent* (1800); and it is perhaps not surprising that this ambivalent creation should be the work of an upper-class woman, who is likely to experience a somewhat parallel conflict between her social power and sexual subordination. Thady recounts with obsequious affection the story of his drunken, profligate, black-hearted employers, who would presumably lack both the nerve and the gumption to tell the tale themselves; and critical interpretation of the novel has revolved on the significance of this eminently dialogical structure, this play of identity and difference between Quirk and his masters, which in a boldly inventive move projects the social relations of a benighted landlordism into the very form of the fiction. How tongue-in-cheek is Thady's toadying to this lineage of moral desperadoes?

If Thady's reverence for the brutal, boneheaded Rackrents is to be taken straight, then his unnervingly uncritical response to the narrative he delivers is bound up with the situation he represents. What puts him thoroughly on the inside of the Rackrent *ménage* is the befuddled mystification with which he observes it from the margin. His genial indulgence of his superiors, like the emotional autism of some of Swift's personae, is a symptom of the condition on which it comments. His obtuse loyalty is a kind of irrationalism grotesquely indifferent to the actual situation, and so curiously reflects the Rackrents' own pathological form of life. The Rackrents may be crass materialists; but they are also fantasists to the core, recklessly indifferent to the empirical world in their compulsive pursuit of self-gratification. As with all dramas of *Thanatos*, there is pleasure to be reaped from the spectacle of this monstrous self-squandering, which is one way in which the tale entices us into enjoying what it officially reproves; but something similar could be said of our response to Thady's fawning fidelity. For fidelity, like sincerity, is a quality we tend to admire regardless of its object or occasion; and the same goes for vitality, which the carnivalesque Quirk has in plenty. The verve and brio of his discourse partly qualify its cringe: he may be a groveller, but the language which betrays the fact is garrulously self-assertive. This robustness then rubs off on the object of his speech – the Rackrents themselves – to present them more favourably than they could themselves; and in this way the form of the narrative helps to defuse its unsavoury content. Sir Kit Rackrent incarcerates his wife in her bedchamber for seven years, but Thady communicates the incident out of the side of his mouth, and his sprightly way with words implicitly forbids us to dwell upon it. His loquacity is a kind of artlessness, an unstaunchable excess of speech; but it is also, so we may suspect, the rhetorical strategy of the 'lower Irish', disarming authority by its rumbustious spontaneity and wrapping unpalatable truths in its endless parataxis. Truth and artifice are thus interwoven in his discourse, as they are in the form of the text itself – a palpable piece of invention which nonetheless claims the status of a historical document.

It is hard, then, to know exactly who or what is being satirized, just as it is at the end of *Gulliver's Travels*. We smile at Gulliver when he imagines himself a Houyhnhnm and his fellow humans as Yahoos, since the Houyhnhnms thought him a Yahoo too; but they would have thought just the same of us, which might qualify our title to be amused. The more Thady exculpates his masters, or can be felt blandly manipulating the narrative in their favour, the worse it is for them: they are now responsible not only for their own squalid conduct but for a monstrous blunting of moral sensibility around them. The act of making light of the Rackrents' crimes is actually part of them, as the deadpan bureaucratese of the *Modest Proposal* projector belongs to the dehumanized situation he seeks to remedy. From this viewpoint, then, Thady is an archetypally unreliable narrator, both comically and horrifically condemning himself out of his own mouth. Yet it could also be claimed that his boisterous idiom serves the Rackrents too well – that by the end of the novel, with the destruction of the pathetic Sir Condy Rackrent at the hands of Thady's scheming son Jason, we have been seduced into finding ourselves witness to the triumph of a new, ruthlessly utilitarian order over what might now seem in retrospect a colourful if corrupt traditionalism. Marilyn Butler reads the narrative as a 'not unsympathetic' record of the demise of the spendthrift old squirearchy, but notes a contrast in this respect between its satirical beginning and elegiac conclusion: 'the book', she comments, 'ends with a totally different meaning from the one with which it began'.[41] To this extent, *Castle Rackrent* can be read as embodying an ideological conflict we can discern elsewhere in Edgeworth, between the values of a vital if anarchic ruling class which is able, whatever its moral shabbiness, to secure the allegiance of its underlings, and the rational virtues of a more sober social order whose austere utility will win it few ardent adherents. It is just this contrast which *Ormond* (1817) enforces between the ramshackle but warm-hearted regime of Corny, Rabelaisian patriarch of a traditionalist Gaelic island, and the calculative pragmatism of Sir Ulick O'Shane, whose geniality is strictly skin-deep. It is true that Thady shares his masters' interests in all the wrong ways, and this might just be read as a sardonic smack at notions of cross-class harmony: such complicities, *pace* a conventional neo-feudalist wisdom, can turn out to be vicious as well as virtuous. This is certainly a truth that the *text* discloses;

---

41. Marilyn Butler, *Maria Edgeworth: A Literary Biography* (Oxford 1972), p. 358. See also her comments on Edgeworth in *Jane Austen and the War of Ideas* (Oxford 1975), and the remarks by Donald Davie in *The Heyday of Sir Walter Scott* (London 1961), Ch. 6.

yet we know that its author was a devout believer in the peaceful co-existence of social classes, and her father a celebrated practitioner of the doctrine; and the spiritual bonding between Thady and the Rackrents could thus be seen as beneficent in principle, if blatantly retrograde in moral content. On the other hand, it may be that *Castle Rackrent* extends no such sympathy, of however nuanced a sort, to the bunch of dissolute exploiters who furnish its theme – that, rather in the manner of *Mansfield Park*, it takes the measure of a certain spurious vitality only to reject it as not worth the ethical price.

The danger with unreliable first-person narration is the lack of a metalanguage by which its flaws might be measured; but, so we might claim, that metalanguage is discreetly present in this text in the form of its normalizing editorial apparatus – in the Preface, footnotes and glossary which supervise and regulate Thady's dishevelled Irish discourse with a very English ironic condescension. It is here, perhaps, that the true negative judgement on Thady and the Rackrents is delivered, and the norms of a more enlightened social order, owing nothing to this gallery of ruffians, may be implicitly discerned. Edgeworth emphasizes in her very subtitle that we are viewing the gentry as they were before the magical Irish date of 1782; and this anxious disclaimer – that things are not now as they were, that the nation or the aristocracy has been reformed – will become a commonplace of subsequent Irish fiction. From this viewpoint, the novel is not after all a masterpiece of Swiftian un-decidability or triumph of dialogical indeterminacy, but plain enough in its controlling imperatives. Published in the year of the Union, symboli-cally marking a brave new anglicizing epoch, it feels able to represent the turbulent prehistory of the present warts and all – to lay boldly before the English reader the very stuff of their anti-Irish fantasies, but now ironically slanted, historically distanced, subtextually normalized. The Rackrents, significantly, are an old Gaelic family, not an Anglo-Irish one; and this allows Edgeworth to put a degree of daylight between herself and her subject matter. The general *impression* the novel gives, taking its Preface, substance and subtitle together, is that an uproarious old feudalist regime is now thankfully passé; but this is to emphasize culture and ideology at the expense of social relations. For the social relations of the Rackrents are no more feudalist, give or take a few residual features, than those of the Edgeworths; and to this extent the work insinuates a dis-continuity for which there is little historical warrant.

Is *Castle Rackrent*, however, really as assured a text as all that? The novel may have been published in the year of the Union; but the manuscript was being prepared for the publishers in the thick of the United Irish insurrection,[42] in which Maria's father suffered the fate of all good liberals and narrowly escaped a hammering by both sides. What if the narrative were a fantastic rendering of all that? – if Thady Quirk were no loyal lackey but a type of the disaffected Catholic peasantry, concealing his subversion beneath a mask of servility and working covertly for the overthrow of the landlords? His story would then be a species of performative contradiction, proclaiming in the ritual act of memorializing a devotion undercut by its satiric content. Such is the interpretation of the novel sponsored by, among others, the historian Tom Dunne, who reads Quirk's fealty in ironic terms and sees him as exploiting his inside knowledge of Castle Rackrent to promote the usurping schemes of his son Jason.[43] On this theory, if the Quirks stand for anything in their author's distraught imagination, it is for the ominous realization of the old Gaelic dream of popular repossession of the land.

In the revolutionary 1790s, previously trusted family retainers suddenly revealed their hostility to their masters; and this was particularly unnerving for genteel women, dependent as they were on socializing with their servants. As with many an Irish peasant, Thady's deference is perhaps only skin-deep, resistance cloaked as complicity; and if these devious rebels are not to lay their hands on the great estates, as Jason does on Sir Condy's, then the rotten social order of the Rackrents must be superseded by the kind of full-blooded 'anglicization' of social relations in Ireland that Richard Lovell Edgeworth so efficiently practised.[44] Only in this way will the landlords secure their hegemony; yet there is a contradiction here which the text fails to resolve. For if an ironic reading of Quirk's servility is plausible, then the hegemony which failed in his case was a *Gaelic* one; and there seems little reason to suspect that an Anglo-Irish project would fare any better. For all his celebrated benevolence as a landowner, Richard Edgeworth found himself confronted in 1798 by pockets of rebellion among his own tenants. *Castle Rackrent*, as Tom Dunne remarks, may display 'some elements of sympathy in its portrayal of traditional social

---

42. For a useful compositional chronology, see W.J. McCormack, *Ascendancy and Tradition*, (Oxford 1985), p. 100.

43. Tom Dunne, *Maria Edgeworth and the Colonial Mind*, (Cork 1984). See also James Newcomer, *Maria Edgeworth* (Lewisburg 1973).

44. For an account of Edgeworth's reformist, anti-sectarian landlordism in Edgeworthstown, see his *Memoirs*, vol. 2, (London 1820), Ch. 18. Volume 1 of the work was written by Edgeworth himself, and volume 2 by Maria after her father's death. For something of the earlier history of the Edgeworth family, see H.J. and H.E. Butler, eds, *The Black Book of Edgeworthstown* (London 1927).

relationships, if only because of their potential in creating class harmony';[45] but by his own account even *those* relations have signally failed to create precisely that. If the meaning of the novel is hard to decipher, then, it may be because of an ambiguity in its assessment of the past forced upon it by present circumstance.

It is an ambiguity evident in Edgeworth's other Irish novels: *Ennui* (1809) and *The Absentee* (1812) are largely dismissive of Gaelic traditionalism, whereas Harry Ormond ends up inheriting the charismatic cultural authority of the chieftain Corny O'Shane, along with his estates.[46] On the one hand, the past is an unruly kingdom which must be decisively abandoned; on the other hand, it possesses, at least potentially, *ideological* resources of which the present stands sorely in need. But such resources are not easily disentangled from the social situations they historically served, which is one of Edgeworth's problems; and in this novel, at least on an ironic reading of Thady, even they turn out to be chimerical, which is another problem. The peasantry are naturally two-faced, even with land-lords of their own ethnic kind. If Thady *is* a hypocrite, then the novel, in its concern to blacken the past, has also jettisoned what the present might politically rescue from it; and if he is not a hypocrite then there is no guarantee that his compatriots under the more culturally alien landlordism of the Ascendancy will not be so. If Thady is the gull he appears to be, then the Catholic peasantry are clearly not fit for power; if he is not, then his treachery is a logical product of the brutality of the old regime, and might yield to a more civilized dispensation. But that new order may fatally lack the 'natural' affinity between landlord and tenant which the Rackrents, at least on one reading, could command; and if, on another reading, all that is sheerly bogus, and the tenantry will be satisfied with nothing less than the land, then there is no reason to expect that they will relinquish that demand in a more benign social order, and every reason to believe, in the Edgeworthstown of 1798, that they will not. In any case, the double reading which *Castle Rackrent* licenses places the Catholic masses in a convenient double bind: if they are loyal to a worthless landlord they are scorned as credulous and collusive; if they pit themselves against him they are perfidious rebels.

The theory that Thady is dissembling his disaffection has some interesting implications. For it is *we* he is fooling – we, the readers, who exert no kind of power over him, but who are consequently placed in

---

45. Dunne, *Maria Edgeworth*, p. 15.

46. For a useful discussion of this ambivalence, see Thomas Flanagan, *The Irish Novelists 1800–1850* (New York 1959), pp. 88–91.

the position of his superiors. His capacity for deception runs so deep that he exercises it gratuitously, with little or nothing to gain. One might claim that he profits from putting his own past conduct in the best possible light; or that this is the most devastating method of casually damning his masters; or that it is less the reader he is conning than the 'Editor' to whom he recounts his tale, a figure who would fall squarely enough for him into the category of class enemy, and before whom it would be natural to keep up appearances. In this sense, curiously, it is Maria Edgeworth who is being taken for a ride by one of her own creations. But if Thady is just chronically incapable of straightness even when he has no reason to fear it, then this raises the further interpretative possibility that he is not so much deceiving as self-deceived. Perhaps he *believes* that he loves his masters, but in fact does not; perhaps he is unconsciously working against them but unable to acknowledge this truth to himself. Like Gramsci's typical proletarian, he may be caught between two contradictory sets of beliefs, one 'official' – what he is formally supposed to hold – and an 'unofficial' way of seeing which provides the unconscious subtext to his piously proclaimed allegiance.[47] Thady is a domestic servant, and so in a sense in the position of a woman; he would certainly seem jealous of his masters' various wives. His narrative, which has a stereotypically feminine intimacy, eye for the stray detail and obliqueness to the public world, is thus at one level that of a wife who knows her husband too well to think anything but badly of him, but who is patriarchally constrained from defining herself as disloyal. Serflike or marital fidelity is just the taken-for-granted frame of one's perceptions, which cannot even be intelligibly called into question, which is ideologically prohibited from being raised to an object of conscious criticism., but which discredits itself in the slips and crevices of one's discourse. Thady's self-serving blunders and oversights – dropping a pen, for example, so as to continue the more conveniently to eavesdrop on his master's affairs – would then be in a precise sense Freudian parapraxes, symptoms of a smouldering animosity barred from the conscious mind. Such a reading of the work is wholly debatable; but it would make the novel an extraordinarily perceptive portrait of the workings of ideology, in which conscious beliefs and unconscious intentions can certainly be at odds; and it would chime with Edgeworth's sense, elsewhere in her writing, that truth and fiction in Ireland are not so much at odds as inextricably intermingled.

---

47. See Quintin Hoare and Geoffrey Nowell-Smith, eds, *Selections from the Prison Notebooks of Antonio Gramsci* (London 1971), p. 327.

One primary place of that intermingling is Maria Edgeworth's own novels. Like any good utilitarian, Edgeworth writes with a moral purpose; but she thus encounters an intractable difficulty with which Samuel Richardson had previously wrestled. The problem is that only an animated, imaginatively engaging presentation will drive your moral point home, and these are the very qualities which are most likely to undermine it. *Castle Rackrent*, which dispenses with a moral metalanguage in the interests of dramatic immediacy, is the most obvious instance of this dilemma, and Edgeworth was understandably rattled by its favourable reception: just as Richardson's readership had perversely idolized Lovelace, so her audience were in danger of sentimentally indulging Quirk. The more graphically unmediated the narrative, the less it can control its own interpretation. Fiction must flesh out its moral diagram in felt experience, instantiate its general principles in concrete particulars; but an unregenerate reader is then likely to plump for the flesh rather than the diagram, and concrete particularity, as Hegel knew, risks subverting the universals it exemplifies. Edgeworth gave *Belinda* the subtitle of 'Moral Tale' rather than 'Novel', for the 'rational' novel she strives for is something of a contradiction in terms, its austerely ethical ends at odds with its imaginative substance. If the 'novel' is that which indulges the vices of a depraved upper class, then Edgeworth faces a clear generic dilemma: the very form she deploys is complicit with the conduct she seeks to reform. On the other hand, a too moralizing or schematic fiction, of the kind *The Absentee* or *Ennui* have seemed to some, will be affectively unappealing and so ideologically ineffective. (William Carleton complained of the 'flatness' of Edgeworth's Irish novels and regretted their lack of 'heart-stirring lovemaking', which is rather like regretting the absence of sodomy in Jane Austen.[48]) One of the most vigorous characters of *The Absentee* is Lady Dashfort, who maliciously misrepresents Ireland to the young hero Colambre because she has her private reasons for not wishing him to live there. Her travesty of the truth is delivered with 'wit, satire, poetry, and sentiment' (Ch. 7), so that the qualities necessary for good literature are denigrated by an instance of it.

The liveliest representations may also be the slipperiest, and when it comes to fiction the devil has all the best tunes. 'In books', Edgeworth writes in *Practical Education* (1815), 'we do not actually suffer by the tricks of rogues, nor by the lies they tell; hence their truth is to us a quality of no value; but their wit, humour, and the ingenuity of their contrivances,

---

48. See David J. Donoghue, *The Life of William Carleton* (London 1986), vol. 2, p. 175.

are of great value to us, because they afford us entertainment...'[49] The novel must serve truth, but its very devices tend to undercut it; indeed Edgeworth herself remarked that 'it is dangerous to put a patch of truth into a fiction, for the truth is too strong for the fiction, and on all sides pulls it asunder'.[50] Lady Delacour in *Belinda* is another spirited yet morally disreputable figure, as superior in fictional interest to the anaemic Belinda as Thady is to the insipid, impeccably upright young protagonists of *Ennui* and *The Absentee*. Indeed she is a palpable poetic symbol all in herself, with her mask of wit and gaiety concealing a hideously cancerous body; but the novel, anxious to disown its own literariness, comments dryly that her concealed medical closet might have come straight out of a novel. The upper class live a double life, just as good novels do: if they have style and verve, they also have practical interests to pursue. It is just that with the gentry the one tends to mystify the other, their levees and masquerades concealing the cold truth of suffering and exploitation, whereas writing must lay bare this structural falsity. But to do so it must itself harness fantasy to utility, and so risk replicating the duplicitous life-style it denounces.

Like the predatory aristocracy, Edgeworth's fictions deploy style and spirit in the service of hard-headed interests, press artifice into the cause of reality; and to this extent they resemble nothing more than Richard Lovell Edgeworth's eccentric inventions, which for all their prosaic service-ability have more than a smack of Swift's Laputa about them.[51] Maria herself took a lively interest in mechanical processes, and some of her novels bear witness to the fact. Too fond an indulgence of generous energies can run counter to one's proper interests, both in the writing of a novel and the management of an estate; but the lack of such *élan* will render one's interests unpalatable, and so undermine them in this way too.

If the English aristocracy are unpleasantly affected, their Anglo-Irish counterparts, inferior in breeding and education, are at least more 'natural'. The French, however, characteristically deconstruct this very opposition: young Ormond witnesses in Parisian high society 'that eagerness to feel and excite a *sensation*; that desire *to produce an effect*, to have a scene; that half real, half theatric enthusiasm by which the French character is

49. *Essays on Practical Education* (London 1815), vol. 1, p. 276.

50. *Memoirs*, vol. 2, p. 350.

51. See his bizarre project for constructing an eight-legged machine to scale high walls (*Memoirs*, vol. 1, pp. 169–70), and his account of his membership of a Parliamentary Committee for Wheels, which debated the respective merits of the conical and cylindrical varieties (*Memoirs*, vol. 2, p. 323).

peculiarly distinguished from the English ... It was real! and it was not real feeling!' (Ch. 29). If truth is theatrical, if the line between fiction and reality is dangerously undecidable, then an Enlightenment rationalist like Edgeworth is in dire trouble; and one name for this blurring of the real and the rhetorical is Ireland. For there are several truths in Ireland, depending on whom one is talking to;[52] and if truth is in this sense elusive it is because it is in the service of power. When you have a divided society in which party feeling runs high, so the narrator of *Ormond* comments, then individuals are 'prone reciprocally to believe any stories or reports, however false or absurd, which tend to gratify their antipathies ... [in] this situation it is scarcely possible to get the exact truth as to the words, actions, and intentions, of the nearest neighbours, who happen to be of opposite parties or persuasions' (Ch. 23). Political strife breeds epistemological opacity, a kind of structural slanderousness: a community of shared knowledge is impossible, since physical contiguity serves merely to highlight this mutual travestying. Gossip, rumour, defamation all thrive in the pages of *Ormond*, and in Edgeworth's work in general language tends either to dissemble social interests or to become a mere blunt instrument of them.

Full of 'a spirit of fiery misrepresentation' was how De Quincey described the Irish character.[53] The Irish may be charmingly spontaneous; but they are also constitutionally bogus, full of bulls, blarney, bombast, hyperbole, and these verbal stratagems are at once an effect of colonialism and a form of resistance to it. Honesty is of the essence of the English, whereas if the Irish have an essence at all, which is questionable, then it is inauthenticity. Truth in Ireland is socially determined; and Edgeworth herself, for all her scrupulous devotion to discerning the situation as it really is, was not above passing on the odd lurid dinner-table tale of what the seditious peasantry were up to.[54] You may love your tenants, but it is dangerous to take what they say on trust, without access to the codes which govern their guileful rhetoric. In *Ennui*, the canny land agent McLeod has such dearly earned knowledge, whereas the *ingenu* Lord Glenthorn does not, and must learn it the hard way. Language in Ireland is a field of struggle and dissimulation, performative rather than constative; and to extract the truth of it you need to be on the spot, which is what

---

52. A fact brought home to William Thackeray in Belfast, who remarks that one would grow old trying to distil the truth from the nine or so diferent politico-religious versions of it on offer. (*The Irish Sketch Book*, 1843, reprinted Oxford 1946, p. 306).

53. Quoted in Seamus Deane, *A Short History of Irish Literature* (London 1986), p. 94.

54. See Michael Hurst, *Maria Edgeworth and the Public Scene* (London 1969), p. 145.

in Edgeworth's view is so wrong about absenteeism. Physical remoteness is epistemologically as well as politically disabling: Lord Clobrony, the London-based landlord of *The Absentee*, is 'at a distance, and cannot find out the truth', whereas his dutiful son Lord Colambre tours his Irish estates incognito to repair this cognitive breakdown. Absenteeism is the divorce of knowledge and power; whereas the enlightened Anglo-Irish settler, moving between different worlds, inside and outside the sphere of the peasantry simultaneously, may hope to mediate different truths to each other from no vantage point in particular.

It is just this elusive location which Richard and Maria Edgeworth seek to occupy in their joint *Essay on Irish Bulls* (1802), which aims to defend colloquial Irish speech from the patronizing calumny of the foreigner. The work is sufficiently *au fait* with Irish popular culture to savour its jokes and anecdotes, but sufficiently distanced to submit them to rational analysis; its elaborate literary allusions betray its remoteness from native speech in the very act of affirming it. If the Irish brogue is to be valued, it is because it represents a pure, Shakespearian form of English, in contrast to the uncouthness of Yorkshire or the absurdities of Cockney; Hiberno-English is thus both praised for its distinctive qualities and judged by the metropolitan norm. It is a tongue marked by wit, eloquence and metaphorical richness; but this figurative force is never far from rhetoric in the pejorative sense, from blarney, wheedling and making the poor mouth. Indeed the essay displays a notably self-undoing moment when an appreciation of the verbal resourcefulness of the peasantry veers suddenly into a genial criticism of them: the rhetorical skills of an old woman complaining about her impounded cow are displayed for our admiration, but the complaint in fact turns out to be unfounded. The landlord must always beware of being verbally mugged by the populace, whose language is lubricious with power and demands a vigilant hermeneutical skill from their superiors. Communications between the two parties are chronically mystified, as the people tell the gentry what they think they want to hear, calculating their own discourse on the basis of its potential misreception by the other or by the practical effects it might engender.

Language is weapon, dissemblance, seduction, apologia – anything, in fact, but *representational*; it is in a perpetual condition of untruth, and truth can thus only be imported from the outside, by those disinterested enough to represent the people accurately both to others and to themselves. But such a viewpoint must naturally repress the conditions of its own representability, which is why Edgeworth's crisp, judicious, eminently reasonable prose is a politics all in itself. Language is strategic for the oppressed, but representational for their rulers. To tell one's superiors only what you think they want to hear, or only what you judge they should know, is at once deference and disrespect, collusion and resistance; it is to refuse to treat them and oneself as members of some universal linguistic community, and so the denial of an abstract linguistic equality which could only mystify inequities of social power. To assume that the other is likely to misunderstand you is at once humbly self-effacing and a subtle put-down, an admission of powerlessness which is itself an act of power. The rulers may speak the truth, but only from within what their subordinates regard as a false situation; as an old woman accused of stealing a cow remarked in court to her prosecutor Daniel O'Connell, 'you know about the roguery of it, but you don't know at all about the truth of it'.[55] It is this 'untruth' of the social relations of utterance which Edgeworth perceives, but which she cannot finally bring herself to accept. It is clear enough from *Practical Education* that she recognizes the social roots of this mendacity: 'oppression and terror', she writes there, 'necessarily produce meanness and deceit in all climates'.[56] But what matters for her in the end is the referent, whereas what matters for her social inferiors is the addressee. Those in power can afford to assume that the truth is always beneficial, whereas those bereft of status are conscious that it can always be turned against them. You may, like the old woman with the cow, lie about a specific wrong, but only on the assumption that injustice is done to you in general; the rulers, by contrast, tend to hold that the general situation is just, and that offences are sporadic and particular. It is a contest between political and juridical notions of truth; and if there can be little dialogue between them, it is because the juridical conception of truth is unable to round upon the political sources of its own authority. That the landlord may be right but also wrong is the kind of Irish bull which finally defeated the Edgeworths' analytic powers.

There is a question, then, for Edgeworth as much as for Swift, of how near to or distant from a situation you need to be in order to pass judgement on it. Thady Quirk, if we take him straight, is too conspiratorially close to see much at all; but between the astigmatism of the insider and the purblindness of the absentee there would seem some narrow epistemological ground, and it is this that Maria Edgeworth seeks to occupy. It is a middle ground between Irish and English, generosity of spirit and rational justice, energy and utility; and we can find it exemplified, among

---

55. See Sean O'Faolain, *King of the Beggars* (Dublin 1938), p. 115.
56. *Essays on Practical Education* (London 1815), vol. 1, p. 269.

other places, in Sir Herbert Annaly of *Ormond*, who speaks sense to his tenants, but 'mixed that sense with wit and humour, in the proportion necessary to make it palatable to an Irishman' (Ch. 23). The ideal landlord, blending sense and sensibility, is thus also the ideal novel; and the formal problem of Edgeworth's fiction – how to reconcile 'life' and rational doctrine – is an index of the difficulty of its attainment. If the Ascendancy fails to mobilize the virtues of *Ormond*'s rumbustious King Corny, or of the feckless warm-hearted crook Sir Terence O'Fay of *The Absentee*, then it will fail to achieve hegemony; but these virtues are always in danger of upending it as well. This strain can be felt in the very form of Edgeworth's Irish novels, which at their worst pull off the improbable feat of being at once too schematic and too romantic[57] – as though the desirous imagination, expelled from the diagrammatic stereotyping of the narrative, is forced to take up its home instead in the fabular devices of the plot. *Ennui*, for example, is at one level a tale of rational reform and moral education, and at another level an improbable saga of long-lost parents and children substituted at birth. The narratives of these works will then try to mediate what their form fails to synthesize, as their protagonists steer a path between callously exploiting the Irish and gullibly sentimentalizing them. Richard Edgeworth feared that his daughter might prove too soft a touch as a landlord when she came to inherit the estate, but he needn't have worried. One must strive 'to preserve a proper medium between the indulging and the repressing of their sensibility', Edgeworth comments of children in *Practical Education*;[58] and for 'children', as so often, one can read 'the Irish'.

In all of these novels, individual character is largely a function of some overall didactic scheme, rather as, for the rational landlord Richard Edgeworth, generosity to individual tenants must be subdued to some rigorously impersonal pattern of justice and utility. The upshot of this is character as stereotype; but this is a pervasive phenomenon in nineteenth-century Irish fiction, as evident in Griffin, Carleton or Lady Morgan as it is in Edgeworth. The typical English novel is crammed with what we are meant to take as lovably idiosyncratic figures, 'characters' in both senses of the term; and this springs at once from the radical individualism of the dominant ideology, and from a characteristically urban way of seeing. In

---

57. One might note the contrast in this respect between the tedious moralism of a work like *Essays on Practical Education*, 1815, penned by Maria with her father, and the exuberance of her correspondence. See Christina Colvin, ed., *Maria Edgeworth: Letters from England* (Oxford 1971).

58. *Practical Education*, vol. 1, p. 377.

the complex industrial-capitalist milieu of nineteeth-century England, social relations are diffuse and opaque (who exactly is the governing class?), the dense, intricate texture of social life is notably hard to totalize, and secreted behind each social persona is some hinterland of inscrutable private experience, which only the omniscient authorial eye can decipher. None of this is likely to be the case in a largely pre-urban society which has no large-scale industry to run, empire to manage or foreign policy to pursue, and where social relations are more salient and sharply etched than in the metropolitan country.

The pattern of social life in such circumstances is rather more predictable, which is doubtless one source of literary stereotyping; and in a network of small agrarian communities, in contrast to the random encounters of the urban streets or labyrinthine reaches of an imperial bureaucracy, individuals are more instantly and assuredly located. So it is that Irish fiction seems to ring the changes on the same parsimonious stock of immediately readable characters – the choleric cleric, the blackguardly land agent or middleman, the saintly mother, the gauger or gombeen man, the nationalist publican or shopkeeper – all of whom inhabit the same physical space, in contrast to the purely abstract relations between banker and millworker, industrialist and housewife, solicitor and shopkeeper, which are more characteristic of the metropolitan nation. These small Irish communities, need one add, are as far from the 'organic' as one could imagine: their characteristic experience is one of insecurity and privation, violent upheaval and gruelling labour. But they are, in Raymond Williams's sense, 'knowable communities',[59] in which individuals are quickly identifiable in their social roles, in which they are often enough in and out of each other's cabins, and in which the dominant class has a physical proximity to its inferiors untypical of British social life. Kingsley's or Gaskell's proletarians would have scant idea of where their employer lived, a felicitous ignorance denied to the Irish landlord. The nineteenth-century Irish novel contains its fair share of aimiable or unprepossessing eccentrics, local idiots of one sort of another, but even these wayward, unassimilable figures are stock types, largely accepted as such by the community, as opposed to the sinisterly inaccessible grotesques of a Dickens. And just as Irish society is in this sense more calculable and transparent in its structure than the obfuscatory social order depicted in *Little Dorrit* or *The Secret Agent*, so one can understand what it means to

---

59. See Raymond Williams, *The English Novel from Dickens to Lawrence* (London 1970), Ch. 3.

describe Irish history, as Denis Donogue has done, as 'intense but monotonous'[60] – a mere set of variations, or so it would sometimes appear, on the three mighty abiding motifs of land, religion and colonialism, which then stamp apparently more far-flung topics (culture, education, sexuality) with their own inexorable impress.

In these conditions, real life already has something of the well-sculpted, prototypical, instantly legible quality of realist fiction; and no finer instance of this could be found than Richard Lovell Edgeworth himself, a figure so purely exemplary of the benign, sagacious landowner that he might have stepped straight out of the pages of a novel, instead of – in the case of his daughter's devoted writing – stepping straight into them.[61] Edgeworth was, in the Lukácsian sense, a historically typical character, indeed sometimes seems little else;[62] even as private, contingent a matter as the date of his migration from England to Ireland – 1782 – has a resonant public significance, as the year in which Grattan's parliament won its so-called independence. It was because she occupied a genuinely world-historical moment in Irish affairs that Maria Edgeworth was able to become the first 'national' Irish novelist. There had, of course, been an Irish novel before her, whatever the English literary historians might consider; but in the work of the eighteenth-century novelists Ireland, where it figures at all, is for the most part setting or backdrop for events which might often enough have occurred elsewhere.[63]

Edgeworth's fiction marks the place where a whole distinctive *object* known as Ireland makes its first fictional appearance, and does so precisely because it has become problematical. Irish society is no longer scenic backdrop or taken-for-granted *Lebenswelt* but dramatically foregrounded as a subject of enquiry in its own right, grasped as a coherent universe,

---

60. Quoted in W.J. McCormack, *Ascendancy and Tradition* (Oxford 1985), p. 4.
61. For Edgeworth's notable virtue, see his comment that 'I have passed some time at two universities, and have been concerned in conducting four or five contested elections, without ever having been intoxicated in my life' (*Memoirs*, vol. 1, London 1820, p. 76).
62. Typical, that is, of the benevolent landowner, not of the landowning class in general. Edgeworth was on the margin of his own class, and Maria, as a woman, was thus doubly peripheral. One might add that the other great Lukácsian type of the Irish nineteenth century is James Clarence Mangan, whose personal misfortunes intersect with uncanny precision with the plight of his people during the Famine, and who probably died, like many of them, of cholera. Mangan, however, recapitulates something of the history through which he lived precisely in his passivity, aberrancy, inauthenticity, lack of identity, rather than in some Lukácsian richness of self.
63. There are some noteworthy exceptions: see, for example, William Chaigneau, *The History of Jack Connor* (1752); and Thomas Amory, *The Life of John Buncle, Esq.* (1756–66).

reconstituted as a cultural entity rather than registered as this or that discrete character, place, event; and all this makes for a notable contrast with the novel in England. For there is no great English novel about England, in the sense of one which takes that topic as its articulate concern. 'A healthy nation', remarks Shaw in his Preface to *John Bull's Other Island*, 'is as unconscious of its nationality as a healthy man of his bones. But if you break a nation's nationality it will think of nothing else but getting it set again.' Not to brood obsessively on one's identity is the privilege of the victor. *Bleak House*, *Middlemarch* and *Women in Love* all reflect on the condition of the nation, but their characters do not typically debate the matter, as characters in Irish fiction interminably do. To introduce such disquisitions would be to risk violating the illusion of realism, about which the Irish novel is characteristically more cavalier. For English fiction, England may be the site of a good many recalcitrant problems; but it is not generally, like Edgeworth's Ireland, viewed as a problem all in itself. It is this newly totalized entity which Edgeworth's fiction seeks to represent as it really is, on the rationalist assumption that prejudice is in large part misunderstanding; but like all such transcendent viewpoints hers was unable to pose the transcendental question, include within itself its own material conditions of possibility, which had consequently to fall outside the representational frame. For this representation is also an intervention, one tendentious perspective within that which it would seek to totalize; and it is thus as much bound to the scene it surveys as Thady Quirk's shameless apologia. Only an outside vantage point, free from nativist *doxa* and self-serving, can deliver the truth; but this epistemological outside is also a site of power, and thus at the very heart of what it dispassionately inspects. The distance which enables true cognition is also what obstructs it. Edgeworth's language trades in power while striving to be innocent of it, negotiates conflicts by which it remains aloofly uncontaminated; but the authority required for any such enterprise is of course formidable. In the end, it is a question of whether the hyphen of 'Anglo-Irish' is bridge or impasse, linkage or sign of contradiction – an enabling passage between terms, or an aporia.

There is no doubt that the inherently contradictory unity known as Ireland finally passed beyond the frame of Edgeworth's representing, as she herself was mournfully to acknowledge in 1834. 'It is impossible', she writes in a familiar passage, 'to draw Ireland as she now is in a book of fiction – realities are too strong – party persuasions are too violent to bear to see, or care to look at, their faces in a looking glass. The people would only break the glass and curse the fool who held the mirror up to nature – distorted nature, in a fever.'[64] This is the Edgeworth who detested democracy and O'Connellism, supported Catholic Emancipation largely in the hope that it would ensure the safety of the Protestant establishment, and is reputed to have sent a present to the judge who condemned John Mitchel to deportation.[65] For the Quirks are now historically on the march, having achieved representation in both a political and literary sense, and are no longer dependent on the looking glass in which another holds the key to their identity. A unifying mode of representation, which is just what the looking-glass image signifies, is no longer able to capture a contradictory reality. For Edgeworth, however, what is twisted out of decent proportion is not the signifier but the referent – not the glass itself, but the feverish masses it fails to reflect. The people are now refusing to peer into this mirror – refusing to acknowledge as their own image and likeness that simulacrum of themselves which lies in an onlooker's possession. Just as popular violence falls outside the frame of constitutional politics, so it cannot find figuration in the realist novel, whose protocols are complicit with that politics. The truth has finally pulled the fiction asunder, shattering the means of representation; and what emerges for the first time from behind these broken shards is the figure of the glass-holder herself, who has previously been effaced behind this medium but is now, as a potential object of verbal violence, an object of the critical representation of others.

Robert Owenson, father of the novelist Lady Morgan, ran a theatre in Galway in which a young amateur actor named Wolfe Tone once played an incompetent butler who failed in everything including an attempt to kill himself. Tone himself was sadly to prove more successful. The co-founder of the United Irish movement was a man much given to melodrama and exaggerated emotionalism, with a habit of speaking in verse and quotations,[66] and he thus represents a curious crossing between

64. Quoted by Tom Dunne, 'A Gentleman's Estate should be a Moral School: Edgeworthstown in Fact and Fiction, 1760–1840', in R. Gillespie and G. Moran, eds, *Long-ford: Essays in County History* (Dublin 1991), p. 118.

65. For Edgeworth's later political views, see Michael Hurst, *Maria Edgeworth and the Public Scene* (London 1969).

66. See Marianne Elliott, *Wolfe Tone: Prophet of Irish Independence* (Oxford 1989), p. 53. This brilliant study has the odd lapse of sensibility: when Tone, unhappily exiled in America, thinks fondly of his native land, he is rapped sternly over the knuckles by his biographer for displaying 'all the emotionalism and chaunvinism of modern nationalism' (p. 274), as though homesickness were a political ideology.

art and life which, as we shall see, has echoes elsewhere in modern Irish history. Owenson himself was a flamboyant, improvident Connaught man who made his living playing stage-Irish roles. He could thus be said to have hammed up what he actually was; and this 'fascinating combination of the authentic and theatrical', as one critic puts it,[67] is everywhere apparent in his daughter's novels. Lord Rosbrin, gay, eccentric amateur Thespian of *Florence Macarthy* (1818), delights in playing Lady Macbeth and dreams of civilizing Ireland with a theatrical touring company, hence prefiguring the projects of the Revival. His English crony De Vere aestheticizes Irish poverty as a charming spectacle, while their host Lady Dunore has the 'inauthentic thirst for scenes and sensations' of her creator, who thus slyly exculpates herself by an act of fictional projection. Lady Dunore thrills to the prospect of conveniently remote dangers, transmutes real-life anger to theatrical quotation and plunders public events for private gratification. She even seizes on the lucky chance of the visit of some circuit judges to her castle to stage a kind of show trial or Star Chamber, rounding up a few local miscreants and placing them in the dock for the delectation of the gentry. The novel is engagingly satirical about these sadistic fantasies, but unlike *Mansfield Park* it is itself every bit as theatrical as the charades it reproves. Its hero, Fitzwalter, is a ludicrously romanticized member of the Wild Geese who has returned from a spell of freedom-fighting in Latin America to reclaim the Norman birthright now usurped by the Anglo-Irish Dunores. Like all such Morgan characters he is an entirely fictional figure uneasily inhabiting an actual social world – just as Morgan herself, in a calculated act of mythological self-fashioning, produced herself, harp, blue cloak and all at the heart of fashionable Dublin and London society.[68] In *Florence Macarthy*, that upper-class world comprises a notable bunch of Peacockian grotesques: the histrionic Lord Rosbrin, the Rosicrucian patriot O'Leary, the frivolous Lord Frederick, the disdainfully aestheticist De Vere, between whom much pointless meta-physical chitchat takes place; yet for all their overbred absurdity, these preposterous figures represent the historically actual ruling class, as opposed to the revanchist fantasy embodied in Fitzwalter. The problem of Morgan's texts, then, is that their imagination is at odds with their ideology: if it is the antique dispensation, Gaelic or Norman, which engages their emotional allegiance, it is the unprepossessing Anglo-Irish gentry of the present who, suitably reconstructed, hold the key to political progress.

67. Tom Dunne, 'Lady Morgan's Irish Novels', in Tom Dunne, ed., *The Writer as Witness: Literature as Historical Evidence* (Cork 1987), p. 140.

68. For her biography, see Lionel Stevenson, *The Wild Irish Girl* (London 1936).

The problem of form, then, is also a problem of politics. Two quite disparate discourses, the one romantic, the other realist, inhabit Morgan's texts without ever fruitfully interlocking; and since romance signifies an ideal, and realism an actual ruling class, this shift and clash of linguistic registers is the site of a genuine ideological dilemma. It is for the former mode that Morgan has been disparagingly remembered – for the mouldering towers and eroticized Milesian chieftains, the forlorn harpist glimpsed at the misty casement of some decrepit fortress – for all, in short, that was processed and aestheticized in the age of Tom Moore as an enjoyably consumable Ireland. But it is not only that this saccharine confection is actually, in her fiction, a good deal more than that – that this vein of vacuously sublimated desire is the symptom of a genuine historical disturbance and dislocation, which offers at every point to burst through the naturalizing constraints of realism and play havoc with a sedate linear chronology. It is also that the image of the Wild Irish Morgan conveniently displaces attention from her considerable literary strengths, which lie precisely in the adroit satirical intelligence she is able to train upon her own adoptive kind. If Rosbrin and O'Leary are mere stage figures, Lady Dunore, for all her compulsive self-dramatizing, is precisely not: like Lady Singleton of *O'Donnel* (1814), she is the kind of vain, spirited, sharp-witted woman whom these works understand wholly from the inside. The problem, then, is that the novels portray best what they most disapprove; and if the most popular of the fictions, *The Wild Irish Girl* (1806), is not the most impressive, it is partly because its cloistered Gaelic world leaves no space for that sharp-eyed critique of Anglo-Irish pretensions at which its author excels.

For all her claims to be a 'national' novelist – and 'national', for her, is effectively synonymous with 'natural' – Morgan is in fact preoccupied with a rather more specific conflict *within* the gentry, between the ruling Ascendancy and those of more ancient lineage who have been routed by it. Like Edgeworth, her theme is leadership; and though the question of leadership is metonymic of the plight of society as a whole, it can come by metaphorical substitution to stand in for it. It is on the traumatic moment of disinheritance that Morgan's historical imagination is fixated; and the strategy of each of her Irish novels is symbolically to repair this rupture through the displacing device of marriage. Thus Mortimer of *The Wild Irish Girl*, son of an absentee landlord whose family have ousted the Gaelic prince of Inismore, will return to Ireland, insinuate himself into the prince's desolate castle and end up marrying his daughter. Fitzwalter of *Florence Macarthy* wins the hand of the eponymous heroine, scion of a ruined Gaelic family, thus effecting a union of Norman Protestant and Gaelic Catholic lineages over the heads of the degenerate Anglo-Irish. Roderick O'Donnel, in the novel named after him, is the dispossessed heir of the Earl of Tirconnell, and having wound his way through a brittle, deceitful Ascendancy world reclaims his birthright by marrying into the family which appropriated it. Murrough O'Brien of *The O'Briens and the O'Flahertys* (1827) is another pauperized Irish chieftain who moves on the fringes of fashionable Anglo-Irish society, while his half-crazed wood-kern foster brother Shane leaps from hill to hill like some Connemara Caliban. Straddled amphibiously between Nature and Culture, the romantic nationalist O'Brien finally weds his cousin Beauvoin O'Flaherty, but only after they have abandoned Ireland for Bonapartist France, to which Irish revolutionary energies must now be exported. In this bleaker novel, then, marriage has shrunk to a personal rather than a political solution; but in the other works it betokens a conciliation between Gaelic and Old or New English, poetry and pragmatism, the political demands of the present and the spiritual resources of the past. What the present needs of the past is its violated legitimacy, its symbolic capital, its aura of cultural authority, as a vital hegemonic link between modern-day Protestant Ascendancy and traditionally minded Catholic masses. Obsessed by a moment of historical expropriation, Morgan's fiction is thus itself an act of ideological appropriation, symbolically undoing past crimes in the name of a politically refurbished present.

The literal implications of this symbolic act, however, need to be strictly controlled. Glorvina, O'Donnel and Florence Macarthy end up repossessing through marriage some of their lost estates; but this is not to be read as *carte blanche* for some full-blooded programme of Gaelic restoration, as the novels are prudent enough to point out. The fact that a few deracinated nobles have won their deserts does not mean that the peasantry should lay claim *en masse* to their land. Indeed it means exactly the opposite: the point of this realignment within the governing bloc is to consolidate its power, resolve its antagonisms, furnish it with the hegemonic resources it so grievously lacks. What takes place is a symbolic trade-off: Mortimer in *The Wild Irish Girl* 'restores' Glorvina's property by marrying her, thus conveniently retaining it for himself; Florence Macarthy 'regains' her possessions by marrying Fitzwalter, but will do little more than grace her Anglo-Irish Protestant husband with the authority of her Gaelic Catholic name. The Anglo-Irish are buying into mythology in order to buy off a disaffected tenantry; and the strategy of Morgan's novels is to regulate this inequitable exchange between cash and culture, power and prestige. Novels are particularly appropriate vehicles for such resolutions, since in realist fiction personal relationships are the medium in which social issues become active and incarnate. Such relationships are in fact metonymic of society as a whole; but it is in the nature of realist writing to convert this metonym into metaphor, recasting social processes as personal transactions. This literary convention then holds open the perpetual ideological possibility of *reducing* social questions to interpersonal ones; and this, one might claim, is a peculiar temptation for the apologists for enlightened aristocracy from Morgan to Yeats. For the programme of regenerating a delinquent aristocracy is essentially an ethical one, much preoccupied with change of heart, personal charisma, strains of blood and breeding; and such an idealist or individualist politics lends itself to the affective intimacies of art more readily than some more anonymously institutional project. Even so, Morgan's metaphor of marriage is ambivalent in its social scope. At the level of ideology, these alliances must be read as symbolizing an essential fusing and revivifying of the ruling bloc; but they are not thereby to be taken as threatening the Ascendancy's property. The Gaelic heritage must be restored, but largely as a matter of symbolic capital.[69] And to this extent the fictional resolutions of the novels are and are not metaphorical of what must happen in political society as a whole. If these texts are to be read as truth, they must also be read as fiction; and their formal dislocations − their peculiar mixture of history and fantasy, antiquarianism and *realpolitik* − lend themselves conveniently to that end.

If truth and fiction are not easy to disentangle in Morgan's writing, it is partly because they are so intimately interwoven in the course of Irish history itself. How is one to produce realist narratives from a history which is itself so crisis-racked, hyperbolic, improbable? How can even the most spectacular of tales not find itself trumped by the lurid theatricality of the actual events it records, which offer to beggar imagination in their epic violence, romantic bravado or tragic despondency? The Breton scholar Anatole Le Braz accounted for the lack of theatre in traditional Irish culture on the grounds that the Irish had quite enough drama in real life.[70] William Carleton notes in his Preface to The *Black Prophet* (1847) 'how far the strongest imagining of Fiction is frequently transcended by

---

69. 'For those from an Ascendancy or "colonist" background the Gaelic world served both as a warning and as the basis for creating new cultural foundations for an eroding social and political hegemony' (Tom Dunne, 'Haunted by History: Irish Romantic Writing 1800–50', in R. Porter and Mikulas Teich, eds, *Romanticism in National Context,* Cambridge 1988, p. 72).

70. See Declan Kiberd, *Synge and the Irish Language* (London 1979), p. 102.

the terrible realities of Truth'; and W.J. McCormack aptly remarks of Sheridan Le Fanu that the sensationalism of his writing is less implausible when read against the background of agrarian agitation in County Limerick than when viewed in the context of Derby or Kent.[71] The events of 1789, wrote the great Belfast radical William Drennan, had 'all the fascination of a novel, attended with the conviction that it is reality'.[72] The Young Irelander Michael Doheny's The Felon's Track, a gripping account of his escape from Ireland after the 1848 insurrection, was published in 1875 by a Glasgow firm in a series of romances that included such titles as The Turkish Slave, The Pirates of the Slave Coast and The White Queen and the Mohawk Chief. Doheny's flight is also recorded in A.M. Sullivan's compulsively readable New Ireland (1878), a work of history which, with its dramatized anecdotes, snatches of dialogue and vivid vignettes, reads much like a work of fiction. Sullivan manages to give the impression that he was an eyewitness to more or less every political event which occurred in the country between 1840 and 1870. Standish O'Grady describes the career of the Ascendancy as one of 'heroic verse, followed by prose, and closed in a disgusting farce'.[73] The humour of Castle Rackrent lies in the farcical discrepancy between Thady Quirk's emollient language and the larger-than-life occurrences it documents. Gerald Griffin despaired of creating a genuine historical novel out of 'centuries consumed in suffering, in vain remonstrance, and idle through desperate struggles for change ... [and of] painting the convulsions of a powerful people labouring under a nightmare for ten centuries'.[74] 'I have nothing more to add', remarks Fitzwalter at the end of Florence Macarthy, having just recounted a hair-raising tale of being sold as a youth into slavery, 'but that my story, strange and improbable as it may appear, belongs to the history of a long disorganised country' (vol. 4, Ch. 6).

A startlingly direct relation is enforced between the disrupted course of Irish history and the non-realist quality of its fictions. Narrative is non-realist because the history is seeks to mirror is somehow the same. If Morgan's novels are formally dishevelled, then this is a more truthful representation of the history they chronicle than the deftly symmetrical diagrams of an Edgeworth. It is because they discreetly close off that fractured narrative that Edgeworth's fictions can maintain their formal equipoise; and when they engage it directly, as in Castle Rackrent, what

---

71. W.J. McCormack, Sheridan Le Fanu and Victorian Ireland (Oxford 1980), p. 46.
72. Quoted by R.F. Foster, Modern Ireland 1600–1972 (London 1988), p. 260.
73. Standish O'Grady, Toryism and Tory Democracy (London 1886), p. 239.
74. William Griffin, The Life of Gerald Griffin (London 1857), pp. 285–90.

emerges is a different literary form entirely, which is as travestying as it is truthful, and which in its paratactic rhythms seems to mime a history of ceaseless upheaval. Charles Maturin writes in his Preface to *The Milesian Chief* (1812), no doubt as a feeble rationale for his romantic excesses, that Irish history, in its blend of 'refinement and barbarity', lends itself particularly well to fiction; and the land agent W. Steuart Trench, in his *Realities of Irish Life*, describes Irish society as typified by 'a kind of poetic turbulence and almost romantic violence, which I believe could scarcely belong to real life in any other country in the world'.[75] In all of this, to be sure, there is a good deal of special pleading on the part of the writers and ritual stereotyping on the part of the observers; but there remains the sense that Ireland gives the slip to realist representation. This may be because its historical events are larger than life; or because its manifold contradictions resist a unifying fictional frame; or because the seismic discontinuities of its past elude the evolutionary rhythms of the classic realist text. This is certainly true of Morgan's writing, in which the present continually threatens to open out into complexly stratified genealogies, and where, as in some Benjaminian constellation, the ancient and the modern are brought into arrestingly immediate encounter. The present is not identical with itself, fissured and hollowed as it its by its relation to a past which at once nurtures and disrupts it. If Morgan did not write 'historical' fiction about her own country, it was because it was plain enough that history, for both good and ill, was what the present was made of.

The present, then, is a kind of allegory, which properly interpreted lays bare the historical forces at its heart. How far one should pursue this project, however, is another question. There is no way of unlocking an intricately historical present without confronting the contentions of the past; yet to do so may be to fall prey to the nightmare of history, and so prove counterproductive. The ancient quarrels which hold the key to the present, and so to a reinvigorated future, may end up by overwhelming both. History is both ruin and redemption; and it was her awareness of the former which inspired Morgan to abandon the original historical setting of *O'Donnel* and transport the action to the present day. She had hoped to use history, so she remarks in the Preface to that work, to 'extenuate the errors' of the present; instead, she found herself uncovering a grisly sectarian violence which would merely scupper her project of conciliation. Past history and present politics are locked in an un-

---

75. W.S. Trench, *Realities of Irish Life* (London 1869), p. vii.

manageable interrelation, as the former both illuminates and undermines the latter.

Where this is less true is in that other more pervasive history of oppression which is the narrative of women, which finds its most powerful expression in her ambitious genealogy of patriarchy, *Woman and her Master* (1840). It is no accident that it was left to a female imagination, relatively remote from the pragmatism of public affairs, to produce for the age its most unabashedly utopian images. For romance, however strained and febrile, always bears such a utopian impulse within it; and if the visions it generates seem idle it is because the workaday world fashioned by men have rendered them so. Morgan's writing has the courage to desire and imagine far beyond the present, even if the only place of that transcendence must be the past. The very forms of her fiction, with their scandalously flaunted play of fantasy, are thus an implicit rebuke to the mean-spirited jobbers and brokers of the male Ascendancy. Her excess and extravagance, both in fiction and real life, are an affront to a certain species of male rationality, which can respond to Oscar Wilde's outrageous camp with amused admiration, but can only condescend to Morgan's exuberant self-transformation into a character out of one of her own fictions. It is the vanity and ridiculousness of this which have been remembered, rather than the provocative, calculatedly histrionic attempt to live a kind of utopia in the present, the admirable narcissism and self-devotion by which she refused feminine obscurity and converted her domestic life into a public stage. That she could accomplish this for the most part only in the stereotypical role of Society hostess, conducting a salon for the male activists of the Emancipation movement, testifies to the limits of patriarchy; but she invested that social role, at once marginal and authoritative, with all the brio and *élan* of her public fictional protagonists, and in doing so troubled the boundary between the domestic and the political. Her delight in patrician elegance was a valuing of the lavishly symbolic in a world which derided it, and she knew how to manipulate those semiotic resources to alchemize herself from the inconsiderable daughter of a second-rate actor–manager to a formidable public figure. In *The Wild Irish Girl*, she manufactured a whole new symbolic matrix for Irish female identity, which for all its breathless idealization and filigree romance drew upon the potent forces of mythology and the political unconscious to create for the Irishwoman an ideal ego more spirited and alluring than the demeaning images of patriarchal power. If she was a menacing figure, venomously denounced by her compatriot John Wilson Croker, it was because she combined this defiant gusto and ostentation with a politics considerably to the left of any other major nineteenth-century Irish writer. If she was a passionate feminist, she was also an admirer of radical republicanism, an advocate of Catholic Emancipation and a dedicated antagonist of the Tory Ascendancy.

By the time of her most convincing Irish novel, *The O'Briens and the O'Flahertys*, it would seem that all these high political hopes have come to nothing. It is a work full of historical cul-de-sacs: the golden age of Grattan's parliament has passed,[76] the United Irish movement (which her hero briefly joins) has been defeated, the catastrophe of the Union has occurred, liberty and elegance have deserted Dublin, and the one brave liberal cause that remains – Catholic Emancipation – is passing from the Anglo-Irish Whig paternalists into the hands of the Catholic demagogues. Gaelic antiquarianism, to be sure, is now no kind of solution, and indeed Morgan was all along more ambivalent about its value than the popular image of her would suggest.[77] That political option appears in the novel in the remarkable figure of Baron Terence O'Brien, class renegade and religious apostate who began life as *Terneen na garlach* or Terry the bastard. From his beggarly origins as a pious mass server, Terry becomes *Terneen na Librach* or Terry of the Books, and manages to haul himself into the Establishment; but little Terneen remains bruised and embittered inside him, and behind his reputable social cover he has reverted to the religious and political faith of his forefathers. But O'Brien has been driven insane by his schizoid allegiances, and there is no trust to be placed in such forlorn restorationist delusions. On the eve of the United Irish rebellion, the Anglo-Irish governing class is as venal, frivolous and boneheaded as were their French counterparts before the revolution; but whereas the French aristocracy was historically superannuated, the Ascendancy still has its time to serve. The histories of the two nations between which the novel moves are depressingly non-synchronous. What is definitively *passé* in Ireland is the old Gaelic order, whatever spiritual energies it might have to bequeath to the present. The dilemma, then, is that spiritual dynamism lies with a historically spent class, while the junta still capable of ruling is disastrously bereft of vision.

The ambiguities of Morgan's ideology reflect the confused crosscurrents of its times. A passionate patriot who appears indulgently at ease in the bosom of the Establishment; an ardent supporter of Catholic Emancipation

---

76. For Morgan's illusions about this period, see her essay *Absenteeism* (London 1825), which is incidentally more of an apologia for its subject of enquiry than a polemic against it.

77. See Dunne, 'Lady Morgan's Irish Novels', pp. 149–50.

who dislikes Catholics and deeply distrusts O'Connell;[78] a republican sympathizer who is also spiritual aristocrat and Gaelic traditionalist; a feminist who wrote to a friend that she was 'every inch a wife'.[79] The brittle unreality of the revivified leadership she offers as a response to Ireland's troubles is betrayed formally in her fiction by its romanticism, just as it is betrayed in Edgeworth by its schematism. Both testify to a solution which can be secured by literary means only; and in both cases, as the Catholic masses begin their long march towards independence, the voices which proffer these panaceas finally lapse into an indignant silence. Edgeworth was to write no more Irish fiction after 1817, or Morgan after 1827. For Maria Edgeworth, the Union is on the whole an auspicious affair, and it now remains to extend that political anglicization to the question of social relations. For Morgan, always less preoccupied with such social issues, the Union has all but put paid to the liberal Whig causes of liberty and enlightenment, and contemporary history would seem in accelerating decline. For Edgeworth, the past is mainly loss, to be relinquished for a reforming future; for Morgan, it is the present which is void, and the past a dangerously two-sided instrument for renewing it.

The woman who began by idealizing antiquity will end up urging that Ireland should obliterate its past.[80] For all her more forward-looking impulse, Edgeworth would seem in the end quite as politically at a loss as her fellow novelist; *Ormond* ends with the young hero gallantly turning over his estates to their true Irish owner, who in tiresomely 'lower Irish' fashion manages to burn down the big house. It is not difficult to read this as a dire omen of the papist future; and though Morgan still trusts to the cause of Catholic Emancipation as the logical consummation of the Whig revolution, she had not gone quite so far as to envisage that the people might be discourteous enough to take this matter into their own hands, rather than obsequiously accept it as a gift from the more liberal-minded of their superiors. What has altered is not the cause, but the question of agency. Morgan would seem incapable of conceiving of history in terms of popular initiative; for her, history is essentially a fable of aristocrats, a pitched battle between Whig and Tory in which the populace are the precious stake to be played for. But the masses have now made their first unruly appearance as a collective actor on the political stage;

---

78. 'O'Connell wants back the days of Brian Borru, himself to be the king, with a crown of emerald shamrocks, a train of yellow velvet, and a mantle of Irish tabinet...'(*Memoirs*, vol. 2, p. 225).

79. *Memoirs*, vol. 1, p. 519, ii 5.

80. See Dunne, 'Lady Morgan's Irish Novels', p. 154.

and though Morgan had good filial reason to know that such acting need
not be bogus, she could find little in it in the end but the bluster of the
stage Irishman.

Both Edgeworth and Morgan tend to work in terms of sharp moral
polarities. There are humane land agents and villainous ones, depraved
Ascendancy lords and wholesome young Milesians, angelically virtuous
women and empty-headed drones. But one can always ask what might
happen if one were to deconstruct these antitheses – if, for example, one
were to retain the hero in all his magnetic splendour, but at the same
time project into the very core of his character the evil by which he is
encircled. What if one were to take the noble figure in a ravaged landscape
and allow that ruined history to be incorporated in his very being? Then
one would indeed have an arrestingly original creation, at once admirable
and appalling, glamorous and deadly; and the name of this figure in early-
nineteenth-century Irish literature is Melmoth the Wanderer.

The early novels of Charles Robert Maturin, *The Wild Irish Boy* (1818)
and *The Milesian Chief* (1812), are lurid parodies of Lady Morgan; but
with *Melmoth the Wanderer* (1820) he fashioned for himself a whole new
structure of feeling, which stands at the source of the powerful current of
Irish fiction known as Protestant Gothic. The fact that Anglo-Irish writers
from Regina Maria Roche, Maturin and Sheridan Le Fanu to Bram
Stoker, Wilde, Yeats and Elizabeth Bowen should have exhibited such
fascination with madness and the occult, terror and the supernatural,[81] is
in one sense surprising: they belonged, after all, to a notoriously hard-
headed social class which habitually chided the Catholic masses for their
infantile superstition. But Protestant Gothic might be dubbed the political
unconscious of Anglo-Irish society, the place where its fears and fantasies
most definitively emerge. To grasp the notion of a political unconscious,[82]
one would need to imagine that our everyday social practices and relations,
with all their implicit violence, longing and anxiety, were all the time
weaving a kind of fantastic subtext to themselves in some entirely imaginary place, a kind of invisible verso to the recto of our waking life, as

---

81. For a valuable survey of this phenomenon, see R.F. Foster, 'Protestant Magic: W.B.
Yeats and the Spell of History', *Proceedings of the British Academy*, LXXV (London 1989). See
also W.J. McCormack, Introduction to 'Irish Gothic and After 1820–1945', in Seamus Deane,
ed., *The Field Day Anthology of Irish Writing*, vol. 2 (Derry 1991).

82. The concept is Fredric Jameson's, in *The Political Unconscious: Narrative as a Socially
Symbolic Act* (London 1981), but I have adapted it somewhat freely here.

intimate and alien to it as id to ego, in which those familiar social processes are refigured in the light of all that they have abruptly repressed, and so as monstrously distorted images through which the shape of every-day political society is nonetheless dimly discernible. Literature, and Gothic literature in particular, is one medium in which this non-place of our fantasized existence can find fleetingly conscious form – in which we find mirrored back to us the recognizable characters, events and locales of daily life, but now shot through with all the guilt, loathing and un-nameable desire which had to be jettisoned from that existence if we were to operate as coherent citizens at all. If this is a *political* unconscious, it is because it weaves the subtext of those actions and relations which make up our collective form of life, as opposed to the events of some uniquely individual biography; and it can therefore achieve expression only in some equally collective phenomenon such as literature. It is as though every drearily predictable process of labour and exchange, every casual act of domination or collusion, is leaving its stealthy impress in some region altogether elsewhere, which will return in the shape of literary fantasy to confront us with the terrifying inner structure of all that we take most for granted.

There are good reasons why the political unconscious of nineteenth-century Ireland should have been rather more turbulent than most. Violent, criminal, priest-ridden, autocratic, full of mouldering ruins and religious fanaticism, it was a society ripe for Gothic treatment, having much of that literary paraphernalia conveniently to hand. And if Irish Gothic is a specifically Protestant phenomenon, it is because nothing lent itself more to the genre than the decaying gentry in their crumbling houses, isolated and sinisterly eccentric, haunted by the sins of the past. Gothic carries with it a freight of guilt and self-torment, and these are arguably more Protestant than Catholic obsessions; in an admirably succinct contrast between the two faiths, Melmoth himself speaks of human beings as 'making their religion a torment; – the religion of some prompting them to torture themselves, and the religion of some prompting them to torture others' (vol. 3, Ch. 16). Yeats writes in *Explorations* of the 'solitude' of the Anglo-Irish, and this too finds its resonance in Gothic, which typically runs its course in some stagnant backwater secluded from the mainstream of history.

As the nineteenth century drew on, the Anglo-Irish had more and more reason to believe that this was their condition; and that most exem-plary of all Gothic states of being – paranoia – was one unnerving consequence of it. For Gothic is the nightmare of the besieged and reviled

– of women, most notably, but in this case of a minority marooned within a largely hostile people to whom they are socially, religiously and ethnically alien. Maturin, like Le Fanu, came of Huguenot stock, and so hailed from a history of religious persecution. The dungeon and locked chamber, the sequestered castle from which there is no escape, is for Maturin Ireland itself, a land thronged with the spectres of the past and haunted by the memory of ancient crimes. Both Ireland and Gothic are typified by extremist spiritual states, in which it is natural to demonize one's opponent: Daniel O'Connell, writes Sheridan Le Fanu, 'who, having seen the victims of his hatred laid in the graves of martyrdom, and those of his perfidy and cajolery exposed upon the gibbets of their country, now approaches the verge of his iniquitous existence, unaffected by the visitings of remorse, with a soul in which every passion, but that of unquenchable malignity has perished, and a heart which so far from being touched by the awful approaches of death and judgement, seems not to anticipate the coldness and corruption of the grave'.[83] O'Connell is for Le Fanu a figure straight out of Transylvanian folklore, a kind of Dracula of Derrynane. But the psychic alienation and anomie which are common to nineteenth-century Ireland, most graphically figured in the person of the blanched-haired, weirdly garbed James Clarence Mangan ('a spectre out of some German romance, rather than a living creation', as Gavan Duffy describes him), assume particularly virulent form in some of the offspring of Ascendancy, whose notorious pugnaciousness and eccentricity can border at times on the pathological. Even the thoroughly modern Charles Stewart Parnell was hag-ridden by superstitition.[84] And it seems plausible, as R.F. Foster argues, that much of the Anglo-Irish obsession with magic, the occult, secret societies and the rest was an attempt to surmount the solitude of the Protestant self – to find in ritual and mystical brotherhood a consoling substitute for that sense of system and solidarity which the Catholic Church was able to bestow on its adherents.[85]

There is, however, a paradox in the idea of the Anglo-Irish as victims of persecution. For are they not after all, from the viewpoint of the masses, the persecutors? How come that those in power should feel so wretched – should share in some measure the spiritual impoverishment of

83. Quoted by W.J. McCormack, 'J. Sheridan Le Fanu's *Richard Marston* (1848): The History of an Anglo-Irish Text', in Francis Barker et al., eds, *1848: The Sociology of Literature* (Wivenhoe 1979), p. 113.

84. See F.S.L. Lyons, *Charles Stewart Parnell* (London 1977), p. 612.

85. R.F. Foster, 'Protestant Magic'. The Limerick poet and landowner Aubrey de Vere went the whole hog and became a Newmanite.

those they oppress? It is possible to read Maturin's astonishing novel as an allegory of this strange condition in which exploiters and victims are both strangers and comrades, and indeed, in the person of Melmoth himself, inhabit the same personality. To read the diabolic Melmoth as a type of the Anglo-Irish ruling class is hardly extravagant: as the brother of a Cromwellian planter, he has survived over the centuries, and what other human subject has a continuous existence over time than a social group or class? The novel may deal in dungeons and the undead, in the Spanish Inquisition and exotic Indian islands; but all this complex *mise-en-abyme* narration, with one crumbling manuscript buried within another, begins and ends in a dilapidated Anglo-Irish big house in County Wicklow, with its miserly, half-mad owner dying squalidly in the bedroom and its superstitious servants muttering fearfully in the kitchen. At the source of all this lies some aboriginal crime, some initial trespass which refuses to lie quiet in its grave but which, in the person of Melmoth himself, stalks restlessly through the centuries in search of expiation. That crime, literally speaking, is Melmoth's selling of his soul, which drives him now to seek out the despairing and destitute to tempt them into exchanging destinies with him. But it is not hard to read this as a metaphor of the original crime of forcible settlement and expulsion, which belongs to the period in which Melmoth's bargain with the devil takes place, or to see his preying upon the dispossessed as a nightmarish image of the relations between the Ascendancy and the people. Time has been suspended since the first trespass, freezing Melmoth in an eternal present; and Oliver MacDonagh has characterized this as a typically Irish view of history, in which a wrong, once perpetrated, can never be undone by chronological succession but is doomed ceaselessly to re-enact itself.[86] Yet Melmoth is also running out of time, like the social class he represents, and by the end of the novel the hour of his damnation will have struck. If he is in one sense outside history, indifferently levelling all epochs and locales, he is in another sense running hard to keep up with it. It is clear, anyway, that whatever its stage properties of water torture and sadistic Spanish abbots, the novel's true subject is Ireland; it is not for nothing that the first topic Melmoth broaches with the innocent child of Nature Immalee, when he arrives on her paradisal island, is, of all seductive gambits, religious sectarianism. Before then we have visited an English madhouse,

---

86. See Oliver MacDonagh, *States of Mind* (London 1983), Ch. 1. A road sign in Donegal today reads 'To the Flight of the Earls', as though this event of 1607 is ceaselessly re-enacted in the present. Britain, by contrast, is singularly lacking in road signs which read 'To the Execution of Charles I', 'To the Industrial Revolution' and so on.

which holds only one inmate 'who was not mad from politics, religion, ebriety, or some perverted passion' (vol. 1, Ch. 3); and it would not be difficult to give a national name to this gloomy asylum.

But Melmoth is much more than some melodramatic stereotype of the dastardly landlords. He is, as the admiring Baudelaire remarked, a living contradiction, a predator who is himself a victim, furnished with a fine sardonic intelligence, able in his perverted way to be stirred by beauty and virtue, and something of a radical social critic to boot. He is, in short, Milton's Satan or Richardson's Lovelace recycled, a man tormented by the moral splendour he is driven to destroy. He is leashed to his victims by a powerful bond, so that (as the novel comments in a different context) they 'cling to each other's hate, instead of each other's love' (vol. 2, Ch. 9). As in Hegel's great parable of master and slave, the exploiter's identity is in the keeping of those he plunders; and he is driven to seek their recognition, as Melmoth stands in need of Immalee's love, if only to ease the intolerable solitude which his exploitation of them has created. This deadlocked dialectic has its theological dimension – the theology, as one character puts it, 'of utter hostility to all beings whose sufferings may mitigate mine' (vol. 2, Ch. 10). The oppressor detests his victims because they incarnate his guilt, and so, having demonized them in this fashion, can gain relief from that self-odium only by torturing them further. The Protestant may vindicate his own righteousness by denouncing the sins of others, but he only has need of such reassurance because he is a wretch himself. There is a spurious kind of fellowship between oppressor and oppressed: if the exploiter is an outcast, then so are those on whom he battens; if they have no identity, then neither has he. What this conveniently overlooks is that if the ruler bears the mark of Cain it is because of his own actions, which is why the oppressed are outcast too; but in Ireland this symmetry can pass as plausible, since the governing class really does have good reason to feel paranoid. Their sense of persecution, in part at least, is a dread of the vengeance of those they have persecuted. Estranged from the populace by culture and religion, the elite can easily mistake itself for the marginal, and so misperceive itself as a mirror image of the people themselves. The hunters become the hunted; and this is surely one reason why the figure of the self-lacerating Satanic hero can strike such a powerful resonance.

Bound together like lovers by their hereditary hatred, ruler and ruled present a kind of negative image of hegemony. Melmoth must elicit the free consent of his victims to be damned, if he is to escape his own fate; but since all he has to offer them is hell, it is hardly surprising that they are somewhat reluctant to close on the bargain. So it is that the great Satanic love scene between Melmoth and Immalee can be deciphered as the Ascendancy's doomed pursuit of hegemony, its need for a loving consent on the part of its subjects which will in fact lead them to their ruin. It is as an allegory of such hegemony that Raymond Williams has read that other Gothic masterpiece, William Godwin's *Caleb Williams*, in which the relationship between Caleb and Falkland can be seen as 'a transcendence of moral contrast by a new process in which both hunter and hunted, persecutor and persecuted, are dynamically though of course differentially formed and impelled by a general condition which is common to both'.[87] In both works, the exploiter has put himself beyond the pale of humanity, and so is curiously on terms with those he dispossesses. In fact Melmoth is in his own macabre way a kind of radical, given to magnificent tirades against social injustice and usually to be found slumming in gaols, madhouses and dens of famine, admittedly if only to find souls to buy up. The novel deploys a Swiftian technique of estrangement to unmask the crimes and follies of humankind from Melmoth's own standpoint as eternal outsider; and these depravities count in a sense in his favour, since a race as vicious as this might well be consigned to hell without compunction. But this Swiftian or Schopenhauerian misanthropy is more the effect of his alienation than the cause of it: only those themselves bereft of human kinship can portray so graphically the brutalities of the world. In a familiar paradox in Irish fiction, the exile can see more of the truth than the natives, but exile is exactly what renders that truth radically suspect.

It is possible, then, to read Melmoth as romantically as Blake read Milton's Satan, and the novel is certainly intent on leaving this perspective open. The Protestant gentry may be doomed; but at least they are figures of high romantic tragedy rather than equestrian idiots, Byronic heroes rather than bumbling country squires. In Yeatsian style, the work raises their destiny to metaphysical status, investing them with all the alluring glamour of the illicit. If Melmoth dispels our sympathy with his rapaciousness, he recoups it in his miserable solitude; if he detests those he destroys, it is – at least in the case of Immalee – with an intensity indistinguishable from love. Predator and prey are fashioned in each other's image, share an ancient knowledge of each another more riveting and intimate than mere affection; and it is not difficult to see in this one of the familiar self-

---

87. Raymond Williams, 'The Fiction of Reform', in *Writing in Society* (London 1984), p. 146.

rationalizing fantasies of a colonial class. The lord has always had a soft spot for the beggar; and Melmoth's repulsive fascination with Immalee presses this perverse attachment to a ghastly extreme.

One of the novel's many narrators speaks of 'that excitement which the sight of suffering never fails to give' (vol. 2, Ch. 9). It is an excitement which belongs to the reader as much as the characters. For reading the Gothic novel involves reaping a sadistic delight from others' terrors, permanently thankful that it is they who face the prospect of dismemberment or incarceration rather than ourselves. This readerly sadism is also of course masochistic: Gothic, like the sublime, is a safely defused way of inflicting pain on ourselves, secure in the knowledge that it can never be actualized. For a fleeting moment, *Thanatos* has its old enemy *Eros* under its heel, as we grapple with all that most threatens life in the exultant assurance that we can never be harmed. If *Melmoth the Wanderer* is in some sense an allegory of Ireland, it is also a sublimating and astheticizing of all that turmoil, a strategy for converting it into pleasurable sensation. But those to whom the sight of suffering never fails to bring excitement are also the religious fanatics who find in this anguish gratifying evidence of the unregeneracy of humankind, and thus testimony to their own spiritual superiority. This, indeed, is the true doubleness of Melmoth, who at once epitomizes the darkness of the human heart and scornfully anatomizes that condition from the Olympian standpoint of a lost soul. The damned are as much a spiritual elite as the angelic, as privy as they are to metaphysical mysteries, and perdition is in this sense only a thought away from paradise. If the reader can feel sympathy for Melmoth, then, it is because he or she is placed precisely as reader in his position, detachedly surveying the carnage of human history and deriving a forbidden pleasure from the spectacle. Like all gripping tales of the diabolical, the form of the novel is thus in contradiction with its moral content, for to fictionalize evil is always to render it appealing. Maturin's novel takes the morally mediocre world of Anglo-Irish society and presses it to an abominable extreme; but if that world is thereby shown up as corrupt, it is also retrieved for romance, and to that extent partly redeemed.

The driving force behind *Melmoth the Wanderer* is not metaphysics but money. Maturin wrote the novel in order to feed his four hungry children; and Chris Baldick has noted how central material possession is to the plot.[88] Protestant Gothic is full of hapless victims imprisoned in sealed

---

88. Chris Baldick, Introduction to *Melmoth the Wanderer* (Oxford 1989), p. xviii. For a brief account of Maturin, see David Punter, *The Literature of Terror* (London 1980), pp. 141–9. See also Dale Kramer, *Charles Robert Maturin* (New York 1973).

chambers, buried alive in dungeons or left to rot in remote asylums; but it is a fair bet that this is because some unscrupulous operator is trying to lay his hands on their fortune. This most subjectivist and supernatural of literary forms is also among the most grossly materialist: at its centre lie disputed wills and struggles over inheritance, secret legacies and financial double-dealing. All this forms the economic base of the guilt, anxiety, paranoia and murderous aggression which is Gothic's psychical super-structure, as well, indeed, as providing a sublunary clue to its obsession with the preternatural. For Gothic is a form in which the dead take command of the living – in which the clammy hand of the past stretches out and manipulates the present, reducing it to a hollow repetition of itself. The present is awash with spectres and revenants, with transmitted curses and rumours of primordial crimes; but it requires no great labour of decipherment to see in all this how the deadweight of property and inheritance moulds an upper-class world, and the novels are not shy of laying bare these connections themselves. The encumbered nature of their estates was the true nightmare of many an Anglo-Irish landowner.

What sustains these decaying Ascendancy settings is the power of capital, itself so much dead labour, a phenomenon in which the past reduces the present to its own mirror image and the inanimate comes to assume an uncannily active force. It is no wonder, then, that these haunted locales are thronged with creatures ambivalently dead and alive, or defined by extreme hallucinatory states of consciousness in which the real and unreal are undecidably mingled. 'The dead and the living cannot be one: God has forbidden it', declares a character in Sheridan Le Fanu's 'Schalken the Painter',[89] but his acquaintance with literature must clearly be confined to realism. What all of this catalyses in Protestant Gothic is then a kind of ontological crisis, in which the past – a country less real than the present – comes to imbue actual experience with a kind of spectral insubstan-tiality, but in a way so neurotically heightened that it seems at once hyperreal and sheer illusion. These states of derangement and delirium, of festering guilt and persecutory terror, are at one level the notorious eccentricity of the Anglo-Irish gentry pressed to a surreal limit, raised to the second power, translated from a humdrum social condition to a meta-physical theatre of good and evil, recoded as demonic possession or family curse. Protestant Gothic is the unconscious screen on which a dying social class projects its fantasies; and it is, then, no wonder that it is so

---

89. See Sheridan Le Fanu, *Ghost Stories and Tales of Mystery* (London 1851).

gripped by the prospect of immortality, or so morbidly quick to discern the imagery of death in the gesture of a limb or the curve of a landscape.

In the sensationalist fiction of Joseph Sheridan Le Fanu, money is usually to be found lurking at the root of the mystery. Indeed his inferior ghost stories, like the gratuitous 'Green Tea' from *In a Glass Darkly* (1886), are typically those in which mystery and sensation are present for their own sake, rather than serving as complex metaphors for a social condition. In a tale like 'The Room in the Dragon Volant', a spooky malevolence turns out to be no more than a front for the mercenary schemes of two of the characters; but in his best work the predatory and the preternatural are more intricately interwoven. Le Fanu knows the roistering, hard-drinking, heavily enmortaged world of the Ascendancy from the inside; and tales like 'Squire Toby's Will' from *Madame Crowl's Ghost* (1923), or 'The Haunted Baronet' from *Chronicles of Golden Friars* (1871) briskly lay bare the Gothic device, showing us how the form's typical subjective ingredients of guilt, fantasy, paranoia and preternatural intimation are engendered by the brutal rapacity of an economically failing class. If the setting of some of these tales is England, the pugnacious, hard-up, socially isolated gentry they portray has more in common with the Anglo-Irish squirearchy than with anything out of *Pride and Prejudice*. What is truly 'Gothic', terrifying in its inhuman violence, is the family feud over property, and it is to this unsavoury world that a work like *Wylder's Hand* (1864) belongs; but Le Fanu is equally adept at sketching this realm in unadorned realist style, as in the impressive early novel *The Cock and Anchor* (1845), with its vivid portraiture of the rapscallion gentry of the early eighteenth century. The novel deploys stereotypically Gothic elements – the black-hearted aristocrat, the incarcerated young woman – in a wholly mundane setting; but this solidly naturalistic world, with its virulent obsessions with money and the marriage market, is so routinely malevolent that it is not hard to glimpse in it something of the material conditions in which Gothic takes root.

Chris Baldick remarks that *Melmoth the Wanderer* 'marries the inheritance plot of realist fiction to the confinement plot of the Gothic novel';[90] and this formal cross-breeding is also demanded by the literary interests of a Le Fanu. If property, inheritance and the domestic strife they generate are themes appropriate to the realist novel, the short story would seem a more logical medium for the handling of mystery and the supernatural. For the supernatural is by definition a realm closed to rational enquiry;

---

90. Baldick, Introduction to *Melmoth the Wanderer*, p. xviii.

and realism is a cognitive form, concerned to map the causal processes underlying events and resolve them into some intelligible pattern. The short story, by contrast, can yield us some single bizarre occurrence or epiphany of terror, whose impact would merely be blunted by lengthy realist elaboration. And since realism is a chronically naturalizing mode, it is hard for it to cope with the ineffable or unfathomable, given those built-in mechanisms which offer to transmute all this into the assuringly familiar. Le Fanu thus tends to reserve his eeriest material for the short stories, while producing realist novels shot through with macabre intim- ations. But this generic division of labour is finally inadequate to his purposes: for if the sensationalist and supernatural are the negative off- print of the domestic and quotidian, then he has need of a literary form which will capture this contradictory unity. If the family is really such a cockpit of feuds and loathings, then a truly realistic anatomizing of it must inevitably press beyond the phenomenally observable – press, indeed, beyond realism itself, into that realm of psychopathology to which Gothic can lend a tongue. For Gothic is the place where this reputable domestic arena offloads its lethal desires and pathological compulsions, the screen upon which the political unconscious of that Hobbesian social order known as the family can be projected; and in his masterpiece *Uncle Silas* (1864), Le Fanu not only yokes these two spheres uncannily together, but suspends the reader precariously between them.

In the topography of the novel, these two worlds figure respectively as Knowl, where the heroine Maud Ruthvyn lives with her eccentric father Austin, and Bartram-Haugh, home of Austin's sequestered cousin Silas. On her father's death, Maud is translated to Silas's decrepit mansion; and this one might view as a shift from the domestic to the Gothic, from the endearing comforts of a childhood home to the cryptic terrors of a suspected murderer's seat. But the novel forestalls any such simplistic reading. For Knowl and Bartram-Hough, Austin and Silas, are mirror images as much as antitheses,[91] and the text cunningly deconstructs the opposition between them even as it affirms it. Austin and Silas are both ailing, reclusive, taciturn figures who exploit Maud in their different ways, and the same sinister grotesque of a French governess persecutes her in both places. The predatory world of Bartram-Haugh is thus ambiguously inscribed within the domestic security of Knowl; and this breeds in both

---

91. See W.J. McCormack, *Sheridan Le Fanu and Victorian Ireland* (Oxford 1980), Ch. 5, along with the same author's Introduction to the World Classics edition of the novel (Oxford 1981), for suggestive readings of these doubling effects.

Maud and the reader an acute epistemological uncertainty, of the kind Tzvetan Todorov finds in the workings of fantasy.[92] The question, here as in the fantastic, is which world is real; and it is an indeterminacy closely allied to the problem of evil. For evil would seem an aberrant, untypical condition and yet, in an exploitative society, part of the stuff of everyday social relations; and the novel can be read as an attempt to hold this shocking paradox together in the mind. There is a parallel here with *Oliver Twist*, which as far as reality goes suspends us undecidably between Fagin and Brownlow, proffering the consolation that the former is just a nightmarish interlude from which one will relievedly awaken, while ominously insinuating that this pantomime devil signifies something a good deal more ontologically solid than anything to be encountered in Brownlow's drawing room.

The evil, after all, might be all in the mind. Even before she has met Silas, Maud is already obediently enacting the Gothic conventions and building him into a Byronic hero, a superiorly disdainful outcast from human society. She makes of him, in short, a Melmoth, a 'long-suffering, gallant, and romantic prodigal' (Ch. 13), complete with thin but exquisite lip and attractively sarcastic nostrils. Since these are the mildly eroticized daydreams of an adolescent girl, the sophisticated reader half-suspects that the novel is here on the point of pulling the carpet out from under us – that the trick about to be turned, *Northanger Abbey* fashion, is that Silas will turn out to be just as prosaically innocent of Gothic menace as his gullible cousin believes him to be. Instead, the text operates a kind of double-bluff: Silas *is* a Gothic villain, though with none of the diabolic glamour of a Melmoth. The fact that he is not out of that particular Gothic novel doesn't mean that he is out of no Gothic novel at all. There are other alternatives besides mythological malevolence and real-life mediocrity, namely a Gothic evil which is alarmingly actual. Silas is after Maud's estate, and will try to murder her for it. The fiction turns out after all to be true; and since it is Austin who has credulously set this deathly process in train, there is a sense in which Bartram-Haugh is the concealed truth of Knowl. It is Knowl happening again with a sinister difference, but one which was woven into it from the outset.

It is not quite, then, that the benevolent father Austin transmogrifies into the wicked one Silas. It is rather that Silas, who as W.J. McCormack points out comes to life as Austin dies, symbolizes the appalling truth of

---

92. See Tzvetan Todorov, *The Fantastic: A Structural Approach to a Literary Genre* (London 1973).

what the kindly father covertly was all along. The novel is thus *inter alia* an attempt to come to terms with the conundrum of paternity: how come that the father of whom one may expect love is also, psychoanalytically speaking, the bearer of the Law? If that Law is punitive and autocratic, by what inconceivable paradox can its embodiment be benign? Or is the notion of a benign authority simply oxymoronic? *Uncle Silas* would appear to confirm this suspicion, at least in relation to that form of paternal authority known as the Ascendancy. For in the complex overlayings of Knowl and Bartram-Haugh, the benevolence of that particular rule turns out to be secretly malign – one contaminated at source, as in Maturin, by a primordial crime (Silas's murder of a gambling crony) which is now, like all such ill-starred histories, about to repeat itself with Maud. The fantasy has come alive, and was always dimly adumbrated in the reality. There is indeed an unspeakable horror at the heart of things, but its names – fraud, coercion, financial dispossession – are as wearily familiar as our own, which is why we thought it imaginary. In the cloistered, decaying world of the Anglo-Irish gentry, reality already contains its admixture of fantasy and alienation, sanity is shot through with madness, and unremarkable adolescents like Maud Ruthvyn find themselves offered major roles in Gothic melodrama.

Maud thinks of Silas as 'a poor and shunned old man, occupying a lonely house and place that did not belong to him, married to degradation, with a few year of suspected and solitary life before him, and then swift oblivion his best portion' (Ch. 30). Silas is in fact English, and the novel set among the bleak Derbyshire hills; but it is impossible not to see in this portrait a strikingly accurate cameo of the Anglo-Irish gentry, along with a prophetic glimpse of their historical destiny. Even when Le Fanu tries to strike a more affirmative note on the subject, the effect is notably inconsistent. *The House by the Church-yard* (1863), an improbable Ur-text for *Finnegans Wake*, begins in far mellower tone, with its nostalgic re-creation of what promises to be the more organic Anglo-Irish society of a century before, in the period of the Protestant nation. We have abandoned the world of the secluded big house for the bustling community of Chapelizod, with its old-world inn and gregarious army barracks, its flourishing social life unriven by sectarian wrangling. There is a potential geniality here, a sense of loose inclusiveness and toings-and-froings between social classes, which the work promises formally to mime in its diffusion of thinly linked subplots, so different from the lean symmetry of *Uncle Silas*. And indeed the narrator, himself a loyal participant in this self-assured Protestant world, sets out in elegaic retrospect by celebrating its unblemished serenity. But this narrational faith is quickly shipwrecked by the text itself, which in typical Le Fanu style revolves around concealed murder, financial ruin and sinister machinations; so that it is hard to appreciate quite what is so organic about a community in which a luckless witness to crime is clumsily trepanned by a drunken surgeon. However far back one presses, the crime which has tainted all subsequent history would seem to recede with you; indeed the novel opens in portentously symbolic vein with the bringing to light of a murdered body at the heart of this supposedly stable community.

Le Fanu's fiction has scant faith in the opposition between life and death, which is continually deconstructed; and whether this takes the form of disinterred corpses, ghostly hauntings or Swedenborgian speculations, it is always a matter of discovering within the living present a criminal history which refuses to be repressed, but which continues in the form of property, mortgage and inheritance to determine the behaviour of those deluded enough to believe they are free. As a child in the 1830s, Sheridan Le Fanu was a victim along with his clerical family of the tithe wars, and then lived through a succession of defeats for his own class: the banning of the Orange order, the abolition of bishoprics, municipal and land reform, the disestablishment of the Church of Ireland. So grievous were these buffetings that this stalwart of the Trinity College Historical Society and proprietor of the stoutly Unionist *Dublin University Magazine*, 'the literary leader of the young Conservatives' as Gavan Duffy described him, was to flirt in the 1840s with the repeal of the Union, and so find himself embarrassingly allied with nationalist insurrectionaries like William Smith O'Brien. His fiction may be seen in this light as the product of his own political unconscious, the negative offprint of his conscious beliefs; and it is hardly surprising that as the record of a disintegrating class, but one continually reanimated by the act of writing itself, it should turn so compulsively on the paradox that life and death, separated from each other by that yawning abyss in which Gothic horror germinates, are at the same time the mere recto and verso of one another.

The title of first 'national' Irish novelist, as we have seen, is usually awarded to Maria Edgeworth. But the word 'national' is ambiguous, and itself a bone of political contention. Is it a social term, designating a kind of fiction which totalizes the nation as a distinctive entity, or a political one, meaning a form of writing which represents the nation in patriotic style? For a certain vein of nationalist thought, the distinction is idly academic: only a nationalist standpoint could totalize the nation as it really is, just as in the Marxist literary paradox of 'partisanship' or 'tendency literature' only a frankly committed vantage point, itself avowedly partial and perspectival, can yield the inner structure of the social formation. Since truth itself is radically one-sided, no mere disinterested assemblage of viewpoints could ever hope to deliver it; and the term 'totality' floats accordingly between the descriptive and the prescriptive. A parallel ambiguity haunts the word 'popular': in one sense Edgeworth was undoubtedly that, a national novelist of international repute, lionized by English aristocrats and French *philosophes*; but she was not popular in the sense of being 'of the people', and she wrote neither for them nor in any central way about them. The title of first Irish national-popular novelist must surely be awarded to John Banim, whose aim in early life was to become precisely that;[93] and the initial volume of his *Tales by the O'Hara Family* (1825) is in that sense an event as historic in its own modest way as Clontarf or the battle of Limerick, signalling the first emergence on the Anglo-Irish literary scene of an apologist for the 'people'. Banim was in fact the son of a respectable Kilkenny tenant farmer; but this middling or petty-bourgeois social status, a cut or so above William Carleton and several cuts below Maria Edgeworth, is exactly what allows his fiction its totalizing 'national' scope. If he can portray the lower peasantry with something of Carleton's forceful imaginative fidelity, his genteel characters are for all their limits a notable improvement on the ham-fisted caricatures of his more distinguished colleague.

Banim's fiction was praised by his fellow countrypeople for being at once tenaciously true to life and for politically vindicating Ireland to the 'sister nation'. When he returned from his indigent, pain-racked life in London and Paris to die in his native Kilkenny, he was greeted with an appreciative address from his fellow citizens couched in much these terms, and ended his days superintending a national school and an amateur theatre in the town. But one might reflect that to portray Ireland as it was, in a state of well-nigh perpetual disaffection, and at the same time to vindicate the nation to its British proprietors, was hardly an easy trick to pull off. There is a tension here between naturalist fidelity and political intent, rhetoric and representation, by which the 'popular' Irish novel is

---

93. See Patrick Joseph Murray, *The Life of John Banim* (London 1857), pp. 92f. Banim enjoyed the collaboration of his brother Michael, and to abbreviate the brothers to John, as I do here for convenience, is not to underestimate Michael's achievement. For a more recent account of the brothers, see Mark D. Hawthorne, *John and Michael Banim: A Study in the Early Development of the Anglo-Irish Novel* (Salzburg 1975).

continually marked, and which would defeat the skills of the keenest dialectician. Only the liberal rationalist assumes that a meticulous documenting of the facts will spontaneously dispel prejudice, or that enmity is essentially ignorance. We have learnt from Mikhail Bakhtin to view the novel as an inherently dialogical form, a conflict or conversation between different codes, languages, genres;[94] but the Irish nineteenth-century novel is dialogical in a rather more precise sense of the term. For what we are listening to when we read it is one side of a fraught conversation with the British reading public, the other side of which can only be inferred or reconstructed from the words on the page. Like Irish political rhetoric, which knew that it would be reported and reacted to on the mainland and crafted itself accordingly, Irish fiction constantly overhears itself in the ears of its British interlocutors, editing and adjusting its discourse to those ends, holding the prejudices of its implicit addressee steadily in mind and constituting itself, at least in part, on the basis of that putative response.[95]

Lady Morgan remarks in the Preface to *O'Donnel* that she has always written in the cause of Catholic Emancipation; but all Irish fiction is in a sense covert propaganda for metropolitan consumption, and the realist novel is particularly convenient in this respect. For literary realism is a kind of proto-sociology, mapping the subterranean causes of apparently unmotivated events, disclosing the stealthy effect of condition upon character and bringing to light those intangible contexts which alone render individual action intelligible. Realism is thus an inherently liberal form, with its implicit nostrum that to understand is to forgive. John Banim is in this sense an Irish sociologist *avant la lettre*, aware that to chart the complex social causes of nationalist discontent is implicitly to overturn certain racist stereotypes of Irish behaviour. Like many a nineteenth-century Irish writer, Banim is cashing in on the dramatic upsurge of post-Union British interest in his country; and his fiction thus constitutes at once an act of demystification, disinterestedly retrieving the true nation from colonial disfiguration, and a variety of political special pleading. As

94. See Mikhail Bakhtin, *Problems of Dostoevesky's Poetics* (Manchester 1984); and Tzvetan Todorov, *Mikhail Bakhtin: The Dialogical Principle* (Manchester 1984). The best theoretical account of Bakhtin's work – Ken Hirschkop's *Mikhail Bakhtin and Democracy* – is still to be published.

95. J.C. Beckett, who argues that the Irish 'national' novel flourishes after the Union in part as cultural compensation for a loss of political identity, points out that such fiction was also made possible by a change in English literary taste involving a new interest in Ireland ('The Irish Writer and his Public in the Nineteenth Century', *Yearbook of English Studies*, vol. 2, London 1981).

Daniel Corkery sourly commented in *Synge and Anglo-Irish Literature*, all Anglo-Irish writing is a species of traveller's tale, an essentially anthropological genre which seeks to account to the alien observer for the bizarre behaviour of the natives; and this is one reason why from Edgeworth onwards it so frequently deploys the 'innocent abroad' device, in which a sweetly reasoned or stirringly impassioned account of Ireland's turbulent affairs is delivered to some visiting *ingenu*, but in fact lobbed adroitly over his head at the British reading public. Indeed at times this indirect propagandizing can amount to a kind of public-relations exercise: Thomas Flanagan describes Croften Croker, author of *Fairy Legends* (1825–28), as 'virtually a travel agent', puffing as he does the charms of the lakes of Killarney for potential tourists from the metropolis.[96]

Puffing the charms of the tithe wars or agrarian strife, however, is a rather more difficult matter. How is the Irish writer to combine truth with partisanship, or either with the wooing of metropolitan sympathies? You can soften the harsh realities of Irish life in the manner of some of Gerald Griffin's work, insisting that the old barbaric days are dead and a civilized moderation now rules; or you can adopt precisely the opposite tactic, as in Carleton's *The Black Prophet* (1847), and dramatize the plight of the nation in the teeth of colonialist complacency. You can ventriloquize the voice of the people, in the knowledge that this will prove disturbing in London or Edinburgh; or you can empathize tactically with a colonialist perspective on your own condition, implying by a certain archness of tone or scrupulously externalized treatment that you appreciate and even endorse that way of seeing. Since both strategies can be mobilized in the same text, the dialogue with Britain registers itself often enough as a division or hiatus within particular works – most evidently, as we shall see in the case of Carleton, in a clash of linguistic idioms. In any case, little about this writing can be grasped unless it is seen as involved in a ceaseless self-censorship, a silent slanting and regulating of itself which seeks to negotiate between the demands of truth and the requirements of political diplomacy. The nineteenth-century Irish novelists are thus among the first historical revisionists, even if their project is a good deal more unstable and self-contradictory than that contemporary enterprise.

John Banim certainly had diplomacy to excess. He speaks of having written his *Tales by the O'Hara Family* (1825) partly to promote the formation of 'a good and affectionate feeling between England and

---

96. Thomas Flanagan, *The Irish Novelists 1800–1850* (New York 1959), p. 173.

Ireland',[97] and describes his work as inspired by a wish to soften the heart of his country's oppressors. This is evident enough in his major historical novel *The Boyne Water* (1826), which as Tom Dunne has shown craftily emphasizes Catholic loyalty to the Crown in its portrait of the war between William and James. But for all its studied reasonableness *The Times* denounced the novel as 'a compendium of mad popery'; and *The Anglo-Irish of the Nineteenth Century* (1828), another Irish *Bildungsroman* in which the priggish young Anglo-Irish protagonist comes finally to love his country, contains so abrasive a critique of the Ascendancy that it had to be anonymously published. Banim is contradiction incarnate, labouring to present a sanitized image of Catholic nationalism to a sceptical British public while castigating their compatriots in Ireland. Writing for him is intervention as well as representation; yet he is sceptical enough of the transformative powers of art in such dire conditions, as is Gerald Griffin. 'You would, I suppose', scoffs one of the latter's personae, 'have a typhus fever, or a scarcity of potatoes, remedied by a smart tale, while you would knock a general insurrection on the head, with a romance in three volumes!'[98] Banim is a fervent O'Connellite with a profound petty-bourgeois fear of O'Connell's mass following, a writer who seeks patiently to master the conventions of an English literary realism which can never quite contain the turbulent materials he brings to it. Thus his finest piece of writing, *The Nowlans* from *Tales by the O'Hara Family*, is a superbly realized portrait of a young ex-priest's alienation which powerfully prefigures Hardy's *Jude the Obscure*, but is finally broken down into inchoate melodrama by the pressures of its own intense psychological exploration. Banim would seem to find realism significantly hard to sustain; and something similar could be said of Michael Banim's story 'Crohoore of the Billhook', where the image of peasant insurrection, at once fearful and fascinating, moves quickly into lurid fantasy.[99] At work in these disorderly texts is some subliminal disturbance or deep psychic dislocation which continually plays havoc with realist figuration and narrative continuity, throwing them out of focus and fracturing them from within; and it is not hard to trace in this conflict of forms a deeper contention of national cultures, between English convention and Irish experience, a language given and a language learned.

---

97. Quoted by Tom Dunne, 'The Insecure Voice: A Catholic Novelist in Support of Emancipation', in *Culture et pratiques politiques en France et en Irlande* (Paris 1989), p. 214.

98. Introduction to *Tales of the Munster Festivals* (London 1827), p. xvi.

99. Though the events recorded actually happened; see Flanagan, *The Irish Novelists 1800–1850*, p. 178.

But it was left to Banim's colleague Gerald Griffin – 'so full of aimiable English sentiment,' as Yeats scoffed[100] – to offer the metropolitan nation the most smugly innocuous portrait of the new, eminently respectable, post-Emancipation Catholic bourgeoisie. His novel *The Collegians* (1829), replete with bogus pastoral and discreetly backdated from the tumultuous present to the palmy Grattanite past, is a triumph of arch literary self-consciousness, with its self-preening presentation of the Catholic middle-class Dalys and demonizing of the fast-living squireens or half-sirs. Griffin's rotund, compulsively periphrastic prose, with its fustian periods and laboured Latinisms, is the style of a man anxious to prove his civility to those otherwise likely to brand him as barbarous; but the project is counterproductive, since linguistic nonchalance is of course the badge of the gentleman. It is a style well adapted to framing and displaying low-life Irish characters for amused English consumption, insinuating a knowing compact with one's readers over the heads of one's characters. With Griffin, the Victorian tone – bland, moralistic, rhapsodically elevated – sounds for the first time in Irish fiction; and Donald Davie notes 'a yawning gulf between the vitality of the peasant's brogue and the frigidity of the more genteel dialogue'.[101] *The Collegians* centres on a conflict of social and religious cultures, between the tediously principled Kyrle Daly and the engagingly profligate Hardress Cregan; but these contentions are scrupulously displaced into moralism and melodrama, so that the work is stripped of all historical dimension, its sensibility rent down the middle between cloying domesticity and stagey tragic gesture. The content of the work belongs to tragedy, but this is belied by the complacent self-indulgence of the style. The novel is the product of a rising rather than a falling class, which is one reason why its grim plot cannot undermine its narrative buoyancy. The anguish remains theatrical; indeed Griffin had an early success on the London stage,[102] and the histrionic is as endemic to his writing as it is to Lady Morgan's.

In the ambivalent, emotionally dishevelled figure of Hardress Cregan, however, there is something struggling to burst through the confines of Griffin's practised colonialist mien. The novel's ideological posture is at odds with its imaginative investment: Cregan is to be written off as a

---

100. *Explorations* (London 1962), p. 234.
101. Quoted by John Cronin, *Gerald Griffin (1803–1840)* (Cambridge 1978), p. 39.
102. For a biography, see Daniel Griffin, *Life of Gerald Griffin* (London 1843). Griffin hailed from a prosperous middle-class Limerick background, and led a struggling life in London as hack journalist, parliamentary reporter and aspirant author. He finally beat a retreat into the haven of the Irish Christian Brothers.

specimen of the dissolute sub-squirearchy, but his moral torment is the most compelling rhetoric of the book. He thus threatens to erode Griffin's binary moral categories: if he is a villain, he is, like Melmoth, a glamorous, self-torturing one, impulsively generous to the people and duly admired by them. He becomes, as a murderer, a moral and social outcast; and though a novelist of the emergent Catholic bourgeoisie cannot formally empathize with this liminal condition, an ex-hedge school writer spurned by the English metropolis certainly can. So it is that Griffin will find a more congenial focus for his imaginative energies in Eugene Hammond, protagonist of 'The Half Sir' in *Tales of the Munster Festivals* (1827). Wedged painfully between social classes, at once poor gentleman and refined plebeian, Hammond has the Catholic rectitude of Kyrle Daly but a touch of the spiritual *angst* of Hardress Cregan, so that Griffin has here found a way of combining a centring of the Catholic middle class with that more smouldering, rebellious aspect of its history that *The Collegians* damagingly dispelled. Politically speaking too, the story has the best of both worlds: Hammond turns from the frigid world of respectable English society to famine-ridden Ireland, converting his social animus into a fervent nationalism; but he also wins the high society woman who formerly spurned him, and ends up with a comfortable enough castle. *The Collegians* effects much the same imaginary solution, reconciling the more civilized aspects of Catholic and Ascendancy traditions in Daly's marriage to Anne Chute, who is also conveniently equipped with a castle.

'The duellist, the drunkard, the libertine, and the gambler', writes Griffin in another of his Munster Tales 'The Rivals', 'have all been exiled from the pale of Irish society, or compelled to wear their vices in a veil' (Ch. 3). But 'The Rivals' is a deeply disturbed narrative, split like *The Collegians* between its formal sympathies and emotional engagements. Its hero is the young Catholic patriot Francis Riordan; but its true focus of attention is the genteel scoundrel Richard Lacey, a Cregan-like figure tormented by obsessive love and unbridled passion. Griffin's fiction works by the psychoanalytic devices of splitting and projection: personal alienation and illicit desire are expelled from the world of the middle class, thus leaving that sphere respectable enough for political power, and projected instead into the dissolute gentry, who are then, as in the significantly entitled *Collegians*, both one's antagonists and alter egos. The spiritual anguish and monomania of an upper-class world on the wane becomes, strangely enough, symptomatic of the repressed emotional subtext of an aspirant Catholic middle class, which can no longer afford to confront directly its own heritage of psychological trauma. By a curious metaphorical device, the one world comes to stand in for the other, allowing Griffin an imaginative catharsis which preserves his scrupulously moderate politics intact. The strategy of his fiction is to effect these structural reversals; but the structure is triangulated by the presence of a woman – Anne Chute in *The Collegians*, Emily Bury in 'The Half Sir', Esther Wilderming in 'The Rivals' – who reconciles virtue with social status, and so provides an alluring rather than repellant upper class for the protagonist to unite with. Any such fictionally engineered resolution, however, must be set against the violent social order starkly exposed by Griffin's tale *Tracy's Ambition* (1829): a world of corrupt legality and brutally oppressive landlordism, which – so the story intimates – sufficiently motivates Rockite peasant rebellion.[103]

When a 'popular' author like Banim or Griffin writes of the 'lower Irish', he engages in a kind of performative contradiction. The message emitted by the content or *énoncé* – that he is intimate with this kind of life, knows it thoroughly from the inside – is at loggerheads with the civilized form of the act of enunciation, which deliberately holds itself on the outside of the experience it mediates. The language of narration thus affirms and disclaims at a stroke, insinuating a distancing judgement on what it purports faithfully to convey, dissociating itself from its own creation and obliquely undercutting its validity. When the 'polite' characters of a Griffin speak, *énonciation* and *énoncé* merge instantly into one – which is not to say that the narrator's voice is now accurately transcribing their idiom, rather that they are now speaking his own florid discourse. Nobody ever spoke like a genteel Griffin character, except perhaps at Drury Lane. But when the lower orders are in question, the text becomes instantly dialogical, each act of popular utterance doubled and infiltrated by the placing voice of the narrator, in what is not merely a clash of linguistic registers but a silent contestation of national cultures. This is not to say that the popular novelists are in the least inept in dramatizing the speech of the people; on the contrary, that they accomplish this so deftly is one of their enduring achievements, in contrast with the often stilted set pieces of an Edgeworth or Morgan. It is just that this speech must be implicitly framed and normalized by the supervening narrative voice, so that the

---

103. Tom Dunne points out that Griffin's native Limerick was particularly marked by popular disaffection in the 1820s. See his 'Murder as Metaphor: Griffin's Portrayal of Ireland in the Year of Catholic Emancipation', in O. MacDonagh and W.F. Mandle, eds, *Ireland and Irish Australia* (London 1986), p. 66.

world of a small Irish farmer or landless labourer is inhabited from the inside by the accents of a Trollope or Disraeli. But those accents are then revealingly unstable: the dialogue is two-way, the authoritative textual voice 'contaminated' by what it mediates, so that the fact that this is indeed not the world of *Mansfield Park* is betrayed by the heavy-handed obtrusiveness of the narrative voice, the sheer fact that it is trying too hard. A stalled dialectic sets up, such that the more convincing and authentic the popular experience grows, the more the narrator must send out meticulously dissociating signals, ransacking his literary lexicon or ragbag of classical allusions to assert his cultural edge over his own characters. Daniel Corkery, true to form, dismissed Griffin as a 'colonial' writer; but though this is far too simple a political judgement, there is a more subtle sense in which his and Banim's texts are colonial in their very letter, enacting in their semantic slippages and verbal torsions the fraught political relations between Ireland and its imperial masters.[104]

Of no Irish writer is this more true than William Carleton, the finest nineteenth-century novelist of all, whose magnificent *Traits and Stories of the Irish Peasantry* (1830–33), much praised by Karl Marx, can surely lay claim to the status of premier work of the century's literature. Carleton, poor peasant, ex-hedge school autodidact turned Protestant man of letters, is inside and outside his subject matter simultaneously, as the Preface to *Traits* makes clear enough: his desire in writing is 'neither to distort his countrymen into demons, nor to enshrine them as suffering innocents and saints, but to exhibit them as they really are – warm-hearted, hot-headed, affectionate creatures – the very fittest materials in the world for either poet or agitator...' Having disowned stereotyping in one breath, he ritually reinstates it in the next; special pleading and naturalist fidelity are once more incongruously yoked within the same writerly enterprise. What the book shows – its sensuous, intensely wrought inwardness with popular life – is at odds with what it says, in its carefully externalized framing and paternalist 'Honest, kind-hearted Paddy!' apostrophizing. But the populist authenticity, and the rhetorical play for the British reader, are not as antithetical as they may seem: simply to describe Irish popular life is to cater to the anthropological curiosity of the outsider, which is why Carleton can relaxedly allow himself long passages of naturalistic observation which do little to promote the plot. Indeed here is another

---

104. For a study of the colonial context, see P.F. Sheeran, 'Colonists and Colonized: Some Aspects of Anglo-Irish Literature from Swift to Joyce', *Yearbook of English Studies*, vol. 13, London 1983.

source of the tenuous, fractured nature of realism in Irish fiction: the fact that the anthropological interest can best be fulfilled by the sketch, the cameo, the brief vignette, whose point is to put the characters on consumable display rather than pitch them into dynamic interaction.

That Carleton's major work should be a collection of short stories is thus not accidental. A sketch like 'Larry McFarland's Wake', for example, starts off with a conventional moralistic plot – one industrious peasant couple contrasted with a shiftless pair who come to a sticky end – but then shifts into an elaborate description of the various carnivalesque customs surrounding a wake, confident that it will not lose the attention of an English reader intrigued by the quaint way the Irish die. Popular Irish fiction can thus resemble soap opera more than classical narrative realism, where the point (as in Charles Kickham's celebrated saga *Knocknagow* [1878]) is less what happens that the pleasurable familiarity we take in largely static characters, a literary form that assures us that life will trundle on much as usual and so helps to assuage our fear of death. It is perhaps worth commenting too that one of the most remarkable and ambitious of nineteenth-century Irish poems, William Allingham's *Laurence Bloomfield in Ireland* (1864), displays just the same set of static scenes, despite its narrative intentions. As Terence Brown remarks, 'it is as if the poet freezes the vigorous conflicts of life into manageable, representable moments, sometimes to a degree that suggests a pandering to an English taste for landscape painting and set pieces'.[105] Here too, the anthropological interest and the difficulty of representing a historical dynamic come significantly together. One might note also Robert Welch's comment on the 'static non-progressive grace' of Thomas Moore's *Irish Melodies*.[106] In his *Study of Celtic Literature*, Matthew Arnold sees the supposed Irish lack of an architectonic capacity in art, as opposed to the brief lyric outburst, as a racial defect, and links it to the nation's political ineffectualness: the inability to construct a narrative is at one with an incapacity to form 'powerful states'. The sensuous impressionism of the Celts, and their unfittedness for self-government, go hand in hand.[107]

Carleton's texts display a high degree of linguistic instability, as the literary English of the authorial voice is bizarrely interwoven with the popular tongue. A *locus classicus* of this discrepancy is the gripping tale

105. Terence Brown, *Northern Voices* (Dublin 1975), p. 51.
106. Robert Welch, *Irish Poetry from Moore to Yeats* (Gerrards Cross 1980), p. 26.
107. Matthew Arnold, *On the Study of Celtic Literature* (1867; reprinted London 1930, pp. 83–4). For other essays by Arnold on Ireland, see R.H. Super, ed., *Matthew Arnold: English Literature and Irish Politics* (Ann Arbor 1973).

'Wildgoose Lodge' from *Traits and Stories*, in which the 'educated' voice
of the narrator describes a meeting of murderous Ribbonmen in which
he suddenly intervenes himself as a Hiberno-English-speaking participant.
The device, no doubt intended to guarantee the narrator's credentials as
eyewitness to these dark doings, merely throws up an unaccountable
linguistic dissonance: has the narrator learnt Standard English since the
events he recounts, was his Hiberno-English speech assumed, or is his
present language counterfeit?[108] Perhaps he is a fifth columnist among the
Ribbonmen, which in a sense, in literary terms, he is. But the speech of
Carleton's characters can also veer from one linguistic form to another
within the same sentence, lurching abruptly from the rude and racy to
the author's own Latinate, mouth-filling, sententious prose style. Young
Dalton, one of the labouring poor of *The Black Prophet* (1847), manages
to produce this earthy, monosyllabic praise of the woman he loves: 'Upon
my honour, Donnel, that girl surpasses anything I have seen yet. Why
she's perfection – her figure is – is – I havn't words for it – and her face
– good heavens! what brilliancy and animation!' (Ch. 13). Dalton's trouble
is that he has all too many words for it; but he is conforming to the
Victorian convention that the gentility of a character's speech is in direct
proportion to his or her moral stature. This poses a problem with
Carleton's young women, since young women are morally virtuous and
so necessarily Standard English speakers even if they have never opened a
book and are perishing of famine in the corner of some squalid cabin.
Kathleen Cavanagh of *The Emigrants of Ahadarra* (1848) talks of 'truth,
pure affection, and upright principle', but she also pronounces 'entreat' as
'entrate'. Connor O'Donovan of *Fardorougha the Miser* (1839) proclaims at
one point: 'Divil a bit 'o that Bartle, nor a morsel of sleepin' in the
meadows is consarned in what I'm goin' to mention to you' (Ch. 5), but
when fired by romantic love he is able to rise to: 'I forgot that, and
everything else but yourself, darling, while I'm in your company. O
heavens! if you were once my own, and that we were never to be
separated' (Ch. 6).[109] When Carleton overlays his own laboriously literary

---

108. Norman Vance notes this discrepancy in his *Irish Literature: A Social History* (Oxford
1990), p. 144. For a study of Carleton's peasantry, see Maurice Harmon, 'Cobwebs before
the Wind: Aspects of the Peasantry in Irish Literature from 1800 to 1916', in Daniel J. Casey
and Robert E. Rhodes, eds, *Views of the Irish Peasantry 1800–1916* (Hamden, Conn. 1977).

109. Stephen Gwynn comments in his *Irish Literature and Drama* (London 1936, p. 70)
that *Fardorougha* could have ranked with Turgenev's 'King Lear of the Steppes' 'if the writer's
art had matched his power of conception'. This is rather like claiming that Sean O'Casey
might have been Ben Jonson if he had had the talent. It is, for all that, an impressive tale.
For a close linguistic analysis of Carleton's *Traits and Stories*, see Barbara Haley, *Carleton's Traits
and Stories and the 19th Century Anglo-Irish Tradition* (Gerrards Cross 1983).

idiolect on his characters' lives, the effect is as striking as filtering the subject matter of a Henry Miller through the style of the late Henry James; and if he can so wickedly satirize the bombastic speech patterns of the hedge school pedagogue, it is because it represents his own literary style raised to the second power. Indeed according to his autobiography it was a style he himself practised often enough as a youth to impress the gullible souls around him.[110]

Raymond Williams has written of the two languages which jostle for mastery within the pages of Thomas Hardy: the 'customary' tongue of his West country locality, and the 'educated' speech which betrays its author's uneasy eye on a metropolitan public searching gleefully for symptoms of the bucolic. To communicate his full experience, Williams suggests, neither language would finally serve: 'the educated dumb in intensity and limited in humanity; the customary thwarted by ignorance and complacent in habit'.[111] One might well see Williams's own distinctive prose style as a strategy for resolving this dilemma; but it is especially acute in Carleton, who when writing of famine in *The Black Prophet* speaks of 'that languid look of care and depression, which any diminution in the natural quantity of food for any length of time uniformly impresses on the countenance' (Ch. 3). Far more blatant instances of bureaucratese could be plucked from his work; the point here is that a language intended to elicit human compassion actively dispels it, deliberately posing itself on the outside of the condition it urges upon our sympathetic attention. The language, in short, is collusive with the very political power finally responsible for the suffering it portrays; if what is represented belongs to one political culture, the means of representation are drawn from another. Carleton's language joins and divides simultaneously, straining to keep clear of what it conveys, intent on its own elaborate integrity while inevitably sharing in what it describes. As with Britain and Ireland, it is not a case of two isolated, uncommunicating cultures but precisely of their baffling imbrication, of a garbled dialogue or mutual interference produced by the inscription of one discourse at the heart of the other. Something similar might be said of Carleton's habitual way of seeing, which at its best is capable of sentimentalizing the Irish in Victorian English style without somehow diminishing the harsh reality of their experience. If he deploys the habitual stereotypes with gusto, he is also curiously capable of transcending them by the very force of his realism — just as the depth of wretchedness his

---

110. See *Autobiography of William Carleton* (London 1868), p. 87.
111. Williams, *The English Novel*, p. 107.

works reveal implicitly challenges the mildly reformist panaceas he offers for its repair.

Just as Carleton's style negotiates its unsteady path between British power and Irish experience, so his politics seek for a compromise between what he sees as the most negative aspects of both. The typical Irish popular novelist – Banim, Griffin, Carleton – is petty-bourgeois in ideological outlook, as horrified by imperial arrogance as he is by the threat of popular insurrection. 'Tubber Dergh' in *Traits and Stories* is virulently anti-landlord, and so is *Valentine M'Clutchy* (1845), which lent Carleton his nationalist credentials; but his sympathy for the destitute in *The Black Prophet* is outweighed only by his apprehension that they will revolt against their misery, and the novel is repelled by the 'wolfish and frightful gluttony' with which the starving gobble down a bit of unfamiliar food. *The Tithe Proctor* (1849) formally examines the rapacious behaviour of the tithe proctor Matthew Purcel, but the novel is easily diverted into one of its author's obsessive assaults on peasant secret societies. (Carleton was himself signed up by the Ribbonmen as a youth, but seems to have joined in a fit of absentmindedness.) O'Connell praised him as the 'Walter Scott of Ireland'[112] but the admiration was by no means reciprocal; and though Carleton had friends within Young Ireland he did not agree with their views. For the average nationalist of the day, he had a good deal more title to the status of 'national' novelist than the upper-class Anglo-Irish Maria Edgeworth; but even he did not have title enough, since his early Evangelical onslaughts on the Catholic masses still rankled, and only the publication of *Valentine M'Clutchy*, complete with some extravagant praise from *The Nation* and a recanting shift to liberal Protestantism, was enough to salvage his reputation.

Valetine M'Clutchy is a sprawling, inchoate, Dickensian monster of a work, full of an anarchic satirical energy loosely organized by the frailest of plots. The novel is really a set of cameos culled from the familiar repertoire of nationalist fiction: rent day, the harrowing eviction in the snow, the drunken Orange lodge meeting, the secret Ribbonite court, the corruption of the grand jury room; and these staged scenes or set literary pieces, like the sectarian slanging match between Fr McCabe and Phineas Lucre, are inherently incapable of inner development. Unlike the great European realists, Carleton is unable to discover a plot in history itself – to organize an evolving narrative in accordance with some deep historical logic, or find in those historical dynamics the driving force of

---

112. See David J. Donoghue, *The Life of William Carleton*, vol. 2 (London 1896), p. 42.

his own fable. As with Banim and Griffin, melodrama must, then, be made to propel the storyline, perform the work of narrative reversal and suspense, while the social contents of the fiction move in some separate, more static dimension. The present is seen, in the odd allusion, as the product of history; but it is not on the whole possible to represent the present *as* history, to grasp it in that powerfully shaping perspective, as it is with a Stendhal or Tolstoy. And this may well have to do with the difficulty of totalizing a coherent tale from the ruptured course of Irish history itself. Nowhere is this hiatus between story and society more painful than in *The Black Prophet*, whose social content (the famine of 1817) and sensational detective plot only arbitrarily intersect. Carleton can find no way of anchoring his narrative in the social conditions he depicts; instead, the latter threaten at times to become a mere context for the former, which irrelevantly revolves on a twenty-year-old murder. Individual destinies, and the social history which shapes them, are dis-articulated, in contrast to their close meshing in the classical realist text; and one effect of this is a displacement of focus from the political to the moral. The black prophet himself, Donnel M'Gowan, embodies a transcendental evil quite unrelated to his social environs, and certainly unconnected to the famine; and though Carleton cannot refrain from making this black-visaged monstrosity a former United Irishman, this was no doubt consequence rather than cause of his fiendish character. By structurally unhinging the murder story from the famine, the novel implicitly suggests that human morality is independent of a material base, which fits its author's petty-bourgeois moralism well enough. A work devoted to exploring the impact of a social catastrophe on human conduct simultaneously implies that such conduct is socially undetermined.[113]

There is much, even so, to be rescued from this powerful text, not least its portrait of the black prophet's daughter, Sarah M'Gowan. Sarah is lawless, passionate and violent (the novel has hardly opened before she takes a knife to her own stepmother), but also resolute, compassionate and courageous; and this *mélange* of moral qualities is for Carleton strictly unthinkable in a female. Women in his work are usually virtuous and occasionally flawed, but to be both at once signals a seismic derangement of his ethical categories. Sarah is a kind of Hardyesque heroine, a

---

113. A smilar discrepancy is at work in *The Emigrants of Ahadarra*, where what threatens to force the McMahon family into emigration is not the usual economic circumstances but the dastardly plotting of Hycy Burke, whose hostility to the family springs from unrequited love. Here again, the driving force of the plot is a personal motivation only loosely linked to social circumstance.

Bathsheba or Eustacia frustrated by a cramping environment; and Carleton has to hand a kind of environmental or social-worker theory of her wilfulness, permitted as she is 'to run into wildness and disorder for want of a guiding hand' (Conclusion). But this headstrong, physically menacing young woman dies of fever helping the destitute, even if, in the manner of a Gaskell heroine, she also strives to deflect their political wrath; and she thus gives the slip to her author's predictably pious stereotyping as surely as some of Hardy's heroines offer to elude his conscious control. The complexity of Carleton's social understanding is at odds with his moral simplifications; and this is one of several ways in which his texts are self-divided.

Carleton's novels end happily, as Victorian novels should; but they do so only by displacing their preoccupations from social to moral, historical to individual, tragedy to melodrama. When the 'social problem' novel of the English 1840s encounters some intractable contradiction in real experience, it tends to reach back for an imaginary closure to the magical stock-in-trade or reach-me-down resolutions of an earlier romanticism: the secret benefactor, the timely legacy, the convenient plunge from the rooftop. *Valentine M'Clutchy* ends by wheeling in that equivalent Irish *deus ex machina*, the returned son of the absentee landlord. 'The doctrine of Poetical Justice, as it is termed, is not always the doctrine of real life', Carleton writes in the Preface to *Rody the Rover*, and history and fiction proceed to battle it out in his work. If the former were allowed to gain the upper hand, then it would disastrously undo the consolations of the latter, and no satisfactory closure could be achieved. A narrative genuinely moulded by historical forces would find no way of consummating itself; and since pessimism for the Victorian writer is ideologically impermissable, one primary function of art being to uplift a dispirited public, this cannot be allowed to happen. But Carleton's remark about poetical justice suggests his ironic consciousness of this contradiction; and as far as history goes, it is hardly a coincidence that his *anni mirabili* are the tumultuous, politically quickening, famine-ridden 1840s. His novels obliquely catch up these raw energies, and draw something of their peculiar intensity from them. And if fiction does not quite measure up to history, it may be because history is itself fictional in a rather different sense of the term. As Carleton writes in 'An Essay on Irish Swearing' in *Traits and Stories*:

> Could society hold together for a single day, if nothing but *truth* were spoken? Would not law and lawyers soon become obsolete, if nothing but truth were *sworn*? What would become of parliament if truth alone were uttered there? Its annual proceedings might be despatched in a month. Fiction is the basis of

society, the bond of commercial prosperity, the channel of communication between nation and nation, and not infrequently the interpreter between a man and his own conscience.

The most popular Irish novelist of the nineteenth century, to the chagrin of all good patriots, was Charles Lever, expert plagiarist, editor of the *Dublin University Magazine* and (along with Samuel Lover) purveyor of stage Irish types to the British reading public.[114] The high jinks and ripping yarns of an early work like *The Confessions of Harry Lorrequer* (1839) have justly earned Lever his reputation as a kind of Hibernian Surtees, full of subaltern swagger and vacuous bonhomie; but technically speaking he is a highly accomplished writer, jovially at ease with the language in the way a Carleton could only envy. This fluency is a sign of his disturbing comfortableness with the world, which is one of his egregious draw-backs; another is the fact that that he has for the most part no ideas on which to put his technical skills to work. But he discovered one or two in his later novels, not least in the impressive *The Martins of Cro'Martin* (1856), which contrasts the ideal quasi-feudal landlordism of the heroine Mary Martin with the shabby actuality. The big house, inhabited by the brutally snobbish Lady Dorothea and her benighted husband, is defeated in a political election, as a sign of the passing of the old haughty, irresponsible gentry; but all the novel can offer in its place is a backward-looking paternalism which its own critique of the Ascendancy calls into question. The vulgar Catholic middle-class bid for Mary's hand in marriage is beaten off, but she herself dies and Cro'Martin is closed up.

The decaying gentry is a constant theme of Irish fiction; but nowhere is that society more brilliantly anatomized than in Somerville and Ross's *The Real Charlotte* (1894), a work published on the very threshold of its final downfall. In this masterpiece of Lukácsian realism, the down-at-heel gentlewoman Charlotte Mullen is at once irreducibly individual and a superbly realized type of Anglo-Irish society, rapacious, mercenary and domineering but full of a rough vivacious energy;[115] and it is a mark of the novel's complex seeing that it allows us to enjoy and condemn her simultaneously. Her ruined, disorderly house, replete with animals and

114. Christopher Morash argues that Lever's huge reputation in Victorian England began to fade as Ireland began to prove more of an irritant ('Reflecting Absent Interiors: The Big-House Novels of Charles Lever', in Otto Rauchbauer, ed., *Ancestral Voices: The Big House in Anglo-Irish Literature,* Hildesheim 1992).

115. Charlotte will reappear as Shibby Pindy, the scheming semi-gentlewoman of *The Big House of Inver* (1925).

lower Irish, symbolizes a traditional order closer to its material base than its English counterpart, bereft of any saving civilized grace, a roisterous space in which conflicts and appetites are out in the open and language is salted with wit and aggression. From this enabling vantage point within the minor gentry, the novel can then glance both up and down the social scale to produce one of the few truly totalizing works of Irish fiction, ranging with all the synoptic assurance of a *Middlemarch* from the aristocratic Dysarts and aspiring rural middle class to a set of convincingly dramatized servants and the urban petty bourgeoisie. If the novel partakes of the verve and pungency of Charlotte's language, sharing something of her hard-headed shrewdness, it is also capable of turning this cold-eyed realism on the shabby crew of egoists, lumpish patricians and social climbers who people its landscape; and its dialectical vision allows it to indulge this world with expansive comic brio while plucking from it an ominous tragic catastrophe.

Three years after the appearance of *The Real Charlotte*, the Dublin civil servant Bram Stoker was to pen another allegory of the collapse of the gentry. Chris Baldick describes Melmoth as an 'absentee villain'; but Dracula is an absentee landlord, deserting his Transylvanian castle to buy up property in London. Like many an Ascendancy aristocrat he is a devout Anglophile, given to poring over maps of the metropolis; and this gory-toothed vampire plans, a touch bathetically, to settle in Purfleet, as a number of the Anglo-Irish gentry were to migrate from the wilds of Connaught to the watering holes of the English south coast. Living in a material world, Dracula is a material ghoul, much preoccupied with leases and title deeds, and has summoned the narrator Jonathan Harker to his Gothic fastness less to bite him in the neck than to discuss his legal affairs. When he is slashed with a knife, it is banknotes and gold coins rather than blood which cascade from his breast. But Dracula, like the Ascendancy, is running out of land: by the end of the novel he is being hotly pursued around Europe, furnished only with the crates of Transylvanian soil he needs to bed down in for the night. His material base is rapidly dwindling, and without this soil he will die. The Ascendancy, too, will evaporate once their earth is removed from them, though to wrench it from them will demand rather more than a sprig of garlic and rather less than a stake through the heart. Like Melmoth, the vampire is both victim and predator: it is hard not to feel pity for this hunted, homeless monstrosity, but the primordial crime must be cut off at source if the deadly chain of contamination is not to perpetuate itself. Those who inherit his curse, like the innocent young Lucy Westernra, are not themselves to blame: the Anglo-Irish ruling class are simply doing a difficult job in extremely trying circumstances, and it is not their fault if their lineage is tainted to its root. There is an unspeakable foulness at the very heart of civility; but if this frightful paradox is not to shatter the mind it must be rationalized by the image of the divided self, the vampiric victim who is sweetly unaware in waking life of the unspeakable horror he or she perpetrates at night. Only thus can one take the full measure of this blood-soaked history, in which sustenance for some is death and debility for others, while exculpating its individual agents.

One of the most celebrated absentee landlords of the *fin de siècle* was George Moore, who reacts in his *Confessions* (1888) to his tenants' demand for lower rents with a practised sub-Nietzschean snarl: injustice is the law of life, and pity and democracy are alike detestable. Moore is rarely exactly sure how serious he is intending to be, given his Yeatsian capacity to pontificate and send himself up simultaneously; like a number of Irish writers, he could never quite see the point of the dreary English distinction between truth and artifice. His self-flaunting aestheticism is in part a defiant rationalization of patrician guilt: in his trek from Mayo to Montparnasse, the young self-exiled Moore disdainfully decathects Ireland to cathect language instead, so that style becomes a kind of willed repression or amnesia, a scrupulously externalizing medium which sets its face against portentous metaphysical depth and operates as suavely ironic detachment from historical reality.[116] For 'metaphysical depth' one could read, among other things, Irish religion, by which Moore was plagued and haunted throughout his life. In place of the fissured, rebarbative course of Irish history he will create the flowing melodic line; in place of discursivity and the whole odious paraphernalia of ideas he will craft the resonant signifer and the detachable *bon mot*. Literary naturalism might seem the reverse of all that, in its scandalous engagement with the squalid and unsavoury; but it is really just aestheticism flipped inside out, the clinical detachment of the sociological *voyeur* set stoically above anything as tediously bourgeois as moral judgement. For all its sensationalist gloom, naturalism is in this sense a profoundly comic form, its consoling fantasies of physiological determinism a massive act of defence and dissociation on the part of its serenely unmoved creator. There is comfort, not least for an Irish landlord like Moore whose property is under siege, in knowing that in the great pre-programmed cycles of Nature nothing could have

---

116. For the early Moore's caustic attitude to Ireland, see *Parnell and his Island* (London 1887).

happened other than as it did – that if one's social class is on the wane, then this destiny is as much inscribed in the laws of cosmic evolution as the blowing of a rose. And since writing is then less an act of intervention in a changeable world than the documenting of an immutable one, its value can lie only in the aestheticist fidelity with which it renders every fold and ripple of this essentially meaningless universe. ('No more literary school than the realists [that is, naturalists] has ever existed', Moore remarks in his *Confessions*.[117]) So it is that, when Moore comes in *Hail and Farewell* to recount his adventures among the Revivalists, his mutedly mocking commentary on the new Irish drama raises that drama to the second power, theatricalizing the theatrical, converting life itself to a consumable aesthetic spectacle.

All of this carefully nurtured flippancy and avant-garde experimentalism is a calculated strike at the English, whose Wordsworthian moralism and Arnoldian high seriousness are profoundly distasteful to the Irish modernist sensibility. Such oppressive moral earnestness is natural to a nation burdened with worldwide responsibilities, from the sugar plantations of the Caribbean to the slums of Calcutta. Moore's enthusiasm for Émile Zola is among other things an impudent assault on such high-toned solemnity, gleefully reducing the delicate complexities of Eliotic consciousness to some hereditarily determined spasm of the neurological system. He was coolly indifferent to Shakespeare, thought the English novel 'negligible, almost non-existent',[118] fulminated against 'trashy Thackeray and rubbishy Dickens and pompous Eliot',[119] and believed Pater's *Marius the Epicurean* 'the great atonement for all the bad books which have been written in the English language'.[120] Moore espouses the French avant-garde against English culture, and exploits it simultaneously to distance himself from Ireland ('no country is so foreign to me', he remarked[121]); but it is not difficult to detect an Irish animus, suitably filtered through a European aesthetic, in his contempt for an English literary tradition which could yield him next to nothing.

Ireland for Moore is Nature, raw, sordid and truculent, from which he will beat a retreat into the artifice of style. But Ireland is also convention, seat of a stifling clerical repression, which he will counter with the pagan and instinctual, with spontaneous self-expression and the cult of the

---

117. *Confessions* (London 1888), p. 184.
118. Quoted in John Eglinton, *Irish Literary Portraits* (London 1935), p. 107.
119. Quoted in Joseph Hone, *The Life of George Moore* (London 1936), p. 213.
120. Eglinton, *Irish Literary Portraits*, p. 107.
121. Ibid., p. 103.

emancipated ego. Oliver Gogarty in *The Lake* (1905) moves from clerical bigotry to pagan liberation through his love for the emancipated Nora, who is figured as mysterious, elusive, instinctual – so that this naturalness, which woman above all incarnates, turns out to be a very conventional prejudice indeed, as indeed is the whole Nature/convention opposition itself. The novel thus ends up endorsing a stereotypically priestly view of women, but merely reverses its value from negative to positive. Nature is Ireland – the countryside for which Gogarty has a quick sensuous feel – but also what points you beyond Ireland to some realm of sensual fulfilment; the symbolically charged lake is part of the local landscape, but also what you must cross to be free. Moore shifts from an unregenerate Irish Nature to the felicities of Flaubertian style, a style which then urges the need to be natural. But this Nature is always ambivalent in his work, both dangerous and desirable, Zolaesque and beneficent, at once the splendour of the Irish landscape and its disfiguring poverty, sexual liberation for Nora but a lifetime's enslavement for those who like Esther Waters yield to a passing impulse. Ireland has at once too much Nature and too little: too many pigs and revolting peasants, but also too much sexual repression, clerical bureaucracy and Castle charade.

Moore's fine writing, his notorious outbreaks of Paterian preciousness, is a kind of temporary escape from the exigencies of narrative and a psychic compensation for its unremitting gloom. These hothouse passages are an elaborate defence against history; but style is also the mark of the privileged sensibility of the very social class Moore is busily detaching himself from, so that he remains bound to that social order by the very medium he deploys to satirize it. If art is a reaction to Ascendancy boorishness, it is also an extension of its leisurely self-indulgence. The raffish aesthete is in one sense the inverse of the lubberly landlord; yet artist and aristocrat share an insouciant individualism, since those who govern society can afford their roguish eccentricity. Moore's Oedipal flight to Paris thus reproduces, as well as challenges, the big house in Mayo; indeed in *A Drama in Muslin* (1886), Alice Barton's landlord father is himself an artist, and as wayward, irresponsible a fantasist as anything to be encountered on the *rive gauche*. Those at the acme of society, and those loitering idly on its margins, are equally without a productive function, and so can find a mirror image of themselves in one another. In this sense, Moore's rebellion against the paternal Law succeeds merely in reinstating it; but at least he can convert his exilic displacement into clinical detachment, into the transcendent non-place of the naturalistic artist. And this Zolaesque aesthetic will then rationalize the contradictions of the internal émigré who finds his own social class distinctly unlovely but is sufficiently part of it to abhor the peasantry too. What appears an Olympian neutrality or scientistic even-handedness in *A Drama in Muslin* – the gentry are drones, their tenants animals – is in fact the bad faith of the upper-class rebel who can now find an avant-garde name for his highly traditionalist contempt for the *canaille*. His style, veering from the iconoclastically crude to the outrageously purple, is then a symptom of this impasse.

In a striking instance of what Raymond Williams has called 'negative identification',[122] Moore's sympathies flow instead to the displaced woman: Alice Barton in *A Drama in Mulin*, Kate Ede in *A Mummer's Wife*, Esther Waters, Evelyn Innes. If the gagged, discarded woman is the wild card of the social system, so is the epicene male aesthete in full-blooded revolt against a patriarchal philistinism. Alice Barton of *A Drama in Muslin* has seen through the fatuousness of Castle society and is gripped by a sense of metaphysical vacuity; but much of her spiritual torment springs from the fact that she feels herself ineligible for marriage, so that she remains like her author leashed to the system she scorns. The frustrated upper-class woman offers an appropriate focus for Moore's emotional disaffection; but her lack of political awareness conveniently obviates the possibility of a fundamental critique of the social order. That critique is displaced from the exploitative social relations of landlordism, about which *A Drama in Muslin* remains largely non-committal, to the glittering trumpery of its social rituals, which costs rather less to satirize. What the novel shows is a social class overripe for extinction; what it says is a rather more ambiguous affair. Alice finally escapes from the regime which oppresses her, but only into the bolthole of a suburban London marriage; she thus combines a rejection of her own class with a fulfilment of its marital expectations. Her friend Cecelia, a somewhat less compromised radical, is portrayed as a deformed lesbian.

The whole of Moore's fiction pivots on some primordial Fall, some originary break from one social condition to another. Kate Ede deserts her Midlands home, Esther Waters is expelled from Woodview, Oliver Gogarty swims the lake, Alice Barton shifts from Irish gentility to English suburbia, Evelyn Innes abandons her father to elope with a rather more personable version of Henry James's Gilbert Osmond. Moore's own career is marked by three such decisive ruptures: from Ireland to bohemian Paris; from Paris back to revivalist Dublin; and from Dublin to literary London.

---

122. See Williams, *Culture and Society*, pp. 178–80.

His autobiographical prose, with its unbreachable *sang froid* and pose of amused detachment, makes light for the most part of these abrupt shifts of allegiance; if the conclusion of Joyce's *Portrait of the Artist as a Young Man* (1916) plucks a momentous symbolic meaning from its author's decision to take a job in Europe, Moore's personal writings just as contrivedly play down the anguish of exile. But it is not hard to read his fiction as some tumultuous return of the repressed, a compulsive revisiting in fantasized form of this traumatic moment of abandonment and self-betrayal, which is always ambiguously lapse and liberation. Moore may have felt entirely foreign in Ireland; but he also felt that the affection for England he was pouring into *Esther Waters* was 'monstrous and preposterous',[123] and as a member of London's high Tory Boodles club insisted on treating the place as some shady dive by disputing minor items of his bill.

Perhaps the most extraordinary moment of *Hail and Farewell* comes with his famous Ebury Street conversion, a veritable road-to-Damascus *metanoia* in which he discovers in himself a sudden impassioned sympathy for the colonized Boers and an inflamed hatred of the British. If this self-fashioning *flâneur* drifted back to Dublin to sniff satirically around its eccentric literati, it was out of a full-bloodedly anti-imperialist motive, as unremittingly radical as anything in Constance Markiewicz but carefully masked, defused, displaced into the anodyne anecdotalism of a minor comic art. Beneath his *übermenschlich* composure and good spirits lurks a shattering crisis of identity, which is then adroitly diverted into the novels to leave his autobiographical fictions of selfhood serenely intact. Kate Ede of *A Mummer's Wife* (1885) abandons her sick husband and dourly Methodist background to go off with a travelling theatre company, thus attaining an artistic freedom which rapidly turns sour with her dipso-maniac degeneration. The emancipation of art turns out to be illusory, as truncated a utopia as Kate's surname; and the novel will deploy its Zolaesque armoury of avant-garde devices to punish its protagonist for her own avant-garde aspirations, briskly reducing her to a pathological specimen and so purging its own puritanical guilt at the very moment that it achieves, through its anaestheticized portrayal of her, a defensive dissociation from it. The oppressive Potteries world from which Kate flees is in one sense the very opposite of Moore's privileged life in Mayo; but it is as though that leisured life is unconsciously 'proletarianized' by the fiction, both to underscore its intolerable spiritual constraints and as

---

123. Quoted in Hone, *The Life of George Moore*, p. 186.

a more persuasive apologia for the urge to relinquish it. Some primordial trespass has anyway occurred, which is both treason and transcendence: Kate's infidelity to her husband, Esther's pregnancy, Gogarty's loss of religious faith, Evelyn Innes's guilt-ridden transition from suburb to stage.

There is something amusing as well as poignant in the idea that this lounging absentee landlord should find his *alter ego* in cruelly exploited working woman. Woodview, the English mansion in which Esther becomes a servant, is perhaps an imaginary transposition of Moore's Mayo big house, its gambling, horse-racing proprietor a kind of English equivalent of the spendthrift equestrian Ascendancy. But if this setting is in one sense alluring it is in another sense alienating, as the scene of hard labour and sexual seduction for Esther herself; and this captures something of Moore's irresolvably ambivalent response to his own class background. Esther is forced by her pregnancy to leave the house, which perhaps rationalizes her author's guilty free choice in deserting his. Her existence in London is one of grinding poverty, which was hardly true of Moore's; but Esther's outcast condition may condense the memory of Moore's first leaving of Ireland with that second rupture in which, confronted in Paris by the news of a tenant rent strike back home, he was compelled to migrate to London to earn his living as a writer. His characters' own fall into material necessity write this experience luridly large, and the upshot of this is ironic: this proletarianized artist can identify with the English working class, or rather with those isolated members of it whose displaced condition reflects his own, but much less with the Irish tenantry whose unjust treatment spurred on his own fall into necessity in the first place. It was the land war that turned Moore into a writer, though not in the sense that he wrote much about it. The lower orders engage his imaginative sympathies, but only if they are unprotected women struggling helplessly for survival, not politically conscious militants who threaten property. *Esther Waters* transcends the demeaning naturalism of *A Mummer's Wife* into genuine realism: it is social forces, not some genetic inheritance or psychological flaw, which impels its heroine's downward trajectory. But it retains, for all that, a naturalistic stress on determining circumstance to the point where Esther's powers of agency are severely circumscribed, which was hardly true of the cottiers and landless labourers who rallied to Michael Davitt. And there is a hint of Zola too in the blind biological instinct which binds Esther devotedly to her child despite her material hardship, a baby which in the case of her author might bear the name of art.

Moore's profoundly self-ironizing return to the Ireland of the Revival[124] allowed him briefly to combine the aesthetic and domestic, enlightenment and tradition, since his native land was now itself becoming aestheticized. The antitheses which his fiction fails to mediate might now be resolved in real life, and art indulged without the pain and guilt of uprooting. It is the solution offered to Evelyn Innes by the portentously Celticist Ulick Dean, a fictional rendering of the self-fictionalizing Yeats. But it could be claimed that Moore's true theme from start to finish is not art but religion, a topic which at times achieves in him the proportions of an obsession, and for which that spilt religion known as aestheticism is no final substitute. Indeed Moore's concern with clerical repressiveness in Ireland displaces attention from colonial oppression. Like many a Romantic, he is torn between expressing the self and abnegating it, stances which are indeed the mere inverse of one another; and the posturing pagan in him has to fight hard against the aloof ascetic, who appears in the guise of John Norton in *Celibates* (1895), and who in the figure of the fanatical Monsieur Martyn will help to transform Evelyn Innes into Sister Theresa. Moore's dilemma is that religion signifies for him at once an oppressively clerical Ireland and a spiritual alternative to it: if the convent provides a welcome refuge from a life of upper-class bad faith and insipid aestheticism, it is also part of the very institution which kills the soul. The ideal would be a suitably aestheticized religion which celebrates the senses while purifying them, thus sublating aestheticism, and which allowed the self free expression through its disciplined submission to order, thus uniting Protestant individualism with Catholic tradition. But these syntheses are simply unworkable: if Moore makes his third break and leaves Ireland forever, it is because of his growing belief that writing is a Protestant activity, and that no Catholic has produced a decent work of literature since the Reformation. *Hail and Farewell* delivers a characteristically self-ironizing account of this stupendous discovery, with Moore rushing frenetically from one sceptical friend to another at any hour of day or night to apprise them of this mighty truth; but he was serious enough about it to insist that his brother's children be brought up as Protestants, and to break with him over this imperious demand. Writing and Ireland are finally irreconcilable; and Moore sails for England to bug the waiters

---

124. 'Nobody will ever write a realist novel again', Moore once remarked. 'We are all gone now, Zola is dead, Huyssmans is in a monastery, and I am in Dublin' (quoted in John Kelly and Ronald Schuchard, eds, *The Collected Letters of W.B. Yeats, vol. 3: 1901–1904*, Oxford 1994, p. 642).

in Boodles, no doubt feeling, like the self-exiled Ned Carmady in *The Untilled Field* (1903), 'at one moment ashamed of what he had done, at the next overjoyed that he had done it'.

Evelyn Innes is an excessively cerebral piece of work, shorn of the density of social texture of the naturalistic fiction, marked by a callow ethereality which hardly transcends the consciousness of its own characters. Its men and women discuss reincarnation over tea at the Savoy, moving in some nebulous realm of *Geist* in which ideas are floated in solemn abstraction from actuality. The realist mould, in which discursive notions must be tactfully naturalized, has been breached by the conceptual ferment of Revivalist Ireland, which can no longer be contained by those traditional literary devices. Indeed naturalism itself presses realism to so self-parodic a limit that it begins to show up as programmatic, theoretically self-conscious, and so as a realism objectified and estranged. And even these more mundane of Moore's works are disrupted by the purple passage or obtrusive symbol, so that their realism is notably impure. But this, as we have seen, is true of Irish fiction as a whole, so that to this extent Moore's modernism seems a logical development of its hybrid forms. It is tempting, in contrasting the Irish novel in this respect with its English counterpart, to overplay the integrity of the latter's realism. For English literary realism is not homogeneous either, as a glance at Dickens or Disraeli or the Brontës is enough to suggest. There is no assured metropolitan norm from which the literary culture of Ireland is a systematic deviation. And one should beware of the temptation to demonize realism itself, as with those poststructuralist commentators for whom everything from Defoe to Dostoevsky would appear to have been a ghastly mistake.

Even so, it is striking how labile Irish realism actually is. Swift writes before a 'mature' literary realism has yet crystallized, predating that division of discursive labour which will fully distinguish imaginative fiction from pragmatic or philosophical writing. Indeed *Gulliver's Travels* trades on this very ambiguity, as witness the eighteenth-century bishop who indignantly declared that he didn't believe a word of it. Maria Edgeworth inaugurates her literary career with a bold generic experiment, mixing in *Castle Rackrent* the forms of oral story-telling with a realism which is scandalous, excessive, larger than life. Her other Irish novels yoke a moral schematism which is less than life to a fabular impulse which is more than it. The satirical realism of Lady Morgan's work clashes head-on with her extravagant idealism, while the histrionic element of her fiction passes on into the writing of Gerald Griffin. The realism of Banim and Carleton is closely interwoven with melodrama, and Carleton crosses easily from the fictional to the didactic, interpolating moral or social commentary into his work without any attempt to naturalize it. Running parallel to this populist literary vein are the full-blooded fantasies of Protestant Gothic, which either transcend realism altogether, as with a Stoker or Maturin, or suspend us precariously between the familiar and the unknown in the manner of a Le Fanu. To characterize the most popular nineteenth-century Irish novelist, Charles Lever, as 'English' is then more than a nationalist sneer: it is to discern in his work a confident realist consistency which cuts against the grain of Irish writing as a whole.

Irish fiction, then, is marked by a hiatus between the experience it has to record, and the conventions available for articulating it. How are those conventions to take the measure of a dislocated, fantasy-ridden society in which truth is elusive and history itself reads like some penny dreadful? Moore's cavalier contempt for an English literary canon which could yield him almost nothing, or Joyce's disdain for Lawn Tennyson, are signs of the resistance of that history to the cultural forms of its rulers, a resistance which, with the emergence of modernism, becomes increasingly self-conscious. That civil stylistic ease and high moral seriousness, all that tonal solemnity and intricate inwardness, proved no fit medium for depicting a fractured, chronically violent, ineluctably political Ireland, since this discourse of Literature had been invented in the first place as an alternative to such sublunary concerns. Yet until George Moore turned defiantly to the French, there were really few other literary models to hand; and the characteristic experience of the Irish novel is thus one of a fraught negotiation between signifier and signified, between the immanent logic of the experience and the forms of its expression.

Walter Benjamin discerns in the writings of Franz Kafka a kind of 'sickness of tradition', a condition in which truth and wisdom have decayed but the forms of their transmissibility are preserved.[125] The Irish equivalent of this phenomenon is James Joyce's *Dubliners* (1914), a work which preserves the forms of storytelling but empties them remorselessly of their content. With Joyce, the realist tale is finally stripped of the aura in which it still bathes in Carleton, transmuted to a scrupulous meanness which reflects its urban environment of mechanical reproduction. For

125. Walter Benjamin, 'Max Brod's Book on Kafka', in *Illuminations*, edited by Hannah Arendt (London 1970), p. 147. I am indebted for this insight to Emer Nolan, who develops it in her *Joyce and Nationalism* (London 1994).

Benjamin, in his great essay on Leskov, the oral tale is the home of tradition and remembrance, of a well-crafted wisdom passed from one teller to another and imbued with all the auratic authority of its legendary origins. *Dubliners* is the death of this originary wisdom, even as it parodies its forms; and it is thus the final refusal of the anthropologist's curiosity, displaying its stock of idiosyncratic natives in the style of the nineteenth-century vignettists only to drain them of all allurement. With this collection of anti-epiphanies and non-events, myth finally shatters on the rock of the modern, an era in which everything is exactly identical with itself, and in which the form of the story stimulates in us a hunger for significance only to deliver us the blankness of the sheerly existent. Once myth has been thus safely dismantled, it can be wheeled in again by the later Joyce as an ironic array of compositional devices, purged of its mystification. Joyce uses realism to secularize myth; but in *Ulysses* (1922) he also uses his mythological framework to ironize and estrange that more tenacious modern myth which is realism itself. And if he can accomplish this so superbly, it is in part because he is heir to a cultural lineage for which such realism, as the fruit of a developed European civilization, had never been less than profoundly problematic.

CHAPTER 6

CULTURE AND POLITICS
FROM DAVIS TO JOYCE

In pre-modern societies, the three great symbolic systems of art, religion and sexuality remained locked into the political order as a whole. It is only with the onset of modernity that these systems will be gradually split off from public life, as art, religion and sexuality are reduced to so many private pursuits which linger on throughout the modern era like some personal hobby or quaintly surviving folk custom. As the grip of an instrumental reason tightens over political society as a whole, the spiritual values which it drives from the public arena have to set up home elsewhere; and they do so in these increasingly marginal enclaves, none of which, as modernity unfurls its course, is any longer of much public importance. The more political and economic life are steadily drained of purpose, the more surcharged, exotically overheated, these symbolic orders become, forced as they are to compensate for this dwindling of affect in the public realm. Their spiritual intensity is at odds with their marginal status; and this fissure between the symbolic and the social runs all the way down the human body, whose erotic or imaginative energies must be syphoned off to that other place known as culture if that body is to operate efficiently as an instrument of production.

Nineteenth-century Ireland, though by no means an entirely pre-modern place, had yet fully to undergo this severing of the social and symbolic.[1] For most of the Irish, religion was hardly a private option; it was a formidable public institution, second in power only to the state and a good deal more authoritative. The faith of the Catholic Church was a matter of corporate rituals, not of some solitary inwardness; and its influence stretched all the way from personal conduct to the spheres of

---

1. There is no question of a Golden Age here: for art, religion and sexuality to be locked into a traditional political system is for them to act, among other more positive things, as bearers of its oppressive power.

politics, culture and education. Irish Protestantism was naturally a more individualist affair; but it too, given the history of the island, was a thoroughly political formation. The whole of social life was caught up in this symbolic network, just as the sexual culture of the nation belonged to a complex economy of land and inheritance, property and procreation.[2] As far as sexuality goes, we are speaking less of the erotic or psychological than of dowries and matchmakers. It is less a question of Jamesian subtleties or Lawrentian intensities than of birth rates, labour requirements, welfare provision, impartible inheritance, clerical regulation, enforced celibacy and emigration. The sexual economy of any nation can of course be discussed in roughly these terms, as Michel Foucault has reminded us;[3] but in Ireland this language would seem closer to the terms in which sexuality was actually lived, which can hardly be said of Romantic Europe. 'Irish history', remarks Joel Mokyr, 'is demographic history.'[4] In pre-modern fashion, the symbolic order remained locked within the economic: for the mass of the Irish people, sexuality was still regulated by a pre-industrial brand of instrumental reason, and had yet to move off into that relatively autonomous sphere which modernity will open up for it. In this context, the sexual nonconformism of a George Moore, Oscar Wilde or James Joyce becomes a more politically charged affair than the emancipated talk of the English *fin de siècle* sexologists or Bloomsbury bohemians. Like Theodor Adorno's modern art, sexuality becomes a metaphor for political revolt at just the point where it appears most privatized, most bereft of social function.

The art of nineteenth-century Ireland moves under the shadow of the political as surely as sexuality remains embedded within the economic. If culture in Britain was increasingly a bulwark against social unrest, in Ireland it was a powerful contributor to it. In the metropolitan country, culture was largely a spiritual affair; in the colony it could prove a formidable material force. It would be hard to underestimate the political impact of Thomas Moore's *Irish Melodies*, the Young Ireland poetry anthology *The Spirit of the Nation*, Charles Gavan Duffy's *The Ballad Poetry of Ireland*, Standish O'Grady's *History of Ireland: Heroic Period*, or Douglas Hyde's *Love Songs of Connacht*. The recycling of ancient mythology, often in sanitized form, provided a cultural frame within which actions such as

---

2. The classic anthropological work is Conrad M. Arensberg and Solon T. Kimball, *Family and Community in Ireland* (Cambridge, Mass. 1940).

3. Michel Foucault, *The History of Sexuality*, vol. 1 (New York 1978).

4. Joel Mokyr, *Why Ireland Starved* (London 1983), p. 30.

the Easter Rising could be deciphered and imaginatively deepened.[5] From Young Ireland to the Revival, culture was often enough grasped in idealist terms; but it could also take on an active material life of a kind rarely matched over the water. Whether or not that play of Yeats sent out certain men the English shot, it was rather more likely to have done so than anything by Sir Arthur Pinero. It is a notable irony that just as the English poetic imagination was effectively spent as a political force, in the transition from Shelley to Tennyson, that whole revolutionary aesthetic was being rekindled in the writings of Thomas Davis and his colleagues on the *Nation* newspaper.

Young Ireland, with its journalism and Repeal reading rooms, its cultural projects and collaborative enquiry, is among the first examples in Ireland of what Jürgen Habermas has termed a 'public sphere'.[6] Just as the bourgeois public sphere of eighteenth-century Europe had sought to carve out for itself a discursive space within traditional society, in which a newly forming public opinion could be consolidated into a political force, so the Young Irelanders launched a programme of cultural re-generation or 'moral force' within the crevices of the existing political system. Deprived of a voice within the state, like the emergent middle class within the *anciens régimes* of Europe, they built instead their own alternative channels for circulating discourse and disseminating values. The cultural forms of the Enlightenment were thus harnessed to radical Romantic ends. In a familiar Irish displacement, culture was called upon to play the formative, unifying role that political institutions might have been trusted to perform in a more developed or emancipated society.[7] The shift from politics to culture is accordingly one from state to nation. Michael Davitt sees Daniel O'Connell as having forged a 'national public opinion' in Ireland, bringing to birth a whole new style of discursive politics in the manner of the classical public sphere.[8] Indeed Davitt himself tried to reconstruct this realm in the period of the land war: the Land League, he considered, had overlooked a vital opportunity in not extend-ing its activities to the field of popular education, and he himself floated

5. See Martin Williams, 'Ancient Mythology and Revolutionary Ideology in Ireland, 1878–1916', *Historical Journal*, vol. 26, no. 2 (June 1983).

6. See Jürgen Habermas, *Strukturwandel der Offenlichkeit* (Neuwield 1962). The first such public sphere in Ireland could be said to have been created by the United Irish movement.

7. See David Lloyd, 'Violence and the Constitution of the Novel', in *Anomalous States* (Dublin 1993).

8. Michael Davitt, *The Fall of Feudalism* (London 1904), p. 35. Oliver MacDonagh speculates that the source of O'Connell's trust in the political force of public opinion might have been his reading of William Godwin. See his *O'Connell* (London 1991), p. 41.

the idea of a 'people's institute' with libraries, reading rooms and club facilities in every barony. 'Waiting for the abolition of landlordism won't do', he declared; the point, in Gramscian style, was to construct a countercultural sphere in the present.[9]

'Ireland, wretched Ireland', complained Lady Morgan in her novel *The O'Briens and the O'Flahertys*, 'has no public opinion, no public to express an opinion.'[10] Gavan Duffy outlines the cultural condition of Ireland on the eve of the founding of the *Nation* in much the same bleak terms: 'Whatever literature existed in Ireland belonged to the party dominant in Church and State. The class who lived by letters was not numerous, but it was in a decisive degree English in spirit and sympathy.' The one prosperous publisher was a Conservative, and the man of 'most authentic genius in fiction' (William Carleton) had allied himself with the ruling political interests. No Irish history books were used in schools, and stage Irishmen dominated theatre and fiction.[11] It was against this coupling of culture and Ascendancy that Young Ireland carved out for itself a countercultural sphere; and just as they politicized culture, so O'Connell aestheticized politics. The great O'Connellite assemblies were carnivalesque festivals as well as political rallies, popular spectacles or forms of street theatre in which music, costume, insignia, banquets, concerts and processions played a key role.[12] It is not for nothing that O'Connell himself was that most theatrical of all public functionaries, a barrister. The Celtic Revival was a far more refined affair; but as Ireland's version of the European avant-garde it would turn back to these collaborative forms, drawing upon an artistic heritage which, whether as epic or ballad, was never much marked by a unique authorial signature. In its recycling of ancient myth and legend, pre-individualist traditionalism and post-individualist modernism mingle curiously together, with little history of liberal humanism to intervene between them. That the public forms of the Revival sometimes contained the most esoteric of contents is only one of its several contradictions, as is the related fact that they were often enough public forms without much of a public.

The problem for a Yeats was how to reinvent a genuinely public art without succumbing to the didactic oratory of Young Ireland. Baffled by this dilemma, he will retreat into a proud, self-delighting autonomy; but

---

9. See T.W. Moody, *Davitt and the Irish Revolution* (Oxford 1981), pp. 514–15.
10. Lady Morgan, *The O'Briens and the O'Flahertys*, vol. 3 (London 1827), Ch. 2.
11. Charles Gavan Duffy, *Young Ireland*, vol. 1 (Dublin 1884), p. 25.
12. See Gary Owens, 'Hedge Schools of Politics: O'Connell's Monster Meetings', *History Ireland*, vol. 2, no. 1 (Spring 1994).

even this is a displacement into the individual life of an image of the free nation. Yeats rejects what he calls the 'anarchic subjectivity of the 19th century', declaring that 'a poet is justified not by the expression of himself, but by the public he finds or creates'.[13] In his epochal division of literature, Ireland is still pre-lyrical, and so pre-individualist.[14] As he moves beyond his early symbolism, he will reach back over the heads of his English contemporaries, the fag-end of a depoliticized Romanticism, to their own great precursors among the early English Romantics, whose art springs out of a politically turbulent moment which can speak across the decades to his own. Irish and English literary history are out of synchrony, so that Yeats must loop time around him, finding a contemporary in Blake as he cannot in Tennyson. It was his good fortune to come to artistic consciousness in a historical period (that of revolutionary nationalism) in which the traditional bardic role – the poet as hero, activist, rhetorician, cultural *Gauleiter*, man of affairs – could be plausibly recreated. Cultural production in Ireland was still folded within a broader political context; in *fin-de-siècle* Britain, the structural separation of private and public, cultural and political spheres, prevented any such recasting of the artistic role. In his history of the Irish literary revival, W.P. Ryan quotes some gloomy words from *Middlemarch* about frustrated St Teresas in search of an epic project;[15] but just as that disenchanted novel is marking the point in English society where such grand gestures no longer seem credible, an epic action of a kind is just about to get off the ground in Ireland.

If art and politics are intimately linked in Ireland, it is partly because they share a common root. In the era of modernity, political life is steadily emptied of the passions and affections, which as we have seen are forced to take shelter in art, religious experience, bodily life. In Ireland, those energies remain active in the public domain, in the political creed we know as nationalism. Nationalism is a spiritual principle before it is a political programme – a discourse of nation rather than state, of *Gemeinschaft* rather than *Gesellschaft*, and so one nourished by those pieties and symbolic allegiances which the politics of modernity excludes from the public realm. This itself, as Tom Nairn points out, is something of an irony: 'the most notoriously subjective and idealist of historical phenomena is in fact a by-product of the most brutally and hopelessly material side

13. W.B. Yeats, *Essays and Introductions* (London 1961), p. 407.

14. W.B. Yeats, 'Nationality and Literature', in John P. Frayne, ed., *Uncollected Prose by W.B. Yeats*, vol. 1 (London 1970), p. 273.

15. W.P. Ryan, *The Irish Literary Revival* (London 1984), p. 6.

of history of the last two centuries'.[16] If nationalism is a matter of subjective sentiment, it is one, so to speak, of a wholly objective kind. Nationalism is a politics of the aura in an age of mechanical repro-duction,[17] rather as Romanticism is a strain of the sacred in a secularized age. The exalted Carlylean rhetoric of Standish O'Grady's *History of Ireland* converts historiography into imaginative ritual. When Daniel Corkery, the Zhdanov of Irish literature, declared that poetry, not prose, is the only fit medium for Irish nationalism, he was giving voice to this internal relation between art and Irish political life.[18]

Unlike market socialism or proportional representation, nationalism is a feeling before it is a theory, which is why its poetry, in the hands of its Irish laureate Tom Moore, aspires to the condition of music. The music of Moore's lyrics is the untranslatable spirit of the nation, a distilled essence of national yearning which resists verbal embodiment; so that the proto-symbolist Moore must pare his words of their referential force, allowing the semantic to approach the condition of pure song.[19] William O'Brien speaks of patriotism as 'the whispered poetry of our cradles', and goes on to produce a fair species of it:

> What the star that shone over Bethlehem on the first Christian night was to the three Eastern Magi; what the vision of the Holy Grail was to the Knights of the Round Table; what the Holy Sepulchre was to the dying eyes of the Crusaders, fainting in the parched Syrian desert, that to the children of the Irish race was and is this tradition that there has been, and the faith that there will be, a golden-hearted Irish nation – the land of song and wit and mirth and learning and holiness and all the fair flowering of the human mind and soul.[20]

It seems a far cry from Prime Minister's Question Time. Nationalism, so Thomas Kettle argues in *The Day's Burden*, is the elevation of sentiment from private experience to political principle; and he goes on to speak in a language redolent of Edmund Burke of the need for a political sensitivity to 'life in its complex richness and man as a complex of remembrances,

---

16. Tom Nairn, *The Break-Up of Britain* (London 1977), pp. 335–6.

17. See Walter Benjamin, 'The Work of Art in the Age of Mechanical Reproduction', in *Illuminations*, edited by Hannah Arendt (London 1970).

18. Daniel Corkery, *Synge and Anglo-Irish Literature* (Dublin 1931), p. 20. For all his prescriptive literary views, Corkery – a disciple of Turgenev – was denounced as a highbrow by fellow nationalists and seen as more concerned with art than propaganda. See Patrick Maume, 'Daniel Corkery: A Reassessment', *Studia Hibernica*, no. 26 (1991–2).

19. See Robert Welch, *Irish Poetry from Moore to Yeats* (Gerrards Cross 1980), Ch. 1.

20. William O'Brien, *Irish Ideas* (London 1893), p. 5. Perhaps it is necessary for me to add, in light of the politics of contemporary Irish historiography, that I find these sentiments a trifle overblown.

instincts, intuitions, and emotional needs'.[21] 'Politics', remarks Lady Morgan in her *Patriotic Sketches of Ireland*, 'can never be a woman's science, but patriotism must naturally be a woman's sentiment.'[22]

Nationalism is an androgynous affair – a matter of feeling, to be sure, but feeling about the *patria*. If politics consorts so readily with art, it is partly because it was aesthetic all along; indeed the analogy Kettle offers for this public rehabilitation of sentiment is the novel. Nationalism is at one with Jürgen Habermas in elevating the 'life world' over the system; and the kind of fulfilment one reaps from belonging to a community of national sentiment is akin to the pleasure the Kantian subject derives from the *sensus communis* of aesthetic taste. Indeed Elie Kedourie baldly describes nationalism as the invention of 'literary men',[23] and it is worth recalling that the founders of Sinn Fein emerged out of the Celtic Literary Society. (It is an intriguing minor detail of modern Irish history that the Fenian John O'Leary shared lodgings in Paris with Whistler and Swinburne, and that a couple of his fellow IRBers lived in the house which Balzac had immortalized in *Le Père Goriot*.) Culture in Ireland may occasionally displace politics, but it is just as much its continuation by other means. The Yeats-sponsored view that politics yielded ground to culture after the fall of Parnell, while one sees what it means, betrays a narrowly parliamentarian view of politics and a curiously depoliticized notion of culture.[24]

What is at stake, then, in Irish nationalism's encounter with British sovereignty, is not simply a political conflict but the clash of two opposed conceptions of the political. For Thomas Kettle, political economy must encompass moral economy, questions of utility be linked to considerations of human welfare. John Eglinton writes in *Pebbles from a Brook* of that 'higher or regenerate patriotism, which has its ground in the relation of man to his fellow men and to nature, rather than in his political relation

---

21. Thomas Kettle, *The Day's Burden* (Dublin 1910; reprinted 1937), p. 10.
22. Lady Morgan, *Patriotic Sketches of Ireland* (London 1807), p. x.
23. Elie Kedourie, *Nationalism* (London 1960), p. 70.
24. See, for a case against this view, R.F. Foster, 'Anglo-Irish Literature, Gaelic Nationalism and Irish Politics in the 1890s', in the British Academy publication *Ireland after the Union* (London 1989). The Yeatsian view is repeated, among many other places, in Richard Fallis, *The Irish Renaissance* (Syracuse 1977, p. 56), an otherwise informative introduction. John Kelly makes the interesting point that although there was indeed such a shift from the anti-cultural, intensely politicized 1880s to the 'literariness' of the '90s, the motive behind it was ironically political – the attempt of the Parnellites to define, through literature, an independent Irish identity, as against those anti-Parnellites who could be portrayed as collusive with British power (see John S. Kelly, 'The Fall of Parnell and the Rise of Irish Literature', *Anglo-Irish Studies*, no. 2, 1976).

to the state'. [25] This nationalist humanism is Ireland's version of England's 'Culture and Society' tradition,[26] and the same figure, Edmund Burke, stands at the fountainhead of both. There is a pre-political strain to both currents of thought, concerned as they are with those ethical or symbolic reaches of social life besides which the business of elections and committees appears singularly unenthralling. Indeed it is remarkable how non-political Irish politics actually were. The Young Irelander Fintan Lalor scorned politics as purely superficial, Isaac Butt disdained party bickering, while Eoin MacNeill preserved a scholarly detachment from revolutionary zeal on the very brink of national insurrection. Douglas Hyde kept a genteel distance from *realpolitik*, and even the politically matchless Parnell harboured a secret distaste for the very public arena in which he excelled. The proprietor of the Irish national theatre specifically banned political drama, while Yeats commended Synge as a man incapable of a political idea. An early historian of the Revival commented that 'relief from politics' was the main condition for intellectual and economic growth in the country.[27] George Russell, in his utopian tract *The National Being*, dismisses the state and representative government ('an English invention') for an aristocratic spirit of freedom on the one hand, and a democratic principle of economic cooperation on the other.[28] Arthur Griffith preferred the role of *éminence grise* to party politician, and early Sinn Fein viewed itself as a 'national' rather than political movement.[29] Patrick Pearse pursued an aestheticized brand of politics, and was a mere Home Ruler as late as 1912. D.P. Moran preached 'language revival and a plague on politics',[30] while the syndicalist James Connolly gave priority to the economic over the political. Irish Irelandism could be quite as dismissive of the political as the Anglo-Irish Celticism it scorned. The Arnoldian large-mindedness of Sir Horace Plunkett was pained by 'political zealotry', and located the nation's woes in its peculiar cultural character. 'The Irish mind', so Plunkett considered, 'is suffering from considerable functional derangement, but not, so far as I can discern, from any organic disease. This is the basis of my optimism.'[31] There is, of course, a political as well as cultural Irish nationalism, all the way from the United Irishmen, with

25. John Eglinton, *Pebbles from a Brook* (Dublin 1901), p. 74.
26. See Raymond Williams, *Culture and Society 1780–1950* (London 1958).
27. Ernest A. Boyd, *Ireland's Literary Renaissance* (London 1916), p. 94.
28. AE (George Russell), *The National Being* (Dublin 1916), pp. 103f.
29. For Griffith, see Richard Davis, *Arthur Griffith* (Dundalk 1976).
30. See Foster, 'Anglo-Irish Literature', p. 76.
31. Horace Plunkett, *Ireland in the New Century* (Dublin 1904; reprinted 1983), pp. 59–60.

their trust in law, state and politics, to O'Connell and Parnell. But the culturalist bent of the creed is nevertheless striking. From the *fin de siècle* onwards, this anti-political animus feeds into a modernism which, in Ireland as elsewhere, replaces political engagement with artistic dedication. But this non-political art was hardly typical of nineteenth-century Ireland. For Victorian England, culture transcends the political; for nineteenth-century Ireland it is the very source of it.

Behind this elevating of culture over politics lies a venerable Irish history. For once the Gaelic political order had been brought low in the seventeenth century, culture in the form of bards and ballads, music and memories, was one of the few remaining repositories of a 'national' consciousness. A people deprived of their own political institutions had to make do instead with the imaginary identity which culture could bestow upon them – an identity to which no political reality now corresponded. But this skewing of the cultural and political can be pressed back even further. For the old Irish bards or *filí*, according to Proinsias MacCana, 'the spiritual concept of a national unity did not require an exact reflex in the realm of secular politics; in other words religious concept and political structure did not necessarily coincide'.[32] In modern Irish history, this non-coincidence is reflected in a nationalism with both cultural and political wings, which sometimes interlocked and sometimes drew apart.

Just as the erotic and economic are hard to distinguish in pre-modern sexuality, so the sexual and political are closely interwoven in much Irish writing, as the poet's object of nostalgia or desire glides ambiguously between a particular woman and the figure of the pillaged nation. Yeats is still making the connection, however scathingly, in the figure of Maud Gonne, rose of Ireland and rancorous demogogue. Sensibility and society are closely allied: the melancholy of a Moore or a Mangan is directly political, while the plangency of a Tennyson is only obliquely so. (Mangan, John Mitchel comments famously in his *Jail Journal*, was really two persons: one well known to the Muses, the other to the police.[33]) Yeats and Joyce

---

32. Proinsias MacCana, 'Notes on the Early Irish Concept of Unity', in M.P. Hederman and R. Kearney, eds, *The Crane Bag Book of Irish Studies* (Dublin 1982), p. 211. For the power of the *filí*, see also Michelle O'Riordan, *The Gaelic Mind and the Collapse of the Gaelic World* (Cork 1990), Introduction.

33. Mangan was in fact a good deal more than just two people. His view of himself as 'a plural [man] – a Protean', his assumption of translations as so many masks, and his deep distrust of anything which emanated directly from himself, are signs of a colonial crisis of identity.

will in their different ways renounce this political aesthetic for the transcendent splendour of art; but no sooner have they done so than they will
reach back from that Olympian standpoint into the profane materials of a
national history, with all the buoyant assurance of one secretly liberated
from it. Yeats may disdain the didactic rhythms of Young Ireland;[34] but
what they give way to in his own work is not some colloquial speaking
voice but the collective forms of myth, public oratory, symbolic system.
Speech in the ancient Irish sagas, so John Wilson Foster remarks, 'is not
self-expression but incantation, song, spell, pledge, or prophecy';[35] and
much the same can be said of Yeats's ceremonious syntax. As for Joyce,
he will no sooner lay claim to his freedom as solitary artificer than he
will surrender it again, decentring this dearly won selfhood into the great
impersonal polyphonies of *Ulysses* and *Finnegans Wake*, celebrating his
unique identity in a language which dissolves all unique identity to
nothing. Joyce's defiantly anti-political aesthetics, like most such modernist
gestures, is a politics all in itself; but its political edge is even sharper in
a society which lacks a mainstream liberal tradition. Such a heritage had
flourished in the eighteenth century, not least in Presbyterian Ulster.[36]
But with the tumultuous birth of the Catholic nation, that creed in the
Protestant north was increasingly under siege; while in Catholic Ireland,
with the sea-change from Enlightenment republicanism to Romantic
nationalism, the language of individual liberty yielded ground to the
discourse of collective emancipation.

In Romantic nationalism, a particularism of people and place begins
to oust a universalism of human rights, so that the revolution, when it
arrives, is lacking in much ontological dimension beyond God and nation.
This style of thought divorces the libertarian impulse of the Enlightenment
from its liberalism, embracing the former while sceptical of the latter.
The idea of national liberation transposes individual freedom to a collective
plane, but in doing so threatens to curb it. 'Rightly understood, intellectual freedom and political freedom are one',[37] writes the liberal nationalist
Frederick Ryan, a sentiment which the illiberal nationalist Arthur Griffith
would have found deeply uncongenial. All of this, along with clerical

---

34. Ironically, Thomas Davis had himself scorned what he regarded as the crude propa-
gandism of much popular Irish balladeering.

35. John Wilson Foster, *Fictions of the Irish Revival* (Syracuse 1987), p. 18.

36. See Seamus Deane, 'Edmund Burke and the Ideology of Irish Liberalism', in Richard
Kearney, ed., *The Irish Mind* (Dublin 1985).

37. Frederick Ryan, *Criticism and Courage* (Dublin 1906), p. 37. A study of this attractive
figure – cultural critic, liberal rationalist, nationalist and internationalist – would be worth
having.

repression, a communally minded countryside and the absence of a developed urban middle class, was enough to stifle any very vigorous liberal growth in Ireland. A key difference between Anglo-Irish and Irish-Irish nationalism was thus how far emancipation was to include freedom from Rome as well as from Westminster, from an authoritarian mind-set as much as from imperial power. One problem for the Anglo-Irish party was that true empathy with the people meant coming to terms with a religious creed which seemed more an obstacle to liberation than an instrument of it. No populist intellectual could simply shelve the mass of the people's deepest beliefs, but few Anglo-Irish free spirits could regard them as anything but a threat to civilized liberal values. The running battle between priesthood and paganism, Catholicism and Celticism, was not one which seemed open to mediation.

The role of liberal was thus left vacant, to be variously filled by Constructive Unionists, dissident artists, Oedipal children of Ascendancy. In industrial capitalist Britain, liberalism had become the dominant ideology; but the governing order in Ireland was still largely pre-bourgeois, led by a dismally unenlightened landowning class. This order was then incapable of bequeathing any fruitful liberal inheritance to its political antagonists: if the nationalists could strike against a repressive state, they were unable to match this dissidence with any very sturdy discourse of individual rights. The point should not be exaggerated: Daniel O'Connell was a liberal, passionately devoted to civil liberties, and so in his own way was Patrick Pearse, with his child-centred theories of education.[38] But the language of Irish nationalism remained largely impervious to what we might now call questions of subjectivity; if the great estates could be shaken up, psychic structures remained stubbornly intact. The two forms of rebellion intersect, of all places, in Anthony Trollope's feeble fiction The Landleaguers, which deals at once with the land wars and women's emancipation, and is equally supercilious about both. John Eglinton in his Anglo-Irish Essays bemoans the absence of free individual spirits in Ireland, and ascribes it to the rigorously collective codes of priest and bard.[39] Eglinton was not the only Anglo-Irish liberal to regard

38. For Pearse's own account of his school, St Enda's, see Seamus Ó Buachalla, ed., The Letters of P.H. Pearse (Gerrards Cross 1980), pp. 152–8. See also Pearse's educational essay 'The Murder Machine' in Collected Works of P.H. Pearse: Political Speeches and Writings (Dublin 1922).

39. See his essay 'A Neglected Monument of Irish Prose', in Anglo-Irish Essays (Dublin 1917). For a similar brand of liberal anti-clerical rationalism, see Frederick Ryan, Crisis and Courage (Dublin 1906).

his own social group as a bastion of civilized intelligence in a conformist nation, a free-thinking modernist intelligentsia marooned amidst a benighted race. Figures like Isaac Butt will strive to assume the role of an Irish Matthew Arnold, but in an inevitably minor key.

In the absence of an Irish John Stuart Mill, then, the role of individual dissent has finally to be assumed by the artists, whose spiritual nonconformism must do service for some more politically framed revolt. What is little more than a sub-Nietzschean cliché in England – the demonic poet loftily transcending the polarities of good and evil – gathers rather more subversive force in a social order where liberalism had never flourished as a dominant doctrine. Yet the situation is more complex than some simplistic opposition of artist and society. As a child of the urban petty bourgeoisie, Joyce hailed from the class which was to spearhead the political revolution; and if his haughty *non serviam* is a refusal to be enlisted in those ranks, it also catches up something of that dissenting impulse. Like the Ibsen he admired so deeply, Joyce belongs to a middle class which is still capable of historic achievement, but which also forms an obstacle to some more deep-seated emancipation. The art of both writers, then, offers a spiritual critique of the very historical forces which helped to shape it.

Art and politics in Ireland may be closely paired; but the question of their precise relationship remains contentious. Is art political weapon; utopian symbol; image of reconciliation? Is it to be mirror or hammer? Should it reflect an oppressive present, give voice to some spirit stirring within it, prefigure that spirit's future realization, or take an active part in its unfolding? The dilemma of a nationalist art is the conundrum of national identity itself, which is at once given and still to be created, present and absent simultaneously, caught in a perpetual tension between actual and ideal. The people will become free; but this is because they are in some elusive sense free already. The Irish nation, so a line of nationalists from O'Connell to Arthur Griffith will claim, has been independent since 1782, and simply needs to remind itself of the fact. There was little these men needed to be told about the concept of virtual reality. An art which portrays the truth of colonial oppression will act as a spur to political action; yet such demeaning images may dispirit the people and erode the will to change.[40] William Carleton's only dramatic piece had to be taken

---

40. The popular Irish pastime of running oneself down is relevant here. Upbraiding one's fellow countrypeople for their cowardice and inertia, in the manner of a John Mitchel or James Joyce, is itself perhaps a symptom of the syndrome it identifies, part of the demoralization it denounces.

off for just this reason. If the masses were not demoralized there would be no reason to transform them; but if they are, then there is no possibility of it. Naturalism, then, must be blended with a revolutionary idealism which will disclose the nation in all its typicality; yoke indicative and subjunctive moods together; illuminate what is, in the light of what might be. The line between truth and edification, disfiguring realism and anondyne idealism, is notably hard to draw; is Synge to be condemned for romanticizing the peasantry, or for portraying them as less than perfect? Are the Irish, in the manner of an O'Connell, to be flattered in their given identity, or in the style of a Thomas Davis to be exhorted into a finer one? Should one complain that the people are shiftless and dissolute in order to indict those who have reduced them to this condition, or praise the people as sober and industrious and reject any less sanguine view of them as a colonialist slur? What, in any case, if realism were the least suitable form for a political art, since the real is what revolutionary desire exists to spurn? 'A man who loves Dickens', writes George Russell with fine condescension, 'may grow to have a great tolerance for the grotesque characters which are the outcome of the social order in England, but he will not be assisted in the conception of a higher humanity.'[41]

Perhaps the only appropriate culture in these conditions is some avant-garde experimentalism which has already crossed the threshold of the future, unleashing the political unconscious of the nation in strange figures and fantasies. Perhaps culture is the laboratory of the nation, its mode of production rather than means of expression. 'To express the whole nature of a race or nation', declares Standish O'Grady, 'the artist needs that absolute freedom which is only supplied by a complete escape from positive history and unyielding despotic fact.'[42] O'Grady himself was certainly never much hampered by the facts. A truly revolutionary art may be one which has transfigured its own forms beyond recognition; but how is such an art to be accessible to a people reared on a diet of Canon Sheehan and the *Brian Boru Song Book*?[43] How is an avant-garde, attuned to a future which may in time be brought within reach of all, to

---

41. AE (George Russell), 'Nationality and Cosmopolitanism in Art', in *Some Irish Essays* (Dublin 1906), p. 16.

42. Standish O'Grady, *History of Ireland: Critical and Philosophical*, vol. 1 (London 1881), p. 57.

43. For a useful account of the enormously popular work of Sheehan, see Terence Brown, *Ireland's Literature: Selected Esssays* (Mullingar 1988), Ch. 5. For all his clericist orthodoxy, some of Sheehan's novels – in particular *Luke Delmerge* and *The Graves of Kilmorna* – are still well worth reading. A survey of 1884 revealed that the two most popular books in Ireland were *The Brian Boru Song Book* and *The Harp of Tara Song Book*.

be distinguished from an Anglo-Irish elite, who are not so much out ahead of the masses as simply over their heads? The relation between political and aesthetic value is a troubling one, since the most artistically distinguished works will tend to be those least amenable to the people, and so the least politically effective. The reverse situation is wryly captured in a comment of Seamus Deane on Thomas Davis: 'among the most important and worst of Irish poets'.[44] But if the populace is as wise and virtuous as some nationalist ideology would claim, how can they be palmed off with any but the most distinguished creations? The clash between radical elitism and populist conservatism may always be resolved by an appeal to the racial unconscious: poets are those who articulate in more sophisticated form what is already broodingly implicit in the popular mind. It is then possible to believe, along with T.S. Eliot, that you have always already been understood, whatever the empirical evidence to the contrary.

None of these issues is peculiar to Ireland, as a glance at early Soviet cultural debates is enough to suggest. The Left Front in Art, RAPP, Proletkult, agitprop, liberal fellow-travellers, the ideologues of socialist re-alism: all of these find their dim echoes in Irish cultural controversy, and some rough analogies can be discerned.[45] Irish Ireland, for example, is not far removed from Proletkult in its emphasis on the unique identity of the revolutionary people – an identity which must find expression in a culture purged of all alien influences and well-meaning upper-class hangers-on. Daniel Corkery's plea for an art in tune with the 'emotional nature' of the peasantry is close to the Proletkultists' notion of a distinctive working-class psychology, which it was the task of art to embody. The callow left Romanticism of some of the Bolshevik avant-gardists, for the people but hardly of them, finds a resonance in the naive idealism of some of the Revivalists. When Arthur Griffith hotly questions the typicality of Synge's profane peasants, he is anticipating a whole history of Comintern cultural debate.[46] Yeats's quarrel with the Young Irelanders prefigures the warfare between RAPP or agitprop and their more liberal

---

44. Seamus Deane, ed., *The Field Day Anthology of Irish Writing*, vol. 2 (Derry 1992), p. 1.

45. There are other Soviet–Irish connections: the Soviet Union was the only nation to recognize the Irish republic in 1919, and the last survivor of the battleship *Potemkin* is reputed to have ended up running a fish-and-chip shop in Galway. Another intriguing con-nection is the nineteenth-century mystical poet Vladimir Pecherin, who ended up as a monk in Ireland. There is a reference to this in John Le Carré's *The Russia House*.

46. See Robert Hogan and James Kilroy, eds, *The Modern Irish Drama, vol. 2: Laying the Foundations* (Dublin 1976), p. 79.

critics, and raises questions of partisan or 'tendency' art which have resounded through the archives of Marxist aesthetics.

In Yeats's view, an art too closely geared to political action fails precisely as art, and so fails to move in some more deep-seated, politically fertile way.[47] His position on nationalist art around the turn of the century was admirably adroit: by serving some immediate political cause, Irish writers have failed to evolve a tradition of their own, a task which demands time and patience, and so surrendered themselves meekly to English literary forms. Yeats can thus assail propagandist nationalist verse while covering his political back, out-lefting and depoliticizing simultaneously. His hostility to Young Ireland's journalistic art is at once nationalist and modernist – nationalist because England was the home of debased popular literature, modernist because modernism is among other things a resistance to the mass culture which was born alongside it. But the dilemma of cultural nationalism is clear. Art must revive the nation, but this suggests a utility at odds with its own autonomy. Culture as political means is at odds with culture as utopian end: if a crudely instrumental art cannot edify, one which plumbs the deepest spirit of the people risks leaving them cold. The more art explores the transcendental mysteries of the nation, the less it can assist that nation into being. Folk art, which is neither esoteric nor instrumental, is then an alluring alternative, combining the popularity of journalism with the symbolism of poetry. But symbolist poetry can be nationalist too, since the purity, unity and autonomy of the work of art can be seen to mirror the ideal qualities of nationhood. In a familiar modernist paradox, such art becomes politically charged in its very apolitical aloofness, bearing the dim outline of the future in its forms while spurning all prosaic commitment in its content. But this culture is inescapably privileged, and so will draw the fire of some political nationalists. The contradiction is plain: an art which has its roots in oppression is elitist and falsely sublimating, but without such art we shall have no images of a transfigured future.

Does culture, then, prefigure the political future, or is it dependent upon it? Is cultural revolution the product, or precondition, of political change? Must a subject class or people have amassed an amount of cultural capital already in order to shake off its rulers, or can it only enter upon its cultural inheritance once it has achieved political power? The former

---

47. Yeats was not above a little suave malice in this respect: 'I have just read in a newspaper that Sir Charles Gavan Duffy recited upon his death-bed his favourite poem, one of the worst of the patriotic poems of Young Ireland...' (W.B. Yeats, 'Poetry and Tradition', in *Essays and Introductions,* London 1961, p. 257).

case is commonly, if mistakenly, ascribed to Antonio Gramsci – mistakenly, since Gramsci was in fact under no illusion that the proletariat could seize hold of the means of cultural production on this side of socialist revolution.[48] The cultural deprivation of the working class is a structural feature of capitalism, and could not be remedied without its overthrow. To claim that a subject *people* may attain cultural power before wresting political victory, however, is rather more plausible. For 'culture' here means less those spiritual goods made available by wealth, leisure and education, than language, customs, religion, tradition, popular art – everything, in short, which constitutes a particular people as distinctive. And since these are primary targets of colonial power, they are inevitably arenas of political conflict. While the imperial powers are busy depoliticizing culture at home, they are inescapably engaged in politicizing it abroad. It is a relief to the colonialist that the natives are ontologically different from himself, in the sense of being inferior; but this difference is also what makes his own foreignness embarrassingly obvious, and so makes it harder for him to naturalize his rule. The difference which props up his power is also what threatens to undo it. What insulates that rule from native influence is also what makes it unstable. Imperial authority, unlike power in the metropolitan nation, can rarely disguise itself, and the ruler in Ireland was never hard to spot: he spoke a different language, or the same language with a peculiar accent, lived in the big house, owned the land you worked on and had scant acquaintance with the Virgin Mary. A governing class may seek to temper and aestheticize its rule by 'civility'; but the 'rapscallion class'[49] of Anglo-Irish landowners had precious little of that. Civility, in any case, is seductive only if it represents a condition to which one might feasibly aspire, which was hardly true of the Irish cottiers and landless labourers. The Ascendancy had a culture of its own, and idealized it in elegaic retrospect; but it was not for the most part a hegemonic *relation* to their inferiors. It was not, on the whole, a field within which the cultures of the governors and the governed could negotiate, interact, inflect themselves in each other's terms.[50] Where that project existed, in

---

48. See Perry Anderson, 'The Antinomies of Antonio Gramsci', *New Left Review* 100 (November 1976–January 1977).

49. Andrew Carpenter and Seamus Deane, 'The Shifting Perspective', in Deane, ed., *The Field Day Anthology*, vol. 1, p. 964.

50. There are obvious major exceptions. The Ordnance Survey project of 1824 was a hegemonic rather than crudely dominative affair, incorporating local knowledge into what remained a British-controlled enterprise. See Mary Hamer, 'Putting Ireland on the Map', *Textual Practice*, vol. 3, no. 2 (1989).

the shape of the Celticizing Anglo-Irish liberals, it was either too marginal or historically too late.

For a colonized people to accumulate cultural capital is clearly a less perilous business than for it to use political force. It was not, in Ireland, wholly without its dangers: there were many aspects of the native culture which were from time to time harrassed or suppressed. In the sixteenth century, the English authorities at once despised the Irish as barbarians and paid a compliment to their culture by threatening their bards with a whipping. But the long revolution of cultural revival was among other things a lateral assault on an enemy too powerful to be directly confronted; and for men like Davis and Yeats this process of moral rebirth was an essential prelude to political success. Many an Irish nationalist recognized the hazards of deferring everything to the insurrectionary moment – recognized that such a crisis would not occur, or would at best be botched, if the agents of the drama did not come to it as already transformed subjects, rather than as the sullen underlings of imperialism to be refashioned *ex nihilo*. 'We have few reserves of intellectual life to draw upon when we come to this mighty labour of nation-building', remarked George Russell in uncharacteristically realistic vein.[51] John O'Leary considered that no political revolution could succeed unless backed by cultural revival. After the defeat of the second Home Rule Bill in 1893, there was a sharpened sense that political victory was no longer imminent, and that cultural renewal could therefore not wait upon it. If a political end is not to make men and women desire uselessly, and so to fall ill of longing, it must be possible to point in the present to what might prefigure its realization. There was this much truth, at least, in the nationalist claim that the spirit of the future was alive, if unwell, in the present; for if it was not then there was no logical sense in which the future could be spoken of.

The opposing case, however, has at least as much force. For if what is at stake is revolution, then how could any identity drawn from past or present be proleptic of such a mind-bending transformation? To speak of it coherently is in that act to betray it; and in this way the most radical rhetoric becomes an unwitting kind of conservatism. Cultural emancipation may be a necessary condition of political power; but to be free to give yourself a name would seem to demand a degree of political liberty in the first place. Without some affirmative sense of selfhood, no political change could come about; yet if one could name oneself with any

---

51. AE (George Russell), *The National Being*, p. 5.

assurance, such change would be unnecessary. The concept of political revolution would thus seem to turn on an *aporia* or *petitio principi*, assuming in its premises an identity which is yet to be defined. Some Anglo-Irish nationalists were inspired by their own self-divided state to view the question of identity as problematic, whereas many of their Gaelic counterparts took it rather more for granted. Like much Romanticism, such nationalism operated with an expression/repression model of the subject: the self is already whole and entire, but is everywhere in chains; if only it could burst through those shackles it could come to full expression. The fact that all effective repression is internalized is then itself repressed. In the Pearsean cult of blood sacrifice, that selfhood was to be ceremoniously surrendered; but it is not hard to see such self-abnegation as the other side of a secure self-identity.[52] How well you must know who you are, if you can abandon your identity safe in the knowledge that it will be restored to you a hundredfold! Something similar, however, might be said of some Anglo-Irish nationalists, whose readiness to renounce their inheritance was among other things a devious means of repossessing it.

If the relations between culture and politics are fraught, it is partly because they belong to different temporalities. A political constitution can be scrapped overnight; the growth of a language or withering of a custom is a matter of generations. Cultural renovation is a fatiguing *longue durée*, in contrast to the punctual time of political insurrection; and the plight of the present might seem to brook no such deferment. The Fenian leader James Stephens, with one cold eye on the Young Irelanders, scorned 'amiable and enlightened young men' imagining that they were re-generating their country while 'pushing about in drawing room society ... creat'ng an Irish national literature, schools of Irish art and things of that sort'.[53] The Parnellite newspaper *United Ireland* wrote in a sideswipe at the Revival that 'the times are highly unfavourable for the cultivation of the intellectual faculties of Irishmen.'[54] 'The nation has to be saved first of all', declared Justin McCarthy in 1890, '...when that is once accomplished the brain and the tongue and the pen can go back to the service of literature, or begin its service under bright auspices and inspiring conditions.'[55] In

---

52. See on this theme W.I. Thompson, *The Imagination of an Insurrection* (New York 1967), Ch. 4.
53. Quoted by D. George Boyce, *Nationalism in Ireland* (London 1982), p. 177.
54. Ibid., p. 232.
55. Quoted by John S. Kelly, 'The Political, Intellectual and Social Background to the Irish Literary Revival to 1901', unpublished Ph.D. thesis (University of Cambridge 1972), p. 52.

one sense this is no more than a commonplace philistinism, evident all the way from Wolfe Tone's infamous irritability with Irish harpers to the Fenians' or Home Rulers' relative indifference to cultural questions.[56] More quaintly, it could spring from a homophobic fear that an entrancement with 'Swinburnian phrases' or 'the dainty trick of Tennyson' was rendering the nation disturbingly effete.[57] But the political nationalists were right to suspect that culture could be displacement as well as deepening. If it was for some a vital point of political engagement, it was for others an obstacle to the very social change it sought to promote. In the manner of Jacques Derrida's 'supplement', culture was in danger of ousting what it sought to subserve. There is a rough analogy here with Leon Trotsky's impatience with Proletkult, doggedly building up a synthetic working-class culture while so many pressing political tasks lay to hand.[58] For Trotsky, the whole idea of such culture was an absurdity, since it was precisely the disappearance of the proletariat which would signal that socialism had finally arrived. One might argue rather similarly that the mark of a truly free nation would be one devoid of nationalist sentiment. But the recovery of a national culture may play its part in securing that freedom; and the debates between cultural and political nationalists thus continued to rage.

Like sex, culture is always in danger of being either underrated or overvalued – reduced, as with the Sinn Feiners, to too functional a role, or, as with Samuel Ferguson and the *Dublin University Magazine*, elevated to an end in itself alongside a Unionist allegiance. If some political nationalists sternly suppressed art, more than a few of their cultural counterparts chronically idealized it. But how was the pure essence of culture to enter upon material existence without thereby entering into contradiction with itself? A concern with meanings and values, however staunchly political, is always likely to conceal a latent idealism at its heart, just as the most materialist of intellectuals is always a prey to theoreticism. There is a thin line between a proper attention to culture and the Marxist heresy known as culturalism, which ascribes it too much weight; and it was a line which some Irish antiquarians and Revivalists were no strangers

---

56. Though as far as Tone goes, the cultural interests of the United Irish movement have been in general neglected. See Mary Helen Thuente, 'The Literary Significance of the United Irishmen', in Michael Kenneally, ed., *Irish Literature and Culture* (Gerrards Cross 1992). Sean O'Casey comments on the philistinism of Sinn Fein in his 'Drums under the Window', in Sean O'Casey, *Autobiographies 1* (London 1992), pp. 616–17.

57. See Boyce, *Nationalism in Ireland*, p. 234.

58. See Leon Trotsky, *Literature and Revolution* (Ann Arbor 1971), Ch. 6. The analogy is indeed inexact, not least because Trotsky is writing on the far side of political change.

to transgressing. And what if the material progress to which nationalism aspired was at odds with its spiritual values? The contradiction is captured in J.M. Synge's befuddled comments on the west of Ireland: 'In a way it is all heartrending, in one place the people are starving but wonderfully attractive and charming and in another place where things are going well one has a rampant double-chinned vulgarity I haven't seen the like of.'[59] It seems a choice between the prosperous philistine and the the aesthetically alluring skeleton. As far as the Young Irelanders went, the quarrel between culture and materiality was finally to be settled by history itself. Few documents of modern Irish history are more painful to read, more finely poised between the tragic and the grotesque, than the later speeches of a Thomas Meagher or a James Fintan Lalor, literary set pieces laced with baroque flourishes delivered just as the Famine was killing off their compatriots.[60] The Young Irelanders were struggling to mobilize a small-holding class which was just about to be decimated; somewhat later, the Land League would have rather more success with a stronger set of farmers. In that most familiar of all Irish tropes – bathos – the material world wreaked its dreadful vengeance on this visionary rhetoric, demonstrating in the cruellest fashion that the material conditions for cultural revival were simply unavailable.

In Ireland, however, culturalism meant something rather more precise than assigning undue weight to symbolic matters. It meant rather the attempt by a whole line of Anglo-Irish intellectuals to find in culture a reconciling, disinterested vantage point in a social order wracked by religious and political strife. From this Archimedean point, they could transcend the social, ethnic and religious differences which estranged them from the majority of the common people, and so buttress their own position as a declining breed. It would also, for good measure, allow them to keep an increasingly untrustworthy Britain at political arm's length. The cultural wing of the Anglo-Irish were to become the new *filí*, the bardic caste of ancient Ireland who, so Proinsias MacCana maintains, had been the linchpin of a system remarkable for its cultural homogeneity.[61] Just as the *filí* had provided a link between the intensely

---

59. Anne Saddlemyer, ed., *Collected Letters of J.M. Synge* (Oxford 1983), p. 117.

60. See Arthur Griffith, ed., *Meagher of the Sword* (Dublin 1916); and *James Fintan Lalor: Collected Writings* (Dublin and London 1918).

61. Proinsias MacCana, 'Notes on the Early Irish Concept of Unity', in Hederman and Kearney, eds, *The Crane Bag Book*.

parochial chiefdoms of ancient Ireland, passing from clan to clan without being regarded as strangers, so the Anglo-Irish intelligentsia would mediate between the various cultures within the island.[62]

This project was the Irish version of Arnoldianism, and was to prove quite as ineffectual. In the words of the antiquarian Sir George Petrie, the common pursuit of ancient Irish culture would promote a 'national concordant feeling in a country divided by religious and political discord',[63] in a scholarly enterprise as altruistic as it was self-regarding. Petrie and his colleagues regarded the Ordnance Survey on which they worked as providing, in its dispassionate historical scholarship, an antidote to sectarian strife, so that 'it would gradually come to be as impossible to make use of the ancient Irish history for the propagation of political animosity, as it is to make use of English history...'[64] The British government thought rather differently, and closed the project down. It is little wonder that the Anglo-Irish were so obsessed by spiritual unity, given their own self-divided status. Culture would be the imaginary resolution of real contradictions – which is to say, at once the sworn opponent of ideology and the very paradigm of it. Even the revolutionist John Mitchel believed at one point that a national literature would be 'in its very essence amalgamating, and may eventually be the great temple of concord'.[65] But if culture had its place for a certain brand of political nationalism, it was even more central to a tradition from Samuel Ferguson to William Yeats which sought to modify or displace those politics. For Ferguson, what will cut beneath the sectarian divisions of the Irish is *sentiment* – and since art is its supreme expression, culture in such a context becomes a politics all of its own.

---

62. For the role of the *filí* in this respect, see Joseph Leerssen, *Mere Irish and Fíor-Ghael* (Amsterdam 1986), p. 177.

63. Quoted by John Hutcheson, *The Dynamics of Cultural Nationalism* (London 1987), p. 79. For an excellent account of Petrie and early-nineteenth-century antiquarianism, see Jeanne Sheehy, *The Rediscovery of Ireland's Past: The Celtic Revival 1830–1930* (London 1980), Ch. 2. Petrie's politically consensual view of antiquarianism is anticipated in the late eighteenth century by Charlotte Brooke, whose *Reliques of Irish Poetry* (1789) is consciously aimed, in a year of revolution, at demonstrating the civilized quality of a supposedly barbarous ancient Ireland and so raising its status in the eyes of the British. See Cathal G. Ó Hainle, 'Towards the Revival: Some Translations of Irish Poetry, 1789–1897', in Peter Connolly, ed., *Literature and the Changing Ireland* (Gerrards Cross 1982).

64. The words are those of an Ordnance Survey antiquarian, quoted in William Stokes, *The Life and Labours in Art and Archaeology of Sir George Petrie* (London 1868), p. 97. For the early-nineteenth-century Celtic revival, see also James Hardiman, Introduction, *Irish Minstrelsy*, 2 vols (London 1831).

65. *Nation*, 21 August 1847.

The tension between a committed and consensual idea of culture is obvious enough in the thought of Thomas Davis, for whom culture is both spiritual ideal and political force.[66] Culture as spiritual ideal is the conciliatory language of the Anglo-Irish liberal, and belongs with the Davis who, as Ireland's answer to Thomas Carlyle,[67] dreams of an organic society of yeomen farmers and paternalist landlords. But the Davis who believed strongly in property rights, and feared the subjection of Protestants to Catholic supremacy, was also the author of bellicose nationalist ballads and the advocate of Irish independence. Young Ireland was both more politically militant than the O'Connellites and more culturally idealist; and both tendencies converge in its aestheticized cult of violence.[68] They blend in its poetry too, which is politically instrumental in form but which elevates Irish spirituality over English utility.[69] The distinction between Young Ireland and the rest of O'Connell's Repeal movement is not just one between culture and politics, but (with many a judicious qualification) between political left and right. Culture, in a reverse of conditions in England, is here on the side of 'extremism', as opposed to the Liberator's cautious constitutionalism.

But this partisan sense of culture is locked in conflict with a more ecumenical vision. Davis called for a history of Ireland from below; but if he wished the past to be remembered, he also desired its religious and political cleavages to be forgotten. If he played up the notion of a distinctive Irish people when confronting the British, he played it down

---

66. Raymond Williams discerns a similar tension in the work of Matthew Arnold, for whom culture is both a concrete social process and an absolute which finally transcends it. See *Culture and Society*, Part 1, Ch. 6.

67. The curious relationship between Carlyle and Young Ireland has been well examined by Christopher A. Morash, 'Imagining the Famine: Literary Representations of the Great Famine', unpublished Ph.D. thesis (Trinity College, Dublin 1990), Ch. 1. There is a touch of the grotesque in the Young Irelander's admiration for the irrationalism, chauvinism, neo-feudalism, and worship of physical force of one of Ireland's most vituperative critics.

68. For an account of Young Ireland, see Richard Davis, *Young Ireland* (London 1987). For Davis, see T.W. Rolleston, ed., *Prose Writings of Thomas Davis* (London 1889); and T.W. Moody, *Thomas Davis* (Dublin 1945). For the conflict between Young Ireland and O'Connell, see R.B. McDowell, *Public Opinion and Government Policy in Ireland, 1801–1846* (London 1952), Ch. 9; and Kevin B. Nowlan, *The Politics of Repeal* (London 1965), Ch. 6.

69. The contrast is only approximate: Young Ireland ideology is itself an intriguing blend of utility and idealism. Its Romantic vision, and its stress on the serviceable and industrious, are linked by a common puristic idealism. The *Nation* was much approved by that apostle of English Utilitarianism, Samuel Smiles, who, in the words of Tom Dunne, 'recognised [its] sentimental bourgeois utilitarianism and [its] preoccupation with moral improvement' as akin to his own concerns. See Tom Dunne, 'Haunted by History: Irish Romantic Writing 1800–50', in Roy Porter and Mikulas Teich, eds, *Romanticism in National Context* (Cambridge 1988), p. 77.

within Ireland itself. The *Nation* newspaper was a fiercely *engagé* publication; but Davis was also intent on fostering a pluralist Irish culture, whether through a national theatre, the patriotic 'Library of Ireland' series or even, prefiguring Matthew Arnold's call in England, an Irish lyceum or national academy.[70] As the son of an Englishman of Welsh extraction and a woman of both Gaelic and Cromwellian descent, Davis was himself a walking instance of cultural diversity. This forerunner of Fenianism was also a large-minded liberal who opposed denominational education and sought to rally the landlords to the nationalist cause.[71] If he was in some ways to the left of the cannily pragmatic O'Connell, he was also a good deal more socially regressive, playing Coleridge to the Liberator's Bentham. The concept of culture among the Young Irelanders is at once radical and reconciliationist; and much the same can be said of their ill-fated uprising of 1848. When the aristocratic William Smith O'Brien led his revolutionary peasant following around Tipperaray, he is reputed to have instructed them not to trespass on private property.[72] Entering a police station with his men, O'Brien politely requested its occupants to hand over their weapons. The officers asked him to retire and return with more supporters, so that they might surrender their arms while preserving their honour; and when O'Brien obligingly withdrew, they naturally made their escape.[73] He was, as a colleague remarked, 'too much of the Smith and too little of the O'Brien'.[74]

In a liberal capitalist society such as nineteenth-century Britain, the prospect of conciliation through culture retains some faint plausibility. For it is in the nature of modernity, as we have seen, to dissociate culture and politics, as the former comes to constitute itself as an ideal by its suppression of the latter. Culture is that which erases the traces of its own production, and along with it the business of material production as a whole. It is innocent of all but spiritual power; and though it may speak of the political and economic, it can do so as art only from some place

---

70. An appeal in which Davis had been anticipated by the novelist John Banim, in a pamphlet of 1822 calling for a national academy of art. See P.J. Murray, *Life of John Banim* (London 1857), p. 84.

71. As indeed did Young Irelanders to his left. See Fintan Lalor's 'To the Landlords of Ireland', in *Collected Writings*. See also John Mitchel in the *Nation*, 16 January 1847. Both men were finally to despair of landlord leadership and advocate popular ownership of the land. For an account of J.F. Lalor, see David N. Buckley, *James Fintan Lalor: Radical* (Cork 1990).

72. See Malcolm Brown, *The Politics of Irish Literature* (London 1972), p. 113.

73. See R.V. Comerford, *Charles J. Kickham* (Dublin 1979), pp. 22–3.

74. Quoted by Charles Gavan Duffy, *Young Ireland*, vol. 1 (Dublin 1884), p. 206.

that transcends them. By the mid nineteenth century in Britain, the poetic and the political have come to be redefined as each other's opposites, in a move which might have come as a surprise to Milton or Blake. There can still be a political art; but the structure of such art is always ironic, contrasting its prosaic subject matter with the spiritual wealth implicit in its form. In the epoch of modernity, then, there are real conditions to support the myth of cultural transcendence; but these conditions prevailed much less in Ireland, where culture was self-evidently political and partisan, and thus part of the problem to which, in its impartial Anglo-Irish guise, it posed as a solution. Culture in the hands of a Matthew Arnold could masquerade as a metalanguage into which all merely sectoral interests might be absorbed; in Ireland, that metalanguage could too easily be identified as the idiom of a disinherited ruling class, and so was all too obviously a sectoral position in itself. Those spiritually on the margin are in one sense well placed to provide an Olympian overview, as *dégagement* becomes disinterest; but that posture is too plainly a way of ratifying their own less than congenial situation, and so can be quickly discredited. If Arnold could turn to education as a solvent of class struggle, no such recourse was possible in Ireland, where the nineteenth-century commissioners on national education had concluded that the teaching of non-partisan history in schools was simply impossible.[75] Nor could the celebrated Arnoldian appeal to the state, as the very locus of sweetness and light, ring quite so persuasively in a country where the state was quite visibly coercive. In Irish conditions, such high-minded mystifications were simply unworkable – and they involved, in any case, an idea of individual inwardness which had rather less resonance in the more collectivist culture of the colony.

In Arnold's view, the political threat of the Populace may be defused if it can absorb a little culture from above; and this in turn depends on its immediate masters, the middle-class Philistines, becoming gradually infused with the grace and panache of the aristocratic Barbarians. Arnold runs just the same case about Anglo-Irish relations: if the Irish are to be properly hegemonized, the English middle class must improve its manners.[76] It is a trickle-down theory of culture, at once canny and far-

---

75. See David Fitzpatrick, 'The Futility of History: A Failed Experiment in Irish Education', in Ciaran Brady, ed., *Ideology and the Historians* (Dublin 1991), p. 171. Fitzpatrick remarks that 'the concepts of "scientific" and impartial history had few Irish exponents' (p. 169).

76. See Matthew Arnold, 'The Incompatibles', in R.F.H. Super, ed., *The Complete Prose Works of Matthew Arnold*, vol. xi: *English Literature and Irish Politics* (Ann Arbor 1973), pp. 272 ff.

fetched. The Anglo-Irish cultural intelligentsia, from Thomas Davis and
W.B. Yeats to Lady Gregory and Douglas Hyde, put this osmotic process
into reverse: it is now the middle class and aristocracy who must go to
school with the spontaneously cultivated populace. Whatever the absurd
idealism of this view, the vision of an organic peasantry bound to a
benign aristocracy might be thought a little more plausible in agrarian
Ireland than in industrial Britain, where it was peddled by Carlyle and
Disraeli as a panacea for the ills of industrial capitalism. The programme
of Young Ireland was certainly regressive, but hardly as much, one might
claim, as the fantasies of Young England. But this would be to mis-
interpret English neo-feudalism. For the aim of its more astute apologists
was not, *à la* Davis, to link peasant and patrician, but to graft aristocratic
leadership on to the captains of industry, thus transforming this uncouth
brigade into a truly hegemonic class which could then incorporate its
own inferiors. Whether this was a realistic ambition or not, there was at
least in England a tradition of patrician *noblesse oblige* to hand, which in
Ireland was a good deal feebler. And the Young Englanders targeted the
right branch of the governing class, while the Young Irelanders directed
their appeals to an obsolescent one. Moreover, the English landed gentry could benefit from the presence of an industrial middle class, which
interposed itself between them and the common people. In Ireland, landowner and common people were locked in direct combat, so that for
the former to pose as sublimely disinterested was a good deal more
difficult.

Arnold's cultural vision rested on a faith that totality was still possible; but to see life steadily and see it whole seemed in Ireland a less
feasible pursuit. In Britain, such overviews were often self-interested
enough; but they had behind them the authority of a flourishing liberal
tradition, and stemmed from intellectuals who, like Arnold and George
Eliot, were themselves relatively separate from the ruling class. The
problem in Ireland was that the mantle of liberal disinterestedness
descended, *faute de mieux*, on those displaced upper-class spirits whose
self-interested stake in cultural pluralism was occasionally all too palpable.
A class which had so dismally failed to provide political leadership was
now eagerly offering itself as a band of cultural commissars, hoping to
fashion a refurbished selfhood for Ireland out of their own crisis of
identity. Two dying cultures intersected, as an Anglo-Irish heritage on
the wane sought a last lease of life by raking over the fading Gaelic
embers. Upper classes, given their relative freedom from material
constraint, are often enough inclined to idealism; and from Samuel

Ferguson to Augusta Gregory[77] that idealism could offer some poor compensation for a decline in political power. In a telling irony, a cultural vision which was in some ways forward-looking sprang up among the liberal gentry as a response to the erosion of their traditional base. What happened in the Revival was that the Romantic idealism of a deviant wing of the upper class fused momentarily with the rather different Romantic nationalism of the very class which was busily digging their graves.

The invaluable contribution of these Anglo-Irish activists to the nationalist cause drew upon all their finest patrician virtues: courage, resourcefulness, self-discipline, selfless devotion, generosity of spirit. Without these men and women, who were of course quite as Irish as Daniel O'Connell or William Rooney, the annals of Irish culture and political life would be immeasurably impoverished. In any case, renegade gentlefolk are always a welcome addition to radical ranks, since they can turn to good use their innate self-assurance, inside knowledge of the enemy and taken-for-granted equality with them.[78] Yet it could not pass entirely unnoticed that if the forefathers of the colonial class in Ireland had been a little less intent on undermining the native culture, their emancipated sons and daughters would have needed to busy themselves rather less with restoring it. Before Lady Gregory came to collect Gaelic folk tales, her future husband William had framed the infamous Gregory clause in the depths of the Famine, a means test which deprived relief-seeking farmers of their paltry piece of land and no doubt despatched some unnecessary extra thousands to their graves. In any case, the late-nineteenth-century Anglo-Irish bid for cultural leadership came only after the group's political fate had been effectively sealed. It was not the first instance of a social order briefly, brilliantly flourishing at the very point of its demise.

---

77. For a biography of Gregory, see Elizabeth Coxhead, *Lady Gregory: A Literary Portrait* (London 1961). See also the same author's *J.M. Synge and Lady Gregory* (London 1962).

78. One gets the flavour of this milieu in Lady Gregory's autobiography *Seventy Years* (Gerrards Cross 1974), which seems one incessant round of dinner parties with the great and the good, laced with a little high-minded nationalist talk. One of Lady Gregory's famous victories over British colonialism was to persuade her friend Lady Lyttelton, wife of the commander-in-chief of the British forces in Ireland, to turn up with her entourage at an Abbey performance of Shaw's *The Shewing-Up of Blanco Posnet*, then under threat of censorship by Dublin Castle. See Lucy McDiarmid, 'Augusta Gregory, Bernard Shaw, and the Shewing-Up of Dublin Castle', *Publications of the Modern Languages Association of America*, vol. 109, no. 1 (January 1994). For an account of upper-class Protestant nationalists, see Léon Ó Broin, *Protestant Nationalists in Revolutionary Ireland: the Stopford Connection* (Dublin 1985), a work which refers throughout to Alice Stopford Green as 'Aunt Alice'. It is an intriguing detail of modern Irish history that Brendan Behan's mother was for a while a servant of Maud Gonne.

It was, in the words of Oliver MacDonagh, 'a miniscule, lonely and beleaguered world, but perhaps, because of that, like late Byzantium or the post-emancipation Russia of the gentry, rich in genius and potential'.[79]

The entry of the literary émigrés into modern English culture is by now a familiar narrative.[80] From Conrad, Wilde and James to Shaw, Pound and Eliot, the high literary ground is seized by those whose very marginality allows them to bring fresh perspectives to the society they have adopted. The result is a bracing combination of empathy and estrangement: the outsider casts a critical eye on his new-found culture, sees more than the natives do and can bring a relativizing or totalizing viewpoint to bear on it; yet his uprootedness often enough impels him to go native, become more English than the English, esteem a heritage he has chosen more dearly than those to the manner born. It is not hard to see the Hydes, Yeatses and Synges as Ireland's homegrown version of this creative ambivalence – though one might claim that a similar duality was at work with the rebels of 1916, who numbered within their ranks two sons of Englishmen (Pearse and Clarke), one child of a Unitarian mother (MacDonagh) and a Scottish immigrant (James Connolly).[81] A mixture of guilt, generosity of spirit and political opportunism spurs the enlightened Anglo-Irish to ally with the Gaelic order, out-Celticizing the Celt; but their marginal status also yields them broader vistas, bringing to bear on Ireland the resources of European culture, English civility, the Anglo-Irish tradition. The self-division of the internal émigré then resolves itself in the notion of leadership – for the leader is at once in dynamic relation with the populace and necessarily set apart from them. If the 'Old English' of Anglo-Norman Ireland could be found assimilating with the natives, the 'New English' of a later epoch largely shut them out; and something of both strategies can be detected in the Protestant Celticists' ambiguous relations with the Catholic masses. It is an ambivalence especially marked in the poetry of Yeats, who can veer from arrogant aloofness to passionate engagement in the course of a single poem.[82]

---

79. MacDonagh is describing the milieu of Somerville and Ross's novel *The Real Charlotte*, in *The 19th Century Novel and Irish History: Some Aspects* (Cork 1970), p. 18.

80. See Terry Eagleton, *Exiles and Émigrés* (London 1970). For the broader intellectual emigration into England, see Perry Anderson, 'Components of the National Culture', *New Left Review* 50 (July–August 1968).

81. See F.X. Martin, '1916: Revolution or Evolution?', in F.X. Martin, ed., *Leaders and Men of the Easter Rising* (London 1967).

82. F.S.L. Lyons discerns in Yeats's writing a tension between the 'overcharged rhetoric of assertion, and the sardonic irony of withdrawal' (*Culture and Anarchy in Ireland, 1890–1935*, London 1979, p. 22). See also his *Ireland since the Famine* (London 1971), Part 2, Ch. 5.

To belong to this social group is, to be sure, a position of a kind; but since by the end of the nineteenth century it has become an alarmingly peripheral one, it can always be translated into that 'non-position' which is the transcendental standpoint. In Yeats as in T.S. Eliot, the fact of cultural disinheritance can be converted into the all-inclusive eye of the outsider. In a familiar Romantic paradox, the remnant becomes the vanguard: those who are actually on the edge may lay claim to spiritual centrality, just as the earlier Ascendancy has rationalized its own minority status with an ideology of elitism. Men and women at odds with the mainstream culture are able to look around and behind it, apparently absolved of all interests of their own. The progressive Anglo-Irish thus come to adopt the role classically reserved in modern societies for the intellectual, who is supposed to be similarly free of all one-sided commitments.[83] What in Arnold is the metalanguage of culture or the state can then become the totality of the 'common name of Irishman'. This is a political notion of a kind, as Arnold's 'culture' might be said to be anti-political; but in so far as it evokes some Edenic Ireland before the fall into race, class and creed, it also functions as a *pre*-political idea, and so as a totality every bit as tendentious as that of *The Waste Land*. For what, in fact, if Irish society were in certain respects untotalizable? What if such a totality were part of the problem to which it proffered a solution?

What was not finally totalizable in Ireland were the divisions of social class; and it was this that the partisan pluralism of the enlightened Anglo-Irish was in the end unable to countenance. Since class in Ireland was for historical reasons deeply bound up with questions of religion and ethnic origin, it seemed natural to assume that a tolerant embrace of difference at those levels should stretch to class conflicts too. This, indeed, was the common assumption of many nationalists, whether Gaelic or Anglo-Irish; and it is the tacit assumption of some liberal Irish commentators today, who, in a postmodern age for which concepts of social class are un-fashionable but notions of ethnicity much in vogue, misread a socialist criticism of, say, the Anglo-Irish ruling class as chauvinist or sectarian. But the mystified pluralism of traditional nationalism, Gaelic as much as Anglo-Irish, which sought to link arms with the landlords rather than abolish them, had a hard time surviving the realities of class struggle in

83. For an Irish version of this theme, see John Eglinton, *Two Essays on the Remnant* (London 1895).

the countryside. The only culture which will totalize all viewpoints is one which engages no specific interest, and so becomes, like the more hollow of Yeats's poetic postures, a mere empty transcendence. Its practical effectiveness is in inverse proportion to its spiritual integrity. In early-nineteenth-century Ireland, a republican universalism had run aground on the rocks of nationalist particularism, and a liberal universalism was later to fare no better.

Culture for the English tradition from Coleridge to Leavis is a non-political politics – at once a salutary deepening of political questions, and a last-ditch displacement of them. Culture for some Anglo-Irish free spirits fulfilled much the same function. In Britain the project was in-effectual, in Ireland self-contradictory. In Britain, culture could pose as a solution to conflict precisely because the conflicts in question were not themselves of a primarily cultural kind. It offered political antagonisms an alternative form of solution; and though this was hardly convincing, it was at least coherent. Culture in Ireland could occasionally play this role too; but the problem in the colony was not, as Arnold thought of England, that there was too little culture, but that there was too much of it. The problem in Ireland was one of colliding cultures, which then ruined any fond hope that culture and discord might prove automatic opposites. Culture was always already political, and so could scarcely offer itself as a substitute for everyday life. When this happened, it could be quickly identified as a move within the power game rather than a serene transcendence of it. Indeed culture's complicity with that system was rarely more obvious than when it sought to soar above it. The English tradition which reaches its high point in F.R. Leavis and I.A. Richards views culture as a redemptive force; but to fulfil that redemptive promise it must take on practical form, which is exactly what culture exists to disparage. To realize itself it must descend to the unseemly rancour of the political arena, which means, in effect, to abolish itself. The ends and means of culture are in this sense mutually antagonistic. In its aloofness from the political sphere, English culture imitates the *hauteur* of the aristocrat, though the latter's apparent indifference to power is precisely the measure of his possession of it. In Ireland, by contrast, culture had no problem in producing material effects, from the *Nation* newspaper to the Gaelic League; but this made its transcendent role harder to sustain.

Where conflict for Arnold is ultimately resolved is in the political state; but culture in Ireland is more closely bound up with the nation. And whereas the state for Arnold transcends all partisan interests, the nation in Ireland is itself an object of contestation.[84] Far from providing the neutral frame within which an array of forces might contend, the nation was exactly what was being contended for. In colonial conditions, the nation is a floating signifier rather than a fixed meaning, and victory will go to those who have successfully appropriated the concept.[85] For the historian J.A. Froude, a nation meant a people capable of defending itself; and since Ireland had been conquered, it was by definition not a nation. In an ingenious neo-scholastic sleight of hand, no act of colonization can violate another's nationhood, since the fact that it can occur at all means that there was no nationhood there to be violated.[86] W.E.H. Lecky, in his monumental history of eighteenth-century Ireland, uses the word 'nation' sometimes to signify the whole Irish people, and sometimes to refer to the propertied elite.[87]

If 'nation' is becoming a descriptive term in Britain, it remains a normative one in Ireland. In Britain, nation and state are – so the theory runs – harmoniously hyphenated terms, the latter space symmetrically overlaid on the former. The political state is an outcrop of the cultural realm of the nation, the point where its identity is gathered and articulated; and the fact that the two orders occupy the same material space makes this view convincing enough. In Ireland, the state is a foreign import, non-identical with the nation, occupying a different spatial and temporal dimension altogether. And within the borders of the island there are competing nations, all the way from the colonial nationalism of the eighteenth-century Patriots to Tone's common name of Irishman, from O'Connell's Gaelic people to Davis's anti-colonial alliance. Nations could be invoked into existence overnight, as in 1916, when Irish history was brought to what Walter Benjamin might have called a dialectical standstill.[88] Sinn Fein of the time believed that the Irish republic had in fact been established by this performative act, even if no attempt to realize it in reality had yet been made. What counted as the country was unclear, as Mary Martin, the spirited young heroine of Charles Lever's novel The

---

84. For the opposition between state and nation, see Donal McCartney, 'MacNeill and Irish-Ireland', in F.X. Martin and F.J. Byrne, eds, *The Scholar Revolutionary: Eoin MacNeill* (Shannon 1973).

85. See Ernesto Laclau, *Politics and Ideology in Marxist Theory* (London 1977), Ch. 4.

86. James Anthony Froude, *The English in Ireland in the Eighteenth Century*, vol. 1 (London 1872), Preliminary.

87. See Anne Wyatt, 'Froude, Lecky and the Humblest Irishman', *Irish Historical Studies*, vol. 19, no. 75 (March 1975).

88. See his 'Theses on the Philosophy of History', in *Illuminations*.

Martins of Cro' Martin, makes plain: 'If you mean, by the country, the lives and fortunes of those who live in it – the people by whose toil it is fertilized – I tell you frankly that I yield to none for interest in all that touches them; but if you come to talk of privileges and legislative benefits, I know nothing of them; they form a land of whose very geography I am ignorant.' For Mary, different interests form alternative topographies. The Arnoldian state, then, as embodying the cultural unity of the nation, was never a very convincing doctrine in Ireland; and neither was Arnold's later nostrum for social discontent, a suitably demythologized religion. It was not the most relevant of proposals to a country where a riot could be provoked at a horse race in which 'Protestant Boy' beat 'Daniel O'Connell'.[89] The Celtic Revival, however, is Arnoldian in this sense too, finding in culture a substitute for religion. Vivian Mercier has pointed to the clerical backgrounds of several of its leading figures.[90] It is as though, for both Arnold and the Revivalists, culture is a *via media* between religion and politics – a poeticized brand of the former which can soften the rigours of the latter.

In seeking to go native, the enlightened Anglo-Irish were out to overcome their own social displacement, and so became part of what helped to displace James Joyce. Perhaps Joyce would have been less easily dislodged if there had been a more vigorous urban middle class around him, rather than an ocean of small farmers. If contending cultures can converge anywhere, it is in the pages of *Ulysses* and *Finnegans Wake*; but this fruitful exchange of idioms can happen only in the non-place of exile, or a book. That it cannot take place in Ireland, either under the Ascendancy or the Free State, is then part of the political meaning of Joyce's work. Joyce's literary experiments are inspired, obviously enough, by his colonial context: it was the lack of any very serviceable metropolitan traditions which drove him to invent his own outlandish forms. What launched him into the vibrant heart of modernist Europe was inertia at home. In moving from Dublin to Paris without lingering in London, he bypassed the culture of the metropolis as surely as the nationalists he despised, who by turning backward to ancient Ireland, and forward to a nation yet to be born,

---

89. See MacDowell, *Public Opinion and Government Policy*, p. 33.

90. See Vivian Mercier, 'Evangelical Revival in the Church of Ireland, 1800–69', in *Modern Irish Literature* (Oxford 1994). It is worth noting too that the Revival was accompanied by a Catholic religious revival centred on the cult of the Sacred Heart. Both currents fuse in the fiction of Canon Sheehan.

hoped to squeeze out the history of British sovereignty which intervened between them. But the free play of the signifier which results from Joyce's literary scavenging has as its referent (Ireland) a place where such freedom is largely absent. Hence the 'free state' of his fiction, in which a ceaselessly mobile discourse moves within a cyclical enclosure.

It is as though the traditional gap between rhetoric and reality in Ireland has now been incorporated into the very forms of the fiction, become the substance of an entire text. A political disability is cheekily transmuted into an aesthetic triumph. And the political point of that is that the referent itself would need to be changed if the plurality to which its signifier bears witness were to be realized in practice. The phrase goes beyond the content, as Marx comments of the great bourgeois revolutions in *The Eighteenth Brumaire of Louis Bonaparte*. The rhetoric and reality of those mighty social upheavals are for Marx farcically at odds; and it is not hard to see the application of this to *Ulysses*, a text which appeared just as the heroic tradition of Irish nationalism was giving birth to the mouse of the Irish Free State. Between the date of the novel's publication (1922) and the date of its setting (1904), a whole revolutionary history had erupted with surreal speed: the First World War, the Easter Rising, the Bolshevik Revolution and its turbulent European aftermath, the Irish war of independence, the outbreak of the artistic avant-garde. At the level of the signifier, *Ulysses* belongs in some sense to this momentous upheaval; but its referent is an Ireland still frozen in pre-revolutionary torpor. As in one of Benjamin's dialectical images, time is brought to a shocking standstill, as the archaic and the avant-garde blend in strange conjunctures. The 'never-changing ever-changing' nature of Joyce's oeuvre thus becomes a trope of the conservative revolution in Ireland, in which everything and nothing seems to have altered. The country has produced a modernism, but failed to enter properly upon modernity. European modernity and colonial backwardness interact in Joyce's own writing as form and content, signifier and signified; but it is vital that they meet ironically, if that writing is to be more than utopian compensation for a fissured world. That it is also this is part of its political double-edgedness.

Joyce levels cultures without homogenizing them, whereas the Celticists do just the reverse. Yeats dreams of a social order which would be at once unified and hierarchical. For him, there is a racial unity to be detected beneath the diversity of history, just as for Joyce there are certain abiding archetypes beneath the cacophony of the sign. But for Yeats, at least in one of his incarnations, the race in question is Irish, whereas for Joyce it is human; so that the cosmopolitan vision of the literal exile outflanks the totalizing standpoint of the metaphorical one. The Revivalists are at once too much outsiders and too little so – too remote from the common people, yet too close to Ireland's rulers. Joyce will resolve this ambivalence by caricaturing both poles of it: in becoming more of an outlander than the Anglo-Irish, removing himself to Paris and Trieste, he ends up by producing a genuinely demotic art rather than a spuriously populist one. The two aspects are related: the satiric realism of those rumbustious texts is at one with the sensibility which drove their author from a clericist, Celticist, chronically idealizing Ireland in the first place. Joyce's contact with the European avant-garde allows him to reach back to Ireland and re-create it in modern rather than atavistic form. His priestly aestheticism turns the tables on the Celticists, treating their nationalist piety with something of the disdain they themselves reserved for the Young Irelanders; but in embracing an autonomous art, one claiming allegiance to no particular culture, he is able to enrol Ireland among the nations. If the dispossessed children of Ascendancy had turned their own marginal position within Ireland into a vision of spiritual centrality, Joyce takes advantage of the 'non-position' of the country, as an afterthought of Europe, to dramatize the relativity of all times and places in modernist space, plucking an art of global significance from the island's very backwardness. Whereas the Revivalists had imported selected aspects of world culture into Ireland, Joyce exports Ireland to the world, at once highlighting its centrality and undercutting its ethnic privilege. His self-imposed exile re-enacts, in its own rather more privileged way, the history of emigration which was to make of the Irish an international people, and for which in the end they had British imperialism to thank.

'Art must be parochial in the beginning to be cosmopolian in the end', remarks George Moore with characteristic glibness in *Hail and Farewell*.[91] Thomas Kettle saw the matter in reverse: 'my only counsel to Ireland is, that in order to become deeply Irish, she must become European'.[92] W.B. Yeats was to second his opinion in Arnoldian style: 'if we do not know the best that has been said and written in the world, we do not even know ourselves'.[93] Was a national art to be a bulwark against foreign decadence, or could it find a place for other cultures? Not all Irish nationalists were as conveniently chauvinist as some of their modern-day critics would wish, though many could be parochial enough. If the

91. George Moore, *Hail and Farewell* (Gerrards Cross 1985), p. 56.
92. Thomas Kettle, *The Day's Burden* (Dublin 1937), p. xii.
93. W.B. Yeats, *Explorations* (London 1962), p. 80.

Irish Irelander Arthur Clery thought nationalism compatible with more global concerns, so of course did the Marxist James Connolly. The journalist W.P. Ryan sought an even more exalted context for the nation, as the title of his euphoric rhapsody *The Celt and the Cosmos* might suggest. A zealous nativist, Ryan could nevertheless make room in his Gaelic heart for the Anglo-Irish, the Pan-Celtic movement and even for the Unionist politics of Standish O'Grady.[94] T.W. Rolleston, luminary of the Irish Literary Society, was steeped in Greek classicism, wrote a life of Lessing and translated Whitman into German. Like Rolleston, John Eglinton, Frederick Ryan and Stopford Brooke all called for a national art shaped by universal motifs, while the notion of some pure Gaelic race was lambasted by nationalist thinkers from George Sigerson and Eoin MacNeill to Aodh de Blacam and Thomas MacDonagh.[95] MacDonagh's last class at University College, Dublin, before he joined the ranks of the Easter Rising, was devoted to his beloved Jane Austen.[96] MacNeill opens his *Phases of Irish History* with a smack at the unscientific notion of race, choosing instead to define 'Celtic' in linguistic terms. Even the Irish Irelander D.P. Moran, the aboriginal Anglophobe and Dublin's answer to Karl Kraus, rejected racial prejudice and tipped his hat in the direction of Thomas Davis's pluralist conception of Irish nationhood.[97] Perhaps the most bizarre encounter between Ireland the the rest of the globe was Augusta Gregory's *The Kiltartan Molière*, a dialect version of the playwright unfamiliar alike to Paris and Kiltartan.

Nationalism, after all, is a thoroughly international phenomenon, as Thomas Davis's early anti-colonial pieces on India and Afghanistan would attest; and the Revivalists campaigned vigorously against the Boer war. As Perry Anderson dryly comments: 'few rhetorics have been more repetitively

---

94. See W.P. Ryan, *The Irish Literary Revival* (Dublin 1894), Ch. 3. Ryan's *The Pope's Green Island* (London 1912) is also still worth reading.

95. See John Eglinton, *Literary Ideals in Ireland* (Dublin 1899), and *Anglo-Irish Essays* (Dublin 1917); Frederick Ryan, *Criticism and Courage* (Dublin 1906); Stopford A. Brooke and T.W. Rolleston, eds, *A Treasury of Irish Poetry in the English Tongue* (Dublin 1900); Arthur Clery, *The Idea of a Nation* (Dublin 1907); George Sigerson, *Bards of the Gael and Gall* (London 1897); Eoin MacNeill, *Phases of Irish History* (Dublin 1919); Aodh de Blacam, *Towards the Republic* (Dublin 1918); Thomas MacDonagh, *Literature in Ireland* (Dublin 1916).

96. See R.F. Foster, *Paddy and Mr Punch* (London 1993), p. 305.

97. D.P. Moran, *The Philosophy of Irish Ireland* (Dublin 1905), p. 11. Moran, to do him justice, was an Anglophobe in the sense of hating the British variety of civilization, not Britain itself; indeed he castigated his fellow countrypeople for expending in hatred energies which might be more constructively used. See his 'The Battle of Two Civilisations', in Lady Gregory, ed., *Ideals in Ireland* (Dublin 1901).

general in this century than claims for the ethnically particular'.[98] But the literary renaissance could never quite decide how cosmopolitan it intended to be, and for a significant reason. To draw into a national art the resources of world culture is in one sense to enrich it, in another sense to displace it. To discover that the myths of ancient Ireland find their echo elsewhere in the world is at once to confirm and undercut their centrality. If myth encodes universal structures of the mind, can there really be a national mythology? Are J.M. Synge's plots Irish or Greek, and does it matter? Is Irish culture privileged because it is unique, or because it is a microcosm of the global mind?[99] If the national culture lacks a universal dimension it is in danger of lapsing into provincialism; but such universality is exactly what threatens its unique identity. The United Irishman lived a different version of this problem: republicanism must be universalist in the best Enlightenment style; yet how could it then embrace an unenlightened Catholicism without contradicting itself? Perhaps Celticism, which is at once national and a community of nations, could provide a mediation here;[100] or perhaps one could argue in a kind of provincial cosmopolitan spirit for the Celtic origins of European literature.[101] In 1900, the *United Irishman* described Shakespeare as 'a Celt born in England', while other Irish critics detected unmistakable strains of Celtic blood in Virgil and Racine. Tennyson, by contrast, felt short of greatness precisely because he was not a Celt.[102]

Great art is supposed to transcend its local origin; but one can always claim that it does so precisely by being so deeply rooted in it. Cosmopolitanism, declared William Yeats in a speech to the Trinity College Historical Society in 1899, had never been a creative force; what was needed instead was a truly national literature. But no sooner does he begin to number the nations which might construct one than his thoughts have strayed into the international realm; and by the end of his address he is speaking of the task of expressing the Irish intellect as one 'not for

---

98. Perry Anderson, *A Zone of Engagement* (London 1992), p. 249.

99. Seamus Deane has pointed to the importance, in some Irish nationalist tradition, of 'the conviction that Ireland represents, *in parvo*, the great historical events of the world. For it was a country which had been transformed by the three great revolutions of the century – the Whig Revolution of 1688, the American Revolution of 1776, the French Revolution of 1789' (A *Short History of Irish Literature*, London 1986, p. 57).

100. For the conflict in the Revival between Pan-Celts and Gaelic Leaguers, see Ruth Dudley Edwards, *Patrick Pearse: The Triumph of Failure* (London 1977), pp. 31–8.

101. As does Gavan Duffy, who claims that the Celts bequeathed rhyme to humanity. See C.G. Duffy, *The Revival of Irish Literature* (London 1894), p. 79.

102. See John Kelly, 'The Political, Intellectual and Social Background to the Irish Literary Revival to 1901', unpublished Ph.D. thesis (University of Cambridge 1972), pp. 185–6.

Ireland only, but for the world'.[103] So it is that Yeats can speak elsewhere, oxymoronically, of creating a national theatre 'after the Continental pattern'.[104] Ironically, his obscurantism was also a kind of international-ism: the occultist mysteries in which he traded were the key to an arcane universal knowledge, and so a convenient corrective to chauvinism. If he himself found Wilde and Shaw too rootlessly cosmopolitan, Arthur Griffith and Irish Ireland were quick to return the compliment to his own creations. Yet even the most apparently homegrown of Irish cultural prod-ucts – Pearse's cult of blood sacrifice, for example – could turn out to be impeccably European, as a glance at James Frazer, George Sorel or Freud's *Beyond the Pleasure Principle* would attest.[105] And if one is speaking of ancient Irish traditions, then cosmopolitanism, in the shape of the nomadic medieval scholar, was a good deal more time-hallowed than any new-fangled nationalism. In this sense it was Joyce, not Griffith or Hyde, who was most in continuity with the island's past. Few pursuits were more native to the country than getting out of it.

A tension between local and global was present in European nationalism from the outset. If its Enlightenment version dreamed of each nation pursuing its own path to universal progress, its Romantic apologists laid stress on the unique destiny of a particular people. At its worst, it is a choice between the empty universalism of republican doctrine and the blind particularism of a national destiny. Where all this comes to a head is in the language question, which is both international in resonance and stubbornly specific. The campaign to revive the Irish language was of course a home-grown affair; but it also belonged to a more general linguistic turn in the modernist period, one which stretches from Viktor Shlovsky to Ludwig Wittgenstein, from Paul Valéry and Martin Heidegger to Karl Kraus and I.A. Richards. It is no accident that J.M. Synge learnt part of his trade in Paris, home of self-conscious literary experiment. It is as though, everywhere in Europe, the frail filaments which bind language to reality have begun to strain at the leash. Signifiers must thus either be cut adrift from their signifieds, as in the various currents of symbolism;

103. Robert Hogan and James Kilroy, eds, *The Modern Irish Drama: vol. 1, The Irish Literary Theatre 1899–1901* (Dublin 1975), p. 60. See also Robert O'Driscoll, ed., *Theatre and Nation-alism in 20th Century Ireland* (London 1971). For Yeats's amalgam of nationalism and openness to international influence, see Philip L. Marcus, *Yeats and the Beginning of the Irish Renaissance* (Ithaca and London 1970), Chs 1–3.

104. Hogan and Kilroy, eds, *The Modern Irish Drama: vol. 3: The Abbey Theatre 1905–1909* (Dublin 1978), p. 82.

105. For Pearse in a European Romantic context, see Seamus Deane, *Celtic Revivals* (London 1985), Ch. 5.

placed in some bold pictorial relation to the world which, as with Wittgenstein's *Tractatus*, cannot itself be spoken of; or nailed vigorously down on their elusive meanings. From the 'de-automated' word of the Russian Formalists to the Imagist ideogram, a language grown threadbare and anaemic must be recharged with concrete life, flushed with all the vital energies of its object. An Irish language 'racy of the soil' is one aspect of this move to restore to an alienated speech its lost flavour, recovering that sensuousness of the sign which an arid rationalism has banished from it. If this linguistic self-awareness is one of the very marks of the modern, it is also, in Ireland and elsewhere, part of a traditionalist retreat from it.

Ironically, then, the Gaelic Leaguers have much in common with the Cambridge Scrutineers. If F.R. Leavis located the organic society in seventeenth-century rural England, Daniel Corkery found it still flourishing in eighteenth-century Gaelic Munster, with its 'common culture flowing up and down between hut and Big House'.[106] In both periods, language is still in pristine condition, intimately at one with its referent. Just as the Irish cultural nationalists turn back in Heideggerian style to an authentic speech before the calamitous fall into modernity, so F.R. Leavis and his colleagues dream of an Elizabethan language as packed and ripe as an apple. This 'new Elizabethanism' links the English critics with J.M. Synge, whose drama was occasionally spoken of in these terms; and on both sides of St George's Channel the recovery of *parole pleine* was a symptom of political integrity, restoring that organic relation between mind and world which technology, or imperialism, or the vulgarity of mass civilization, had all but severed. Some of the terms in which Ireland hoped to re-create its national identity were thus the very terms in which some of its colonizers were busy recreating their own. Indeed Ireland comes to figure not just as the other of Britain but as its origin, the very image of the integral past from which it has declined. In Synge's and Yeats's sense of affinity with those Elizabethan or seventeenth-century writers celebrated by the Scrutineers, Britain's past is, as it were, afloat off its shores, spatially coexistent with it.[107] What more marvellously convenient for those metropolitans in quest of the organic society than to have a

---

106. Daniel Corkery, *The Hidden Ireland* (Dublin 1925), p. 58. For a critique of the 'hidden Ireland' concept, see L.M. Cullen, *The Hidden Ireland: Reassessment of a Concept* (Dublin 1988), which argues that much of the eighteenth-century Gaelic poetry Corkery claims as 'peasant' is in fact aristocratic in allegiance and middle-class in provenance.

107. The Irish interest in the English Elizabethan and Jacobean periods, evident also in the criticism of Thomas MacDonagh, is in part an interest in an epoch when England was itself forging its nationhood.

nation of lords and peasants a mere twenty or so miles away, rather than to seek for that society in the substitute form of a sensuous literary text? All the same, it would be hard to imagine a return to the Metaphysical poets in England taking on the dimensions of a mass political movement, which is certainly what the Gaelic League grew into. By 1904, there were some six hundred registered branches of the League throughout Ireland, and their splendidly energetic efforts had ensured that the teaching of the language was now ensconced in the national schools. As the first major urban-centred mass movement in the country, the League was to spawn an industrial committee, take an active interest in temperance, technical education and industrial reform, and stamp a whole future generation of political leaders.[108] It was the most precious achievement of the so-called Celtic Revival, with an influence far beyond the charmed circle of the Abbey Theatre.

The ironies of the language movement are nonetheless striking. Branded as inferior and uncouth, ousted by the English of education, commerce, politics and the pulpit, driven from the countryside by famine and emigration, the Irish language took up its home instead in the hearts and minds of the intelligentsia.[109] A speech which the Irish people were rapidly abandoning as a badge of backwardness was eagerly taken up by their cultivated superiors. It was not, to be sure, an intellectual matter alone: the Gaelic League was a genuinely popular movement, and the language was still spoken in the *Gaeltachti*. But it was also a classic instance of the belated flight of Hegel's owl of Minerva. Philosophy for Hegel arises when the real world becomes problematic, and is thus as much symptom as solution. The discourse of aesthetics emerged in the mid eighteenth century to clarify an art pitched into crisis; but aesthetics was also to play its part in that art's tormented self-awareness. Once a human practice has been forced into self-reflection, it can never be quite at one with itself again. This was certainly true of the Irish language movement, which in self-consciously re-creating the most spontaneous of human activities was bound to be something of a self-contradictory project from

---

108. See S. Tuama, ed., *The Gaelic League Idea* (Cork and Dublin 1972); and Brian Ó Cúiv, 'The Gaelic Cultural Movements and the New Nationalism', in Kevin B. Nowlan, ed., *The Making of Easter 1916* (Dublin 1969). See also Brian O Cúiv', ed., *A View of the Irish Language* (Dublin 1969). For a caustic review of the language revival, not least the pro-kilt 'down with trousers' campaign, see Declan Kiberd, 'The Perils of Nostalgia', in Peter Connolly, ed., *Literature and the Changing Ireland* (Gerrards Cross 1982).

109. It is a suitable irony that the first thing J.M. Synge heard on arriving on the Aran islands in eager pursuit of Gaelic purity was a good deal of English spoken. See 'The Aran Islands', in *The Works of J.M. Synge* (Dublin 1910), p. 3.

the outset. The act of retrieving a dying language in the context of a new medium is always profoundly ironic, eroding that heritage in the act of preserving it. So it was that the *Gaeltachti* or Irish-speaking regions were later to become the targets of social development which – since much of it involved the use of English – threw open to 'alien' influence the very precious pockets which were to be shielded from it. Under-mined as a social practice, the language reappeared as an aesthetic object for the more Romantic of its resuscitators. The tongue of the peasant and patrician past was to be the speech of the middle-class future.

The quarrel over literature between aesthetes and utilitarians was reflected in the drive to restore the language. For the Anglo-Irish Douglas Hyde, co-founder of the Gaelic League, the language offered a terrain on which all the Irish could meet.[110] It was thus yet another instance of the transcendental viewpoint, providing a common currency for those riven apart by class, religion and ethnic origin. For Arthur Griffith, the Irish language was less cultural resource than political weapon, more valuable for breeding anti-English sentiment than for its intrinsic merits. But for political radicals to devote themselves to the language question is in one sense paradoxical; for language is one of the least fruitful models of radical change. Languages, after all, change only slowly, and not as the result of concerted action; and to share a language is to enjoy an abstract equality which may mask deeper forms of division. A national language is always a host of diverse idioms, and so hardly the image of ethnic purity some nationalists demanded; and the fact that one needs no theoretical knowl-edge of a language in order to speak it may have dubious implications when translated into political terms. Languages develop; but they do not progress, as societies may occasionally be said to do.[111] In all of these ways, a radical politics which assigns a high priority to language is likely to end up with a conservative theory of history; and though this was by no means entirely true of Irish nationalism, the conflict between its actual politics and the implicit politics of the linguistic model is nevertheless telling. If the former laid emphasis on will, action, revolutionary change, the latter projected an image of spiritual community and unruptured

---

110. For Hyde, see Dominic Daly, *The Young Douglas Hyde* (London 1974); and Janet E. Dunleavy and Gareth W. Dunleavy, *Douglas Hyde: A Maker of Modern Ireland* (Berkeley 1991). Hyde's plays are still worth reading: see the selection in G.W. Dunleavy and J.E. Dunleavy, eds, *Selected Plays of Douglas Hyde* (Gerrards Cross 1991). See also Brendán Ó Conaire, ed., *Douglas Hyde: Language, Lore and Lyrics* (Dublin 1986). For a valuable commentary on the language question, see Declan Kiberd, *Synge and the Irish Language* (London 1979), Introduction.

111. See Gyorgy Markus, 'The Paradigm of Language: Wittgenstein, Lévi-Strauss, Gadamer', in John Fekete, ed., *The Structural Allegory* (Minnesota 1984).

evolution. Like culture as a whole, language is both partisan perspective and comprehensive standpoint, and the tension between the two was not slow to emerge in the ranks of the Gaelic League. As an abrasive national-ism gradually seized the initiative from Hyde's more ecumenical vision, he felt forced to resign his presidency.[112] In the end, there could be no accommodation between two equally flawed versions of language – as the expression of a racial essence, and as a symbolic solidarity in which real conflicts could be resolved. What began life as an attempt by Protestant patriots to discover common ground among the Irish ended up as a weapon in the hands of those out to dispossess them. The Anglo-Irish had helped to give birth to their own gravediggers, and not for the first time: Irish nationalism, after all, had been their idea in the first place.[113]

What was at stake, however, was not just the rebirth of Irish, but the fraught question of its relation to English. Was the continued use of English, as the cultural separatists insisted, simply a resting place en route to a thoroughly Gaelicized Ireland? Or was there more value in Yeats's vision of a dialogical relation between the two tongues, a living fusion of vernaculars in which each would transmit its most precious qualities to the other? No finer parody of such dialogism can be found than in George Moore's proposal for the writing of the play *Diarmuid and Grainne*, which was to be composed by Moore in French, translated by Augusta Gregory into English, rendered into Irish by Taidgh O'Donoghue, turned back into English by Lady Gregory and 'have the poetry put on it' by Yeats. Translation in Ireland was a troubled affair, sign of the vexed relation between past and present or one culture and another. The work of James Clarence Mangan, the Baudelaire of Baggot Street, is full of fake trans-lations,[114] while the bibulous Cork colleagues William Maginn and Francis

---

112. For Hyde's views of Irish language and culture, see his *A Literary History of Ireland* (London 1967).

113. D.G. Boyce notes that the ideology which inspired the Easter Rising was largely an Anglo-Irish creation: an amalgam of Tone's separatism, Davis's nationalism, Hyde's nativism, even James Fintan Lalor's communalism. The Rising was thus a kind of recapitulation of past Anglo-Irish-led rebellions, though one now firmly under Catholic middle-class control. See Boyce's *Nationalism in Ireland* (London 1982), p. 311.

114. Mangan's body was as inauthentic as his translations. With his flaxen-coloured wig, outsize dark green spectacles, false teeth, waxen countenance, exotic hat and cloak, two bulky umbrellas (one for each arm) and bottle of tar war, he seems a kind of proto-postmodern self-parody. One of his personae remarks regarding his cloak that 'my personal identity is here at stake ... I lose my cloak and my consciousness both in the twinkling of a pair of tongs; I become what the philosophy of Kant (as opposed to the Cant of Philosophy) denominates a *Nicht-ich*, a Not-I, a *Non-ego*' (D.J. O'Donoghue, ed., *Prose Writings of James Clarence Mangan*, Dublin 1904, p. 285).

Sylvester Mahony ('Fr. Prout') sported with spoof renderings, spurious personae, polyphonic word-play. In his essay 'The Rogueries of Thomas Moore', the proto-Derridean Mahony – a spoilt priest – pens in several tongues the 'original' poems of which Moore's lyrics are supposedly derivative, castigating him for plagiarizing works which had not yet been written.[115]

At just the point when the early-nineteenth-century Celtic revival is struggling to retrieve an authentic Irish past, with which any currently valid work will necessarily be continuous, Mahony impudently inverts this temporal relation, striking Tom Moore's works retrospectively illicit by the power of the derivative. It is a practice to which Mangan gives the name of 'anti-plagiarism': whereas plagiarism proper claims the parasitic text as original, this mischievous reversal reduces the source text to secondary status. Rather as *Tristram Shandy* contains a denunciation of plagiarism which is itself plagiarized, so the inauthentic 'Father Prout', whose title lays claim to an authority of which he had in fact been ignominiously stripped, turns Moore into a literary pilferer by filching his writing. The present has the power to delegitimize the past, in a subversive smack at antiquarian ideology. In Maginn's 'O'Docherty Papers', the rollicking adventurer O'Docherty delivers a learned disquisition to a Scottish antiquarian society on a Roman frying pan found in a Kilkenny bog.[116] This mixture of pokerfaced pedantry and knockabout humour, with its carnivalesque lurchings from the erudite to the everyday, is, one might claim, a characteristically Irish genre, and can be found in Mangan too, who veers unsteadily from apocalyptic doom to a treatise on a pair of tongs.[117] Mangan, Maginn and Mahony are adrift between tongues, styles, cultures – hacks, parodists and *bricoleurs* who in the absence of a settled literary tradition shuttle from one (sometimes invented) language to another, brilliant wastrels who lavish their considerable philological talents on poems in praise of port or wicked burlesques of Wordsworth. A pathology of punning marks their linguistic inbreeding, which gives off all the sense of a fragmented, frustrated, self-involved colonial culture; and Mangan drifts between styles of handwriting as well as languages, depend-

---

115. For Mahony's writings, see *The Reliques of Fr. Prout* (London 1860).

116. See R.W. Montagu, ed., *William Maginn: Miscellenies in Prose and Verse*, vol. 1 (London 1885), p. 19. There is a brief commentary on Maginn in W.B. Stanford, *Ireland and the Classical Tradition* (Dublin 1971), pp. 170–71.

117. See, for example, his 'Treatise on a Pair of Tongs', in D.J. O'Donoghue, ed., *Prose Writings of James Clarence Mangan* (Dublin 1904). For carnivalesque humour in Irish literature in general, see Vivian Mercier, *The Irish Comic Tradition*, (Oxford 1962).

ing on his whiskey intake.[118] A busy intellectual energy finds little enough to expend itself on, and the learned Irish poet can shift easily into the role of Grub Street scribbler. The group find their echo in the literary dilettante Joe Atlee of Charles Lever's novel *Lord Kilgobbin*, whose delight is 'to write Greek versions of a poem that might attach the mark of plagiarism to Tennyson, or show, by a Scandanavian lyric, how the laureate had been poaching from the Northmen' (Ch. 4). With Atlee, a nationalist of sorts, this textual dialogism is turned against the most revered literary figure of the metropolitan nation.

But the linguistic dilemma – to write in Irish or English? – remained, despite the Corkmen's intertextual high jinks, a weighty one. Even Thomas Davis, despite his enthusiasm for Irish, had come to accept English as a fact of life, and was rapped over the knuckles for such apostasy by Daniel Corkery. Turning from those Gaels who, in Frederick Ryan's phrase, were content 'to let the substance of liberty go for the gee-gaw of a new grammar',[119] Yeats and his colleagues hoped to make a distinctively Irish contribution to European culture in the medium of English. The Anglo-Irish would thus put their hyphenated identity to productive use, providing a pivot between colony and continent. Dispossession would become empowerment, as those at home in no single culture felt themselves free to mediate between several. But was there not something inevitably shamefaced and compromised about an Irish literature in English, devoting one's energies to culturally enriching the very nation one politically opposed? Was this not the cultural equivalent of Home Rule? 'Did we come into the world merely to wreathe laurels round the brows of our conquerors?', as the *Fortnightly Review* rhetorically enquired in 1891.[120] Such was the position of polemicists like D.P. Moran, for whom the whole notion of Anglo-Irishness was an absurd oxymoron.[121] The precise literary meaning of the couplet was in any case in doubt. For Thomas MacDonagh, Anglo-Irish literature meant that English-language writing in Ireland which postdated the adoption of English by the mass of the Irish people; so that on this theory Carleton was acceptably Anglo-

---

118. See O'Donoghue, *Life and Writings of James Clarence Mangan*, p. 208, though the point has been questioned. The minor poet Joseph Brenan wrote of Mangan as one who 'Drinks at the fount Of old Teutonic awe and mystery!', though this was not in fact the poet's most regular form of consumption.

119. Frederick Ryan, 'Is the Gaelic League a Progressive Force?', in Deane, ed., *The Field Day Anthology*, vol. 2, p. 999.

120. Quoted by Kelly, 'The Political, Intellectual and Social Background', p. 58.

121. For Moran and Irish Ireland, see Donal McCartney, 'Hyde, D.P. Moran, and Irish Ireland', in Martin, ed., *Leaders and Men of the Easter Rising*.

Irish but Swift was not.[122] For Daniel Corkery, 'Anglo-Irish' denoted less a pedigree than a posture, embracing only that Irish writing in English which revealed a spiritual inwardness with the peasantry.[123] In this view, an authentically nationalist literature is one produced *for* and ideally *by* the people, and little of Anglo-Irish writing – a form of literary expatriation in Corkery's eyes – could claim this distinction.

But it was hard to avoid the uncomfortable truth that the texts of ancient Ireland had, after all, been dexterously translated by Ferguson, Hyde, Gregory and others, and that if this were so then the spirit of Ireland could not be quite so *sui generis* as all that. If Irish can be effectively rendered into English, then it cannot be entirely self-identical but must always have been intrinsically capable of this difference from itself. And if English can translate Irish, then this alien medium must be in some sense inherent in the Irish language itself. If language is in one sense too conservative a model for radical politics, it is in another sense not conservative enough. Since languages are porous, hybrid and eternally unfinished, they are the last thing to offer an edifying image of racial unity. 'If language becomes the criterion of statehood,' writes Elie Kedourie, 'the clarity essential to such a notion is dissolved in a mist of literary and academic speculation, and the way is open for equivocal claims and ambiguous situations.'[124] The paradox is plain: language in colonial conditions will tend to the hybrid, the parasitic, the intertextual, as with the macaronic scribblings of the Maginn set; but at just this point a brand of cultural nationalism will turn to it as the very paradigm of spiritual integrity.

Yeats and Synge sought to enrich the English language; Moran and the Irish Irelanders struggled to stem its corrupting influence. There was, however, a way of combining both projects – of at once outstripping and overturning English linguistic accomplishments, deploying the language with such breathtaking virtuosity that you simultaneously took it apart.[125] The name for this alternative strategy was *Finnegans Wake*, the non-Irish-speaking Irish author's way of being unintelligible to the British. If the high-minded Yeats envisaged a dialogical relation between cultures, the

---

122. See MacDonagh, *Literature in Ireland*, Ch. 2.

123. See Daniel Corkery, *Synge and Anglo-Irish Literature* (Dublin and Cork 1931), Ch. 1.

124. Elie Kedourie, *Nationalism* (London 1960), p. 70.

125. Neil Sammels argues a similar case about Oscar Wilde: 'His characters speak with an elegance and an almost extraterritorial precision which exploits English to its own destruction' ('Oscar Wilde: Quite Another Thing', in Paul Hyland and Neil Sammels, eds, *Irish Writing: Exile and Subversion*, London 1991).

carnivalesque Joyce pressed this to the point of promiscuity. This is one reason, indeed, why he proved so scandalous to the Scrutineers. For the Leavisian ideology assumes an intimate relation between the peculiar qualities of the English language, and a distinctively English form of experience. To use English to give voice to non-English experience, in the manner of colonial and post-colonial writing, is then to drive a dangerous wedge between signifier and signified. Joyce turns the medium of English against the nation which nurtured it, thus reversing the colonial power relation at the level of discourse. If the cultural separatists fear that the English tongue will appropriate their native experience, Joyce impudently appropriates that language for his own egregiously non-English ends. In thus estranging the English language in the eyes of its proprietors, he struck a blow on behalf of all of his gagged and humiliated ancestors. He did, in fact, just what Thomas Davis had most feared, in his eloquent English protest against the use of the English tongue: 'To impose another language on such a people is to send their history adrift among the accidents of translation – 'tis to tear their identity from all places – 'tis to substitute arbitrary signs for picturesque and suggestive names – 'tis to cut off the entail of feeling, and separate the people from their forefathers by a deep gulf...'[126] These, of course, are precisely the terms in which Joyce returned the compliment to the colonizers. One is tempted to comment that it is not as if Davis did not understand the post-structuralist project, merely that he disapproved of it.

Joyce's politico-linguistic triumph, however, was bought at an enormous cost. He had little but scorn for the Irish language, and shared with his friend Samuel Beckett a withering contempt for much of Irish culture. The arrogance of the exile is in this sense the inverse of the piety of the native. Like many a modernist, Joyce severed himself from what was diseased in his native culture only by uprooting himself from what was still potentially creative in it.[127] If the Gaelic Leaguers were too keen to forge an iconic link between language and homeland, Joyce was too quick to adopt the callow modernist credo that language can be a sufficient home in itself. The verbal brio and euphoria of the avant-garde are genuine enough, as art is flushed with the exhilarated rhythms of modernity; but they are just as much the self-rationalization of men and

126. T.W. Rolleston, ed., *Thomas Davis: Selections from his Poetry and Prose* (Dublin 1920), p. 172.

127. For this general paradox of early-twentieth-century modernism, see Raymond Williams, *The Politics of Modernism* (London 1989), Chs 2 and 3.

women who have become citizens of the world by dire necessity, driven from their native habitats by philistine ridicule, clerical censorship or political oppression. Art, or language, are then the only frail shelters left to inhabit; but the heady emancipation they yield is always secretly overshadowed by solitude and loss. It is these less palatable truths of cosmopolitan exile that much postmodern theory damagingly represses. If Joyce finally wreaked a magnificent vengeance on both Christ and Caesar, he paid for that pleasure with a lifetime's lonely labour. Only exile could breed a language to confound the patriarchs, yet exile was precisely an index of their power. In this sense even the *Wake* remains bound like its own characters to what it opposes, traced through by a burdensome history in its very conditions of production. Both Yeats and Joyce seek to elude that history by repressing the tragic: as the gyres whir and the Viconian cycles spin, nothing can be absolutely lost to the human spirit. It is their version of the death-and-resurrection scenario of 1916: in Yeats's case, the Nietzschean hauteur of the indestructible aristocrat whose hour will strike again; in Joyce's case the ceaseless repetitions of the biological cycle. Both are fantasies of omnipotence, and both compensate for different forms of powerlessness.

Finnegans Wake can blend diverse cultures as indifferently as it does because they have all been magically levelled, released by the signifier from the power relations which hold between them in everyday life. Its author's sceptical distance from the political is in this sense one source of its subversive force. The project of the Revivalists is another version of this premature utopia, able to imagine a unity of cultures within Ireland only because it has suppressed their social antagonisms. Such a view affirms of the present what could only be true of a politically transformed future, and so helps to defer its arrival. The doctrine of cultural diversity was a profoundly valuable antidote to ethnic supremacy; it was also a way of securing a survival for the Big House, and thus of just the kind of class relations which hindered a deeper emancipation. The more politicized culture becomes, the more decisive a role it assumes in social life; and the more plausible it becomes to believe that it forms the most vital centre of it. Liberal pluralism and postmodern culturalism are, then, contemporary versions of this mistake: if the liberals wish power away, the postmodernists diffuse it to the winds in a way which denies all fundamental contradiction. But culture is always most important when it speaks of more than itself; and to this extent culturalism subtly devalues it. In reducing the political to the cultural, it becomes an inverted image of the very philistinism it finds most offensive.

At the same time, as the more astute of the nationalists recognized, cultural development cannot wait obediently upon political change, which then becomes a convenient rationale for present inertia. If the nationalists meant by this that Ireland must evolve a culture of its own before throwing out the British, the point can be extended to the question of cultural pluralism. Whatever cultural understanding can be built here and now, between communities structurally and politically at odds, should be eagerly pursued, and indeed may play its part in some more thoroughgoing political resolution. The point applies as much to men and women as to Catholics and Protestants. The enlightened wing of the Anglo-Irish remains an object-lesson in such *rapprochement*, and one whose magnanimous spirit Irish history has yet to surpass. Scorned by their own class, reviled by Gaelic chauvinists, trapped painfully between two worlds, they dedicated themselves, sometimes at considerable personal cost, to a nation which all too often responded with ingratitude and disdain. In doing so, they fashioned for the country some of its most enduring artistic and intellectual monuments, as well as lending it some of its most imaginative political leaders. With impressive courage, they spoke up in the teeth of a swaggering ethnic supremacism for a respect for cultural difference, and put those who paid mere lip service to the ideal of a tolerant, diversified society to a searching test. Civilized, cosmopolitan and generous-spirited, they represented at their best the finest liberal current of a deeply illiberal society; and had that society been more receptive to their humane values, much in its subsequent tragic history might have been mitigated.

The fact that these Anglo-Irish values were often enough bound up with paternalism, self-interest and political opportunism is no denial of their inherent worth. But it serves to shed light on why their critics should have treated them with a degree of suspicion. When a previously dominant group begins to speak the language of cultural unity or diversity, it is understandable if their subordinates detect in this rhetoric a way of perpetuating their privileges in displaced form. When men begin to speak of how much, after all, they and women share in common, feminists are properly on the alert. There is a certain species of whingeing men who protest that the power relation has been inverted – that it is now *they* who are victimized by a group of militant separatist women who essentialize their identity and assert spiritual superiority over males. And there are Unionists in Northern Ireland who feel much the same about their situation vis-à-vis Catholics. One should seek to understand rather than scorn these anxieties, and give no leeway to essentialism or supremacy; but erstwhile dominant groups who, having fallen upon hard political times, present themselves as victimized minorities should not be surprised if they evoke the odd exasperated reaction from others. And commentators who, in doctrinaire postmodern style, regard all margins or minorities as inherently positive – an absurd enough attitude, to be sure – should be sensitive to the difficulties of those who have become accustomed to knowing such a besiegied minority as their far-from-hangdog overlords. This was the situation of the mass of the Irish people when confronted with Anglo-Irish enlightenment, and there are clear echoes of it in Ireland today.

It was the just destiny of the Anglo-Irish to lose their political power in Ireland; their tragedy was to lose their liberalizing influence along with it. Dismantling an unjust power involves values which are to some degree at odds with that liberal vision – for justice, unlike the society it hopes to create, is a necessarily one-sided affair. It is this which the middle-class liberal pluralist finds so hard to stomach. The two sexes must indeed negotiate what *rapprochement* they can in the present, but not to the point where this blunts the truth that men, if they are truly to speak to women, will have to forego much of their power. To foster a tolerantly multiracial society means intransigently opposing fascism. There is a tension between the goal of a pluralist society and the process of confrontation involved in achieving it. To ignore the necessities of conflict and partisanship, blandly projecting some future ecumenism upon the present, is just as one-sided as to imagine that the pluralistic end justifies the most sectarian means. Means and ends here are neither continuous nor contradictory, mutually conditioning but not of a piece. There were those who believed in abolishing the Anglo-Irish, and others who believed in welcoming them as equal partners into the Irish fold. Both parties were in the right: until the Anglo-Irish were brought low as a political ascendancy, there was no hope that they could make their full cultural contribution to the nation. The narrative of political justice, and the narrative of cultural diversity, are related but distinct, and one must beware of those who recount one but not the other. The more banal kind of liberal pluralist wants to replace political conflict with cultural difference. The more radical kind of pluralist understands that, without deep-seated political transformation, cultural difference will remain locked and frozen within cultural stereotype. In this sense, culture and politics entail one another; but they are not synonymous either.

CHAPTER 7

THE ARCHAIC AVANT-GARDE

The last great assembly of the fairies took place in 1839. In an unseemly sectarian brawl, the little people debated whether their existence was any longer necessary, and a defeatist wing of them glumly abandoned the country the day after their convention.[1] Ireland was growing gradually disenchanted, as its semi-paganized Christianity yielded ground to a more orthodox Catholicism. Religion in pre-Famine Ireland had blasphemously mingled the sacred and profane, and the Catholic Church did battle with this hybridized creed by frowning on patterns and stations, wakes, holy wells and crossroads dancing. At its most extravagant, this popular culture could erupt into carnivalesque riot: nudity, cross-dressing, indecent phallic games, mock marriages, sexual horseplay, grotesque parodies of Christ's passion, all of it documented in 1853 by the appropriately named antiquarian J.G.A. Prim. But the days when the corpse at a wake might be dealt a hand of cards, have a pipe stuck in his mouth or even be dragged around the dance floor were numbered.[2] From the mid century onwards, the ultramontane authority of the redoubtable Paul Cullen was everywhere to be felt, as the Archbishop, later to become Ireland's first Cardinal, chastised a lax clergy, centralized religious celebrations in a spate of newly built churches and struggled to purge his flock of their heathen practices. The Irish Catholic Church of the nineteenth century was in

---

1. See K. Theodore Hoppen, *Ireland since 1800: Conflict and Conformity* (London and New York 1989), p. 66. The religious ambiguity of the Irish people of the time is captured in the reply of an elderly west Cork woman when asked if she believed in fairies: she did not, she said, but they were there all the same. A belief in fairies, however, is perhaps no more superstitious than a belief in angels – a truth which mught be recalled by those historians who somewhat patronizingly stress the pre-Christian elements of popular Irish faith.

2. For an absorbing survey of popular customs, see S.J. Connolly, *Priests and People in Pre-Famine Ireland* (Dublin 1982).

fact a thoroughly modern phenomenon, not at all the traditional formation it is often mistaken for; but like many a modern phenomenon it
back-projected a venerable pedigree for itself.

Cullen's streamlining of the spirit was matched by a modernizing of
the economy. In the wake of Famine death and emigration, a society of
cottiers and landless labourers yielded to one dominated by strong and
middle farmers, and the population fell as the Irish converted from being
one of the earliest marrying to the latest and most rarely marrying people
in Europe. The country was in the process of shifting from a traditional
tillage economy to modern large-scale pastoral production, and was
gradually reaping the gains of this agrarian revolution. By 1850, Ireland
had one of the most commercially advanced agricultures in the world,
and was fast developing one of the world's densest railway systems. It also
contained the fifth greatest industrial city on earth. The consumer market
expanded, as imports increased five-fold between 1850 and 1914. The
literacy rate was impressively high, the number of National Schools, along
with the number of newspapers, doubled from 1850 to 1900, almost all
of the Irish now spoke English, and a professional Catholic middle class
had begun to burgeon. O'Connell's political machine prefigured in almost
every respect the modern political party, of which he could justly be said
to be the pioneer.[3] Later in the century, the Irish parliamentary party –
the first modern political party at Westminster – could compare favourably in effective organization with most of its continental counterparts,
and outmatched them all for the swiftness with which it had made the
transition from loose local groups to tightly centralized movement.
Presiding over these developments was an unusually modernized state, the
fruit of colonial intervention.[4] A largely pre-industrial society displayed all
the political forms of a more developed social order.

Unlike the parliamentary party, however, the country as a whole had
not leapt at a bound from tradition to modernity. Instead, it presented an
exemplary case of what Marxism has dubbed combined and uneven
development.[5] Cormac Ó Gráda remarks how in nineteenth-century
Ireland 'the decline in the south coincided with an industrial revolution
quite as dramatic and thoroughgoing as anything happening in Preston or

---

3. See Oliver MacDonagh, 'The Contribution of O'Connell', in Brian Farrell, ed., *The
Irish Parliamentary Tradition* (Dublin 1983).

4. See Joseph Lee, *The Modernisation of Irish Society 1848–1918* (Dublin 1973).

5. Jonathan Harker of *Dracula*, trapped in the ghoul's castle, remarks that he has 'taken
with my Kodak views of [the castle] from various points'. This bizarre blending of technology and Transylvania seems an apt symbol of the Irish mixture of tradition and modernity.

Middlesborough'. The structure of the pre-Famine banking economy, he adds, 'bespoke both commercialization at one level and mass poverty at another'.[6] Ireland's rate of income growth remained the slowest in Western Europe, and what affluence there was was drastically ill-distributed. The strong farmers had done well, but the lot of the humbler smallholders was arguably as wretched as before, and those of the rural proletariat who had survived the near-extinction of their class in the Famine were probably as poorly off as ever. Much of the rural economy remained archaic far into the present century; in 1917, there were a mere seventy tractors in the whole of the country.[7] There were marked regional variations, with much of the west still locked in a pre-Famine form of economy. The country as a whole was growing gradually more well-heeled; but it had started a good deal further back than many a European nation, with drastically low standards of living in the seventeenth century, so that even a dramatic increase in production could fail to raise those standards much above subsistence level. Having extricated itself from the calamity of the Great Hunger, an event into which it had drifted despite an agricultural revolution and a sustained growth in foreign trade, Ireland was now heading straight for the most ferocious class struggles it had ever witnessed, in the land wars of the late 1870s. Tradition and modernity were intimately interwoven, just as a commercial and a subsistence economy, one cash-based and the other largely a stranger to money, had long existed cheek-by-jowl in the Irish countryside. If rural Ireland was a land of immemorial custom, it was also one of the earliest examples in Europe of a modern agrarian economy, with a classical capitalist rent system implanted by its seventeenth-century invaders.[8]

In the Victorian epoch, the old and the new continued to form strange conjunctures. Perhaps no country with so high a rate of literacy had so low a per-capita income in the second half of the nineteenth century. Belfast, the country's most economically advanced centre, was ideologically speaking one of its most atavistic, awash with ferocious sectarian strife. The most industrially progressive region of the island, Ulster, had also been the last redoubt of traditional Gaelic civilization. The stringent traditionalist morality of the post-Famine epoch – sexual repression,

---

6. Cormac Ó Gráda, *Ireland Before and After the Famine* (Manchester 1988), pp. 27, 29.
7. For an account of the *fin-de-siècle* economy, see David Fitzpatrick, 'Ireland since 1870', in R.F. Foster, ed., *The Oxford History of Ireland* (Oxford 1992).
8. See Kevin O'Neill, *Family and Farm in Pre-Famine Ireland* (Madison, Wis. 1984), p. 14.

deferred gratification, enforced celibacy, clerical regulation[9] – was partly in the name of a modernizing drive to ensure impartible inheritance and preserve the farm intact. An archaic moral superstructure thus served an increasingly modern base. Conversely, the fact that the state in Ireland was of a modernizing kind, with its centralized structures of education, public health, law and order, was partly a function of the country's traditional backwardness, as the burden of public administration in a conflict-ridden colony shifted from an incompetent or indifferent land-lordism to central government itself. As far as education went, Ireland gained a modern school system before Britain; but the content of that education – classics, mathematics, literature, but no science, commerce or modern languages – was of a timorously traditionalist kind. A different kind of mixture of tradition and modernity had appeared in the schooling system of the eighteenth century, where the very teachers who transmitted to their pupils a Gaelic tradition of political rebellion were also at the centre of a revolution in English-language literacy.[10] And nothing could symbolize a more bizarre conjuncture of ancient and modern than 1916, when it was as though the slain and resurrected fertility gods of Jessie Weston and James Frazer had taken to the streets of Dublin armed with rifles, some of them almost as antique as the deities in question. Indeed it is possible to see the Rising as a watershed between two strains of nationalism – between the Romantic, idealist, traditionalist version of the creed which carried out the insurrection, much of it with Anglo-Irish roots, and the modernizing, Catholic, petty-bourgeois variety which reaped the fruits of it.

The post-Famine Irish economy was on an uphill trek, aided by the permanent haemorrhage of emigration; but the pre-Famine period had witnessed the deindustrialization of much of the society beyond north-eastern Ulster, and the country proved slow to recover. The Irish peasantry were cusped between backwardness and material progress: poorly housed and clothed, but (apart from the semi-starvation months between harvests each year) tolerably well-fed and in impressive physical shape. Irishmen were on average taller than Englishmen, as we know from the statistics of the British army, one-third or more of which was supplied by Irish recruits in the nineteenth century. As a consequence of the land wars, a still impoverished class of labourers and small tenantry combined their material

---

9. The Irish priest who commented in 1974 that he knew of 'many happy couples ... who have abstained from sexual intercourse for over twenty years' was doubtless an heir to this epoch.

10. See David Dickson, *New Foundations: Ireland 1660–1800* (Dublin 1987), p. 195.

backwardness with a remarkably up-to-date political consciousness. Daniel O'Connell had accomplished the extraordinary feat of harnessing the traditional sentiments of the Irish masses to his secular, liberal, utilitarian programme, and Parnell had repeated the experiment with striking success. 'The supporting masses', R.V. Comerford comments of the O'Connellite campaigns, 'were entering a modernising world of ordered, pragmatic politics, while at the same time expressing themselves ... in terms of an Irish version of the millennialism characteristic of the old European peasantry.'[11] The Repeal movement was in one sense a nostalgic affair, with its totemic appeal to Grattan's parliament; yet to re-create that parliament in post-Emancipation conditions would have proved disruptively radical. As Patrick O'Farrell writes: 'Irish archaicism was so profound, so much at variance with English ideas of what should be, that it exhibited a most revolutionary complexion, especially in view of its violent expression.'[12] What the Irish saw as reform, O'Farrell adds, the British viewed as revolutionary; what the British defined as reform the Irish received as a threat to their traditional way of life.

In Britain, the industrial middle class had been deeply stamped, ideologically speaking, by a traditionalist landowning order. But that landowning class was itself the oldest *capitalist* formation in Europe, modern in its economic rationality whatever its neo-feudalist spirit. And its middle-class underlings, the spearhead of the world industrial order, were to prove a powerfully progressive force within British society as a whole. Ireland, by contrast, was saddled with a peculiarly archaic, unreconstructed style of landlordism. It was, every bit as much as its British counterpart, a capitalist formation, and the Anglo-Irish were accustomed to seeing themselves as the sole modernizing force in a nation of benighted peasants. But it was a woefully inert brand of rural capitalism, an old-fashioned form of modernity which lacked the challenge of an industrial middle class to spur it into life. What class of that kind existed was largely confined to north-east Ulster. So it came about that the mantle of revolutionary modernism in Ireland passed to the rural middle class – passed, in a word, to one of the most conservative formations in Western Europe. It was left to this parochial presence to accomplish the modernizing process in Ireland by sweeping away a retrograde landlordism and installing a reactionary ruralism in its place. One internally contradictory

---

11. R.V. Comerford, 'Nation, Nationalism, and the Irish Language', in T.E. Hachey and L.J. McCaffrey, eds, *Perspectives on Irish Nationalism* (Lexington 1989), p. 22.

12. Patrick O'Farrell, *Ireland's English Question* (London 1971), p. 112.

class – a gentry with a capitalist base and a traditionalist ideology – gave way to another of much the same ilk. And a similar mixture of the modern and the traditional applied to Anglo-Irish relations. British rule in Ireland had been a force for both progress and paralysis: if it modernized the country it had also, in Patrick O'Farrell's words, 'arrested the internal development of Irish self-awareness, preserving it in a pre-modern condition...'[13] At just the point when the idea of national autonomy was seizing Enlightenment Europe, Ireland meekly surrendered what meagre independence it possessed in the Act of Union.

There was no question, then, of an eyeball-to-eyeball encounter between tradition and modernity.[14] Irish society was stratified in this respect, made up of disparate time scales. Its history was differentiated rather than homogeneous, as the anglicized and the atavistic existed side by side, and a commercialized agriculture still bore a few quasi-feudal traces. Modernity and peasant society are not in any case necessarily at odds: as Samuel Clark and James Donnelly point out, modern capitalism actually increased the size of the European peasantry.[15] The 1830s and '40s in Ireland witnessed an accelerating decline of traditional popular culture, as a modern democracy began to take shape; yet 'Gaelic' culture was already from the eighteenth century a contradictory affair, as a politically self-conscious Catholic middle class itself took a hand in burying a traditional Gaelic order with its modernizing projects.[16] Ireland, according to L.M. Cullen, was 'the last western European country to abandon the medieval world',[17] with a landed class which still occupied thatched houses as late as the early eighteenth century. But it was also, so Cullen considers, a society remarkably ready to jettison its traditions, 'exceptionally open to and receptive of change',[18] more insouciant about preserving its native language, for example, than any other Celtic people.

The Irish are supposed to fetishize the past; but in quite what sense this constitutes a backward-looking mentality is debatable. As with Walter Benjamin's anti-historicist spirit, it would seem less a question of grasping

---

13. Ibid., p. 8.

14. The tension between the two is obvious in the slogan of the *Nation*: 'to create a foster public opinion in Ireland and make it racy of the soil' – in which Enlightenment and Romanticism are yoked together.

15. Samuel Clark and James S. Donnelly, Jr, *Irish Peasants: Violence and Political Unrest 1780–1914* (Madison, Wis. 1983), pp. 11–12.

16. See Eamon O'Flaherty, 'Atavism and Innovation: Reflections on Culture and Nationality in Ireland', *Irish Review*, no. 2 (1987).

17. L.M. Cullen, *The Emergence of Modern Ireland 1600–1900* (New York 1981), p. 25.

18. Ibid, p. 135.

the past as the prehistory of the present, than of constellating an image plucked from that past with a quick sense of the contemporary. '[The Irish people]', grumbled John O'Leary, 'have a most vivid recollection of Brian Boru ... but they frequently forget all about the day before yesterday'.[19] And Tom Garvin reminds us of how Irish nationalism's view of the *recent* past, in contrast to an idealized golden age, was often enough implacably negative.[20] What is recent is not last week, but antiquity. For James Joyce, the fact that it was an Irish ruler who had invited the English into the country in the first place, with the connivance of the Pope, was an excellent reason for not being a nationalist; but this backward glance to the twelfth century is precisely a nationalist habit of mind.[21] Anti-historicist consciousness blends the archaic with the absolutely contemporary, squeezing out the dreary continuum between them; and this, as we shall see, is as true of Ireland's modernism as it is of its nationalism. It is a time-warping obvious enough in the idealizing of the West, the home of an *echt* Irishness which, as Kevin Whelan indicates, was permanently settled in some of its larger sectors only in the late eighteenth and early nineteenth centuries.[22] Luke Gibbons points out that much of what is now taken to be traditional Irish values is of fairly recent vintage.[23] It is worth adding, too, that the timeless Aran islands of a J.M. Synge had a fishing industry directly linked by large trawlers to the London markets.

But the time-warping runs deeper. For what is afoot in nineteenth-century Ireland, with the cataclysm of the Famine, the agrarian revolution, the sharp decline of the language and the sea changes in popular culture, is the transformation *within living memory* of a social order in some ways still quite traditional, and so a peculiarly shocking collision of the customary and the contemporary. The time of artistic modernism is a curiously suspended medium, a surreally foreshortened temporality in which the laws of orderly narrative are lifted so that time, much as in the dream or the unconscious mind, seems at once fantastically speeded up and fixated upon certain images dredged from the depths of some ancient

19. John O'Leary, *Recollections of Fenians and Fenianism*, vol. 2 (London 1896), p. 216.

20. Tom Garvin, 'Great Hatred, Little Room: Social Background and Political Sentiment among Revolutionary Nationalists in Ireland, 1890–1922', in D.G. Boyce, ed., *The Revolution in Ireland, 1879–1923* (London 1988), p. 99.

21. See E. Mason and R. Ellmann, eds, *The Critical Writings of James Joyce* (New York 1959), pp. 162–3.

22. Kevin Whelan, 'The Bases of Regionalism', in Proinsias Ó Drisceoil, ed., *Culture in Ireland: Regions, Identity and Power* (Belfast 1993), p. 43.

23. Luke Gibbons, 'Coming out of Hibernation? The Myth of Modernity in Irish Culture', in Richard Kearney, ed., *Across the Frontiers: Ireland in the 1990s* (Dublin 1988).

collective memory. This, for a Walter Benjamin, is also the rhythm of political revolution, which blasts a space pregnant with possibility in the continuum of conventional history;[24] and it is perhaps not too fanciful to detect this modernist consciousness, at once traumatized and enraptured by the new, mournfully arrested and dynamically open to the future, in the course of Irish history after the Famine, when in an apocalyptic twist the primitive and primeval – the atavistic event of the Famine itself – *have only just happened*, and happened in a way that at once brings you face to face with a paralysing past, and briskly disposes of its debris for the creation of the authentically modern. The present is now a weightless moment precariously balanced between the ancient and the avant-garde, a condition of absolute loss which nevertheless brims with unborn potential, a mere empty passageway between a past which – since it is only yesterday – cannot be relinquished, and a wholly transfigured future which is just about to arrive. 'From the time of the famine,' writes Patrick O'Farrell, 'the strongly developed sense of the past which was so powerful in Ireland ceased to exercise a conservative social role, and came to be a dynamic prediction of the future.'[25] Perhaps an element of this consciousness was the extraordinary *rapidity* of the post-Famine economic recovery, which seems to have been well under way by the early 1850s. And when the land settlements finally arrived at the end of the nineteenth century, they offered the peasantry in modernizing style what they themselves regarded as their traditional rights.

The modernist sensibility we are describing is not of course synonymous with *modernity*. On the contrary, it is in one sense its sworn enemy, hostile to that stately march of secular reason which was precisely, for many a nineteenth-century Irish nationalist, where a soulless Britain had washed up.[26] Anglo-Irish aesthete and Gaelic ascetic could join hands here in a common censure. If modernism is among other things a last-ditch resistance to mass commodity culture, Irish nationalism would set its own ancient spirit of aristocracy against the dismally standardized society on its doorstep, and so act out in its own way the radical conservatism of so

---

24. See Walter Benjamin, 'Theses on the Philosophy of History', in *Illuminations*, edited by Hannah Arendt (London 1970).

25. Patrick O'Farrell, 'Millennialism, Messianism and Utopianism in Irish History', *Anglo-Irish Studies* 2 (1976), p. 50.

26. Edward Martyn, Unionist landowner turned Gaelic Leaguer, Abbey playwright and president of Sinn Fein, was one of the more vociferous exponents of this view. For a biography of this intriguing figure, see Stephen Gwynn, *Edward Martyn and the Irish Literary Revival* (London 1930).

much modernist art. The Irish may have felt crushed by the British, but they tended to feel superior to them as well. If Britain stands for Enlightenment, and nationalism is a child of Enlightenment too, then one can resolve this embarrassing contradiction by a nationalism which is modernist rather than modern, one which links the venerable and the very new in a common front against empty, linear time. In one sense, it is ironic that Britain should have come to represent for Irish nationalists the very nadir of the modern – vulgar, materialist, spiritually polluted, industrially devastated. For if it was all of that, it was also in its own way a thoroughly traditionalist culture. Ireland may have been arrested in its own development by a backward ruling class, but that class was simply a more uncouth, caricatured version of a traditionalist landowning oligarchy over the water. If Ireland was in many ways an archaic country, so was the land of its proprietors; and the two conditions were by no means unrelated.[27]

If the histories of the two nations were out of step at one level, they were parallel enough at another. The 'modernist' time of nationalism then solves this problem by moving off in two directions at once. Turning its back on a callow British modernity, it sets off in search of its own ancient spirituality; but in doing so it takes a modernizing leap forward, one which will break beyond the history of the merely recent into an authentic future. Like Walter Benjamin's *Angelus Novus*, it will move backwards into the future with its eyes fixed sorrowfully upon the past, impelled into that new creation by the winds let loose from a paradise it has lost. Since the recent past of British colonialism is a mere aberration, it forms an empty passage of time through which the past can return in all its plenitude, this time as the future. It is precisely the remote past, un-contaminated by recent time, which can provide the most stirring image of the future. Like modernism, nationalism will outflank the merely modern by turning to advantage the shattered time to which that era has reduced it. Since those who are the sheer waste products of modernity are less in thrall to that epoch, they are able to shift on ahead of the present, exposing the moderns as yesterday's men. If a one-way history has disintegrated around you, then it is just as easy, in this adrift, emancipated condition, to move forwards as well as backwards. Virtue can be plucked from necessity – just as the art of Samuel Beckett, with its starved

---

27. Tom Nairn writes of Britain's 'containment of capitalism within a patrician hegemony which never actively favoured the aggressive development of industrialism or the general conversion of society to the latter's values and interests' *(The Break-Up of Britain*, London 1977, p. 32). Ireland, to this extent, seems Britain writ theatrically large.

landscapes that are at once Ireland and anywhere, shows well enough how to be stripped of your particular culture is to become a citizen of the world.

Both nationalism and modernism turn on a play of difference and identity. In asserting its equal right to freedom with other nations, and so its identity with them, nationalism finds itself affirming the uniqueness of its own culture.[28] An identity with others modulates into self-identity. For the more Romantic brands of nationalism, all nations have an equal right to autonomy, but each will achieve it in its own inimitable style. The nationalist aspiration is for the people to enter as free and equal partners onto the global stage; yet the intense self-awareness which this brings with it risks driving the nation back upon itself in solitary self-communing. In any case, the equality at stake conceals a disabling difference: the very conditions of backwardness which drive a people to claim equal status with others will also render that equality depressingly unequal once it is achieved. 'Why is it', enquires Partha Chatterjee, 'that non-European colonial countries have no historical alternative but to try to approximate the given attributes of modernity when that very process of approximation means their continued subjection under a world order which only sets their tasks for them and over which they have no control?'[29] The nation should not be governed by a foreign power because it has as much right to independence as those who rule it, and so is commensurate with them, but also because it is entirely *sui generis*, and so incommensurate.

In one sense, colonialism is a false differentiation of equals; in another sense it is the political equivalent of a category mistake, deceptively linking two distinct realities. But to assert your difference from the colonizers is to risk taking on board their own belief in a national essence, and so to end up identical with them. Ironically enough, Ireland made its strike for independence at just the point where it was coming most to resemble the society which held it down. At a time when the most powerful nations have long since thrust their own national–bourgeois revolutions into historical oblivion, the striving of small nations to be free is bound to

---

28. 'Nationalist thought, in agreeing to become "modern", accepts the claim to universality of the "modern" framework of knowledge. Yet it also asserts the autonomous identity of a national culture. It thus simultaneously rejects and accepts the dominance, both epistemic and moral, of an alien culture' (Partha Chatterjee, *Nationalist Thought and the Colonial World*, London 1986, p. 11).
29. Ibid., p. 10.

appear quaintly archaic, not least in a multinational world in which the leading powers are beginning to surrender something of their own national sovereignty. But this difference is in fact a question of deferral, a time-lag between more and less 'successful' nations, and so conceals an identity between them. Indeed it is partly because multinational capitalism brings with it a deepening exploitation of its neo-colonial fringes that those nations are driven to seek an independence which can then only seem antediluvian. In the build-up to the nationalist revolution in Ireland, the elegantly sceptical John Eglinton is already speculating that 'the day of nations ... is passing away', and this in 1906.[30]

The idea of the nation, as Benedict Anderson has argued, is an abstraction.[31] Yet the community implied by it is not entirely imaginary. Nations are not self-identical; but the fact remains that colonized peoples, however unevenly, are indeed oppressed precisely *as peoples*. What gives them their unity is not some racial essence, but the negative fact of being held down as a whole. It is colonialism, not nationalism, which makes of the nation something more than a fictive entity. The fact that some of the colonized reap more benefit from this arrangement than others is no argument against this point. If the idea of a people subdued as a whole were simply a fiction, the rhetoric of nationalism would be a good less persuasive than it has proved to be. The idea of woman is an abstraction too; yet the blunt fact remains that women are oppressed precisely as women, whatever their differences of class or colour. All human community or solidarity is at some level imaginary, even that around the village green. Ideologically speaking, the abstractness of the concept of the nation can prove a problem: it will take the people, with their inevitably local allegiances, some time to learn it. The conflict between the republican universalism of the United Irishmen and the more humdrum concerns of many of their followers is a case in point. But few modern political ideas have survived transcoding into those vividly concrete terms with so little loss − certainly not the idea of proletarian internationalism. If nationalism is a bourgeois abstraction, it is equally a matter of passionate popular sentiment; and much of its appeal springs from the fluency with which a translation can be made from one to the other.

---

30. John Eglinton, *Bards and Saints* (Dublin 1906), p. 11.
31. Benedict Anderson, *Imagined Communities* (London 1983), Chs 2 and 3. On the artifice of the concept of 'nation', see Eric Hobsbawm, *Nations and Nationalism Since 1780* (Cambridge 1990), Introduction. See also Horace B. Davis, *Towards a Marxist Theory of Nationalism* (New York 1978).

Modernism, too, moves at a level of abstraction, to the point where Theodor Adorno can read the purity of its forms as indebted in part to commodity exchange. With its deep structures and universal archetypes, its cosmopolitan artists cut loose from parochial traditions, modernism appears in some ways as the very opposite of nationalism, as the work of the anti-nationalist Joyce would suggest. Yet modernism, like nationalism, is out to translate those abstract forms into the aesthetic experience of difference, uniqueness, of the ineffably particular and stubbornly specific, of all that escapes the levelling commonness of modernity. Like nationalism, then, it is dependent on that modernity for its universal forms, while resisting them in its idiosyncratic content. Both movements are fuelled by the very modernity against which they constitute, in part, an anxious defence.[32] Both pit image and intuition against what they see as the reified rationality of the modern world, a rationality which for nationalism reaches its grim apotheosis in the bureaucracy of the colonial state. To reclaim that state for the people is to fuse tradition and modernity, race and rationality, the communitarian and the contractual, converting the barren forms of *Gesellschaft* into the living medium of *Gemeinschaft*. The fact that pre-Norman Ireland was a politically decentralized society, lent what unity it had by the cultural forms of language, religion and custom, could then supply a persuasive pedigree for this enterprise in Ireland.[33] It was, to be sure, a contradictory sort of project – for how was cultural nationalism to translate itself into political terms without betraying its spiritual essence to anglican forms? Modernism, rather similarly, depends on material structures from which it would prefer to remain icily aloof. Both nationalism and modernism are the work of the spiritually disinherited children of the bourgeoisie; but whereas the modernist artist makes her lonely rebellion against an oppressive order, the nationalist intellectual turns instead to a collective act of freedom, to an affective community which will prove a more congenial place to live in than the atomized society of the colonial conqueror. Rather than find a home in the alternative community of art, the uprooted intellectual forges an imaginary identification with a dispossessed people. The contrast should not be too sharply drawn: the modernist artist is also often enough in

---

32. On the need to discriminate the more progressive and more regressive faces of nationalism, as against a postmodernist thought which carelessly conflates them, see Aijaz Ahmad, *In Theory: Classes, Nations, Literatures* (London 1992), Introduction.

33. Tom Dunne points to the central role played by poetry in traditional Gaelic society, and sees the society as lacking a modernizing political dimension. See his 'The Gaelic Reponse to Conquest and Colonisation: The Evidence of the Poetry', *Studia Hibernica*, no. 20 (1980).

hot pursuit of some spiritual collectivity, whether as Tradition, 'primitive' society, an organic precapitalist order or the European Mind.

Both nationalism and modernism eclipse the prosaic time of modernity, placing this whole epoch in brackets by the power of a thought which, in striving for some post-bourgeois form of life, finds its models for this in the pre-bourgeois world. In Ireland, the weakness of the liberal individualist tradition, the relative absence of a mature industrial middle class, made this a plausible kind of manoeuvre, curving time back upon itself in a loop which, like William Morris's blend of socialism and medievalism, forced out what history had intervened as so much deviation from an abiding, if buried, continuity. If the past is seen in the style of Irish antiquarianism as a high point of civilization, then what Benjamin dubbed the 'tiger's leap' into it appears at the same time historically progressive.[34] And if the linear time of modernity is treated with suspicion, it is partly because backward nations cannot afford to wait upon that long march of enlightened progress, needing as they do here and now to take a quantum leap into a future which is another people's present. It is a commonplace that revolutionary nationalism unites the archaic and the avant-garde, inflecting what is in fact a modernizing project in the rhetoric of ancient rights and pieties.[35] Nationalism is a desire to be modern on one's own terms; and since one is not yet modern, those terms can be nothing but traditional. 'The return to the folk', as John Hutchinson puts it, 'is not a flight from the world but rather a means to catapult the nation from present backwardness and division to the most advanced stage of social development'.[36] Like T.S. Eliot's ideal poet, the revolutionary nationalist is at once the most primitive and progressive of creatures, poised at the cutting edge of the present yet drawing upon some visceral resource of traditional feeling. The Irish had

---

34. For some eighteenth-century antiquarians, the Irish past was more or less the high point of *all* civilization. It was the ancient Irish, of Egyptian and Phoenician origin, who had taught these peoples their arts, and who for good measure had also invaded and civilized the British. A language something very like Irish was probably spoken in the Garden of Eden. For a representative work, see Charles Vallancey, *A Vindication of the Ancient History of Ireland* (Dublin, 1786).

35. See, for example, Nairn, *The Break-Up of Britain*, pp. 340 f; Ernest Gellner, 'Nationalism', in his *Thought and Change* (London 1964), and his *Nations and Nationalism* (Oxford 1983). Jacqueline Hill makes an interesting application of the theory of the displaced nationalist intellectuals to Ireland in her 'The Intelligentsia and Irish Nationalism in the 1840s', *Studia Hibernica*, no. 20 (1980).

36. John Hutchinson, *The Dynamics of Cultural Nationalism* (London 1987), p. 33. Gellner, by contrast, tends to view cultural nationalism merely as regressive.

little to learn from Eliot's insistence on the contemporaneity of the past.[37] If the nationalist memory was not exactly as old as the Flood, it was at least as old as Flood. Even the uncompromisingly radical Constance Markiewicz had a horoscope which showed Uranus on the Descendant, Pluto at the Nadir and Capricorn on the Ascendant, irrefutable evidence that she was a revolutionary with a fondness for hierarchy and tradition.[38] Antiquarianism in Ireland had typically been a mildly progressive pursuit, and Irish nationalism was traditionally both radical and aristocratic. The Revival witnessed the most recondite of doctrines (druidism, theosophy, Rosicrucianism) being pressed into the service of universal brotherhood, national liberation and a utopian synthesis of religion and science. The esoteric elite who indulged in these spirit summonings and table-rappings were a mirror image of the exoteric vanguard of the political future.

Sociologically speaking, nationalism is the creed of a displaced, frustrated sector of the native middle class, which finds its ambitions blocked by the colonial system and in doing so suffers a double alienation, at once from that modern rational state and from the traditional culture of the people.[39] Caught in this crisis of identity, it turns to a doctrine which provides it at once with a rooted identity and a vocational future. A traditional culture which is now being increasingly abandoned by the people themselves, under the influence of metropolitan manners, is re-invented by an urban intelligentsia for its own political ends. But the sociological case is in the end too reductive, since nationalism, even for its critics, is clearly more than just cynical self-interest. If these men and women were after jobs in the post-colonial state, they were also driven by a passion for social justice. Like socialism, the nationalist idea is a response to a modernizing process which seems to have escalated out of control, not least in its shattering impact on a still largely traditional social order. Like socialism too, it acts as an *immanent* critique of that order, seeking to turn the techniques of modernity against the alienations they have bred. Irish nationalists could thus call for native manufactures in one breath

---

37. T.S. Eliot, 'Tradition and the Individual Talent', in *Selected Essays* (London. 1932). Oliver MacDonagh, discussing eighteenth-century antiquarian debates in Ireland, remarks that 'Time was being so foreshortened that the character of druidical Ireland was being treated as validating or otherwise, in some significant degree, the early nineteeth century political and social order' ('A View of Anglo-Irish Relations', *Anglo-Irish Studies*, no. 4, 1979, p. 3).

38. See Anne Haverty, *Constance Markiewicz: Irish Revolutionary* (London 1988), p. 192.

39. See Hutchinson, *The Dynamics of Cultural Nationalism*, for an illuminating application of this theory of nationalism to Ireland. See also A.D. Smith, *Theories of Nationalism* (London 1971), and *The Ethnic Revival* (Cambridge 1981).

while denouncing the evils of British industrialism in the next; and Yeats's revolt against English materialism drew part of its inspiration from a very English humanism. And just as capitalism for Marx gives birth to its own gravedigger, unable to function without bringing into the world a proletariat capable of supplanting it, so colonialism, in seeking to integrate a native middle class into its own political culture, finds that the natives have turned those resources to ends it did not anticipate.

Like most nationalisms, then, the Irish version was a curious amalgam of the traditional and the modern. On the whole, it looked forward to a modernized, modestly industrialized Ireland with its traditional culture preternaturally intact. If its Anglo-Irish wing was archaicizing in one mood while self-consciously liberal and cosmopolitan in another, its more Gaelic manifestations – the Gaelic League, for example – were just as self-divided, nostalgic for a dying culture yet eager for industrial development. From Thomas Davis to Patrick Pearse (an enthusiastic modernizer despite his cult of *sanitas* and sacrifice), these opposed visions unite in a typically petty-bourgeois sensibility: the ideal Ireland is a country sober, disciplined, industrious and self-reliant, values which lend themselves equally to material progress and spiritual conservatism. Yet that unity was not so easily achieved in practice. Taken as a whole, Irish nationalism was a political movement with a modernizing base and a Janus-faced superstructure, ambiguously forward-looking and elegiac; but there was real conflict within it between its more political wing, heir to an aspiring Catholic middle class which had sought since the eighteenth century to advance its cause within a thoroughly modern framework of civic rights,[40] and its more Romantic or culturalist sector, whose aim was to recast the entire modern notion of civil society as such. Indeed 'Romantic nationalism' comes close to being an oxymoron, since nationalism suggests a set of hard-nosed political realities with which Romanticism feels distinctly uneasy. Like most radical movements, Irish nationalism veered between ultra-leftism on the one hand and pragmatic compromise on the other, seeking to locate the elusive line between immanence and transcendence. Whatever these problems, if one is excluded from full membership of

---

40. The definitive study is Thomas Bartlett, *The Fall and Rise of the Irish Nation* (Dublin 1992). Bartlett points to the irony that in the period of the penal laws and the consolidation of Protestant Ascendancy, a prosperous Catholic bourgeoisie was beginning its steady advance. C.D.A. Leighton, however, reminds us that the resurgence of the Catholics was more a matter of property than of consciousness: 'this was a resurgence from a very low position indeed' *(Catholicism in a Protestant Kingdom*, London 1994, p. 2). See also Maureen Wall's classic essay 'The Rise of a Catholic Middle Class in Eighteenth-Century Ireland', *Irish Historical Studies*, vol. 11, no. 42 (September 1958).

political society, then 'culture' remains an alternative form of belonging. But it was not the least of that cultural nationalism's embarrassments that it arose, phoenix-like, out of the ashes of the very traditional order it struggled to re-create, and so was always radically belated. 'The most belated race in Europe', Joyce wrote of the Irish.[41] Indeed it may be that one can only ever objectify one's culture as a whole, grasp it as a complete entity, by the power of a backward glance, when it has already come under historical threat. A language becomes 'native' at just the point where someone else is trying to uproot it.

Nationalism, in any case, is surely the most contradictory of all modern political phenomena, which is why it is curious that anyone should take an unequivocal stand either for or against it. In our own century, nationalism has liberated oppressed peoples, from India to Angola, from the arrogance of imperial power; it has also led straight to the death camps. It has salvaged cultures and languages in danger of extinction, and restored the damaged self-esteem of those to whom they belong; it has also been known to celebrate those cultures as inherently superior. Nationalism has been the strategy by which disregarded nations could break dramatically on to the world stage, and a form of festering spiritual introversion which has imprisoned them within their own frontiers. It has been both the valiant struggle of a Finland against tsarist autocracy, and the lethal expansionism of the Axis powers. If it has provided downtrodden peoples with a concrete image of their freedom, it has also regularly handed them over to the self-interest of a native middle class, as socialists have consistently warned. Nationalism is the mould in which imperialism itself has cast the politics of its dependents, since nations are oppressed precisely as nations; yet that imposed identity has proved a more dramatically successful force than any other revolutionary movement of the modern period.

Nor can an angelic and a demonic nationalism be neatly distinguished: some arms of the movement which have proved of most value to the destitute have also carried with them some dangerously irrationalist baggage. Tom Nairn's comment that 'all nationalism is both healthy and morbid'[42] is surely an overstatement – what precisely was healthy about Nazism? – but it captures, however hyperbolically, an important truth. The nationalism of a Wolfe Tone involved an appealing form of identity politics: Ireland should share the right of all nations to be free, without privilege or partiality. The nationalism of an Arthur Griffith carried a

---

41. Quoted by Herbert Gorman, *James Joyce* (London 1941), p. 73.
42. Nairn, *The Break-Up of Britain*, p. 347.

much less savoury notion of identity — that of the supposed self-identity of a radically divided society. Irish nationalism has spanned Thomas Davis's fellow-feeling for Afghanistan and John Mitchel's contempt for African-American slaves; it has consorted equally with the Marxism of a James Connolly and the high Toryism of a Samuel Ferguson. Some Irish nationalism has been provincial, racist and exclusivist, and the British variety has often been much the same.[43] Like gender and ethnicity, nationalism has no obvious class bearing, but is itself, as Connolly recognized, the site of a class struggle.[44] As far as what Lenin called the 'democratic content' of nationalism goes — the right of a people to self-determination — it is hard to see how any Enlightenment liberal could deny it; nationalism in this sense is no more than a requirement of democracy. But that political content has come often enough swathed in ideological forms which exclude and denigrate others, and retrieving the democratic kernel from the mystical shell is a delicate enough operation.

'We are', announced Kevin O'Higgins, Minister of Home Affairs in the first Free State government, 'the most conservative revolutionaries in the world.' He could say that again. Despite a steadfast British faith in the extremism of the Irish, the truth is that even their radicals have been by and large a signally conservative crew. The Catholic Committee in the eighteenth century supported Britain in its war against America, and was prodigal of obsequious declarations of allegiance to the Crown. Wolfe Tone, a cross between swashbuckling adventurer and classical civic humanist, was autocratic and elitist in political style, paternalist in his attitude to the peasantry and morbidly fascinated by military insignia. A reluctant separatist and doughty defender of private property, he was by no means averse to the notion of monarchy. The social and economic content of his politics was notably thin, extending to perhaps little more than a kind of Manchester-school model for Ireland.[45] Daniel O'Connell, opportunist and authoritarian, informed on peasant secret societies and advocated increased military repression of them. A champion of peasant protection rather than peasant proprietorship, he was prepared to flirt

---

43. A point well made by Seamus Deane in Seamus Deane, ed., *Nationalism, Colonialism and Literature* (Minneapolis 1990), pp. 7–8.

44. See Ernesto Laclau, *Politics and Ideology in Marxist Theory* (London 1977), Ch. 4.

45. For a somewhat tendentious portrait of Tone, see Tom Dunne, *Wolfe Tone: Colonial Outsider* (Cork 1982).

with federalism as a solution to Anglo-Irish relations. Strongly anti-socialist, paranoid and despotic in his declining years, he evinced throughout his lengthy political career a craven servility to British sovereignty, and allied with the very Whigs who were sending thousands of Irish to their graves by their criminally incompetent handling of Famine relief. His zeal for justice was matched only by his horror of the radical measures it required. Peasant agitators were on the whole social conservatives, theoretical if not actual respectors of the property system.

Thomas Davis, traditionalist and idealist to the core, was nervous of Catholic democratic power, and his newspaper the *Nation* could be soft on American slavery, an institution his racist colleague John Mitchel enthusiastically endorsed. The *Nation* also spoke out at various times against Chartism, socialism, higher wages, the restriction of working hours and indiscriminate charity to the poor. Cooler in the cause of the Irish language than is sometimes imagined, it occasionally succumbed to demeaning British stereotypes of the Irish. If it was patronizing in its attitude to women, it was considerably more respectful in its stance towards the landlords. Some of the leading Young Irelanders were little more than genteel liberals in revolutionary clothing, and the movement was not unqualifiedly separatist. It clung absurdly late to the illusion of benevolent landlordism, and apart from John Mitchel renounced the idea of class struggle; even the radical Fintan Lalor considered that the land-lords should be allowed to keep their estates. Thomas Meagher, one of the more leftist of the group, declared himself no democrat or republican and professed himself incapable of imagining a society without an aristocracy. The Confederation, the left-wing successor of Young Ireland, believed in a union of all social classes. Several of the leading IRB luminaries were bigoted, puritanical and loftily remote from social struggles. Charles Kickham, president of the movement, did not consider landlordism an evil in itself, denounced the Land League as communistic, and like some of the Young Irelanders looked for support to a paternalist upper class. His anxieties about the Land League, a movement which betrayed the labourers and small tenants to the interests of the graziers and strong farmers, were farcically unfounded. The Fenian John O'Leary's main reaction to the land wars was to worry that they might deprive him of his *rentier* income. Isaac Butt was an imperial nationalist who wanted to see Ireland reap a fuller share of the fruits of empire, while some Anglo-Irish clamoured for Home Rule in order to preserve Ireland from the pollution of British democracy. Charles Gavan Duffy rejoiced that in Britain's colonies 'the word of command is not infrequently uttered with

an Ulster burr, or an unequivocal Munster brogue'.[46] Charles Stewart
Parnell believed in a unity of all social classes and devoted much of his
energy to defusing radical demands. Arthur Griffith was a monarchical
anti-Semite, a Bismarckian and anti-Dreyfusard, an anti-socialist chauvinist
loyal to the cause of British imperialism. For the ultra-nationalist D.P.
Moran, almost every previous nationalist trend was to be dismissed as
insufficiently Irish; even the Fenians were a 'Pale movement'. Yet Moran
finally declared himself a royalist. Even Patrick Pearse was prepared to
contemplate a constitutional monarchy for Ireland. The revolutionaries of
1921 settled for dominion status for Ireland under the Crown, and their
military cohorts violently suppressed rural agitation among the labouring
poor.

It is hardly a portrait of fanatical revolutionism. But neither, for all its
limitations, is it a record to be scorned. If its blind spots must be
registered, so too must its courage, resilence, political resourcefulness and
imaginative flair. The political genius and generally enlightened views of
Daniel O'Connell, to choose merely one example, warrant the highest
praise. Irish nationalism transformed popular consciousness and brought
low an awesome imperial power. If its political history is fairly chequered,
the history of British radicalism is at least as much so. The blunders and
illusions of both movements pale into insignificance beside the greed and
violence of their superiors. If the Irish revolution was to prove a
conservative one, it was in part because 1916 was its coffin as well as its
cradle, wiping out some of its most gifted and radical leaders. And the
record of Irish women revolutionaries, while hardly unblemished, does
much to trim the balance. On the whole, radical Irish women out-lefted
their menfolk – hardly surprisingly, given that women were traditionally
excluded from the public sphere, and so on entering it (usually, in Ireland,
as supports or substitutes for their male colleagues) were less likely to be
bound by its protocols. The Ladies' Land League, under the guidance of
Anna Parnell, fought with impressive courage and resilience, in the teeth
of mockery and venomous abuse, to salvage the radical content of a
movement increasingly under the heel of conservative interests. Its funds
were finally cut off by Charles Stewart Parnell, in a shabby sellout to
British Liberalism. Disgusted in equal measure with both men and Irish
politics, Anna Parnell retired under a pseudonym to an artists' colony in
Cornwall, and never spoke to her brother again. Her sister Fanny, penner
of politically forceful if artistically feeble verses, was like Anna a radical

46. C.G. Duffy, *The Revival of Irish Literature* (London 1894), p. 52.

republican and a champion of class politics.[47] Alongside these middle-class luminaries, some hundreds of ordinary women took part in the Land League and its Ladies' counterpart, preventing evictions, delivering speeches and organizing boycotts.

The Ladies' Land League provided in effect the first public sphere for women in modern Irish history, and involved ordinary countrywomen with remarkably high levels of political awareness. It was women who often took the brunt of police violence during evictions, both because defending the home belonged to their traditional role and because they were on the whole less likely to be arrested. But they were no shrinking violets either. At Carraroe in County Galway in 1880, according to Michael Davitt, a Mrs Mackle 'succeeded in throwing a shovelful of burning turf upon Sub-Inspector Gibbons and thereby driving him from the house'.[48] One or two other unorthodox weapons could be wielded too: at a Land League meeting in County Galway, one Margaret Sheehan moved 'that we, the young girls of Waterford, Tipperary and Kilkenny, resolve and promise before this vast multitude to reject with scorn and contempt any matrimonial proposals from Michael Hickey as a punishment for his heartlessness to a poor labourer and his young and helpless family of seven'.[49] Effectively excluded from office in the male-dominated Land League, the female rank and file nevertheless did more than fulfil their stereotypical functions of relief and assistance.

Some decades later, *Inghinidhe na hEireann* (Daughters of Erin) was an uncompromisingly revolutionary organization which in ultra-leftist spirit rejected all parliamentary politics for an allegiance to the separatist, physical-force tradition of the Irish Republican Brotherhood.[50] Constance Markiewicz, one of the greatest of all Irish political militants, was born to a wealthy aristocratic family in Sligo, studied art at the Slade and made her first contacts with Irish nationalism through Arthur Griffith's Sinn Fein and the Theatre of Ireland, a dissident breakaway group from the Abbey Theatre. Rapidly outlefting Sinn Fein, she joined *Inighnidhe na hEireann*, allied with the IRB leaders Tom Clarke and Bulmer Hobson,

---

47. See Jane McL Coté, *Fanny and Anna Parnell* (London 1991). See also R.F. Foster, *Charles Stewart Parnell: The Man and his Family* (Hassocks 1976), Part 5, Chs 3 and 4.

48. Michael Davitt, *The Fall of Feudalism* (London 1904), p. 217.

49. Quoted by Janet K. TeBrake, 'Irish Peasant Women in Revolt: The Land League Years', *Irish Historical Studies*, vol. 28, no. 109 (May 1992).

50. For a useful account of radical Irish women, see Elizabeth Coxhead, *Daughters of Erin* (Gerrards Cross 1979). See also Margaret Ward, *Unmanageable Revolutionaries* (London 1983); and Carol Coulter, *The Hidden Tradition* (Cork 1993).

and wrote for *Bean na hEireann*, the first women's newspaper in Irish history. A member of Sinn Fein's executive council, she founded and organized *Fianna Eireann* (Ireland's revolutionary answer to the Boy Scouts), taught them how to drill and shoot and set up a short-lived commune for their members. Introduced to socialist ideas through her friendship with James Connolly and Jim Larkin, she played a central role in organizing soup kitchens during the Dublin lockout of 1913 and joined both the Volunteers and the Irish Citizen Army. Armed to the teeth, she was easy to mistake, in the view of the *Irish Worker*, for a representative of an enterprising firm of small-arms manufacturers. As a Major in the Irish Citizen Army and second-in-command on St Stephen's Green during the Easter Rising, she was sentenced to death, reprieved on account of her sex and endured the first of several spells of imprisonment.

In 1917 Markiewicz was elected president of the women's organization *Cuman na mBan*, and became Labour spokeswoman in the Sinn Fein provisional government, where she was widely regarded as the chief inheritor of James Connolly's socialism. Interned in Holloway Prison in 1918, she was returned for parliament as the first woman MP in Britain, and became Minister of Labour in the first *Dail*, where she rescued some vital state papers from the British army by carting them around Dublin in a taxi and despositing them in the window of an antique shop opposite the Black and Tan headquarters, protected by a forbiddingly high price tag. As Labour Minister she intervened in industrial disputes (including one at a rosary-bead factory) on the side of the workers, was imprisoned once more, and during her stint in a thoroughly bourgeois *Dail* insistently pressed the claims of labour and the cause of socialism, while soviets sprang up in Munster and landless labourers sought to expropriate the great estates. Imprisoned yet again, and court-martialled for conspiracy, she joined the anti-Treaty party in the *Dail* split of 1922, supported by the five other female members of the chamber. *Cuman na mBan* rejected the Treaty overwhelmingly, and Markiewicz, on the run during the civil war, was finally imprisoned by the Free State. Still campaigning among the destitute of Dublin, though snatching time to run a republican theatre company, she joined De Valera's *Fianna Fail* in 1926, was re-elected to the *Dail* and died in 1927, burnt out in the cause of feminism and socialist republicanism. The Free State government refused to allow her body to lie in state. Shunned by her upper-class friends, brutally beaten by the police, ridiculed and reviled by those whose manhood she threatened, she sacrificed her money, marriage and beauty in the service of the dispossessed, helped to keep a starving working class alive during the great lockout, and carried little to her grave but the love of the Dublin poor.[51]

Markiewicz was the greatest, as well as the most eccentric and flamboyant, of a rich array of feminist republicans in those years: Charlotte Despard, Helena Maloney, Eva Gore-Booth, Kathleen Clarke, Dorothy McCardle, Sheila Humphreys, Eithne Coyle, Hanna Sheehy-Skeffington, Mary MacSwiney and others. The male-centred historiography which has largely written them out has nonetheless seen fit to salvage Maud Gonne, chiefly as an appendage to William Yeats. Born in Surrey, the daughter of an English army officer, Gonne anticipated her exotic career by accepting at the age of fourteen a proposal of marriage made in the moonlight in the Colosseum in Rome. Her political apprenticeship began in true cloak-and-dagger style in Paris, where she fell in through her French lover with an unsavoury bunch of right-wing anti-Semitic monarchists and embarked on a clandestine mission to Russia to enlist tsarist support for a conspiracy against the Third French Republic. Back in Ireland, she became deeply involved during the Plan of Campaign period in struggles against evictions in the west, encountered William Yeats and struck him, in his own phrase, 'like a Burmese gong'. She joined the Order of the Golden Dawn, worked for political prisoners and became a vice-president of the National Literary Society. She and Yeats would sometimes lie in the west with their ears to the ground, listening to the music of the fairies. After launching a nationalist newspaper in Paris, she took a leading role in the anti-Jubilee celebrations of 1897 and had her first taste of police brutality. Lecture tours and a visit to the USA followed, before she returned to Mayo in 1898 to help organize famine relief. Active in the pro-Boer campaign and the protest against Victoria's visit to Ireland, she became a close associate of James Connolly and was elected president of *Inghinidhe na hEireann*, as well as a vice-president of *Cumann na nGaedheal*.

Gonne played the part of the Countess Cathleen in *Inghinidhe na hEireann's* celebrated production of Yeats's play, and having married John McBride[52] concocted a plot to assassinate the king while on her honey-

---

51. See Diana Norman, *Terrible Beauty: A Life of Constance Markiewicz* (London 1987); and Anne Haverty, *Constance Markiewicz: Irish Revolutionary* (London 1988). Sean O'Faolain's *Constance Markiewicz* (London 1935) speaks of how Markiewicz, 'in her woman's way, had no intelligible ideas but many instincts' (p. 74), and either buries her for long stretches under a general account of Irish history or views her from the standpoint of her supposedly long-suffering husband Casimir.

52. McBride was not the most intellectually gifted of Irish republicans. While in Paris with Gonne, he once delivered a speech in French so bad that the audience thought he was speaking Dutch.

moon. She took an active part in the production of the feminist newspaper *Bean na hEireann*, campaigned for the childen of the poor and was gaoled after her return to Ireland from Normandy in 1917. In 1919 she worked in Sein Fein's publicity department, was later a judge in the Sinn Fein courts, and continued her relief work among the working class of Dublin. In 1921, after initially supporting the Treaty, she swung against it as the Free State, with the aid of British military hardware, ruthlessly suppressed republican forces among whom her son Sean was prominent. She nursed republican casualties, became involved in negotiations between the warring parties, and formed the Women's Prisoners' Defence League ('The Mothers'), in which cause she was imprisoned and went on hunger strike. Unlike Markiewicz, she refused her support after the civil war to De Valera's *Fianna Fail*, and along with the octogenarian socialist-feminist Charlotte Despard and James Connolly's son Roddy threw in her lot with the short-lived Workers Party of Ireland, soon to be dissolved by Stalinist ukase. Continuing her work for IRA prisoners, she joined with Hanna Sheehy-Skeffington in the protest against Sean O'Casey's *The Plough and the Stars*, and liaised with Indian nationalists.

It was, by and large, women like Gonne who in the 1920s spearheaded the opposition to the repressive new state, just as during the civil war, while the IRA were organizing in the south, it was women who, under intense state harrassment, mounted the political opposition in the metropolis. In 1932, on the election of De Valera, Gonne's lifelong campaigning in support of political prisoners achieved final victory, as the gaols were emptied of them. The amnesty was to prove shortlived, as the Free State began to reimprison its republican opponents. Gonne continued to support the IRA, clamoured against the Free State's denial of women's rights, and stood as a candidate for *Cumann na Poblachta na hEireann* (Republican Party of Ireland) on an ultra-leftist, anti-constitutional ticket. An article of 1938 reveals pro-fascist and anti-Semitic leanings, mixed in with her customary Anglophobia. She lived to see Ireland sever its final links with Britain in 1949, and died four years later.[53] Like Constance Markiewicz, Gonne resisted the left-utilitarianism of some of her male comrades with a concern for style, elegance and ornament, an attention to the small beauties and stray pleasures of life which could be easily dismissed as female vanity. Throughout her tumultuous political career, she preserved her two favourite ballgowns from her days as a debutante.

53. Among the various accounts of Gonne, one of the most informative is Margaret Ward, *Maud Gonne: A Life* (London 1990). See also the brief note on her in Denis Donoghue, *We Irish*, vol. 1 (London 1986).

'Maud Gone Mad and Charlotte Desperate', as the Irish knew Gonne and Despard. Charlotte Despard, born of the celebrated French family, was known in *fin-de-siècle* London as the 'Mother of Battersea', renowned for her work among the destitute. She published seven novels of indifferent quality, joined the Independent Labour Party and became active in the Marxist Social Democratic Federation in the 1890s. She was later to join both the Labour Party and the British Communist Party. As honorary secretary of the Women's Social and Political Union, she endured a spell in prison and in her late sixties spearheaded a suffragette splinter group, the Women's Freedom League. She was prominent in the campaign against the First World War, and as an animal lover found time to express her love for horses as mounted police bore down upon her in Parliament Square. A Theosophist and Catholic together, and friend of the anarchist Edward Carpenter, she established table-rapping communication with Mazzini and opened a teetotal pub on the Hampstead Road called the Despard Arms. In 1921, at the age of seventy-seven, she moved to Ireland, where her brother had been appointed Viceroy, and joined Maud Gonne in the Women's Prisoners Defence League. She also threw in her lot with the Irish Vegetarian Society, whose president was Mrs Ham and whose vice-presidents were Mrs Joynt and Mrs Hogg.

Active among the anti-Treaty forces in the civil war, Despard opened a jam factory for the unemployed and retained close connections with British leftists like Harry Pollitt. In 1926 she joined the Irish Workers Party, and after the assassination of Kevin O'Higgins was officially branded a dangerous subversive ripe for expulsion from the country. Among her other achievements, she was deeply disliked by W.B. Yeats. Having enthusiastically welcomed the new Bolshevik state in Russia, she travelled to the Soviet Union in 1930, and in 1932 campaigned for De Valera. A workers' college she founded in Dublin was sacked by an angry mob, and at the age of ninety, half-blind, arthritic and rheumatic, she moved to the North to continue her work in Belfast. When the Spanish Civil War broke out two years later, she was insistent upon going to Spain, but contented herself with speaking in defence of the republican forces at various international conventions. She died three years later a bankrupt.[54]

None of these women was free of illusion: about the nature of the Soviet Union, the pointlessness of constitutional politics, the Romantic spirit of Ireland, the inveterate degeneracy of the British. Nor were they all as unequivocally feminist as figures such as Margaret Cousins, Hanna

---

54. See Margaret Mulvihill, *Charlotte Despard: A Biography* (London 1989).

Sheehy-Skeffington, Jennie Wyse Power and the other leading militants of the early-twentieth-century Irish Women's Franchise League. It was that flourishing tradition of Irish suffrage which insisted – from a radical rather than liberal position – that feminism must not be unduly subordinated to republicanism, that women must do more than service patriarchal nationalists, and that women's rights could not wait upon national liberation.[55]

The sources of nationalism and those of modernism have much in common. In an illuminating essay, Perry Anderson has sketched what he sees as the three preconditions for a flourishing modernism: the existence of an artistic *ancien régime*, often in societies still under the sway of an aristocracy; the impact upon this traditional culture of breathtakingly new technologies; and the imaginative closeness of social revolution.[56] Modernism springs from the estranging impact of modernizing forces on a still deeply traditionalist order, in a politically unstable context which opens up social hope as well as spiritual anxiety. Traditional culture provides modernism with an adversary, but also lends it some of the terms in which to inflect itself. That culture, so Anderson argues, can be put to use by modernism in its quarrel with the more negative aspects of modernity. It is not hard to trace something of this diagram of forces in the emergence of Irish modernism, or indeed of the nationalism with which it was so closely linked. Irish nationalism takes root in a still traditionalist landowning order, which provides it with a political target; but the Revival, with its distinctively 'aristocratic' cast, will turn some of those cultural forms against the detested modernity of the merchant and the clerk. And this artistic experiment, for all its elitist tone, is part of a broader revolutionary current, that of political nationalism itself.

It is no accident, then, that the one major flourishing of modernism in what were then the British Isles should have taken place in its most backward region. What 'British' modernism there was in the late nineteenth and early twentieth centuries was largely of Irish origin. Of Anderson's three conditions, England itself, one might argue, was able to muster only one and a half. It was, to be sure, a traditionalist society, with a remarkably hidebound culture; but it was also the oldest industrial

---

55. For the Irish suffrage movement, see Rosemary Cullen Owens, *Smashing Times* (Dublin 1984); and Cliona Murphy, *The Women's Suffrage Movement and Irish Society in the Early Twentieth Century* (Hemel Hempstead 1989).

56. See Perry Anderson, 'Modernity and Revolution', *New Left Review* 144 (March–April 1984).

capitalist nation in the world, one which had long since naturalized and absorbed the shocks of modernization. And though it was hardly a tranquil place in the decades of high modernism, threatened with civil war and regional disintegration in the years before the First World War, this scarcely matched the revolutionary ferment of Ireland. Unable to breed a major modernism of its own, England was forced to import its modernist artists, from James and Conrad to Eliot and Pound.[57] Realism in art and empiricism in philosophy, the spiritual fruits of a mature middle-class civilization, could offer no fertile ground for a futurism or surrealism. And since modernism is nothing if not cosmopolitan, crossing national frontiers as nonchalantly as it shifts between art-forms and coteries, it struck little response from an inward-looking imperial Britain, which had never been much enthused by the pretentious antics of a bunch of bohemian foreigners.

There are other reasons why modernism, then as now, can thrive more vigorously on the colonial or neo-colonial margins than at the metropolitan centre. In an increasingly unified world, where all times and places seem indifferently interchangeable, the 'no-time' and 'no-place' of the disregarded colony, with its fractured history and marginalized space, can become suddenly symbolic of a condition of disinheritance which now seems universal. It is in this sense that the stagnant, parochial, never-changing/ever-changing Dublin of *Ulysses* can make its bid for cosmopolitan stature. Modernism, so Anderson claims, needs a traditional culture against which to react; but it can also, as in Ireland, turn a fragmented cultural history to its own advantage, exploiting the very absence of a stable system of representation for its own audacious experiments. As Luke Gibbons puts it: 'Irish culture did not have to await modernity to undergo the effects of fragmentation – the cult of the fragment was itself the stuff from which history is made.'[58] And if the political history of the nation is fissured and disrupted, subject to the authority of another, it is less likely to throw up those realist notions of coherent narrative and self-determining characters which are England's alternative to the digressive storylines and depleted figures of a Samuel Beckett. In Yeats, the moral notion of character gives way to the aesthetic cult of personality. Joyce's leading player, Stephen Dedalus, is that most unEnglish of fictional characters, an intellectual rather

---

57. The two major home-grown modernists in England were a radical woman and a provincial coal miner's son – both of them significantly askew to the cultural Establishment.

58. Luke Gibbons, 'Race against Time: Racial Discourse and Irish History', *Oxford Literary Review*, no. 13 (1991).

than a moral hero. Ireland also lends itself to modernism because on the colonial edges the world is less easy to totalize in classical realist fashion, precisely because some of its central determinants lie elusively elsewhere, in the metropolitan country. And since the 'real' in this situation is hardly a source of consolation, art is quick to discover for itself an inward world or compensatory fantasy life which merges easily with the modernist unconscious. Seamus Deane has listed the striking number of modern Irish writers – Joyce, Beckett, Francis Stuart, Patrick Kavanagh – for whom 'politics is regarded as a threat to artistic integrity',[59] writers who cast a cold eye on the political realm precisely because its unseemly clamour was too much for them. The stance of much European modernism is apolitical; in Ireland this is intensified by the boisterous presence of politics. Yet reaction is a relationship; and to this extent the art of a Joyce or Yeats or O'Casey remains on terms with the political even when it turns contemptuously from it, or offers itself in its place.

We have seen that modernism, like nationalism, has both a progressive and regressive face, as a product of the very modernity it puts into question. But the ratio between these tendencies varies from place to place; and what is striking about Irish modernism is its overwhelmingly conservative tenor.[60] If there is a high modernism in Ireland, there is little or no avant-garde – little of that iconoclastic experiment which seeks to revolutionize the very conception and institution of art itself, along with its relations to political society.[61] There could be no exhilarating encounter between art and technology in such an industrially backward nation. There is no Irish Dada or Constructivism, though the exception, as far as avant-gardism goes, is Joyce. What we have instead is a peculiarly mandarin modernism in which, by and large, the archaic triumphs over the contemporary. And the reasons for this are not hard to discover. For one thing, Ireland was in general a profoundly conservative society, with only a weak ideology of modernization. Yeats remarks on the absence of a developed scientific tradition in the country, for which his own highly systematized magic had to do service. For another thing, a good deal of

---

59. Seamus Deane, *Celtic Revivals* (London 1985), p. 15.

60. Though Christopher Butler considers that most modernisms started life this way: 'The major Modernists have an extremely respectful relationship to tradition. None of them began their careers as confrontational or avant-garde. This innate conservatism, which only arrives at a technical breakthrough after an exploration of the past, is one of the extraordinary strengths of early Modernism' (*Early Modernism*, Oxford 1994, p. 25).

61. The most authoritative account is Peter Bürger, *Theory of the Avant-Garde* (Manchester 1984).

its modernism was monopolized by the Anglo-Irish. It was precisely because they were a *politically* dispossessed group that the Anglo-Irish could shift, as though by way of compensation, to *cultural* production; and their social privileges, in stark contrast to the mass of the Irish, were a precious advantage in this respect. Culture was the territory which the Anglo-Irish were especially equipped to occupy – one of the few territories, indeed, which they still *could* occupy; and they brought to it, naturally enough, the tones and assumptions of their genteel inheritance. The liberal Anglo-Irish were remarkably well-placed to provide the country with a modernist vanguard, as a displaced coterie with elitist instincts and cosmopolitan sympathies. Their 'in-betweenness', wedged as they were between London and Dublin, Big House and peasant cabin, was a version of the hybrid spirit of the European modernist, caught between diverse cultural codes; and for both parties the conflict was as invigorating as it was undermining. Just as Futurist euphoria and Expressionist angst are the opposed faces of continental modernism, a manic-depressive movement if ever there was one, so the Anglo-Irish modernists were swept up in heady enthusiasm for the new Ireland about to be born while anxiously unsure of their role within it. For some of them, as for many a European modernist, art could offer an ersatz kind of identity and belonging, a community of sorts which was painfully lacking in historical fact; so that the celebrated formalism and aestheticism of the modernists, their scandalous insistence that one could live inside myth or language or archetype, that the art-work was its own origin, audience and *raison d'être*, was among other things a defiant rationalization of their own rootless condition.

The Anglo-Irish intelligentsia were used to seeing themselves as the civilized spearhead of Irish society, its finely disinterested spirits; and this view blends easily with the Olympian dispassionateness of the modernist artist, set apart from anything as vulgar as social engagement. 'A forlorn advanced guard', was how Sir Samuel Ferguson described the Ascendancy. Yet the Anglo-Irish could also draw on an antiquarian tradition stretching back to the eighteenth century; and in this combination of archaicizing and freethinking they reproduced within Ireland the divided sensibility of modernism as a whole. It was just because the political turmoil which produced the Revival was of a nationalist rather than a socialist stripe that the Anglo-Irish were able to play such a key role within it. For nationalism ranks culture – the stock in trade of liberal Ascendancy intellectuals – among its most vital concerns; it values spirit, ideal, sentiment and subjectivity, all of which were amenable to a Romantic upper class; and it fosters the backward glance, a vision to which that historically obsolete class was no stranger. And just as modernism mingles radicalism and elitism, so the aristocratic idea in Ireland could always be given a rebellious twist, implying as it could an anti-colonial affection for the old Gaelic nobility. Throughout nineteenth-century Ireland, a democratic nationalism cast itself often enough in the language of ancient aristocracy. In one sense, the nationalist Anglo-Irish were in the process of trying to convert themselves from an elite to a vanguard – to step down from their traditional aloofness from the people, yet preserve something of that privileged status by placing themselves at the head of the army. In another sense, it was possible for them to keep up their coterie practices, as with Yeats's esoteric dabblings, in the knowledge that these were in some oblique way related to the wider nationalist cause.

There are those who imagine that to criticize a writer's politics is necessarily to impugn his or her art. With Yeats and the other great modernists, almost the contrary is true. What helped to produce much of the major art of the early twentieth century was political reaction. It is not accidental that Conrad, Yeats, Eliot, Pound and Lawrence were all on the radical right, or that Heidegger is among the most original of modern philosophers. The radical right finds conventional middle-class society supremely distasteful, and confronts it with a critique far more searching and fundamental, if also a good deal more wrong-headed, than anything a liberal realism can muster. In the absence of a revolutionary aesthetic, it is the great reactionaries who stand askew to a degraded present, invoking spiritual values whose political implications are occasionally odious, but whose artistic depth and intricacy resonate far beyond the workaday decencies of an E.M. Forster. Yeats is the supremely fine poet he is, not despite his politics but in some measure because of them – a truth which offers little comfort to either liberal aesthete or reductive leftist.

If Ireland gave birth to a distinctly conservative modernism, much the same can be said, for quite different reasons, of the land of its masters. What modernism Britain produced was largely implanted by émigrés who sought out the country precisely for its settled, traditionalist character, fleeing as they were from political upheaval or 'inorganic' social orders elsewhere.[62] Indeed British modernism was a good deal less radical than its Irish counterpart. It maintained on the whole a disdainful distance from politics, whereas Irish modernism, for all its genteel nostalgia, was

---

62. See Perry Anderson, 'Components of the National Culture', *New Left Review* 50 (July–August 1968). See also my *Exiles and Émigrés: Studies in Modern Literature* (London 1970).

actually helped to birth by the existence of a militant revolutionary project. Just as the theatre of Bertolt Brecht would have been unthinkable without the socialist movement of the Weimar republic, so the poetry of Yeats, whatever its ideological *parti pris*, is inseparable from a nationalist political history. While British modernism cast a cold eye on politics, Irish modernism, however ambiguously, bore some relation to the political from the outset, precisely because the politics in question lent themselves more readily to an upper-class idealism than did, say, the socialism of the German working class. 'Spirit' could provide a precious link between art and the political nation, realities which in modernist Britain were largely at each other's throats. By forging an identity between their own aristocratic Romanticism and the very different Romantic strain of middle-class Gaelic nationalism, the Anglo-Irish Revivalists could hope to realize for themselves that most cherished ideal of every displaced intelligentsia, an active relationship with the people. For a brief moment, the backward-looking ideology of a benevolent aristocratism, one now almost bereft of a material basis, was able to lend itself a final lease of life by linking hands with a progressive movement of the bourgeoisie.[63] An alliance of Protestant gentry and Catholic middle class which had proved singularly hard to achieve in Irish society as a whole could now be cobbled together in opposition to that order. Both groups had in common a certain purism – with the Anglo-Irish of an idealizing flavour, with the Gaelic middle classes of a distinctly puritanical bent. The materialism of Joyce, at once somatic and semiotic, is an assault on both kinds of sublimation.

This union of Celt and Gael was, to be sure, a fraught, unstable affair, soon to be overtaken by history; but it did more than allow the Anglo-Irish narodniks a brief illusion of roots. It also meant that they could revive their traditional dream of leadership at the very moment of its historical collapse. A native Catholic culture forced down since the seventeenth century from patrician to peasant status would now be raised up again to its true aristocratic grandeur, this time by progressive Protestants. This, in effect, was an Irish version of the Arnoldian project in England: just as for Arnold a traditional culture had now to sweeten and refine the oafish captains of industry, so the Celticist project was as much about the edifying of the nationalist middle class, harnessing an antique

---

63. There is a need to distinguish the social and ideological here. Socially speaking, Yeats and Synge were, like Patrick Pearse and Thomas MacDonagh, of the middle class; they were not, like George Moore, Edward Martyn and Augusta Gregory, literally of the landed gentry, though both had landowning affiliations. Ideologically speaking, however, they identified themselves to varying degrees with that class.

culture to modern political ends, as it was about a flight to the Aran islands. What for a modernist like Eliot could only remain a wistful hope – the ideal of a common culture in which an illiterate farm labourer might subliminally pick up the resonances of *Four Quartets* – could be turned in Ireland into a whole cultural programme. If for Eliot this meant a certain style of art, in Ireland it meant the founding of a theatre. The ideology of both Yeats and Eliot could be described as conservative populism;[64] it was just that Yeats had the rare good fortune to live in a time and place where this happened to be part of a major political movement.

There is another sense, too, in which Irish modernism was politically in advance of its metropolitan counterpart. The Revival was not, in the classic sense of the term, an avant-garde affair: apart from some nebulous agitprop notions (travelling libraries for the peasantry, theatre for the common people) it did little to transform the existing modes of cultural production.[65] Individual works of art were still framed and autonomous – once more with the exception of Joyce, who succeeded in exploding the whole genre of high fiction, transgressing the border between high and demotic art[66] and exploiting the materiality of print for his own devious ends. The Abbey presented modernist plays; but it was hardly an avant-garde *institution*, refashioning the relations between play, actors and audience in the manner of Brecht's Berlin theatre. Indeed it was soon to set into a rigidly naturalistic mould, an apt expression of the arthritic nationalism of the Free State. The most avant-garde playwright it produced was Sean O'Casey, whose loose, non-linear, intensely physical later drama is an Irish equivalent of Brecht's social Expressionism; but O'Casey's experimental pieces were written only after his break with the Abbey, which preferred to pigeonhole him as a slum realist. To take the Revival as a whole project, however, rather than as this or that play or poem, is to observe a quite astonishing transgression of the frontiers between the aesthetic and the social, of a distinctively avant-gardist kind.

---

64. Though Yeats shifts emphasis between populism and elitism at different stages of his career. The populist, anti-intellectualist tendencies of an Eliot, fully compatible with his conservative elitism, are often overlooked. His ideal culture is at once common and stratified (see my 'Eliot and a Common Culture', in Graham Martin, ed., *Eliot in Perspective*, London 1970).

65. In 1903 Yeats hatched a plan for a People's Theatre along the lines of the working-class *Freie Volksbuhne* in Berlin, but it came to nothing. See John Kelly and Ronald Schuchard, eds, *The Collected Letters of W.B. Yeats, vol. 3: 1901–1904* (Oxford 1994), p. 433.

66. The contrast with the Revivalists is instructive. Aspects of Joyce's work are genuinely popular in the sense of incorporating the culture of the people; but Joyce is not a populist in the Yeatsian sense, a doctrine which involves constructing an ideological image of the people for political ends.

'Literary' Revival or Renaissance is surely a misnomer: it was always a good deal more than that, and the term is damagingly academicist. James Connolly lecturing backstage at the Abbey Theatre; the theosophist poet George Russell helping to set up cooperative creameries; Yeats organizing political demonstrations, and a gentle Gaelic scholar fronting the Irish Volunteers: the years of the Revival are full of such bizarre intersections. The Irish National Theatre grew out of the women's movement, its first performance a Daughters of Erin production, and James Connolly regarded his *Labour in Irish History* as belonging to the literature of the Irish Renaissance.[67] One of the most popular forms of culture – sport – rapidly became a revolutionary weapon.[68] As the political revolution heats up, the barriers between fiction and reality gradually crumble to leave a set of surreal images lingering in the mind. The Citizen Army staging an attack on Dublin Castle one particularly foggy night without knowing whether it was real or simulated (and which exactly was the Easter Rising itself?).[69] Jim Larkin smuggled into a Dublin hotel to harangue the crowds from its balcony, disguised in Count Markiewicz's cloak and a false beard. An Ascendancy Countess drilling street urchins in how to shoot British soldiers. Gun-running into Howth harbour by the daughter of the Archbishop of Meath, the Committee Clerk of the House of Commons and the niece of the British Ambassador to Washington. A Tolstoyan, Captain Jack White, training the Citizen Army, and a Lord Lieutenant arriving in Ireland in 1918 to be demonstrated against by his suffragette sister Charlotte Despard. James Connolly reading detective fiction while lying wounded inside the General Post Office, and meetings which were ambiguously literary salons and military councils. Men and women of mystical or occultist persuasion who believed at once in political revolution and in the unreality of the material world. The Limerick Cooperator W.L. Stokes, Buddhist and butter merchant, devouring *The Light of Asia* and the *Grocer's Gazette* with equal relish.[70] A performance of a play which was also a political riot. Maud Gonne disguising herself as an aged crone

67. See Margaret Ward, *Maud Gonne*, pp. 72–3; James Connolly, *Labour in Irish History* (reprinted London 1987), p. 22.

68. See W.F. Mandle, *The Gaelic Athletic Association and Irish Nationalist Politics 1884–1924* (Dublin 1987).

69. See F.X. Martin, 'The 1916 Rising – a *Coup d'État* or a "Bloody Protest"?', *Studia Hibernica*, no. 8 (1968).

70. See R.A. Anderson, *With Sir Horace Plunkett in Ireland* (London 1935), pp. 6–7. Anderson, known as 'R.A.' to his English cronies and as 'Plunkett's Man Friday' to the Irish farmers, writes in his book of how, having met the great Plunkett, his youthful bumptiousness instantly evaporated, a claim undercut by the style of his work.

in *Cathleen ni Houlihan*, and doing just the same to smuggle herself into Ireland in 1917 when banned from the country. A cocker spaniel belonging to Constance Markiewicz taken solemnly into custody by Dublin Castle detectives.

Yeats, Gonne and Markiewicz brought a theatrical panache to revolutionary politics, more at home with the grand gesture than the finance committee; and Connie Markiewicz ran her bit of the Irish revolution with all the imperious authority with which she ran her servants. On the Sunday before the Rising, the Abbey actor Sean Connolly played the leading role in his namesake James Connolly's drama *Under Which Flag?*; both men were to be killed in the insurrection which followed. Actors rehearsing a Yeats play at the Abbey are said to have abandoned their production to join in the rebellion. An Irish nurse attending the wounded in O'Connell Street was awarded a bit part in a West End review called *Three Cheers*.[71] An acquaintance of Patrick Kavanagh refused to believe that the civil war was real: 'It's only a dodge to fool England', he would remark.[72] When Yeats announces in his Nobel Prize address that 'It is too soon to say what will come to us from the melodrama and tragedy of the last four years',[73] it is unclear for an intriguing moment whether he is referring to the Abbey's bill of fare or independence and civil war. And all of this, for the Karl Marx of the *Eighteenth Brumaire of Louis Bonaparte*, is in the nature of bourgeois revolutions, events which he sees as inherently fictive or theatrical, full of panache and breathless rhetoric and historical cross-dressing, rising to an exuberant crescendo before sinking back, like some prolonged binge, into the 'crapulousness' of everyday life.

If fiction and reality mingled in the history of the period, so did they in the forms of the Revival themselves. Much of its art is representational, in contrast to the abstractions of the European avant-garde; but it is for the most part that curiously hybrid artistic form, *non-realist* representation, art faithful to an action which is itself realistically improbable, or one which represents it in a non-realist way. It is mimesis which Yeats melodramatically denounces: 'False art is not expressive, but mimetic, not from experience but from observation, and is the mother of all evil.'[74] The

---

71. See Edgar Holt, *Protest in Arms* (London 1960), p. 109. For a graphic eyewitness account of the Rising, see James Stephens, *The Insurrection in Dublin* (Dublin 1916).
72. See Patrick Kavanagh, *The Green Fool* (London 1975), p. 135.
73. W.B. Yeats, *Autobiographies* (London 1977), p. 571.
74. W.B. Yeats, *Essays and Introductions* (London 1961), p. 140.

novel for Yeats sums up all that is awry with both art and bourgeois
England: empirical, sentimental, moralistic, utilitarian, in contrast to an
art which is gestural, extravagant, ceremonial, reckless, decorative, lavish
and fantastic. It is a war, in effect, between naturalism and Nietzsche. The
anti-mimetic impulse of the Revival is thus both modernist and patrician
together: aristocrats can become avant-gardists precisely because they reject
bourgeois realism from a pre-bourgeois standpoint. That realism was also
the cultural dominant of Britain lent this dismissal a sharper edge. Like
Martin and Mary Doul, the vagrant couple of Synge's *The Well of the
Saints*, the Anglo-Irish cast a cold eye on a harsh reality and plumped
instead for their own fictions.

If Yeats lavishes such attention on dramatic texture and theatrical technique, on the sound of a phrase or the colour of a costume, it is because
it is here that for him ideology is crystallized, in the very forms of the
work itself, in practice and production rather than in text.[75] Symbolism
refuses common experience in the name of some deeper essence which
is its abiding truth; and this is at once an anxious disavowal of reality on
the part of those adrift within it, and a superior form of cognition and
control. The gap between phenomenon and secret essence in the work of
art is a version of the split between the hot-faced money changers and
the true aristocratic spirit of the nation. By being buried from view, that
spirit is preserved from the pollution of a degraded reality; yet since it is
the hidden truth of that world, it has the final edge over it. To re-create
the phenomena in the light of their essences – the programme of literary
symbolism – is thus to recast middle-class Ireland as a society with its
hereditary rulers still secretly in command. The elusiveness of these secret
essences is both an assault on a bourgeois positivism which prefers its
truths clear cut, and the effect of a Celticist politics which could never
quite succeed in saying what it meant.[76] The spirit of the nation is at
once what is most real about it and eternally ineffable, that which resists
expression and so can be shown but not said. Only if the earthly forms
which express it could be induced to transcend and abolish themselves

75. As far as colour goes, Yeats insisted that the red cloaks designed by Annie Horniman
for a production of *On Baile's Strand* should be abandoned, since they made the actors look
like fire extinguishers or a bunch of Father Christmases. See James W. Flannery, *Miss Annie
F. Horniman and the Abbey Theatre* (Dublin 1970), p. 15.

76. Lady Gregory writes that 'I myself never quite understood the meaning of the "Celtic
Movement" which we were said to belong to. When I was asked about it, I used to say it
was a movement meant to persuade the Scotch to buy our books, while we continued not
to buy theirs' (*Our Irish Theatre*, Gerrards Cross 1972, p. 72).

would that spirit shine forth in all its fullness, but it would then be a mere bodiless cypher.

Theatre mediates here between mind and society, since it is a realm of mysterious symbols with a materiality of its own, a materiality to which Yeats, inspired by dance or Gordon Craig or the Noh drama, paid studious attention. At one pole lies a purely non-mimetic theatre, in which as in dance or circus or the theatre of cruelty the dramatic signifier is utterly non-representational, figures nothing but itself, collapses together the time and space of signification with the time and space of the signified.[77] At the other pole lies the despised mimetic theatre, in which the signifier is robbed of its materiality, obediently effacing itself before its referent. But midway between these forms is the art of non-realist representation, an ontologically ambivalent theatre which, as with Brecht or Beckett, is both material and representational together, both real and fictional; and this divided space lends itself particularly well to the politics of the Celtic Revival, for which on the one hand the creative mind triumphs over the drearily actual, but which on the other hand celebrates the real, the soil, the sensuous peasant life where all the symbolic ladders start. Like art itself, that organic peasant order is at once more and less real than the middle-class normality which overlays it – its underlying truth, to be sure, but precisely because underlying condemned to a shadowy, fantastic existence.

The time of this patrician art is a sacred one, in contrast to the mere empty, homogeneous time of, say, the *Playboy* riots. It is a mythic temporality, static and frozen, which thus has a troubled relation to the profane history whose truth it seeks to lay bare. In arresting that history, it creates a still point through which some more ancient, eschatological time may emerge from its depths – a time which may therefore illuminate profane history, but only at the risk of robbing it of its dynamic and so falsifying it. Yeats's 'Easter 1916' is a case in point, a poem which turns to advantage the fact that the British have gathered the Post Office rebels into the artifice of eternity by repeating the gesture itself, this time as mythopoeic. The Rising, a kind of comic theatre in the first place, is constituted as real by the performative power of Yeats's fiction, which with typical Anglo-Irish idealism promulgates it after the event into authentic existence. In this sense the poem imitates the action of the

---

77. 'Can I say that a play has a time of its own, which is not a segment of historical time? I.e. I can distinguish earlier and later within it but there is *no sense* to the question whether the events in it take place, say, before or after Caesar's death' (Ludwig Wittgenstein, *Culture and Value*, Chicago 1984, p. 10e).

Rising itself, which proclaims into being something which plainly does not exist. It is not clear whether that act of utterance from the Post Office steps was 'avant-garde', ushering into the world something inconceivably new, or purely traditional, affirming a state of affairs – an independent Ireland – which had never ceased to exist. Whatever the answer, Yeats's own creative act is an instance of Benjamin's anti-historicist consciousness, blasting the Rising out of the continuum of history as the British have just blasted the rebels out of it. Benjamin advocated this surrealist historiography as a way of liberating some stirring event from its actual historical consequences, which in the case of past insurrections usually meant failure, and gathering it instead into that storehouse of dialectical images which would be the poet's contribution to the revolutionary movement. What he desires, so he remarks in his great essay on surrealism, is 'to expel moral metaphor from politics and to discover in political action a sphere reserved one hundred percent for images'.[78] This is exactly Yeats's ambition too, to have done with all that tedious English moralizing, mimesis and opinion-mongering and fashion in its place a sphere of non-discursive images which would structure the revolution rather than reflect it.

The 'subjective' or idealist strain of nationalism lent itself to this task rather more readily than some more materialist politics. 'Neither the grammars of the Gaelic League nor the industrialism of the *Leader*, nor the *Sinn Fein* attacks upon the Irish party, give sensible images to the affections', Yeats writes in *Autobiographies*.[79] In seeking to replace the detestable abstractions of politics – a matter for shopkeepers and shameless women – with the concretions of myth and image, he seems unaware that this is just another form of politics – that a conservative politics is usually one which denies the very category of the political itself. In any case, in pitting the proudly singular image against the discursive prose of middle-class reason, Yeats, like Blake, will soon enough have to avoid being enslaved by another's mythology by weaving those images into a total system, which then turns out to have all the abstraction of the politics he scorns. In the meanwhile, however, the fact of the executed leaders is one such mute image, as death, re-enacted by the poet's own mythopoeic ritual, turns them into signifiers as purely expressive as the death's head of Benjamin's *Trauerspiel*. Yet the idealist Yeats, conjuring events

---

78. Walter Benjamin, 'Surrealism', in *One-Way Street and Other Writings* (London 1979), p. 238.
79. Yeats, *Autobiographies*, p. 494.

into being with all the bravura of Berkeleyan epistemology, is also too canny a realist not to throw an anxious glance sideways at the possible effects or non-effects of this impetuous political action, half-tempted to reinsert it into the very continuum of history from which his lordly myth-making has just lifted it free. If England delivers Home Rule after all, what was the point? History is itself an effect of rhetoric; but this is only half the story, since the poem acknowledges its own belatedness vis-à-vis a history beyond its control in the very act of trying to place itself at its creative source.

Anglo-Irish realism, humbly aware of its own marginal place within a Gaelic nationalist narrative, sits cheek by jowl with a compensating epistemic authority. This tension between the symbolic and the imaginary, between acknowledging that the world turns its back on you and insisting that it would vanish without your presence, is common enough in Yeats. If he is sometimes to be found cavalierly converting the real to the symbolic, turning a swan into an emblem the instant it glides into view, he is also to be found anxiously querying the 'fit' between symbol and stubborn reality, asking himself whether a particular figure will suffice, setting up his creaking allegorical machinery in full view of the reader, or wondering aloud whether these images are not in any case so much straw in comparison to the imperfect business of the heart. It is thus never quite possible to know how seriously he is taking his own mythic powers, as when he solemnly mythologizes a group of Cheshire Cheese poetasters he must have known were a bunch of dopeheads and spongers, or prudently qualifies a description of leprechauns spinning on their pointed hats with the scholarly reservation 'but only in the north-eastern counties'.[80] When Yeats announces in oracular vein that 'I dreamed the other night that I was being hanged, but was the life and soul of the party',[81] it is well-nigh impossible to separate mask from reality, the poseur from the sincere eccentric. A poet who literally lives in one of his own symbols is either peculiarly self-mythologizing or unusually self-ironizing, and the question with this passionate, posturing man is sometimes undecidable.

If Yeats's images go to compose a myth, Benjamin's are out to undo that entire sphere. Myth for Benjamin is the realm of the naturalized, which he remarked would survive as long as the last beggar; and the revolutionary image must strike disruptively into these organic narratives. Yeats, by contrast, fashions his images and then claims to have stumbled

---

80. J. Frayne, ed., *Uncollected Prose by W.B. Yeats* (London 1970), p. 180.
81. Quoted by Lady Gregory, *Our Irish Theatre*, p. 37.

across them in the immanent structure of the real. He is forever conjuring from the world with one hand what he has just slipped into it with the other, to the point where in 'The Fisherman' he can address an entire poem to one of his own images, treating the mind-created as an autonomous object. The faith that reality is a construct of the mind, which allows a sinking Ascendancy to assert a last edge over a history which flouts them, is not entirely at one with the equally ideological enterprise of giving authority to your myths by projecting them into the world. It is the difference between subjective and objective idealism, and Yeats draws on either epistemological strategy as it suits him.[82]

To close the gap between mind and world by seeing the world as the upshot of a performative act of mind is to merge the language of the subject with that of the object; and this, among other things, is a way of narrowing a traditional Irish dichotomy between rhetoric and reality. The extravagant discourse of the Young Irelanders is grotesquely at odds with their political situation, just as the bombast of an O'Connell overshoots his cautiously pragmatic purposes. (Though one can put the point in reverse: what kind of political language would have been adequate to the horror of the Famine?) As with the slipshod poetry of the bourgeois revolutions of Marx's *Brumaire*, exorbitant forms conceal a painful paucity of content. The impassioned rhetoric needed to unite a diverse range of interests behind a programme of modest political demands becomes farcically disproportionate to that programme itself; and there is usually the need to placate your left wing with some suitably apocalyptic talk while playing for the political centre ground. The real political issues in Ireland are often enough drably prosaic, a matter of rent and potatoes, but in a colonial context these commonplace questions open up a much more dramatic scenario of conquest and subjection, which is enough to raise the rhetorical temperature. And that florid language can become often enough a poor compensation for political impotence.[83] The very

---

82. Were it not an undue concession to the tyranny of metanarrative, one might mention here that much the same is true of the great medieval Irish theologian John Scottus Eriugena, for whom 'knowledge is the absorption or subsumption of reality into thought', and for whom 'the mind contains and circumscribes the whole world and ... the spatio-temporal world is essentially immaterial and incorporeal' (Dermot Moran, 'Nature, Man and God in the Philosophy of John Scottus Eriugena', in Richard Kearney, ed., *The Irish Mind*, Dublin 1985, pp. 103, 104).

83. Though a more positive reading of the gap between rhetoric and reality is also possible: 'For the Irish, language did not merely obsequiously and oppressively reflect the real, it foreshadowed future plenitude' (Thomas A. Boylan and Timothy P. Foley, *Political Economy and Colonial Ireland*, London 1992, p. 124).

colonial conditions which confront the Irish with the need for an action of epic grandeur simultaneously ensure that they will never really be up to it.

The greatest of all Irish novels turns on an ironic unity-cum-discrepancy between a humdrum text and a heroic subtext. Like the Easter Rising, *Ulysses* remains ambiguously suspended between the mythic and the real. Seamus Deane reads the work as a performative act which reflects the structure of Irish political rhetoric: '[Joyce] had learned from Irish nationalism the power of a vocabulary in bringing to existence that which otherwise had none except in the theatre of words.'[84] But this time it will be a successful performative, in contrast to the flailing rhetoric of Young Ireland, since in fiction the reality signified is at one with the means of signification. If language cannot correspond to the world because the world isn't up to it, then it can always take itself as its own reference point. Joyce's fiction aims for a utopian equivalence of discourse and reality, and Yeats's mind-made history aims for another. To assert that a preposterous, pragmatical world lives only in the poet's mind is to proclaim an imaginary relation between subject and object, and so to resolve in fantasy a real contradiction. As his fellow fantasist George Moore put the point in *Hail and Farewell*: 'reality can destroy the dream, why shouldn't the dream be able to destroy reality?'[85]

So much is evident too in the drama of J.M. Synge, which explores a conflict between ideal and reality in its content while holding the two together in its forms. Individual and society, heroism and the common life, may be at loggerheads in Synge's theatre, but this conflict is contained within a sumptuous wealth of language, so that the form of the plays celebrates a utopian community undercut by their bleakly realist narratives.[86] Idealism, unceremoniously shown the door in the dramatic action, re-enters as verbal exuberance. That dramatic language hovers in its turn between the realist and non-realist: as one commentator puts it, there is no phrase in Synge that a real Irish peasant might not have used, but

---

84. Deane, *Celtic Revivals*, p. 105.
85. George Moore, *Hail and Farewell* (Gerrards Cross 1976), p. 120.
86. Much the same is true of some of Synge's prose accounts of the Irish peasantry, which are realist in content but Romantic in form: the elderly tramp encountered on the lonely glenside who delivers an eloquent tale of deprivation. See, for example, 'The Vagrants of Wicklow' and 'The Oppression of the Hills' in *The Works of John M. Synge*, vol. 4 (Dublin 1910). There is a similar interplay of realism and idealism in some of the dramas of Lady Gregory. See Ann Saddlemyer, ed., *The Comedies of Lady Gregory* (Gerrards Cross 1970), and *The Tragedies and Tragic-Comedies of Lady Gregory* (Gerrards Cross 1970).

nobody talked like that all the time.[87] Naturalism is socially engaged but disenchanted, whereas symbolism is idealist but socially irresponsible; Synge will therefore outflank them both with an idealized brand of realism, and so with a poetics marvellously well-suited to Anglo-Irish populism. It also meant that he could be shot down from both sides of the fence, accused alike of sentimental idealism and scurrilous realism.

But if form and content are at odds at one level in Synge, they are united at another. Within the drama, fiction often enough gives birth to reality; and in this sense the plays brood obliquely on their own epistemology, displacing it in a kind of *mise en abyme* into the action on stage, finding their own formal operations mirrored in the topos of the life-giving lie. The plays claim truth to a referent – peasant life – which at the same time, by an artful construction of language, they bring into being; so that like Yeats Synge is both anxious to conform his language to a world independent of it, and actually brings that world to birth in the process. This double operation is then an allegory of progressive Anglo-Irish politics, which looks to some humble integration with the peasant masses, yet fashions them in its own image. An aesthetic hegemony replaces the failed search for political leadership. The peasant is 'other' to the upper-class intellectual, who must therefore transform his own language to capture this difference, yet the peasant is also, as natural aristocrat, a kind of mirror image of himself. The loneliness of the disinherited intellectual finds its echo in the collective isolation of peasant life, but discovers there too a community which might compensate for it. It is not for nothing that Synge felt wonderfully at home on the Aran islands, and a complete outsider. And if the peasant is a natural aristocrat, then he or she overturns the opposition between Art and Nature, allowing Synge's drama to follow suit. By discovering a gorgeously wrought language among the people themselves, his plays are able to suppress their own status as verbal constructs, displacing this opulence from their form to their content.

Like the society he inhabited, then, Synge is both modern and traditional together. If he estranges language in modernist style, it is because the speech he uses is so quaintly archaic as to appear enthrallingly new. If his plays criticize traditional society in their content, they affirm it in

---

87. L.A.G. Strong, quoted by Alan J. Bliss, 'The Language of Synge', in Maurice Harmon, ed., *J.M. Synge: Centenary Papers 1971* (Dublin 1972), p. 45. For Synge and the west of Ireland, see Luke Gibbons, 'Synge, Country and Western', in C. Curtin et al., eds, *Culture and Ideology in Ireland* (Galway 1984).

their forms. His focus on the lone character breaking loose from a coercive society is a familiar modernist motif; but the figure around whom it turns is usually the traditional one of the vagrant. It is in the beggar, the outcast, the social misfit that the Anglo-Irish artist can find an objective correlative of his own solitary nonconformism, rather than in some more collective political revolt.

If the verbal profusion of Synge's plays is, among other things, a utopian compensation for the barrenness of their reality,[88] something of the same can be said – though with a good deal more qualification – of the theatre of Sean O'Casey. Raymond Williams sees the paradox of *Riders to the Sea* as lying in 'the depth of its language and the starved, almost passive experience', and in similar vein notes O'Casey's habit of indulging in gratuitous colour imagery to enliven an equally sterile world.[89] But the blather and and compulsive alliterating of O'Casey's 'deprived, fantasy-ridden talkers', as Williams describes them,[90] are clearly more part of the problem than the solution. Indeed O'Casey dramatizes the condition to which the performative art of Yeats and Joyce is a response: a mismatch between language and reality, at once farcical and tragic, in which the more men and women are victimized by history, the more a self-consciously poetic speech freewheels impotently around the action. Other Irish dramatists may seek to heal this division by projecting the ideal into the common life, but O'Casey's naturalistic space is so constructed as to split them down the middle.[91] The typical space of naturalism, so Williams argues, is a closed room in which characters react passively to a history which is always offstage. The forces which shape these men and women are thus condemned by the dramatic form itself to remain invisible and opaque, impossible to bring on stage without breaking beyond this mould into some less claustrophobic form of theatre.[92] O'Casey's typical room is part of a tenement building with a good deal of toing and froing, and so hovers between a private and a communal space in the way that an

---

88. For the ways in which form in modernism is sometimes compensatory in this sense, gratuitously decorating an alienated exprience, see Fredric Jameson, *The Political Unconscious* (London 1981), Ch. 5.

89. Raymond Williams, *Drama from Ibsen to Brecht* (London 1968), pp. 133, 150.

90. Ibid., p. 149.

91. There is, of course, more to O'Casey's theatre than naturalism: farce, music hall, fantasy, melodrama and a good few other forms mingle freely with it. But Williams's general point is, I think, valid. For an account of the importance of the non-naturalistic in O'Casey, see Ronald Ayling, 'Sean O'Casey and the Abbey Theare', in David Krause and Robert G. Lowery, eds, *Sean O'Casey: Centenary Essays* (Gerrards Cross 1980).

92. Williams, *Drama from Ibsen to Brecht*, Conclusion.

Ibsenite or Chekhovian living room does not; nobody in O'Casey ever seems to knock at a door. The stage can thus accommodate a community alongside the lone individual of classical naturalism, and find in this group of grotesques and good neighbours a spontaneous politics more vital and warm-hearted than anything that nationalism has to offer. The structure of feeling of naturalism, with its trapped, isolated protagonists, is crossed with the popular forms of music hall and burlesque, as the parlour becomes a pantomime.

Even so, nothing in Irish drama fits Williams's case quite so well as O'Casey, whose men and women gabble colourfully away while just beyond the door their destinies are being determined for them by a history which is always elsewhere. This divided theatrical space incarnates what for O'Casey is the eternal rift between rhetoric and reality, heroism and a seedy humanity; in *The Plough and the Stars*, nothing of the Easter Rising appears on stage but the shadow of Patrick Pearse as he spouts his revolutionary oratory just outside the pub window. It is a stagey brand of rhetoric, but no longer in the literal sense of the word. The scene is a caricature of Williams's point, and one that caters well enough to contemporary liberal prejudice: grand political gestures are one thing, everyday life quite another.[93] But as an image of Irish nationalism in general, O'Casey's naturalistic space is significantly falsifying. For what distinguishes that tradition, from the United Irishmen and O'Connell to the Land League and Sinn Fein, is exactly its mass popular base. It was a politics which engaged the active participation of thousands or even millions, in contrast to a liberal politics which demands of its supporters no more than their votes. That the United Irish movement involved both the common people and – from time to time – a degree of heroic courage, or that O'Connellite compaigns were at once common and spectacular, is then silently suppressed by the forms of O'Casey's drama, as it is by a jaded liberal wisdom for which the folk are spontaneously non-political and fancy ideas the preserve of the few. It is a curiously elitist form of anti-elitism. O'Casey's image is true in its fashion to a *particular* political event – the vanguardist insurrection of 1916 – but false on the whole to the history from which it flowed.

Whereas Yeats and Synge oppose the commonplace political world with an aesthetic truth, O'Casey counters it with his own strain of sentimental

---

93. A view uncritically endorsed by David Krause in his *Sean O'Casey: The Man and his Work* (New York 1960). For an alternative viewpoint, see C. Desmond Greaves, *Sean O'Casey: Politics and Art* (London 1979). O'Casey's *The Story of the Irish Citizen Army* (Dublin 1919) is still of interest.

moralism. Ideal and actual can fuse only in the figure of the woman, who is at once more realistic than her fantasizing menfolk and more morally heroic. The heroism which in Synge was at odds with domesticity has now itself become domesticated, and the family, in fiercely patriarchal Ireland, offered as a model of the non-political. In Yeats, myth displaces history, but only to shed a deeper light upon it; with O'Casey, history is sidelined by a domestic rather than mythical space which is secretly part of it. O'Casey is the insider trying to get out, and his objectifying forms reflect it; Yeats and Synge are semi-outsiders trying to get in, as their idealizing forms suggest. In the end, O'Casey is as much caught between populism and elitism as Yeats himself, swinging from Rabelaisian raciness to the ivory tower, from a celebration of the folk to a sense of the artist's superior mission.[94] The attitudes are not as opposed as they seem: both belong to a complex Romantic heritage, which counters the debased realm of politics either with an earthiness that cuts below it, or a spiritual wisdom which soars above it.

The Revivalists, then, combine tradition and modernity, but largely under the sway of the former. If the building which the Abbey Theatre took over was that token of modernity, a Mechanics' Institute, part of the site on which it stood had contained a morgue. With no sign of semantic strain, Theodore Roosevelt could celebrate the Abbey as 'one of the healthiest signs of the revival of the ancient Irish spirit which has been so marked a feature of the world's progress during the present generation'.[95] The theatre's chief luminary was later to assemble a group of eighteenth-century forebears (Swift, Berkeley, Goldsmith, Burke) who were all in their different ways indebted to Enlightenment, and turn them by a brazen sleight of hand into an unequivocally anti-modern heritage. And though this backward glance was soon to be eclipsed in Ireland by a more briskly modernizing brand of nationalism, the Free State to which it finally gave birth stood for an introverted form of capitalism languishing under an archaic superstructure.

With Joyce, the archaic and the avant-garde also come to form strange combinations, but this time under the dominion of the latter. When

---

94. The Rabelaisian raciness is most irritatingly on show in the prose style of O'Casey's autobiographical writings, with its self-consciously rollicking quality. Even so, the auto-biographies are a valuable record of the Irish revolution and its bloody aftermath. For the latter, see Sean O'Casey, *Inishfallen, Fare Thee Well* (London 1949).

95. Quoted in Lady Gregory, *Our Irish Theatre*, p. 245.

Stephen Dedalus speaks of his ambition to embrace the loveliness that has not yet come into the world, he speaks as an avant-gardist. As for nationalism, Joyce could see nothing in it but regression: 'The Irish nation's insistence on developing its own culture by itself is not so much the demand of a young nation that wants to make good in the European concert as the demand of a very old nation to renew under new forms the glories of a past civilisation.'[96] The fact that it might be both together apparently did not occur to him. Joyce's work reveals how the modern, pressed to an extreme, curves back into the sphere of primitive mythology – how the newly emergent world of international monopoly capitalism, with its tight-meshed connections, global forms, cyclical rhythms, interchangeable human beings and deep determining forces, issues once again in a mythical form of consciousness.[97] The difference-in-sameness which in the case of myth is a constant permutation of a few invariable elements turns up in modern capitalism as that eternal recurrence of the slightly modified which is the commodity. The proto-structuralist Joyce was fascinated by the fact that a mere twenty-six marks could yield an infinity of words; the ruthless parsimony of Samuel Beckett, conjuring an evening's entertainment out of a pitifully meagre clutch of components, is a later instance of this ascetic cast of mind. With Synge, a tribal or village form of community exists on the margins of modernity; Joyce's work is already prefiguring the global village of twentieth-century life. *Finnegans Wake* has all the synchrony of the pre-modern world of mythology, as well as of that more up-to-date invention, the Freudian unconscious.

And if Joyce's blend of the progressive and the primitive can be turned against the tedium of modernity, it can equally be deployed to undo the aura of the archaic. The modern itself can be unmasked as just another myth; but it follows that any other myth can be relativized too, which undermines the numinous authority which Yeats and his colleagues would claim for that way of seeing. Joyce projects the logic of the modern into mythology itself, transforming it into a world of perpetual motion in

---

96. E. Mason and R. Ellmann, eds, *James Joyce: The Critical Writings* (London 1964), p. 157.

97. A point which Ezra Pound appreciated in his own way: in *Ulysses*, he remarked, Joyce had 'presented the whole occident under the domination of capital' (quoted by Deane, *Celtic Revivals*, p. 105). For an interesting Marxist critique of Joyce, though one unduly dismissive of his Irish context, see Franco Moretti's chapter on Joyce in *Signs Taken for Wonders* (London 1983). I have discussed these matters more fully in my 'Joyce and Mythology', in Susan Dick et al., eds, *Omnium Gatherum: Essays for Richard Ellmann* (Gerrards Cross 1989).

which mythemes merge and split, exchange and circulate, with all the promiscuity of the commodity form. For Yeats and Synge, myth is more than a formal device; it is also, as it was for Nietzsche, a privileged mode of cognition. And this, as with T.S. Eliot, is always a mark of modernism's darker, more irrationalist face. Joyce, mythologizer *par excellence*, is also the great demythologizer for whom myth is more formal technique than source of superior knowledge, for whom no single myth is privileged, for whom a seedy middle-aged cuckold can play Odysseus, and who – as a good scholastic – prizes a verbal and analytic reason while taking the measure of what it fails to encompass. With his grocer-like, compulsively cataloguing mind, he is not especially enamoured of the ineffable, which is usually obscurely linked with right-wing mystification.

The Ibsen whom Joyce so deeply admired centres his dramas on that moment of tragic deadlock in which the present, in the very act of reaching out for a liberated future, is crushed beneath the burden of the past.[98] The demand for emancipation from the past is absolute; but as the present stretches eagerly forward it confronts that past as a barrier blocking its path, breaking down the movement to freedom from the inside. In a tragic version of modernism, the present is suspended between an unbreachable past and an unattainable future, and slowly withers to death between them. It is not hard to read this stalemated moment as allegorical of the fate of so many modern movements of political emancipation, which like Irish nationalism carry the burden of the past with them into the future. And it is not hard either to see just what it is about Ibsen which Joyce might have found so appealing. Bourgeois independence movements run up against their own structural limits and are thrown into self-contradiction; and Ibsen, born into an overwhelmingly rural society which like Ireland had a newly emergent middle class, is exploring among other things the spiritual equivalent of this tragic self-thwarting. Between the end of the *Portrait* and the beginning of *Ulysses*, Stephen Dedalus has run into something very much like this deadlock; but Joyce parts company with Ibsen by refusing to press it through to its tragic finale. Instead, this privileged moment – always for Ibsen a starkly individualist encounter – is relativized within the great polyphony of discourses which is *Ulysses*, and implicitly upbraided, through the figure of Leopold Bloom, as a refusal to accept the fact of material limitation. Stephen must learn to cling to the actual rather than live so kinetically, and this tough-minded naturalism, so it would seem, is part of his author's debt to Ibsen. But the

---

98. See Williams, *Drama from Ibsen to Brecht*, Part 1, Ch. 1.

problem for Ibsen himself is that the actual *is* kinetic, driven by a desire for freedom which can be neither abandoned nor realized. Joyce resolves this dilemma by displacing that desire into language itself, which will then in its infinite plurality figure as a utopian image of the freedom of which Ibsen's lonely, tormented figures can only dream. It is in this sense that Joyce's writings act as a critique of the bourgeois revolution. But the ceaseless dynamism of their language coexists with an equable acceptance of creaturely limit; and this is small comfort to the Ibsenite protagonist, or indeed the political revolutionary, whose problem lies not in a refusal of materiality but a refusal of *these particular* material conditions.

In the end, Joyce converts tragedy into comedy by prising apart the Ibsenite deadlock and combining its forces in new ways: the confrontation of freedom and limitation is now inherent in the synchronic play of language, which endlessly permutates its elements in a world where everything changes and nothing does. The tragic oppressiveness of history is overcome by comic simultaneity.[99] By embracing the actual, you are set free to celebrate its infinite combinations; but this cannot address a situation in which what blocks your freedom is not a failure to acknowledge the actual, but its specific historical nature. Joyce thus wins his image of liberty at the price of obscuring the process by which it could actually be achieved, in contrast to those nationalists who bent their energies to achieving freedom but whose version of it was a travesty. For all his modernizing scorn for the world of a Synge, he too finds the utopian element of a barren social reality in the language let loose to depict it. The wealth of that language is an implicit satire of the seedy world it records; but it also graces and dignifies that world, in democratic defiance of the Coole Park idealism which would belittle it.

Joyce thus buys his opposition to that idealism at the price of a naturalism which implies that no radical change is really possible, that everything is a recycled, intertextual version of something else, and so undercuts Yeatsian apocalypse and the fantasies of the radical right at the risk of a serene celebration of the given or a mild Bloomian reformism. The limits of his textual politics are thus the limits of a naturalistic aesthetics; and there is no question of how radical that aesthetics could be in the face of an idealism like Synge's, which could embrace common

---

99. Much the same can be said of Joyce's fantasia of the unconscious – for though Freudianism is hardly a comic doctrine it is certainly an anti-linear one, conflating past and present or reading their relations backwards in (for example) the conundrum of the Oedipus complex. Here too, as it the play of freedom and limitation within language, the drive for emancipation, and what obstructs it, are born together, synchronic rather than successive.

experience only in aestheticized form, or of a naturalism like O'Casey's, which could be little more than a high-sounding name for despising ordinary people. But naturalism for Ibsen meant both an openness to the actual and an emancipation from its most death-dealing aspects; and it was the final clash of those values which made of him a tragic artist. Joyce circumvents that tragedy by displacing the emancipation into a language which revels in the actual, and so unleashes in the here and now a plurality to which the Ibsenite hero, single-mindedly pursuing his goal, must damagingly close his eyes. Much the same can be said of the Irish nationalists whom Joyce opposed. As Brecht knew, those who attempt to create the conditions for human freedom can rarely be the best examples of it themselves. It is in this sense that, in becoming the utopian mythologer of the revolution, Joyce was unable to be its political supporter.

CHAPTER 8

OSCAR AND GEORGE

George Bernard Shaw was a Lamarckian, or so he thought. But what the English *fin de siècle* understood as Lamarckianism was very different from the genuine article. In his *Système des animaux sans vertèbres* (1801), Jean Pierre Antoine de Monet, Chevalier de Lamarck, argues that structural adaptations in living organisms are the result of their acquisition of new needs, and that these changes are genetically transmissable. The theory can be summarized in the slogan 'need precedes structure': organic modifications arise from an organism's response to fresh needs, so that – in a hackneyed example – the giraffe acquired its long neck from aeons of straining, not because shorter-necked creatures confronted with edible but inaccessible tree tops inevitably died out.[1]

There is nothing necessarily idealist about this doctrine. On the contrary, Lamarck himself was a full-blooded materialist who declares in his *Recherches sur l'organisation des corps vivants* of 1802 that life is a completely natural phenomenon, and sees the medium of the 'feelings' which compel organisms to adapt their structures as some kind of 'nervous fluid'. There is no stress here on some dim spiritual striving or intimation of a higher state which impels an animal to transform its material being. The 'feelings' which motivate such adaptations are symptoms of physiological need, not stirrings of subjective desire: the bird does not 'wish' to land feet-first on water but is compelled to do so by environmental necessity, and over immense periods of time will develop the webbed toes essential for a successful put-down. Material necessity produces an excitation in the 'nervous fluid' of the organism, which in turn gradually effects structural transformation. Nor is there any suggestion here of a singular 'life force' driving on these various developments; Lamarck holds

---

1. See A.S. Packard, *Lamarck: His Life and Work* (London 1901). See also Lamarck's *Philosophical Zoology*, translated by Hugh Elliott (London 1914).

to a tree-like complexity of the origins of life, not to some single linear principle.[2]

The most influential English disciple of Lamarck, Herbert Spencer, first ran across the theory in Lyell's *Principles of Geology*, where it is expounded only to be refuted.[3] Spencer was nonetheless impressed, and in his *Social Statics* made the vital positivist move of translating this biological hypothesis into a theory of social evolution. His essay 'On the Development Hypothesis' explicitly expounds the Lamarckian doctrine;[4] but in Spencer's hands this has now become the grandiose vision of a human history which progressively shucks off outmoded forms until human consciousness, and the material structures of society, converge in the telos of moral perfection. Lamarck's own modest theory of local structural adaptations to new biological circumstance has been boldly projected into a mighty cosmic law:

> The modifications mankind have undergone ... result from a law underlying the whole of organic creation ... As surely as the tree becomes bulky when it stands alone ... as surely as the skin of a labourer's hand [tends to become] thick ... so surely must the human faculties be moulded into complete fitness for the social state; so surely must evil and immorality disappear; so surely must man become perfect.[5]

We have leapt from the long-necked giraffe to the utopian state, from webbed feet to the cessation of warfare. The humble claim that environmentally bred needs result in organic transformation has now evolved into the doctrine that there is at work in Nature a law by which social institutions are constantly moulded to a progressively self-perfecting humanity. If Lamarck holds that organs can become degenerate through disuse and be replaced by others, Spencer conjures from this a perfectibilist history of the human species. If Lamarck claims that acquired physical characteristics are transmissable, Spencer plucks from this a theory of cultural evolution. The law which he identifies as impelling the whole of creation is still a scientific affair rather than a spiritual force; but the way

---

2. It is arguable that he differs here from Erasmus Darwin, who anticipates some of his findings in his *Zoonomia* (London 1794), but holds that all animals originate from 'a single living filiament'.

3. See John Burrows, *Evolution and Society* (London 1966), p. 188.

4. See Herbert Spencer, *Essays*, vol. 1 (London 1858). Spencer also claims in his late work *Factors in Organic Evolution* (London 1887) that natural-selection theory needs to be complemented with the Lamarckian hypothesis, and repeats the claim in his pamphlet *The Inadequacy of Natural Selection* (London 1893).

5. *Social Statics* (London 1851), p. 65.

has been prepared for its translation to semi-mystical status. The determinism of this law belongs with its autonomy of the human race: confronted with this implacable dynamic, human agency is in danger of being radically devalued.

It is Samuel Butler who will press this thesis in the direction of a full-blown vitalism. In his *Evolution, Old and New*, Butler quotes a lengthy passage from Spencer's 'Essay on the Development Hypothesis' and comments admiringly: 'This leaves nothing to be desired. It is Buffon, Dr. Darwin, and Lamarck, well expressed.'[6] In his earlier *Life and Habit*, Butler posits an unconscious memory in the human species which, as the accumulated heritage of acquired ancestral characteristics, has some loose affinity with Lamarckianism. The root causes of evolution, *pace* Darwin, are to be found in the 'needs and experiences' of creatures themselves – in 'faith and desire, aided by intelligence'.[7] But if 'needs and experiences' is an acceptably Lamarckian phrase, 'faith and desire' is hardly true to the master's scientific materialism. Butler marks a point where that doctrine, while preserving something of its scientific status, is becoming steadily subjectivized and idealized. Lamarck had insisted that the roots of structural transformation lay in the organism's experience of need, and to that exent the motivating force of the evolutionary process is 'subjective'; but this felt need is for Lamarck the reflex of environmental necessity, not some state of consciousness which transcends material conditions altogether.

In *Evolution, Old and New*, Butler steadfastly avoids the term 'desire' in his account of Lamarck, clinging instead to the more prudent 'need' and 'want'. He also points out that Lamarck's concern with environment as the moulder of need is closer to the Darwinist account than the disapproving Darwinists like to think. Yet 'want' is of course an ambiguous word, equally suggestive of an objective lack and a subjective desire; and there are points in the book where Butler's case swerves towards an unLamarckian emphasis on the dominance of will or intelligence over material circumstance, subjective striving over objective necessity. He quotes with apparent endorsement Erasmus Darwin's claim in his *Zoonomia* that structural modifications spring from the 'desires and aversions' of animals, and criticizes Lamarck for his materialist reduction of intelligence to the brain. 'Who can tell', he asks, 'what ideas a worm does or does not form?'[8] Whatever the inherent fascination of the question, is it

---

6. *Evolution, Old and New* (1879; reprinted London 1911), p. 332.
7. See *Life and Habit* (London 1877), Appendix. See also Basil Willey, *Darwin and Butler: Two Versions of Evolution* (London 1959).
8. *Evolution, Old and New*, p. 255.

not the kind of inquiry which would have much enthralled Lamarck. Butler rejects the notion that all self-adapting organisms have some conscious sense of purpose and design; but he upbraids Lamarck, along with Buffon and Erasmus Darwin, for overlooking the teleological implications of their own theories. All three men were too myopically intent on scientific minutiae to recognize that they were, in effect, positing a continuity of intelligent purpose in Nature. What Butler has done, in the wake of Spencer, is to abstract Lamarck's local teleologies into a single life force at work in creation. Unlike Spencer, however, he presses this belief to a religious extreme. In *God the Known and God the Unknown*, and *Luck, or Cunning?*, the mysterious purposiveness which informs the whole of Nature is now a synonym for God. The essence of his work, he writes in 1886, 'is to insist on the omnipresence of mind and intelligence throughout the universe to which no name can be so fittingly applied as God'.[9] The long-necked giraffe has now been elevated into a spiritual alternative to the dismally mechanistic world of Victorian rationalism.

As Lamarckian theory moves from pigeons to pantheism, it comes to adapt to fresh needs in a way remarkably parallel to its own propositions. In the eyes of a utopian anarchist like Edward Carpenter, Lamarckianism suggests that 'there is a force at work throughout creation, ever urging each type onward into newer and newer forms...'[10] It is in this vitalized, idealized form that the doctrine will pass into the hands of George Bernard Shaw, where it merges with an equally reductive version of Nietzsche. Shaw's Lamarckian faith, paradoxically enough, is both the Romantic's refusal of a dreary scientific orthodoxy, and the revolt of a rationalist who sets a high value on sheer intelligence against a world sinisterly drained of human wit. Darwinism for Shaw suggests a chapter of senseless accidents against which he reacts with unwonted passion; but the other pole of his rejection is the subversively commonsensical assumption that any child could show Darwin to be mistaken. Lamarckian evolutionists 'have observed the simple fact that the will to do anything can and does, at a certain pitch of intensity set up by the conviction of its necessity, create and organize new tissue to do it with'.[11] The final vulgarization of Lamarck, long in the preparation, has been triumphantly carried through. The 'pitch of intensity' which triggers organic change is no longer, as in Lamarck, a physiological crisis in the 'nervous fluid', but an affirmation of faith and

9. Quoted by Willey, *Darwin and Butler*, p. 107.
10. Edward Carpenter, *Civilisation, Its Cause and Cure* (London 1889), p. 140.
11. Preface to *Back to Methuselah* (London 1945), p. xvii.

will; it is a subjective 'conviction of necessity', rather than objective biological need, which now holds sway. With a simple-mindedness strikingly at odds with his defence of cosmic intelligence, Shaw interprets Lamarck as holding that 'living organisms changed because they wanted to', and the whole theory can be summarized in the tag that 'when there's a will there's a way'. What Lamarck means, according to Shaw, is the banal credo that 'If you have no eyes, and want to see, and keep trying to see, you will finally get eyes.'[12] Lamarck's way is 'the way of life, will, aspiration, and achievement'; Nietzsche, 'thinking out the great central truth of the Will to Power', is a parallel figure. The fact that the Nietzschean will to power has precious little to do with willpower – that it is not a *psychological* category at all – is not a point over which Shaw lingers. Instead, a crude misprision of Lamarck, yoked to a voluntarist misreading of Nietzsche, provides him with the cosmic rationale for a Fabian programme of progressivist social engineering: 'If you can turn a pedestrian into a cyclist ... without the intervention of Circumstantial Selection, you can turn an amoeba into a man, or a man into a superman, without it.'[13] For 'you' here one may read the elite, who figure in Shaw as a cross between the Fabian technocrat and the Nietzschean *Übermensch*.

The creed of Creative Evolution, as Shaw calls it after Henri Bergson, resolves a number of awkward Victorian problems. It offers, as we have seen, a riposte to mechanical materialism; but since it is a spiritualized version of scientific laws it can combine a metaphysical teleology with well-founded scientific truth. 'My creed of Creative Evolution', Shaw remarks in his Preface to *On the Rocks*, 'differs from the old Dublin brimstone creed solely in its greater credibility; that is, in its more exact conformity to the facts alleged by our scientific workers...'[14] Like much Romanticism, evolutionary vitalism is ersatz religion, but of a tough-minded strain suitable to the Shavian sensibility. If the life force is the pith and essence of Nature, then the disabling duality of spiritual and material, noumenal and phenomenal, can be overcome. But so can the equally recalcitrant opposition of freedom and determinism. Herbert

---

12. Ibid., p. xxi.

13. Ibid., p. xxiii. For dicussions of Shaw's doctrines, see Eric Bentley, *Bernard Shaw* (London 1950), Ch. 2; and Julian B. Kaye, *Bernard Shaw and the 19th Century Tradition* (Norman, Okla. 1958), Ch. 5.

14. Preface to *On the Rocks*, in *Bernard Shaw: Collected Plays with their Prefaces* (London 1973), p. 606.

Spencer can ascribe a progressive purpose to the laws which drive history onwards and upwards; but those forces remain as relentlessly determinist as the iron laws of a mechanistic world. It is just that Spencer is able to add a benevolent telos to this implacability. In the hands of Butler and Shaw, however, the opposition between freedom and determinism can be deconstructed; for the life force lies at the very source of one's creative will, just as for orthodox Christian doctrine one's dependence on God lies at the very root of one's personal freedom.

Much the same is true of the Nietzschean will to power, which lives us far more than we live it, but which the *Übermensch* can wrest into the service of his own free self-fashioning. For Nietzsche, the world is utter chaos and the will to power absolutely bereft of purpose; so it seems odd for Shaw to yoke this resolutely anti-teleological vision to that of Creative Evolution. If he can do so without strain, it is because his version of the life force is in fact less Nietzschean than an upbeat version of the Schopenhauerian Will. The Nietzschean will to power is in no sense a subject, whereas the purposive, self-determining force which propels Schopenhauer's creation is exactly that. But the point of the coupling is to blend the consolations of cosmic determinism with the triumph of the free spirit. If a displaced form of Lamarckianism allows you to feel spiritually at one with the universe, since your very will is no more than its stealthy workings within you, the *Übermenschen* are both part of this cosmic process and a free-standing elite. Like the Hegelian philosopher or Carlylean hero, the superman is the one in whom the life force has finally achieved self-consciousness, and so can further its inscrutable purposes all the more effectively. Shaw thus adroitly combines dualism and monism, freedom and determinism, the solace of being at one with Nature with the audacity of an avant-garde. Nature is suffused with mind; but in the figure of the superman, mind simultaneously gains a victory over matter.

It is possible, perhaps, to detect in Shaw's vision of progress a mythified version of the ideology which inspired the Irish revolution.[15] It is as though he lends a cosmic setting to the briskly modernizing bent of men like Arthur Griffith and D.P. Moran. The social context of that revolution was Shaw's background too: urban, petty-bourgeois, modernist, upwardly mobile. As the son of a Dublin corn factor, he became an estate agent's

---

15. Douglas Hyde was a kind of unconscious Lamarckian: he once commented that the Irish vocal organs, given generations of Irish speaking, had developed differently from English ones, and thus were no fit instrument for the English language. See Tom Garvin, *Nationalist Revolutionaries in Ireland, 1858–1928* (Oxford 1987), p. 87.

clerk, then an émigré journalist and writer; and this, leaving aside his religious pedigree, was a fairly typical trajectory for an Irish nationalist of his day. Indeed Shaw was himself an Irish nationalist, though of a characteristically equivocal kind.[16] His triumphalist view of history, which he believed might finally come to abolish death itself, reflects the buoyancy of a rising class, whereas Yeats's cyclical vision of time is the outlook of a failing one. The Yeatsian cycle is compensatory: if your fortunes are presently plummeting, then the next whirl of the gyre might always spin you back on top.

Oscar Wilde sprang from a failing class too; indeed his life-span is more or less coterminous with the decline of Ascendancy fortunes. He was born a few years after the Famine, at a time when the Catholic middle classes were starting out on their long march to political power. The Church of Ireland was disestablished in his adolescence; the first Home Rule Bill was drafted around the time of his early literary success; and his death in 1900 coincides with the passing of the Land Acts which were to destroy the Ascendancy's economic power. Wilde's origin, as Lady Bracknell remarks of Jack Worthing, is thus a kind of terminus: he was born in a cul-de-sac, if not exactly a railway station, and his own crisis of identity shares in the chronic insecurity of an Anglo-Irish caste who, like some of the characters of *The Importance of Being Earnest*, were never quite able to say who they were. His rake's progress through English society seems an image of this crumbling splendour. One can feel, in Wilde's too-brilliant career, the gathering hubris of a man who is riding too high, hanging on by his wits, and who seems at times to be perversely courting disaster. Like the effervescent wit and intoxicating high spirits of *Earnest*, written at a time when the policeman's hand was just about to feel his collar, his life seems giddily sustained by nothing but its own exhilarating momentum. As with his Anglo-Irish countryman Charles Stewart Parnell, he is at first admired, then thrust out as immoralist and sexual transgressor. Just as his own profligate class in Ireland finally pulled the roof down upon their own heads, so Wilde's spendthrift lifestyle and flamboyant flouting of convention seems a race towards self-destruction, as though he was intent on wresting the initiative from others even in this, cutting himself down before the Establishment stepped in and did it for him.

---

16. Shaw was a Home Ruler vehemently opposed to Sinn Fein. For his views on Ireland, see David H. Greene and Dan H. Laurence, eds, *The Matter with Ireland* (London 1962). Shaw thought it a mistake to view nationalism as an end in itself; for a similar Shavian view, see Terry Eagleton, 'Nationalism: Irony and Commitment', in Seamus Deane, ed., *Nationalism, Colonialism and Literature* (Minneapolis 1990).

It is intriguing, then, that like Bernard Shaw the young Wilde was a disciple of Herbert Spencer. In a very early essay, 'The Rise of Historical Criticism',[17] he emerges, surprisingly enough, as a full-blooded scientific rationalist in the high Victorian tradition. The essay is a two-finger exercise in the Spencerian philosophy of history, full of tough-minded stuff about inexorable historical laws. The germ of the philosophy of history, Wilde writes in Comtean vein, is the discovery of 'some one formula of law which may serve to explain the different manifestations of all organic bodies, *man included* ... the one scientific basis on which the true philosophy of history must rest is the complete knowledge of the laws of human nature in all its wants, its aspirations, its powers and its tendencies...'[18] Though the essay rejects 'pure necessitarianism in its crude form', it interprets Aristotle approvingly as holding that 'nature, including the development of man, is not full of incoherent episodes like a bad tragedy, that inconsistency and anomaly are as impossible in the moral as they are in the physical world, and that where the superficial observer thinks he sees a revolution the philosophical critic discerns merely the gradual and rational evolution of the inevitable results of certain antecedents'.[19] The study of facts is to be valued, since it is in them that we find inscribed the great laws of development; and the historical critic, the great epigrammatist sternly admonishes us, must not 'falsify truth for the sake of a paradox or an epigram'.[20]

The groundwork for Wilde's essay is to be found in his Oxford Notebook and Commonplace book; and in an Introduction to these texts, the editors point to Wilde's Irish background as one influence on his scientific thought.[21] Both of his renowned nationalist parents busied themselves with the philological, ethnological and archaelogical sciences, while as a student at Trinity College Wilde felt the influence of the historical philosopher J.P. Mahaffy. At Oxford, a combination of Ruskin's cultural criticism and neo-Hegelian philosophy reinforced these intellectual tendencies; indeed the historicism of Wilde's early essay is quite as much Hegelian as materialist, and his notebooks seek for a synthesis of idealism and evolutionary theory. 'Every true philosophy', he writes, 'must be both

17. Wilde entered the essay in 1879 for the Chancellor's English prize at Oxford.
18. 'The Rise of Historical Criticism', in G.F. Maine, ed., *The Works of Oscar Wilde* (London 1949), pp. 1061, 1063.
19. Ibid., p. 1064.
20. Ibid., p. 1081.
21. See Philip E. Smith and Michael S. Helfand, eds, *Oscar Wilde's Oxford Notebooks* (New York and Oxford 1989), Introduction.

idealist and realist';[22] and this is the thrust of 'The Rise of Historical Criticism', which discerns in the evolving laws of matter a progressive growth of mind.

It is hard to recognize the author of *Dorian Gray* in this solemnly positivist piece, which conflates the natural and historical orders, holds to the underlying unity and rationality of the universe, and leaves scant room for the random, creative or inconsistent. The historicist bent of the essay, a tribute to Wilde's mentor Walter Pater, firmly downgrades the individual will, a phenomenon so moulded and modified by circumstance that its agency dwindles almost to nothing. There are, to be sure, one or two aestheticist undertones to this rigorously scientistic tract, harbingers of its author's future. The historical critic, so Wilde claims, views history as 'an organism containing the law of its own development in itself, and working out its perfection merely by the fact of being what it is'.[23] History, in short, is a work of art, autotelic and self-determining; and when the later Wilde comes to transpose this radical autonomy to the individual life, the result will be his aestheticist ethics. For Wilde as for Comte, Spencer, George Eliot and Walter Pater, there is a quasi-religious fulfilment to be reaped from contemplating the sublimity of this self-inventing artefact: religion is 'that transcendental attitude of the mind which, contemplating a world resting on inviolable law, is yet comforted and seeks to worship God not in the violation but in the fulfilment of nature'.[24] Scientific rationalism banishes spirit from the universe only to readmit it through the back door – for this self-moving world from which all contingency has been expelled resembles nothing quite so much as the Almighty.

At the basis of scientific law, for the early Wilde as much as for Herbert Spencer, lies an unfathomable mystery, and Wilde will carry over this sense of mystery into his later aesthetics. Moreover, the individualism which he will later come to celebrate is the telos of this whole cosmic process, which in Spencerian style evolves from simplicity to complexity, unity to hetereogeneity. As Bruce Haley aptly comments, the later Wilde was to retain the values of multiformity and differentiation he derived from his early Spencerianism, while abandoning the scientific rationalist approach to phenomena which went along with them.[25] Evolution, Wilde comments in 'The Critic as Artist', is the law of life, and there is no

---

22. Ibid., p. 127.
23. 'The Rise of Historical Criticism', p. 1065.
24. Ibid., p. 1083.
25. Bruce Haley, 'Wilde's "Decadence" and the Positivist Tradition', *Victorian Studies*, vol. 28, no. 2 (Winter 1985).

evolution except towards individualism. There is thus a secret pact between Wilde the historical determinist and Wilde the anarchic aesthete: what the former sees as an inviolable law of Nature, the latter transfers to the absolute law of one's individual being. There is also some continuity between his early hard-nosed determinism and the later cult of hedonism, since both creeds are in their different ways offensive to an orthodox liberal humanism. To dissolve the self into the laws of evolution, or into its moods and sensations, are both strikes at the autonomous moral ego. A similar shift can be observed in the career of Roland Barthes, who moves from scientific semiology to post-structuralist libertarianism, both of them profoundly distasteful to a conventional humanism. And Oscar Wilde is in all kinds of ways the Irish Roland Barthes.

Even so, it would seem a far cry from this austere early exercise in Enlightenment to the hedonistic iconoclasm of Wilde's later writing. Does Wilde, when he arrives at his full immaturity, simply abandon this middle-aged fantasy? It is not in fact clear that he does so entirely. What he does, one might claim, is to retain a sense of natural determinism while stripping it of its rationality, and to preserve his vision of an evolving collective mind while divorcing it from the material world. Nature for the later Wilde is still an inexorable force; but is now more Darwinian than teleological, exactly the chapter of senseless accidents that he had earlier interpreted Aristotle as rejecting. 'What Art really reveals to us', remarks Vivian in 'The Decay of Lying', 'is Nature's lack of design, her curious crudities, her extraordinary monotony, her absolutely unfinished condition.'[26] Wilde will later regard his own downfall in this light, as grotesquely styleless rather than sublimely tragic. The later Wilde retains a good many traces of his earlier scientific progressivism; but Nature is now also seen as blind, aleatory, the enemy of mind rather than the paradigm of a universal reason.[27] The monism of 'The Rise of Historical Criticism' thus yields to a thoroughgoing dualism: whereas for the early Wilde human consciousness is at one with an orderly material evolution, the later essays will give the name of art to the revolt of the mind against Nature. And Nature here often enough includes society, with its oppressive, drearily naturalized institutions. The Spencerian unity of social and material spheres is to this extent preserved. For the early essay, the laws of spirit and the laws of

---

26. 'The Decay of Lying', *Works*, p. 909.
27. There is the odd Lamarckian qualification of this view: Nature is said in 'The Critic as Artist' to be 'matter struggling into mind'. But this is untypical of the essay's general emphasis.

matter are intimately interwoven; the later Wilde will subdue the latter to the former, finding in art or language the mind's anarchic transgression of natural law. If 'The Rise of Historical Criticism' is content to assign only a puny power to the will, this for the Wilde of *Dorian Gray* has become the noxious creed of Lord Henry Wotton, who holds that good resolutions are useless attempts to interfere with scientific laws. What Bernard Shaw's mixture of Lamarck and Nietzsche holds together – a unity of mind and matter, along with the triumph of the former over the latter – are for Wilde less easily reconciled. In principle, to be sure, the two cases can still be run in tandem: if the whole of Nature is groaning and travailing towards the birth of the supremely individualist mind, then mind and Nature are at once continuous and distinct. In practice, however, Wilde shifts the emphasis from their organic unity to their eternal antagonism.

There is a sense, then, in which Wilde moves from Comte to Kant: from a unity with Nature which all but cancels the creative will, to an affirmation of inner freedom which is now quite at odds with the realm of fact. The Kantian duality of noumenal and phenomenal reappears in Wilde as the conflict between a blindly determining world and the sweet waywardness of subjectivity. This, presumably, is the meaning of Gilbert's claim in 'The Critic as Artist': 'When man acts he is a puppet. When he describes he is a poet'.[28] To act, for Wilde as much as for Joseph Conrad, is to risk keeling over at the very high point of subjective resolution into the condition of a passively determined thing.[29] Action, Gilbert remarks, is 'a blind thing dependent on external influences, and moved by an impulse of whose nature it is unconscious. It is a thing incomplete in its essence, because limited by accident, and ignorant in its direction, being always at variance with its aim'.[30] Wilde has not reneged on his early vision of a necessitarian world.[31] It is just that this social or corporeal sphere is now one of alienation, reified fact, degrading accident, from which consciousness must be jealously demarcated. Art represents that quirky deviation by which we can take a momentary leap out of the realm of necessity into

---

28. 'The Critic as Artist', *Works*, p. 963.

29. This is one reason why Conrad is so fascinated by jumping. To jump is to take a free decision which then surrenders you inescapably to the determining laws of gravity.

30. 'The Critic as Artist', *Works*, p. 962. The idea that actions, once performed, elude the control of one's subjectivity, assume a momentum of their own and return to plague you in alien form, is a recurrent motif in the *fin de siècle*, and accounts in part for Thomas Hardy's interest in Greek tragedy.

31. Declan Kiberd discusses *The Importance of Being Earnest* as a parody of determinist thought in his 'Irish Literature and Irish History', in R.F. Foster, ed., *The Oxford History of Ireland* (Oxford 1989).

the kingdom of freedom, as the latter offers some fantasy compensation for the *longeurs* of the former. The danger, to quote Henry Wotton's Kant-like formulation, is of being split between 'a realism that is vulgar, [and] an ideality that is void'.[32] Ironically, it is just the fact of scientific determinism which licenses our freedom; for the theory of heredity tells us that all action is pre-programmed, and thus liberates us from moral responsibility for our deeds into the freedom of pure contemplation. Once one has leapt out of reality, one can turn back and coolly aestheticize it, 'set[ting] ourselves to witness with appropriate emotions the varied scenes that man and nature afford'.[33] It is a mixture of Arnoldian disinterestedness with a Schopenhauerian serenity which, having given the slip to the voracious Will, is set free to treat the world as a work of art.

Wilde, who hailed from the city his compatriot Joyce spelt as Doublin, is a fissured subject in all kinds of ways: English and Irish, socialite and sodomite, dandy and republican, upper-class and underdog, a respectable paterfamilias who consorted with rent boys, a shameless bon viveur who laid claim to the title of socialist. There is in any case something intriguingly divided about the aristocrat, who is at once overlord and immoralist, commanding and cavalier, an inverted anarchist with all the iconoclasm of those unquestionably in control. But beyond these purely social polarities, Wilde's work urges an ontological division between history and consciousness, one which splits the human subject down the middle as thoroughly as the Kantian self is strung out between phenomenal object and free subject. Vivian in 'The Decay of Lying' explicitly repudiates the historicist perspective on art which his author had learnt from Pater, and the essay contains a negative allusion to Herbert Spencer. If facts for 'The Rise of Historical Criticism' are the very locus of mighty cosmic laws, the later essay will dismiss them, in lofty Arnoldian vein, as usurping the domain of Fancy. 'The Rise of Historical Criticism' deploys an aesthetic image to assure us that Nature is inherently purposive: it is not, Wilde maintains, 'full of incoherent episodes like a bad tragedy'. 'The Critic as Artist' exploits the same theatrical metaphor to illustrate exactly the opposite point: life is deficient in form, its catastrophes happen in the wrong way, and its tragedies seem to culminate in farce.

To pit mind against reality, however, is not necessarily to pit the *individual* mind against it. 'The Critic as Artist' speaks of the determining law of heredity as having 'hemmed us round with the nets of the hunter,

---

32. *The Picture of Dorian Gray, Works*, p. 24.
33. 'The Critic as Artist', *Works*, p. 981.

and written upon the wall the prophecy of our doom. We may not watch it, for it is within us'.[34] So necessity is not after all just external; on the contrary, it informs human consciousness from within, just as it did for the scientific evolutionism of 'The Rise of Historical Criticism'. If, then, subjectivity is just as determined as biology, where does freedom have its source? Wilde resolves this difficulty by mobilizing his earlier Hegelian idea of collective mind. Just as Samuel Butler resorts to the notion of race memory as the motivating force of human action, so 'The Critic as Artist' sees the imagination as distilling a kind of racial unconscious. It is this, not individual creativity, which lies at the origin of art; our soul is 'no single spiritual entity' but the precipate of this collective history of spirit.[35] So creativity and determinism are preserved together – but only at the cost of sacrificing the uniqueness of the individual imagination, which is now decentred into the dreams of the species as a whole. For Wilde as for Butler, individual creativity is paradoxically quite as programmed as Nature itself, since it is merely the workings within us of a vital transindividual force. But whereas for the Creative Evolutionists this force is a dynamic within material history itself, for Wilde its creativity is increasingly confined to the mind. The very law of heredity which breeds exotic fantasies in the subjective sphere is also the force which enslaves us in the objective one. The evolutionary vitalism which, for Butler and Shaw, overcomes the distinction of mind and matter thus serves in Wilde's case to reinforce it. There is one great Necessity which works itself out in both mind and world; but this monism instantly bifurcates into a dualism, since the dreams it generates in the mind lead us blessedly *away* from material reality. The law of heredity 'can lead us away from surroundings whose beauty is dimmed to us by the mists of familiarity, or whose ignoble ugliness and sordid claims are marring the perfection of our development'.[36] It is in this way that Wilde can simultaneously cling to his determinism, open a space for the imagination, and deconstruct the individual psyche.

The tension in Wilde's work here is the sign of a familiar Romantic dilemma. If the human subject is integrated with Nature, it gains a secure foundation but sheds its freedom; if it breaks with Nature, it achieves an

---

34. Ibid., p. 979.
35. Wilde may have derived this doctrine from the anthropology of Edward Tylor, with which he seems to have been familiar. See Tylor's *Primitive Culture* (London 1871). For his interest in heredity, see John Wilson Foster, 'Against Nature? Science and Oscar Wilde', *University of Toronto Quarterly*, vol. 63, no. 2 (Winter 1993/4).
36. 'The Critic as Artist', *Works*, p. 980.

autonomy which is disturbingly ungrounded. The point of Creative Evolution (and, indeed, of Hegel's philosophy) is to have it both ways: if Nature is secretly a subject, then one can unite with it with no detriment to one's freedom. But there may also be a more specifically Irish context to Wilde's thought here. For the anti-mimetic aesthetic which his dualism involves – art must invent its own world, or at least transform Nature rather than slavishly reproducing it – has a venerable Irish lineage, all the way from the fantastic hyperbole of the ancient sagas to the myth and symbolism of the Revivalists. Like Yeats, Wilde carried over this anti-mimetic creed into life itself, denouncing heteronomy, refusing to submit to the law of another, taking himself as his own supreme model. 'There is no mode of action, no form of emotion, that we do not share with the lower animals', comments Gilbert in 'The Critic as Artist'. 'It is only by language that we rise above them, or above each other – by language, which is the parent, and not the child, of thought.'[37] Once again, Wilde retains his earlier scientific naturalism, but in the same gesture separates out human consciousness from it. A naturalistic anti-humanism, which regards humanity as just one more animal species, instantly breeds its own opposite – a humanism for which language is the mind's lonely edge over a determining environment. Language, as often in Irish history, compensates for a history in which you are more determined than determining, more object than agent.

The gap between consciousness and action is among other things a familiar Irish discrepancy between rhetoric and reality; and when Wilde speaks of language as the parent rather than the child of thought, he is adopting a performative rather than representational epistemology which has a lengthy Irish provenance. The more the body becomes the plaything of external forces, the more you must just keep talking, as Samuel Beckett's grotesque figures continue to stammer out the ghost of a narrative as the flesh disintegrates around the mouth. Language is the one frail enclave of freedom in an oppressive world; and its supreme form of expression, art, does not merely displace that world but actively wreaks vengeance upon it, refashions reality until fact is just the passing creation of fancy and life a slipshod imitation of art. 'Nature', comments Vivian, 'is our creation. It is in our brain that she quickens to life. Things are because

---

37. Ibid., p. 962. The thought is probably Max Muller's, with whom Wilde studied at Oxford. For Muller, language was 'the one great barrier between the brute and man: Man speaks, and no brute has ever uttered a word. Language is our Rubicon, and no brute will dare to cross it...' (quoted by Smith and Helfand, eds, *Oscar Wilde's Oxford Notebooks*, p. 9).

we see them, and what we see, and how we see it, depends on the Arts that have influenced us.'[38] Like Yeats, Wilde dips back into Berkeleyan idealism in the teeth of a recalcitrant history, asserting with a certain Ascendancy arrogance of mind that the world is whichever way we wish it.[39] Or perhaps it would be more accurate to say that it is a way of seeing which combines the cavalierness of the Anglo-Irish with their sense of being under siege. It will be left to the even more audacious Shaw to suggest that the point of such mental acts is not only to interpret the world but to change it – that if only we will hard enough, life will deliver us our desire.

If Wilde despises Nature, it is also because, as for Roland Barthes and Michel Foucault, it suggests an oppressive normativity. Nature is the family, heterosexuality, stock notions, social convention; and Wilde had only to be presented with a convention to feel the irresistible urge to violate it. His whole instinct was to improvise, experiment, self-fashion; and if he disliked the natural it was because, as one who made a fetish of originality, he found it repetitive and predictable. One is tempted to speculate that one reason for his homosexuality is just the fact that he found hetero-sexuality intolerably clichéd; and Wilde was more terrified of a cliché than he was of appearing on Piccadilly in the wrong cut of waistcoat. So it is that he brandishes the epigram as a lethal weapon; for the epigram is the mind's momentary triumph over the dead matter of conventional wisdom, a piece of linguistic deviancy, a sagacious saying gone suddenly awry. 'A paradox', comments an early Wildean critic, 'is simply the truth of the minority, just as a commonplace is the truth of the majority.'[40] The epigram inverts, deconstructs, turns inside out, displays that capacity of the mind to dismantle and transmute the actual which we know as wit. This compulsion to invert runs much deeper in Wilde than sexuality, though the frisson of the epigram is erotic: 'What the paradox was to me

---

38. 'The Decay of Lying', *Works*, p. 925.

39. An emphasis on the creative mind which can be found as far back in Irish thought as the ninth-century theology of John Scottus Eriugena. For Eriugena, humanity is an image of God in the boundlessness of its mind, free from all external authority and necessity. Eriugena's term for such bondlessness is *anarchos*: the human individual is entirely free be-cause he or she is ruled only by the utter freedom of the divine will. Just as art for Wilde is the intervention of the mind in Nature, so for the idealist Eriugena knowledge is less an adequation to the real than an absorption of reality into thought. See Dermot Moran, 'Nature, Man and God in the Philosophy of John Scottus Eriugena', in Richard Kearney, ed., *The Irish Mind* (Dublin 1985).

40. Ernest Newman, 'Oscar Wilde: A Literary Appreciation', reprinted in Karl Beckson, ed., *Oscar Wilde: The Critical Heritage* (London 1970), p. 203.

in the sphere of thought,' Wilde writes in *De Profundis*, 'perversity became to me in the sphere of passion.'[41] The Wildean epigram is a satiric cut, a negation of the given; but it also has the utopian dimension of the Freudian jest, which delights in its own exuberant play of spirit at the very moment it scores a deadly point. Both Wilde and Shaw are court jesters to the English upper classes, practitioners of paradox, estrangers of the tediously naturalized; but Shaw's more terse, cerebral wit, while quite as iconoclastic as Wilde's, is less languidly self-pleasuring, more briskly demystifying, more pointedly in the service of a hard-headed common sense. The Romantic and the rationalist, unified in Shaw's supposedly scientific theory of evolutionary vitalism, are also curiously comminged in his wit, which couples an intuitive flash of knowledge with a lethal shaft of realism. Shaw is brittle, bumptious, intolerably opinionated – though many of his opinions are admirably enlightened; Wilde presses through this cult of the ego to an extravagant extreme, raises it to the second power, so that its fictional or pose-like quality ironically qualifies it. The last person to whom it might have occurred that the subject was a fiction, for all his theories of the composite self, was George Bernard Shaw.

In what sense for Wilde, though, *was* the self a fiction? There is no doubt that he was a postmodernist *avant la lettre*, with his belief that interpretation is endless, criticism a form of creative writing, truth more aesthetic than cognitive, the human subject an ephemeral construct, the world a product of the sign, the body and its pleasures a subversive undoing of a pharisaical ideology. It is not hard for the émigré to perceive the constructed nature of social reality; if English stage comedy has been dominated by the Irish, it is partly because nobody is better placed to appreciate the comic arbitrariness of conventions than those who, while insiders enough to manipulate them with aplomb, never took them wholly for granted in the first place.[42] Wilde hijacked the social and theatrical forms of the English to demonstrate that he could deploy them even more dexterously than the natives, parodying their conventions by obeying them so exactly. Whether this was flattery or mockery was never easy to determine. If he was fascinated by the life of English high society, it was

41. *De Profundis*, *Works*, p. 857.

42. For a discussion of the Irish influence on the English comic stage, see Thomas Kilroy, 'Anglo-Irish Playwrights and Comic Tradition', in M.P. Hederman and R. Kearney, eds, *The Crane Bag Book of Irish Studies* (Dublin 1982).

partly because its social forms seemed at once absolutely binding and flagrantly gratuitous; indeed in its meticulous formality of manners, English aristocratic society was for him a work of art all in itself. So it is that his formalism is at once an assault on bourgeois moralism, and a devotion to the truth of masks or substance of style on the part of one whose whole existence was a carefully wrought illusion.[43] But 'illusion' might suggest a concealed or distorted reality; and the question is whether Wilde believed that a true self lay behind his manifold masks, or whether he thought it merely an effect of them.

If there is a Nietzschean strain in his work which suggests that identity is a chimera, there is also an older Romantic drive to absolute self-realization. These need not be logical opposites: you can view identity as fluid, multiple, provisional, while holding that each of its passing phases demands complete expression. But such expression would seem to be of the essence of the self; and it is hard to see where this essence lies if the self, like truth, is just one's latest mood. Dorian Gray rejects 'the shallow psychology of those who conceive the Ego in man as a thing simple, permanent, reliable, and of one essence';[44] the self for him is protean, intertextual, composed (as for Samuel Butler) as much of the dead as of the living. Yet the narrative he belongs to works with the logic of the doubled, rather than decentred, subject, which is indeed essentialist: Dorian's hideous portrait signifies his true selfhood behind the alluring appearance. Guilt and remorse – the 'mediaeval emotions', as Henry Wotton scornfully dubs them – are a negative clue to who you are. Wilde pins together these conflicting views of the self by paradox: 'we are never more true to ourselves than when we are inconsistent ... through constant change, and through constant change alone, will [the individual] find his true unity'.[45] But if the essence of the self is evolution, this still does not resolve the Kantian problem of how this particular development comes to be mine rather than someone else's. The unity of the self may persist through change, but it cannot logically be identical with it.

Wilde's problem here is that he values the non-identical, but is committed to a notion of individualism which depends on self-identity.[46] The

---

43. Wilde's formalist bent anticipates the doctrines of Russian Formalism: when he writes in 'The Critic as Artist' that the poet's idea follows from his choice of the sonnet form, he is very close to the Formalists' notion of content as the mere 'motivation' of form.

44. *The Picture of Dorian Gray, Works*, p. 112.

45. 'The Critic as Artist', *Works*, pp. 984, 987.

46. It is not clear why a view of the self as non-identical should be thought of in our own time as inherently radical. If this is so, then David Hume was certainly a radical.

Schillerian and Arnoldian language of self-perfecting he inherits posits the very unified self which his more Nietzschean doctrines seek to undermine. On the one hand, he calls for a multiplication of personalities; on the other hand, he values the individual who is 'perfectly and absolutely himself', and imagines true personality as a simple, flower-like growth.[47] The self is pose, mask, persona; yet true individuality 'comes naturally and inevitably out of man', and 'The Soul of Man under Socialism' will even reach back to its author's early flirtation with Spencer by imagining this progressive differentiation as a force inherent in life itself. There is still a conflict, in other words, between evolutionary naturalism and its alternatives − only now this is one between different images of the self, not just a conflict between its unity with and separation from Nature. 'The Critic as Artist' tells us on one page that 'we are never more true to ourselves than when we are inconsistent', and portrays the critic as a decentred subject, a practitioner of negative capacity able to evaluate the object from every point of view. On the next page it speaks up for a strongly partisan self, remarking that 'the man who sees both sides of a question is a man who sees absolutely nothing at all'. 'Man', comments Gilbert, 'is least himself when he talks in his own person. Give him a mask, and he will tell you the truth.'[48] Does the image identify mask and true selfhood, or is the former merely a means to the latter?

Wilde adopts an idealist language of authenticity, while being mightily suspicious of the whole idea. It is, in part, a conflict between the European Romanticism to which he was heir, and the self-ironizing consciousness of the colonial mimic man, for whom truth can only mean the wry knowledge of one's own fictionality. Wilde was an accomplished impersonator of himself, holding that the posture created the subject as surely as you could fall in love by lingering over the vowels of a love poem. In Brechtian or Wittgensteinian fashion, he believes that interiority is a product of the signifier. If he was a phoney, then he would justify the fact by setting out to expose all identity as ungrounded and evanescent; the outsider would become the fifth columnist in the enemy camp, unmasking his own apparently assured identity for the poor pretence it was. The misery of colonial non-identity could thus be turned to advantage, converted into a utopian alternative to the politics which had produced it. But Wilde was also a sexually, ethnically and socially divided subject who for that very reason felt, like Yeats, the allures of absolute self-identity,

---

47. 'The Soul of Man under Socialism', *Works*, pp. 1026, 1023.
48. 'The Critic as Artist', *Works*, p. 984.

and exemplified that condition in *De Profundis* in his aestheticized portrait of Christ.

'Truth in art is the unity of a thing with itself', Wilde comments.[49] If the human subject really is fluid, multiple, diffuse, then it is hard to see how it can have the self-identity of the work of art; yet Wilde's whole ambition is to aestheticize that subject. Art is not a substitute for life, as in the more stereotyped forms of aestheticism, but the very model of it. Gilbert remarks in Kantian vein that the sphere of art and that of ethics are absolutely distinct;[50] but this just means that the aesthetic should be kept free from the clutches of bourgeois morality. Wilde does not seem to realize that he himself has conflated the ethical and the aesthetic by aestheticizing ethics. To live well is to conduct yourself like a work of art, which means realizing one's creative potential, savouring each sensation with the intensity of a poem, valuing experience as an end in itself, and bowing to no authority but the law of one's own being. Anarchism and the aesthetic consort naturally together, the antinomianism of the one mirrored by the autonomism of the other. Every impulse which is truly of the self must find expression; but if the self is nothing but its impulses, how can it transcend them sufficiently to judge which ones are really authentic? If the answer is 'all of them' – if the only crime is the stifling of the self's free development – then one must either hold in naively libertarian fashion that all human desire is positive, or explain away why one has just enshrined the right to murder. 'Whatever is realised is right', Wilde comments dangerously in *De Profundis*. Moreover, if the subject's moods are diverse and conflictive, the imperative to express them all will lead to a contradictory selfhood, not a unified one.

Wilde has no real solutions to these problems, and neither does the Romantic lineage he inherits. Ethically speaking, he is a consequentialist who believes that morally right conduct is whatever promotes the non-moral good of free individual self-realization. In this, he is more or less at one with Karl Marx. But Marx himself qualified such consequentialism with certain deontological imperatives – the claim, for example, that such self-realization must take a form which allows it to be universalized.[51] For Marx, it must be a matter of mutuality, such that the self-realization of

---

49. *De Profundis*, *Works*, p. 864.

50. Wilde is also Kantian in his belief, recorded in 'The Soul of Man under Socialism', that new works of art cannot be measured by the standards of the past – precisely Kant's argument in *The Critique of Judgement*.

51. See on this topic R.G. Peffer, *Marxism, Morality, and Social Justice* (Princeton 1990), Part I.

each is the condition for the self-realization of all. Wilde accepts the universalizing, but not the reciprocity. He is aware that his own liberty is deformed by its offensively privileged character, in a society where so many others are oppressed. This is why socialism is for him the precondition of genuine individualism: under socialism, everyone will live as he lives now. He is not thereby prepared to abandon that freedom, partly because he is enjoying himself too much, partly because one needs proleptic images of utopia. Just lie on the couch all day and be one's own communist society. But though Wilde wishes, like Marx, to universalize individual self-development, this will not for him be achieved through mutuality. On the contrary, it will be achieved by each individual leaving the others alone. It is in this sense that his political vision is finally more anarchist than socialist, and in this sense too that his individualism is at once a spiritualized version of commonplace bourgeois egoism, and one which threatens to subvert that ideology by pressing it to an outrageous extreme.[52] The self for Wilde may be mutable, pluralist, decentred; but it is not at root relational, and so is in the end more Nietzschean than Marxist. The self is inded relational for the early Wilde of the Oxford commonplace book, who in Hegelian fashion views ego and non-ego as interdependent. It is also relational in so far as it is the product of a whole racial unconscious, a mere intertexual tangle in the evolution of *Geist*. But Wilde rarely views the human subject as constituted by its practical relations to others of its kind. The human being under socialism stands essentially alone, but will reap joy from sympathizing with others; and this is exactly the situation of Nietzsche's *Übermensch*, who recognizes no moral claims on his compassion but will exercise it, if he so chooses, for essentially aesthetic reasons.

Wilde's socialism is sometimes a naturalistic affair, in the manner of nineteenth-century libertarianism. There is a force at work in Nature making for individual freedom, and if only it were to be prised loose from artificial political institutions it would lead us by its own momentum into a higher social state. Resonances of this doctrine, which is in effect Spencer's Law of Equal Freedom, can be found in 'The Soul of Man under Socialism', and they hark back to the evolutionary naturalism of 'The Rise of Historical Criticism'. But the essay can also be read in a way more consonant with Wilde's later, more dualistic thought. The argument of 'The Soul of Man under Socialism' is that socialism, by

---

52. The same may be said of his homosexuality, which is at once a radical strike against convention and a covertly accepted part of Victorian ruling-class male practice.

automating labour and abolishing poverty, will release men and women from the claims of others and allow them to evolve as genuine individualists. This case, for all its perverse panache, is closer to Marx than to William Morris, whose *News from Nowhere* Wilde would probably have read in serialized form. Morris believed in making labour creative, whereas Marx believed in doing away with it as far as possible, so that individuals could fulfil their powers and capacities in some more fruitful way.

Both Marx and Wilde recognized that an economic revolution was necessary if economics were to cease binding so much precious human energy. Socialism for Wilde is a way of escaping the material world by reorganizing it; and the consequent division between self and society is a social version of the ontological duality we have examined earlier. Just as, for 'The Decay of Lying', Nature operates by certain laws from which the mind must keep its disdainful distance, so for 'The Soul of Man under Socialism' socialism will convert society into a 'thoroughly healthy organism', an automated sphere which the individual can then thankfully leave to look after itself. Society for Wilde is 'blind' and 'mechanical',[53] which is how Nature is too; but the point of socialism is to mechanize it even further, not to transform it into a creative medium. History is not, *pace* the Lamarckian vitalists, to become an expression of mind; instead, subjectivity must detach itself from the tedium of social life, relieved of all fatiguing responsibility for it. Just as Wilde argues in 'The Critic as Artist' that an awareness of determinism frees us from responsibility for our actions and allows us to dream, so his essay on socialism transplants this doctrine to the political sphere. Socialism will liberate us from the demands of altruism, which for Wilde is as much the flip side of possessive egoism as sentimentality is of cynicism. Few were as well placed as he to appreciate the selfish delights of self-sacrifice.

For Theodor Adorno, the identity of the subject, if one can speak in those terms, lies in suffering. This is what Wilde means in *De Profundis* when he remarks that pain, unlike pleasure, has no mask. But the work undercuts its own pronouncement. The Wilde of Reading Gaol, who urges meekness, simplicity, spontaneity, has simply discovered a fascinating new persona. The Jesus whose artistic genius and 'charm of personality' prove so seductive bears a remarkable resemblance to Oscar Wilde, a man now so humbled that he remakes the Son of God in his own image. *De Profundis* is all about how deeply its author has changed, and how utterly self-identical he remains. Bernard Shaw was quick to note this fact,

---

53. *De Profundis, Works*, p. 882.

remarking approvingly of the essay that Wilde 'comes out the same man he went in'.[54] In the very crisis of conversion, there must be no revolutionary break with a past self: it is just that whereas he previously fingered the flowers of evil, he will now, for the sake of Hellenic completeness, extend his aesthetic sympathies to the good. His prose is hushed, grave, tremulous with pathos, even as the old wisecracks keep breaking through. This spiritually chastened penitent is all he ever was, only more so: having unaccountably overlooked the aesthetic delights of moral virtue, he is now resolved to savour them to the full.

For all his exquisitely calculated pathos, Wilde is a genuinely tragic figure; and it is here, finally, that he has the edge over Shaw. Shaw praised De Profundis as exhilaratingly comic, commenting that 'it annoys me to have people degrading the whole affair to the level of sentimental tragedy'.[55] There can be no real waste or breakdown for the hubristic philosophy of evolutionary vitalism, with its callow insensitivity to the material limitations of the human creature.[56] Sin, crime, failure will all finally be recycled as success, in a perspective to which the equally anti-tragic Yeats was in his own way no stranger. Wilde sometimes flirts with this idea too, adopting the theory (a kind of evolutionary deism) that evil is misperceived good; but in him, in contrast to Shaw, Romanticism has confronted Darwinism rather than taking the Lamarckian detour around it. The universe is not spontaneously on the side of the individual, and neither, as Wilde was to discover, is society. The imaginary bond between mind and world has been ruptured, and the mind must now turn back on its own resources in that gesture of cosmic defiance we know as art. One would not wish Oscar Wilde's calamity on Bernard Shaw; but his art would no doubt have been the better for it.

---

54. Letter to Robert Ross of 1905, reprinted in Beckson, ed., *Oscar Wilde: The Critical Heritage*, p. 244.
55. Ibid., p. 244.
56. For an eloquent statement of this theme, see Sebastiano Timpanaro, *On Materialism* (London 1975), Ch. 1.

INDEX